RECOLLECTIONS OF A
HAMBURGER

RECOLLECTIONS OF A HAMBURGER

◆

GROWING UP GERMAN, 1941–1962

Christel Behnke Gehlert

To Dorothy

Christel Behnke Gehlert

iUniverse, Inc.
New York Lincoln Shanghai

RECOLLECTIONS OF A HAMBURGER
GROWING UP GERMAN, 1941–1962

iUniverse books may be ordered through booksellers or by contacting:

iUniverse
2021 Pine Lake Road, Suite 100
Lincoln, NE 68512
www.iuniverse.com
1-800-Authors (1-800-288-4677)

Because of the dynamic nature of the Internet, any Web addresses or links contained in this book may have changed since publication and may no longer be valid.

The views expressed in this work are solely those of the author and do not necessarily reflect the views of the publisher, and the publisher hereby disclaims any responsibility for them.

ISBN: 978-0-595-46145-5 (pbk)
ISBN: 978-0-595-70782-9 (cloth)
ISBN: 978-0-595-90445-7 (ebk)

Printed in the United States of America

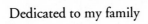

Dedicated to my family

Contents

Acknowledgments ix

Preface xi

CHAPTER 1   Birth and early childhood in Hamburg 1
1941—1943

CHAPTER 2   Escape to the Sudetenland 30
1943–1945

CHAPTER 3   Childhood years in post-war Hamburg 49
1945–1948

CHAPTER 4   Elementary school and family life 78
1948–1954

CHAPTER 5   High school
Class trip to Sylt 135
1954–1955

CHAPTER 6   Last year of high school and dance lessons 178
1956–1957

CHAPTER 7   Business school, infatuations and religion 204
1957

CHAPTER 8   Class trip to the Rhine 223
1958

CHAPTER 9   Graduation from business school, first job and
first trip to England 232
1959

CHAPTER 10   Goodbye Germany, hello England 252
1960

CHAPTER 11   Au pairing in England 297
1961

CHAPTER 12   Off to America 345
1962

Afterword 359

Acknowledgments

Thanks to my family for urging me to finish the book. I am grateful to my family and friends in Germany whose stories triggered long-forgotten memories.

Thanks to Kate Musgrave, one of the first friends I made in the United States and a published author herself, for contributing what she knows about writing and editing.

Thanks also to Avon Crismore, my English professor, for her vigorously wielded red ink pen, her never-ending questions, and her unceasing encouragement.

Over the years, these conscientious readers have given me valuable advice: Julie Adams, Lois Colburn, Julie Ervin Bennett, and Dick Gehlert.

Reference material at the beginning of chapters for the years 1949–1962, with the exception of 1961 (my year in England) were selected from *50 Jahre Deutschland—Das deutsch-deutsche Geschichtsbuch von BILD*: Econ, 1999.

I chose two photographs of World War II Hamburg from *Hamburg im Bombenkrieg 1940–1945: Das Schicksal einer Stadt,* by Christian Hanke and Joachim Paschen. Hamburg: Medien-Verlag Schubert, 1993.

The *Nordamerikanische Wochenpost,* a German-American weekly published in Detroit, Michigan, provided excellent details in their column, "Historisches Kalenderblatt—Diese Woche vor 50 Jahren."

Lachmund, Fritz. *Das Alte Barmbek.* Verlag Hans Christians, 1976.

The internet proved to be a valuable resource.

Preface

This book was born in 1988 when I first mentioned to friends my desire to recount the story of my German girlhood. I wanted to write an account of events in my life from the time I was born to when I left Germany at age twenty-one. I felt that sharing my thoughts and feelings about my experiences was especially important for my children. Doubts came immediately, and many times I gave up without ever having written the first word. At age forty-seven, would I be able to recall what happened so long ago?

I had kept diaries, written between 1955 and 1961. In rereading them as an adult, I laughed and cried both and then felt inspired to translate them from German to English, having decided to write the future book in English. I began taking notes, looking at photographs that triggered memories—details about clothes, food, living conditions, life. All in reaching back to September 17, 1941.

Some memories came easier than others, but many were so deeply buried that it took me years to pull them up. Some, particularly those of the immediate post-war years, were so painful that I would burst into tears on recalling them. But tears also led to the sheer delight of recalling some long-forgotten moments.

When my children wanted funny or sad stories, stories about what I ate as a child, the clothes I wore, songs I learned and especially lullabies, and what I did in school, I told them many a tale of my growing up in Germany. My experiences were quite different from my children's and their fascination with my stories was endless. They would say, "Mom, tell us that story again, the one when you were two and you walked to the bomb shelter all by yourself." The more details I could muster, the more they liked the stories.

All the tales I told eventually led me to revisit my homeland on a mission. Since my parents had been dead for many years, I interviewed my brother, who was seven when I was born, asking about wartime conditions in Hamburg. I taped the questions and answers, and additionally he wrote down for me some of the neighborhood events, invaluable information about our life in the Sudetenland and the subsequent return trip to Hamburg at war's end, and the successive years. My sister also contributed, though she was less inclined to dig around in her memory. She did tell me about some of the games we played as children. Both siblings supplied me with many telling snapshots, such that my whole being flooded with memories. The stories my parents, aunts, and uncles had told me over the years came back to me in fragments at times, and often in surprising detail.

On my 1998 German sojourn, then, I contacted a genealogy researcher for information about my grandparents. A visit to the state archives in Hamburg amazed me with the number of documents that had survived the bombings. Gradually, I began to see the war as a backdrop against which all Germans' destinies had been played out. Having been given a script, we followed it. Then the wartime backdrop receded, and the Germany of the 1950s emerged to let everyone take a deep breath and begin to enjoy the present.

After I finished my research, I essayed a first draft, more or less in stream-of-consciousness style. I gave it to my English professor at Indiana/Purdue University, where I was taking writing classes. When she returned it to me, it was pretty well covered in red ink, so armed with a notebook full of her questions I made another trip to Germany, where I pumped relatives, friends, and former neighbors. Some were distinctly uneager to talk yet again about the war.

Armed with evidence of the past, then, I began revising. Eventually I was able to get past the war years to write about my pre-teen and teen years, my year in England, and my decision to discover America. Through it all my purpose was to tell what it was like to grow up German.

For the most part, the book is written chronologically. When chronology seems abandoned, especially in the beginning of the book, it is done so intentionally, tangled sometimes as only memories can be.

1

Birth and early childhood in Hamburg

◆

1941—1943

The year was 1941. Germany was stretching itself to its limits, starting a war and killing many people. Still, this is not a story about Germany at war but rather about how my family and I coped with the enormity of events that befell us. There are lots of history books about the war, but this is my personal story about my twenty years in Germany.

On about New Year's Eve of 1940, I was perhaps a glint in my parents' eyes because I was conceived around that time. Maybe between Christmas Eve and New Year's Eve when they were trying to forget all the bad things that were going on around them, bombs raining down for one. Of course, their timing was all wrong. I can't imagine being a woman pregnant in wartime, running to shelters day and night, worried about the life she is carrying.

Two days before my birth, on September 17, 1941, the British were bombing Hamburg, where my parents lived. It was a nuisance attack, meaning that the British wanted to keep the people in Hamburg on their toes, jittery, scared almost to death, terrorized in short. It was one of the many attacks that continued until July 1943, when Hamburg was fire-bombed. After that, there wasn't much left to bomb, though still the bombings continued.

September 17 began like many other fall days, I imagine. The air was probably crisp, especially in the morning and a little foggy until the sun broke through. It was a Saturday just like any Saturday before the war when the man who would become my father would walk to the bakery at the corner to buy fresh rolls. But now there was only black bread to eat, and only a little of that. A smidgen of margarine was scraped onto the bread, and the gooseberry jam the woman who

1

would become my mother had made from the gooseberries in our back yard added some sweetness to breakfast.

Everyone—my parents, my brother Klaus who was seven, and my sister Doris who was two enjoyed what little food there was and so did I, though indirectly through my mother's womb. After clearing the table and washing dishes in the kitchen sink, my mother went back to bed because she wasn't feeling all that energetic. She felt dizzy just watching her belly heave with her unborn child's foot first here and then a fist there and all felt only by her. My father and Klaus went outside to rake the courtyard in the back of the house and clean out the chicken coop. They put my sister Doris in a buggy from where she watched them, her fat, rosy cheeks bursting with good health. I heard later that she was a happy baby, in contrast to me.

My mother went into labor sometime after 1:00 p.m. My father, who had gone through this twice before, asked Klaus to run to Tante Hensel, the midwife, and tell her that Anna was in labor. The midwife told Klaus to come back when the pains were five minutes apart, then he ran home where my father was busy getting ready for my birth. This meant that he sat by his wife's bed, holding her hand and talking reassuringly with her. Our closest hospital, the huge *Barmbeker Krankenhaus,* was only four minutes away from our house, but my mother insisted on delivering her baby at home.

Only two days earlier the British Air Force had bombarded Hamburg, leaving everybody anxious, but still my mother insisted on delivering me at home. Later in the afternoon of the 17th, Klaus ran back to get Tante Hensel, and this time she walked back with him, holding her big leather bag while my brother danced around her, prodding her to hurry up. But she was ready to deliver her umpteenth child and wasn't about to be rushed. She knew from experience that most unborn babies waited until she got there. Tante (*aunt*) Hensel wasn't our real aunt but a close-enough friend of the family to be called that. Of course, I didn't know her yet. Neither did I know about the German etiquette of titles and when and how to use them. More about that later.

According to my family, Tante Hensel asked my father to help her, or rather told him what to do. She was, as I later found out, a no-nonsense woman. "Henry, get me some sheets," "Henry, boil some more water." Evidently, she needed lots of water for delivering me, and he was happy to oblige so he could leave the bedroom for a while as my mother and Tante Hensel attended to my being born properly. Tante Hensel was a big woman, not fat but sturdy and quick on her feet, and with a few deft motions she placed sheets, blankets, washcloths, cloth diapers, and all the things she needed to clean me up on my father's side of the bed.

By this time, our neighbor Tante Schütt arrived to pick up my sister Doris and her toys and take her to her house across the street. My brother Klaus was sent upstairs to wait with his best friend Ernst, whose parents rented the upstairs flat from us. Two years earlier, when Doris was about to be born, he had also been sent upstairs. Neighbors were more like friends on our street since they had all lived there for many years and they always helped each other. Klaus told me later that he thought he was waiting for the stork to appear, and to speed up the process he put sugar cubes on the kitchen windowsill. Everybody knew that storks liked sugar cubes. There he stood looking out the window and reciting a rhyme:

> *Storch, Storch bester*
> *Bring mir eine Schwester*
> *Storch, Storch guter*
> *Bring mir einen Bruder*

> (Stork, stork dearest
> bring me a sister
> good stork, good stork
> bring me a brother).

When nothing seemed to be happening, he gave up on his rhyme and played with Ernst. Meanwhile, downstairs, Tante Hensel said, "Anna, push." My mother did and suddenly I appeared. My birth probably wasn't that fast, but I don't want to dwell on this event because I don't remember any of it. In the habit of the times, Tante Hensel wrapped me up tightly in several layers of cloth beginning with a diaper, a pair of plastic underpants meant to keep in the wetness, a shirt, then a *Lure* or cloth that fit tightly around me from my waist to my toes to make sure that my legs grew straight. Finally came a blanket. By now I looked like a cocoon. Safe, for now. I was a package Tante Hensel thrust in my Mutti's arms with, "Here's your *Deern*," a Northern German dialect word for "girl." Then she ministered to Mutti, while Papa helped rinse washcloths, towels, and sheets that had been soiled in the birthing process.

When Ernst's mother heard my first cry, she snatched the sugar cubes from the sill, and as far as my brother was concerned the stork had come and gone and brought him another sister. Then Klaus ran up and down the street, yelling proudly, "I have a sister, I have a sister." He was seven to my few minutes old, and he hadn't even seen me yet.

When I was much older, I often wondered what the woman who was now my Mutti was thinking at the moment I was put into her arms. Was she happy to have a baby at this time, considering that her country was at war, material things were severely limited, bombs were falling, and she was cuddling another mouth to feed? I can't begin to guess what she thought, but I hope that she was able momentarily to forget the brutish world outside, the better to enjoy looking at the baby girl in her arms who will end up looking so much like her.

My parents named me Christel Marie—Marie, after my paternal grandmother, whose name was Emma Maria. Close enough, that. My birth certificate stated only that I was born on September 17, 1941, in Hamburg, Hartzloh 38, to the musician Henry Ernst Behnke and Anna Olga nee Schmidt, both of the Lutheran faith and residents of Hamburg.

Two days after my birth, Mutti developed thrombosis in her legs which meant that she could fall victim to dangerous blood clots, and she and I had to go to the hospital after all. I went with her because she was breastfeeding me. We stayed a week, because in those days patients were not sent home unless they were well and able to function normally. After all, Mutti had two children at home waiting for her return to care for them. While Mutti and I were away, Tante Klara, my mother's older sister, helped Papa.

When finally the two of us returned home, my life began in earnest. Relatives came to visit, unbeknown to me. My paternal grandmother Emma swung her large bosom over my bassinet and agreed to be my godmother; my grandfather, who has the princely name Georg Heinrich Wilhelm Ernst, more than likely played practical jokes on members of my family because that's what he liked to do at every opportunity.

My brother kept my sister busy by having her watch him dig around in the backyard dirt. Aunts, uncles, and cousins come by to say, *Ach, das ist aber ein süsses Baby* (What a sweet baby!), and other such tender nothings said about a newborn. Of course, I didn't know any of these people yet, but as I grew up my aunts, especially Mutti's sisters, would be ever-present in my life.

I imagine myself warm in my cocoon in a white wicker bassinet stuffed with blankets and breast-fed by my Mutti whenever I wanted.

◆   ◆   ◆

Outside, war raged and brought its ugliness inside my home. For the approaching winter, Hamburg's populace was urged to prepare potatoes in their skins so that no vitamins would be lost. Potatoes were precious, skin and all. But at this point in my young life, I wasn't aware of the shortage of food any more than the alarming air raids.

About two months after I was born, the sirens wailed as they did each time British planes came into our sky. Papa grabbed my bassinette, Mutti grabbed me, my brother held my sister's hand, and in the dark we five hurried into the supposed safety of our home bomb shelter. No time to waste, the bombs were on their way! Germans had been told to build bomb shelters or to convert a room in their basements into a retreat for use during air raids. These rooms weren't a hundred percent safe, since a bomb could always destroy a house and bury the occupants alive in the basement. It just depended on how a bomb hit a house and how the walls crumbled.

In our house we were fortunate to have a basement. Our basement room had a cement floor, black-out paper on the windows so that the enemy had no beacon to guide them to us, a few wooden chairs, blankets, toys, a bucket of sand, and a first-aid kit. The room also had a heavy, grey metal door with a big handle, the kind of handle I have since seen on meat lockers. I remember this door very well, because when I was five or six, I had to stand on my tiptoes to reach the handle and then pull with all my might to open it. I wondered why a room where my Mutti hung clothes to dry if it was raining or snowing, and where she kept food cold, needed such a heavy door. No other room in the basement had a metal door. It wasn't until I had heard war stories that I understood this door's purpose. If a fire broke out above us and the flames reached the basement, this reinforced steel door would hold back the flames and give us time to crawl outside through the shelter windows.

We had been lucky so far and our house hadn't been hit, although there were plenty of apartment houses in the neighborhood that had window panes and bricks missing and some that had only partial walls standing. People who endured raids in bunkers never knew what they would find of their homes after the explosions ceased. Maybe they had a home to return to, maybe not.

On this particular day, shortly after we reached the safety of the shelter and the family from upstairs descended to crowd us, a firebomb crashed through the roof of our house, fell through the second and first floors, and then with an awful thud bored into the floor of the shelter, about twenty inches away from the bassinette where I was sleeping peacefully, unaware of the war raging around me. My sister wailed as my brother stared at the bomb while my Mutti in a flash moved my bassinette as far away from the bomb as possible. What was this bomb going to do? Some bombs didn't explode because they didn't have powder in them. Still, they were bombs that caused a lot of damage just by crashing through things including people. My Papa threw a shovelful of sand on the small fire that the bomb had ignited. Everybody kept a watchful eye on the thing until the siren sounded the end of the raid and we stumbled upstairs. We had been spared again. Nobody ever said what happened to the bomb to this day. It just fizzled out, I imagine, and was thrown in the garbage, in the place of the potato skins.

The story got retold a thousand times, and each time the patch in the wooden living room floor was pointed out and the storyteller said, "After the bomb crashed through the living room floor, it barely missed hitting our Christel sleeping in her bassinette in the shelter!" It seemed that each time the story was told, the bomb fell just a tiny bit closer to me than before. Sometimes, as I learned later, stories got changed in the recollection depending on who told the story. So years later the wooden floor became covered with an imitation Persian rug and nobody mentioned the near-disaster any more, except when I did.

When I was older, I listened to these stories, all told without self-pity, with only one ear, bored with the repetition of so much suffering and thinking "Please, please, enough of the war, tell me something else!" I didn't understand then that telling and retelling war stories was a way of purging the horror until the pain diminished. But even though I was only half-listening to the stories, they managed to attach themselves to me and stay alive, and I carried them around, thought about them, told them, and, finally, put them to paper.

Regard this story: when I was about eighteen months old and Hamburg was being bombarded repeatedly, I up and took matters into my own hands. Already I had learned what it meant when sirens interrupted my world, and I acted on this subconscious knowledge. Each family member had a small suitcase, just big enough for a change of clothes, a washcloth, a favorite toy, marbles, a book, and maybe some socks that needed darning and could keep Mutti's hands busy. My parents had an additional suitcase with important papers and jewelry. To this suitcase they held on very tightly the entire time we spent in the bunker at the end of the street. Not everyone could be trusted, since people other than immediate neighbors also used these bunkers. Our suitcases were always lined up in the hallway of our apartment in the same order, so even in the dark of the night we knew where to grab our own the minute the sirens screamed, and if there was time to run to the shelter a block away that's where we headed. Sometimes we had a little extra warning from the dentist Alfred Kimmel down the street, who had become the neighborhood watchdog. He would come running out of his apartment, shouting through a megaphone *"Vorarlarm."* This alarm meant that anti-aircraft guns had been activated to give us some protection while we ran to the bunker, our hearts pounding.

One day as the sirens blared and my family rushed out the door, I was nowhere to be found. Imagine the terror my parents felt not knowing where I was but knowing that the rest of us had to get to safety immediately. They broadcast my name, but there came no response. Finally Papa ran outside to look up and down the street, and there he spotted me, halfway down the block going in the direction of the shelter, dragging my suitcase. He scooped me up and carried me to the shelter as the rest of my family zigzagged their way down the street toward us. Then it was only few stairs down to the supposed safety of the gas-proof door.

Sometimes we had as many as three raids a day. Once would have been enough to endure, I think. "Stop the madness," my parents wanted to scream. The anticipation of inevitable bombings created much anxiety that affected us children as well, though I was hardly aware of it at the time. Having to stay in the house or yard, in plain sight, and not being able to be out and about in the neighborhood was hardest on my brother.

One day after the war as I walked down a busy street to the streetcar stop, I passed the bunker we had used. Its grey concrete roof was flush with the sidewalk. It looked so ominous, almost evil, more an eyesore now than a place of safety. Weeds grew up around it and the steps were covered with litter. The place smelled of urine from drunks peeing on the stairs. I hurried past it on the way to meet a friend. There was no time to think about bunkers. Peace had broken out.

◆　　　◆　　　◆

In the summer of 1943, peace was only a dream. Sirens screamed. Bombs fell. What happened one night to friends of my parents', Ulla and Karl, happened to my family too and differed only in detail. Family friend Ulla told me the story: shortly before midnight, warning sirens blared. Inside their apartment, Ulla's family was instantly awake. In the darkness, breathless with fear, they hurried into their coats even though the air was still mildly warm on this July night. Ulla touched the gold, heart-shaped pin on her blouse. She never went anywhere without it. The family grabbed their suitcases which stood ready like soldiers by the front door, packed with a change of clothes, documents, and a little money. Ulla slung a bag with bread and margarine over her shoulder, because they never knew how long they would have to stay in the bunker. Then they flew out the door—Ulla, her husband Karl, nine-year-old Max, and four-year-old Eva. Max held Eva's hand and pulled her along as fast as her little legs would allow. Because Charlotte was only two, she was carried by her father. She was fussing because her sleep had been interrupted again. "Hush," said her mother, kissing her little girl's thin face.

They heard the rat-tat-tat, rat-tat-tat of machine guns in the distance and then a huge explosion. The sky somewhere on the horizon burnt bright orange from the flames shooting up high into the sky. Then another hit, closer now. They heard screams and cries for help as bricks crashed down. The safety of the shelter was only minutes away. It seemed so much longer when running on trembling legs. Ulla and Karl tried to stay close to buildings that were still standing, or at least part of them stood. So many apartment houses already lay in ruins from previous raids. Neighbors were running alongside them. Labored breathing. Such an effort to run carrying children and suitcases. Not a word was said until they reached the door of the shelter and scuttled down the few steps. The gas-proof chamber was within reach. The big iron door slammed shut behind them in the chamber designed to protect them from the bombs. It had always sufficed.

The city had been bombarded for over a year at unpredictable intervals, and most of that time Ulla's family's basement shelter with the reinforced iron door served them well. Once, a bomb hit their apartment house roof, crashed down through all the floors, lodged in the dirt below the basement floor, and then failed to explode. They were scared out of their wits, but their home, their belongings, their future past and present were spared one more time.

Tonight, Ulla felt exhausted. A heavy air-raid two days earlier had left her physically and mentally drained from fear and worry for her family. Her anxiety was heightened by the feeling that tonight's air raid was somehow going to be different. She told her husband, "Karl, I feel that the British will retaliate tonight for our bombing of Coventry." Everyone around her agreed. This raid would be worse than any of the others, and they were numb with fear. The senselessness of war was so overwhelming, it dulled their will to live while also kindling a stubborn desire to overcome each new obstacle.

The bunker normally held fifty people, twelve to fifteen in each of the four chambers, but tonight well over 150 people were sharing the air. Seats were given first to the sick, old, and pregnant. Ulla, pregnant, sat down on the wooden bench running the length of the chamber wall. Eva sat close to her on the floor, holding onto her mother's leg with one hand and with her other hand gripping her beloved rag doll. The shelves for personal belongings across from where Ulla sat were packed to overflowing, so Ulla stowed her small suitcase under her seat. She preferred it this way. When she needed to get into it, she would do it quickly. Her bag of jewelry was hidden under some clothing and clothing was what people would see. But she also realized that everybody used the same ruse. Desperate times bred distrust, and although Ulla was not by nature distrustful, she was well aware of how the war has changed her opinion of people. Trust was a luxury reserved for peacetime.

Max sat on his suitcase in front of her, his head resting on her lap. She stroked his head until the worried look on his face disappeared. She hated it that her children had to play on a street filled with rubble. Why couldn't they have a childhood like the one she had? Hers was peaceful and exciting, with relaxing vacations with her parents and brothers at Timmendorf on the Baltic Sea as well as many stimulating trips to big cities in Germany.

Another hit. Ulla clutched her son's hair as her anxiety momentarily carried her away, then she relaxed again. The adults shrieked with fear and then sighed with relief until the next big explosion. Ulla said to her son, "Max, why don't you see if you can get a game of cards started with some of the boys." He wanted to stay with his mother, but she knew that once he joined children his own age, for awhile at least, he wouldn't have to look at the worried faces all around him. She picked Eva up from where she had been sitting on the floor and put her on her lap, loving putting her face against her daughter's soft, generous cheeks and feeling the toddler's sweet breath on her face. They were safe; the bunker warden had reassured everyone that this underground chamber bunker was the safest of all the bunkers because of its double iron doors. All was well for now.

But even now, as the air-raid was well under way, Ulla heard people banging on the shelter door, crying, "Open up, we can't breathe up here. Please let us in." Ulla moved Eva aside a little and started to get out of her seat to talk to the bunker warden. Maybe there was a way of admitting a few more, but Karl pushed her gently down and said, "Don't." This one word expressed the way it really was at this time in Germany—you looked after yourself and neighbors be damned. It wasn't the way Ulla wanted to live when all this was over. Still, she agreed with her husband for now. There was no way of knowing how long they would have to be here, confined to this small space, when the lack of oxygen would eventually pose a problem. The enemy was raiding the air outside, depriving people of oxygen, but down in the bunker Ulla and her family were still able to breathe. That's all she cared about for the moment. "Merciful God, watch over those outside," she prayed.

Even though space was scarce with 150 people in the bunker, blankets were spread out on the floor wherever possible for the children to sleep on. Adults took turns sitting or standing. By now, Ulla and her family had been in the bunker for well over two hours. She took five slices of bread and some margarine from her food supply bag (her wartime picnic basket, as she called it although now, every time the sirens wailed and she grabbed that bag, she faced the potential for her own destruction). She scraped the margarine on the bread, preparing two extra slices for her friends Ulrike and Wolfgang because she couldn't eat in front of them and not share. Ulla then broke her slice into tiny pieces, crumbs almost, hiding the food in her cupped hand because hungry eyes were all around her, looking at her, wanting sustenance for themselves when she couldn't afford to share more. Her family came first, always. She tucked the rest of the bread back into her bag for later. God only knew how long they would be confined like this.

The knocking on the door continued for awhile, then stopped. In the bunker, Ulla and her family and all the others napped fitfully.

Another hit, this time closer. Ulla jerked awake to screaming. She looked at little Charlotte snuggled in her father's arms and her eyes teared up. Ulla cried easily these days. Her Charlotte and Eva had never known peace, and how could a mother ever make up for the insanity of the war raging around them and restore normalcy for her children?

She touched her gold pin and thought of the time two years ago, when her mother pressed the pin into her palm and said, "As long as you have it pinned somewhere on your clothes, Ulla, you and your family will be all right. The pin once belonged to your grandmother, and she survived the Great War." Ulla doubted the power of talismans, but she couldn't give any other explanation for why they had thus far survived these bombings, hunger, and freezing cold winters. Maybe her family would survive. Maybe.

The inferno outside continued. Someone turned on a radio, at which they learned that the situation outside was as grave as they feared. A firestorm was raging out there, the extent of which nobody had ever seen before. What would happen when they left the bunker this time? Ulla's anxiety rose with each explosion.

By now, all 150 people had been in the bunker for well over eight hours. When Max asked for something to eat, Ulla pulled him close to her and whispered to him that soon, very soon they would be eating something. Potatoes maybe, though most likely there wouldn't be any gas for cooking them. For now they had exhausted their supply of food, their stomachs were growling, and they felt lightheaded. Sometimes Ulla felt that hunger was a defense against all the ghastly things happening in her homeland. Hunger was all-consuming, an invisible enemy so threatening that anything else paled in comparison.

The lack of air made the smell of sweat and fear less sharp, and the bodies curled around each other on the floor seemed less defined. The air ventilators had stopped working a long time ago. For awhile children had hand-cranked them, but the air outside was so full of smoke that the ventilators were left idle.

The noise outside picked up—crashing, thundering, exploding sounds. In the bunker, someone wept hysterically. Children sobbed.

Ulla stared at the writing on the wall as she had done so many times before, reading the same lines over and over again. Someone had written one of Wilhelm Busch's famous sayings, "So live moderately, think smart, if you don't want for anything, then you know you have enough." Hadn't she lived moderately? What had she done to deserve this? And why was she even asking herself these questions when she knew she had no answers? Did anyone have any answers for the madness around them?

Ulla rose and walked to the other end of the bunker to use the chemical toilet yet again. Somebody had poured a little water over a washcloth, and she used it to wipe her hands. When this was all over, she would never again use water sparingly. In the future, there would be enough bath water for each of her children, and water aplenty for drinking and cooking.

On one of her earlier trips to the other end of the chamber, many hours ago, Ulla had stopped by a group of people playing cards and watched them for awhile. People were smiling then and talking with each other. Now there was only murmured conversation and the inertia of weary bodies trying to nap. Somber, exhausted faces looked at her, mirroring her own. She walked by a poster addressing the comrades of the NSDAP (National Socialist Workers' Party of Germany) with "When you need advice and help, ask the NSDAP." What could they do for her now? She wanted the inferno up there to stop, the crashing of buildings to cease, to escape this bunker with her family intact.

On her way back to her bench seat, she only heard deafening silence. The whistling of bombs crashing into whatever was left up there had stopped. Everyone in the bunker came to attention and listened, speechless, fearful but anxious to get out and yet not moving. The warden held back from opening the iron door because the bombing might resume as had happened so many times before. When finally the warden did open the iron door, Ulla and her family along with their friends and neighbors slowly stepped up onto the moonscape that Hamburg had become. On that night in July, more than 35,000 people had died.

The enemy was not done yet and the bombing continued for three more nights, further pulverizing Hamburg.

◆   ◆   ◆

Fast forward.

Sometime in the 1950s most of the bunkers were demolished, but one or two were left standing for the curious, like me. Years after I had been in one as a small child, I revisited a bunker armed with a tape recorder on a research mission for a story I wanted to write. What I didn't foresee were the feelings that came flooding over me, for as I walked around this shelter it seemed to reverberate with the anguish of the people who had used it. All the fear, misery, distress, and agony of my parents' plight washed over me, and I cried bitter tears for what they had had to endure as well as for the utter stupidity of war.

The "tourist" bunker I visited was in Hamm, a working-class neighborhood heavily bombarded during the war. For 90,000 people, there had been only 8,907 places in the community bunkers. Bunkers were meant to protect people from the effects of air-raids, but only about ten percent of the population ended up protected. There were three thousand home bunkers like my family's, and some people preferred to stay there although they were not considered to be as safe as the community bunkers. What was worse, Jews were not allowed in the bunkers. Sometimes, only Aryan women and children were allowed, but often the women would say, "I'm not going in without my [Jewish] husband." Then the whole family had to run to another shelter which might admit all of them.

Construction of the bunkers had begun in 1940 and continued through the war. The construction spoke to German thoroughness, with walls made of reinforced concrete about forty inches thick and the shelter dug more than five yards underground. Even so, below-ground bunkers were not considered safe because of the chance of being buried alive. Often, apartment houses came crashing down on them, blocking the exits with debris.

By 1942, however, more and more people used the community bunkers rather than the basement air-raid shelters, and overcrowding became a serious issue. Admission cards were issued giving the card holder the right to use a certain chamber along with so many children. Some people with reservation cards put their names on their seats. The bunker I visited had seating for fifty, but many times 150 were admitted and people ended up sitting on the floor for as long as necessary, sometimes as much as several hours. Another above-ground bunker was built for 1000 people, but sometimes 4000 exhausted, sweating people squeezed together, most of them standing. Worry, sadness, and lack of oxygen added to their exhaustion. Fear of being hit by a bomb kept most adults silent, in contrast to the young people who played as best they could in their crowded potential tombs.

I walked down twenty steps before I reached the gate that, during the war, was locked by the warden who was the only one with a key. Behind the gate was the gas-proof door opening into four chambers, each forming a tube. Each tube had a gas-proof door and benches lining its sides. Hatches connected the chambers through which people could escape to get to the emergency exit without struggling to open heavy doors that were always locked anyway. Once through the hatches, there was a hallway with built-in metal ladders leading to a tiny emergency hut on the outside. Escaping the bunkers in this way became necessary when buildings crashed on top of them and blocked the entrance.

I tried to imagine myself in one of these bunkers at age two, but I couldn't. I looked at the photographs on the walls collected after the war, showing groups of people sitting around a table with coffee cups, a coffee pot, and a bottle of schnaps, and they were all smiling. The pictures were taken in 1940, and people didn't know all the bad things that were yet to happen. There were gas masks, small ones for the children, but there were never enough to go around. Air ventilators were on most of the time, unless static on the radio indicated that an announcement was coming, at which the ventilators had to be stopped because their noise drowned out the messages. The announcements kept people informed about what was happening elsewhere in the city. This only added to the general anxiety if a part of the city was hit where relatives and friends lived. Whenever the power went out, which was often, candle holders kept in the bunkers for this purpose were brought out and candles were placed either on the tables or hung from the ceiling. Such a bunker atmosphere, with all lights extinguished save for the candles that cast an eerie light on the sea of anxious faces. And then I remembered that I was in a bunker just like that, sitting on Mutti's or Papa's lap, or playing with Klaus and Doris. Is it my own memory that replays the scene, or is it a story I heard? Odd sensation, this.

Alike the wailing of the sirens: in later years, even the sound of a fire engine blaring down the road made me want to run and hide, ears covered and heart racing. This reaction I have to fire engines continues to the present, but I've learned to take a deep breath and look at the bomb-free, friendly skies.

I hadn't done much so far in my life since I was only two. I had been to the bunker and home again and failed to note the relief on my parents' faces when they saw that their house was still standing.

At age one and a half, I got vaccinations, including the ones for small pox which are still visible as dime-sized scars on my right upper arm. I have a picture that shows Mutti, my sister Doris, our neighbor Wilma, age sixteen, and me in front of the building where the vaccination took place. I look grumpy, probably because I am the only one vaccinated that day. My sister has a golden smile on her face and a toy in her hand. And where is my toy? I must have a toy! I am the one who was stuck with a needle!

It must be fall or winter because we are dressed warmly. My coat and hat match, as do the fur collar and trim around the hat. Everyone else is looking at the camera while something is distracting me on the photographer's right side. Wilma's pretty face is smiling. She takes care of us often, being a *Pflichtjahrmädchen*, a girl serving her country for a one-year period because girls can't be soldiers. Since we are a family with three small children, we get to have her. She helps around the house, plays with us, and runs errands for my mother. In the photo, Wilma keeps her left hand on my shoulder as though to steady me, because the vaccinations may have made me weak-kneed. Something about Wilma that catches my eye is that the sleeves of her coat are not long enough, exposing too much arm and wrist. Her coat has outgrown her, but she has no other.

But the most striking person in the photo is Mutti, who is wearing a knee-length black coat with two rows of three buttons each across the upper body and a smart leather belt around the waist. On her head sits a hat with a bow on the front, a little to the side. The top of the hat reminds me of an oversized muffin. But the most gorgeously frightening item of her attire is the fox fur wrapped around her neck, one fox leg dangling down the side of her sleeve. Mutti is wearing a dead fox! She smiles but her graceful face cannot hide the strain of the war heavy in her eyes: she is alive but looks haunted. Her left hand cups the side of my sister's face, a tender, protective gesture and one I use to this very day when I want to comfort someone.

There are only a few pictures of me from this period, probably because taking pictures of anyone was at the bottom of the list of things to do, coming well after procuring food, and dodging bombs. Such are priorities.

There is one last, formal picture taken by a hired photographer. Mutti, Klaus, Doris, and I are posing for the camera before a backdrop of drapery. Papa is not in the picture because he wanted only Mutti to pose with their children. The year is 1943. Mutti sits on a wooden chair, wearing a pale yellowish-white, buttery-to-the-touch silk dress with a Peter Pan collar and a row of fabric-covered buttons from the top to the middle of the skirt pleated down the front. I don't know why I like this dress so much, but when in later years I see it hanging in her closet, I think how elegant it looks, especially with the right accessories. At least I think I see it hanging in her closet, although I never see it on her again, in person or in pictures, so maybe it didn't survive the Big Trip, about which I will explain later.

On this day, along with the elegant dress, Mutti is wearing dark, heavy, war-issue stockings and flat brown shoes with laces. Her dark hair is combed back and held in place with combs, in a very casual fashion. She and Klaus are the only ones smiling at the camera. My handsome brother is wearing either pants that are too short for him or shorts that are too long. Whatever they are, they are held in place by suspenders worn over a short-sleeved shirt. The look on his face is cheerful and bright, and probably he doesn't care what he is wearing. His shoes are sturdy and dark, just like my sister's and mine and even Mutti's although they hardly complement the light silk dress she wears. Shoes were severely rationed during the war, and people wore whatever pairs they were given. Doris is staring at the camera, with quite a stern look on her face, a sourpuss face, a fearful face, as though she is expecting something dreadful to fly suddenly forward from the camera. Maybe she wants to sit on Mutti's lap but her younger sister has beaten her to it. Maybe she fussed and was reprimanded. She stands to the left of Mutti, who holds her arm. More of a grip than a hold, I would say, to get her to smile for the camera. Doris wears a short white, embroidered dress that looks as if it had once been a tablecloth somebody has given sleeves and a neckline. Mutti has combed my sister's hair into a *Hahnenkamm,* a rooster's comb, which means that at the top of her head, her hair is parted from the sides and the remaining hair in the middle is wrapped around combs, like a taco sitting atop her head. The rest of her hair lies flat against her head on either side of her face. It's a fashionable hairdo, popular at that time and for many years afterwards for keeping girls' hair up and neat. I don't have enough hair to make a *Hahnenkamm,* so mine is just combed and looks like my brother's only a little longer. Being the youngest, I sit on Mutti's lap, and I'm grumpy again, wearing a let's-get-this-over-with look. In the middle of a war here we are, looking well-scrubbed although a little run-down in the clothes department. On the one hand we do ordinary things like posing for pictures, and on the other we run from bombs. We endure, the picture says.

◆   ◆   ◆

Rewind.

It hadn't always been like this for Mutti—running from bombs and not hav-ing enough to eat—although this war wasn't the first she had endured. Anna Olga Schmidt was born in her parents' apartment in Hamburg at 1:15 p.m. on Saturday, April 20, 1901. She would share this birthday with a archvillain, one who would change her life drastically, but in 1901 no one had heard of Adolph Hitler. My mother was the youngest of four children of Johannes Schmidt and Julie Ida Jordanski. They live only in my imagination, because I have never seen a picture of them or even of my mother as a child. I assume that some pictures once existed but that they were lost or that someone else got them. My mother doesn't exist photographically until she is in her twenties.

I imagine that my grandfather had a bushy mustache that he twirled at the ends. Maybe he had a goatee as well; in any case, his hair was short. And his eyes twinkled such that in my eyes he was handsome. Opa was a house painter and varnisher by trade and so good with his hands that he built or helped build the house in which I was born. In 1901, the family, which now included my mother, moved into the house on Hartzloh in the working/middle-class district of Barm-bek.

Opa Johannes and his twin Johann were born on February 22, 1863, in Höll-rich, Bavaria. Their parents were Johannes Schmidt and Margaretha, Johannes' second wife. His first wife, Eva Elisabetha, died at age twenty-nine on September 17, 1861. Coincidentally, on that day eighty years later I was born. Nine months after Eva's death, Johannes married my great-grandmother, and my Opa and his twin brother were born eight months later. Perhaps the twins were preemies.

My Opa visited the local pub just around the corner from the house, and there he kept his beer mug engraved with his name and the current year as was the cus-tom. It now sits on a shelf in my kitchen in Indiana. The men at the pub who liked to sing formed a group, and my Opa became the leader of the *Barmbeker Gesangverein*. The group was well-known in the neighborhood for singing at every social opportunity and not just for themselves. Opa had a love for music which was handed down in various degrees to his grandchildren, mainly in the form of singing.

I see my grandmother Julie as a woman with high cheekbones and hair swept up in the fashion of the day, a high collar on her lacy blouse that made her neck appear very long and swan-like. I attribute looks to her that I fancy for myself, in a way seeing her without ever having seen her. She certainly passed her olive-colored complexion on to my mother and me. My mother told me that Oma Julie loved children and that, had she been alive longer, she would have doted on us. I have always thought that a precious thing to know about my grandmother—that she liked children. It was important to me that she would have loved me, although she couldn't tell me so herself. If my mother told me more about my grandmother, I don't remember, and it haunts me that I don't remember. Certain facts attach themselves to me and come alive and others I search for but can't retrieve. Like sheets fluttering on a clothesline, my thoughts float but I cannot pin them down. As much as I would like to, I cannot go back in time in an "I was there" way.

A photograph of my mother with her sisters and friends tells of middle-class life: the living room is decorated in Victorian style, with flowered wallpaper, a crystal chandelier, heavy drapery, and a coffee table covered with a white cloth. There is a cake on the table; they are celebrating some occasion or just having coffee and cake in the afternoon. All the women are holding cigarettes, mugging for the camera. The smile on my mother's face and the affected way she is holding a cigarette with her pinky sticking out, tell me that she thinks this is good fun but she herself doesn't smoke. The seven women, in their twenties, have their hair swept up or back and the ends probably held in a kind of bun. Everybody is smiling; they look carefree and comfortable with each other and the two men in the picture. The time is post-World War I.

My mother's teenage years, though, were a time of deprivation. In 1917, when she was sixteen years old, the country suffered a lack of food, and I imagine that she looked pale and skinny and tired from having too little to eat, which like many children her age made it difficult for her to follow lessons in school. Her clothes were made from old curtains, her boot soles from wood. Those are the few details I have retained from the tales of my mother's first encounter with war.

My mother was only nineteen when my Oma died a few days before Christmas 1920 at age fifty-eight. Officially, she died of an aneurysm, but my mother always said that she died of a broken heart because her only son Hans had been killed in World War I. I was only a child when my mother told me this and I often wondered how a heart could break inside a body. Did Hans' heart break and cause his death? What if one of we three children had died during World War II? Would my mother's heart have broken? War apparently broke things that couldn't be replaced.

When my Oma died, my mother kept house for her father, because she was the only one still at home to help him. Tante Gretchen, my mother's middle sister, had married Onkel Max, and her oldest sister, Tante Klara, had married Onkel Heinrich. Both left their parents' home.

Inflation begins in 1920 and by 1923 reaches its pinnacle. Prices rise every hour; on payday, workers drag their money home in clothes baskets. Average weekly pay for a skilled worker is 185000 Marks or about $25 at that point. Not enough to feed a family. At the end of 1923, a loaf of bread costs an incredible 200 million Marks. Unemployment and poverty are rampant. Inflation stabilizes by November when the Rentenmark is introduced.

By the summer of 1923, inflation was at its highest. A postage stamp cost two million Marks, a streetcar ticket 600,000. Paper money became scarce and companies paid by check or emergency money printed on short order. In 1918, one dollar had cost 6,59 Marks, whereas by 1923 four billion Marks were needed.

I had to think very hard about these numbers because by 1920 my mother was keeping house for her father, and I'm wondering how she made ends meet. All I ever heard were stories about her dragging around bags full of money to go shopping. As soon as her father gave her some money, she spent it on food, because prices often went up every hour. From this she got good training for all those later years when my father was a freelance musician and money thus tight.

Before the death of my grandmother, my mother worked as a teacher at a Kindergarten near our house. When I was a child, I never expressed any curiosity as to what kind of training she had received beyond her nine years of compulsory schooling. Probably she got hands-on training in taking care of children. Women were thought to be suited for that sort of thing that gave them all they needed to know against the day they married and had children of their own. But marriage wasn't in my mother's future until she was twenty-nine years old, which was practically spinsterhood for women at that time.

In the meantime my mother had fun being an actress in an amateur theater group. There is a photograph of her and her fellow actors in which she poses in a dark Victorian dress topped by a huge hat of feathers and ribbons. I examine this photograph with the help of a magnifying glass, looking at the chiseled face of my mother's youth, trying to see me in her. This is the woman who doesn't know yet she will become my mother. I'm thinking that I would have liked to have known her then, this woman who wasn't a mother but an actress.

My mother had black shoulder-length hair that she parted in the middle and pulled back into a bun in the fashion of the day. Her skin had an olive tone which darkened immediately in the sun. Her nose had a little upturn, and we often teased her about her "ski-slope" nose, the shape of which I have inherited. Her chocolaty eyes were warm and loving but could take on a menacing, piercing quality whenever she fixed them on her children to stop us from doing something naughty, like taking a second helping before dinner guests had taken theirs. Then her eyes would focus and stare, and that look made us behave more than any words she could have used.

There are many photos of my mother from the years before she met my father, pictures in which she poses in a bathing suit while standing by a lake or sits in a wicker chair clad in pretty dresses and hats or clowning with female friends and relatives. In all of them she looks well-groomed, smiling, happy. In one picture from her marriage she lies on a chaise lounge in the backyard of the house, looking quite pregnant with my brother in the summer before his birth on November 25, 1934. The picture has an enchanting quality, with my mother in the foreground smiling happily at the camera, her head resting on a pillow, and in the background a trellised gate which then separated the backyard from the courtyard. Around and over the gate hang a profusion of leaves, perhaps even flowers. Like so many pictures of the time, this one has a sepia tint, and my mother with her olive complexion blends into the earth and grass and leaves as though she is part of a secret, enchanted garden. The picture makes me cry because I never knew my mother when she was carefree and unburdened first by the horrors of war and then by the deprivations of the post-war years.

◆   ◆   ◆

My father, Henry Ernst Behnke, was born on October 1, 1905. I have very few photos of him as a boy. One shows him in an all-boy class in 1918, when he was thirteen years old and the Great War over. Another shows him with a group of young men, all dressed up in shirts and ties: they might have been fellow students where my father was training as a draftsman. My favorite photo is a sepia image of my father in a white shirt with open collar and a full shock of reddish-brown hair, his actual hair color. This color was of great concern to his sister who remarked once, when she didn't know I was listening (I was a teenager then and so eavesdropped) that you could never trust people with red hair. I was so shocked by that remark, coming from a sister about her brother, that I never trusted her again. Indeed, I disliked her intensely from that moment on, because I loved my father and knew him to be honorable to the core.

My mother and father met in 1928, when she was twenty-seven and he was twenty-three. Details about their courtship are skimpy. Their courting was probably done under the watchful eye of my grandfather. In order to have time alone together, my mother would meet my father at the Conservatory of Music where he was studying the violin. It must have been my mother's beauty and kindness and romantic nature that spellbound my father, because music was not what they had in common. My mother always sang off-key and couldn't hold a tune, but that was only a minor obstacle to her because she would keep right on singing. For a little privacy, she would meet him after his lessons and he would walk her home before taking the streetcar to the other part of town where he lived with his parents. In my imagination they took romantic walks through the *Stadtpark*, Hamburg's huge park.

My father was twenty-five years old when he and my mother were married in 1930. He was trained as a draftsman but was also taking lessons at the Conservatory and eventually learned to play the violin, double bass, and trombone. My paternal grandparents were middle-class store-owners. My father's mother had come from a long line of respectable vegetable farmers in Moorfleet, south of Hamburg, and my grandfather had worked on farms in the same area all his life. Emma and Ernst insisted that their son learn a "respectable" trade, but they also recognized his musical talent and agreed to stake him to music lessons. Operating a store, going to work every day, was "regular"; playing music was done in "spare time."

My father made a good living, and in his spare time he made even more money by playing in a band. Summers, the band played at resorts on the Baltic Sea, and between 1930 and 1939 my mother accompanied him many times with my brother in tow after 1934. This was a carefree time and I later envied my brother for having had this time with my parents. Time in the sun, fun digging in the sand, his mother's tanned face smiling down on him. They didn't know what was coming, at least not in the mid-30s. Or they weren't paying attention. Looking at my mother's picture, she in her bathing suit with a matching headband and the tranquil sea behind her, I want to change the course of history and spare her and my father and brother and all my relatives from the horrors of the coming war. But I'm not alive yet, and the thirties are a blank that live only in pictures. By the time I became aware of my parents, their city had been bombed, and they had moved to a region of the country previously unknown to them, dragged a cart with their belongings back to their hometown Hamburg, known starvation and survived countless days and ways of deprivation, their comfortable past in tatters.

On May 16, 1943, I was baptized in our neighborhood church, St. Gabriel. We were Lutherans, although I can't comprehend yet what that means. I was less than two years old and probably screamed when Pastor Deter sprinkled cold water on my head. Oma Behnke, my Papa's mother, was chosen to be my godmother. If that meant we two were in a special relationship together, it didn't turn out that way, because I never felt special when I was around her. The psalm chosen for this occasion, I assume by Pastor Deter, was Psalm 103, 22 "Praise the Lord, all his works everywhere in his dominion." I couldn't have cared less about what it said and didn't even know what a psalm was, but when I think about it now, I'd say there was a heavy dose of irony in that psalm considering what the Lord was actually permitting to happen everywhere in his dominion, what with everything being bombed to smithereens with worse to come.

Opa Behnke bounced me on his lap playing *Hoppe, Hoppe Reiter,* one of my most favorite things to do. When he came to the end of the rhyme, he would drop me through his legs just far enough to give me a thrill. I shrieked and giggled, and then he did it all over again. Every night, Papa or Mutti or both sang lullabies to Doris and me, like *Schlafe, Prinzesschen, es ruhn* and *Guten Abend, gute Nacht,* my two favorite lullabies which I sang to my daughters Julie and Amberley as they were growing up and now sing to my granddaughter Makenna. While I played with toys I can't recall now, sat on Papa's lap, watched Mutti hang up clothes on lines strung all over the courtyard in the back of our house, wondering how she could reach so far up because the clotheslines were so high that they looked as if they held up the sky, my parents were making momentous decisions without my knowledge.

Unbeknown to me, Papa went to work every day as a draftsman at the *Vereinigte Deutsche Metallwerke,* a large company with branches in other parts of Germany. In peacetime, this company made machinery of some kind for constructive purposes. Papa drew blueprints in his meticulous hand and trained apprentices in the skills they needed to make fine pieces of steel that would eventually become machines. Knowing Papa, he was very patient with and kind to his students and very supportive of their efforts. Every now and then, he and they would go on field trips to a forest or a lake near Hamburg, just for the fun of it. And for comradeship and developing loyalty to the company.

What happened to this company? Well, I think that at some point the management decided, or was forced to switch to supplying components for military aircraft and bombs. At that time, Hamburg was the largest port on the European continent, shipping enormous tonnage to keep Germany's war machinery well-supplied. While the company geared up for war, they allowed a tradition to remain intact for the benefit of their employees or to keep up morale—the company had an orchestra.

Since Papa was a musician as well as draftsman, he directed the VDM company orchestra composed of at least twenty volunteer musicians. They practiced together and then put on concerts for all the employees. This sounds strange, knowing what companies are like now, but then many big companies had orchestras.

If it hadn't been for the constant bombing, we probably would have stayed in Hamburg. Papa was employed and, although food was rationed, we had almost enough to eat. By the end of 1942, each adult was entitled to seven ounces of meat, four ounces of butter, seventeen ounces of wheat flour, eight ounces of sugar, four ounces of legumes, two ounces of cheese, and about two ounces of coffee per week. We were hungry most every day though not starving on a diet of ten ounces of bread per month (one and a half slices per week), and four-tenths of an ounce of fat per week were amounts hardly worth mentioning. The quantity of rationed food varied from month to month depending on what was available, and sometimes protein couldn't be had at all. Knowing now what it takes to feed a family of five, I find it hard to imagine how to improvise with those miniscule amounts to satisfy even one member of the family. Other necessities such as shoes, clothing, coal, detergent, and soap were rationed as well.

Papa (second from left) and Kapelle Ahrens, 1924

Mutti (second from left) in a play, 1920s

My parents are engaged, 1929

My mother, 1927

My father, 1920s

My parents—
Anna and Henry Behnke,
early 1930s

The house where I was born

My parents and brother Klaus at the Baltic Sea, 1930s

Doris, Klaus, and I in our backyard in 1943

Vaccination Day for Christel, 1943
Wilma, our *Pflichtjahrmädchen*, my mother, and Doris

Hamburg-Barmbek—the suburb where we lived—in 1943

Treks and trips

2

Escape to the Sudetenland

◆

1943–1945

As the family trips to the bunker came more frequently, my parents decided to leave Hamburg. The raids were causing immense fear and distress, coming as they did at all hours of the day and night, and it was time now to get out. Luckily, the Vereinigte Deutsche Metallwerke, Papa's employer, had a subsidiary in the territory of Silesia, about 320 miles southeast of Hamburg. Papa requested a transfer to VDM's subsidiary in Görlitz, out of the range of bombs, and the company agreed. And so we went on our desperate way, virtually into the unknown.

Of course, I recall nothing of the trip. When would I become conscious of what was happening to me? I didn't even know my neighborhood in Hamburg yet, and now I was going somewhere else that I was bound to forget as well. I had to trust my brother Klaus to flesh out this time in our lives. That is, when I got around to asking him many years later.

I was two and Klaus was nine when we moved in the late spring of 1943. He was middle-aged when I finally asked him, and this is what he told me.

In 1943, we packed what we could carry in our suitcases and left behind all our household belongings including furniture and dishes. Tante Klara and Onkel Heini moved into our house since their apartment had been bombed and they needed a place to stay. Mutti decided to leave our cat, Moritz, with this aunt and uncle, but she cried and cried because she loved him so much. Her cat proved to be in good hands, but Mutti yearned for him the whole time of their separation.

It was a good thing we moved in the spring of 1943, but we didn't know this until later. Between July 24 and 28, in the middle of a hot summer, Hamburg was firebombed. Fifty thousand people died and forty thousand were wounded. The center of Hamburg was destroyed entirely. Firestorm winds reached temperatures of 1800 degrees Fahrenheit and leveled many neighborhoods completely.

First, aerial mines lifted the roofs off apartment houses as doors and windows imploded. Then, fire bombs rained from the sky and ignited hundreds of fires. These were followed by the phosphor bombs that crashed through several floors into the basements of apartment houses where they burned everything from the bottom up. Firestorms then raged through the city neighborhood by neighborhood, enveloping homes and people and sucking them into the fire. People ran but not fast enough to outrun the raging fires, and thousands died of asphyxiation. It took fine minds to think of weapons which would kill thousands of people so efficiently.

Of course, by this time, Hitler had set in motion the "final solution to the Jewish question," efficiently murdering the Jews in concentration camps. I didn't know what the Führer was up to.

While the firestorms raged through Hamburg, we were making a home of a small and peaceful village, Voitsdorf, surrounded by beautiful mountains that were part of the *Riesengebirge*, or "giant mountains" of *Rübezahl,* the beloved and feared subject of legends. *Rübezahl* was a capricious rascal, a fickle mountain spirit who could send lightning and thunder, fog, rain, and snow down the mountain at any time, and his footsteps could make the earth tremble. The first time I saw pictures of him in books my parents read to me, I was frightened of the mere size of him. Such a giant! I wasn't able to distinguish between legend and life, and I wanted to take cover until I realized that he could also be friendly and helpful if I were good. And I wanted to be good so Rübezahl wouldn't blow me away from my Papa and Mutti.

The train we had boarded in Hamburg took us east to Schwerin and south to Ludwigslust, and then we were in Görlitz east of Dresden. This sounds easier than it was, because it wasn't one continuous journey on a single train. Sometimes we had to get off a train when it arrived at its destination and wasn't going any further. Then, if no other trains were running, we would hitch a ride on a horse-drawn wagon with other people who were going in our general direction. Often, rather than ride in a passenger train, we sat on freight car floors, which my brother for one found more adventuresome. When we arrived in Görlitz, we took a bus to Voitsdorf (now Fojtovice). Mutti and Papa did their best to keep us three kids happy, but it must have been a difficult trip though, we had no way of knowing then, not as harrowing as the return trip in 1945.

What I will relate next, I heard only from my brother Klaus and never from anyone else. When he told me, my parents were already dead. I still can't quite believe it, and when I think of it even today I feel a mixture of sickness and sadness, although the players have been gone a long time. It seems that my father had a *Freundin* named Irene in Voitsdorf, a little village then of about three hundred. We lived with Irene and her mother, Frau Drexel. Irene's father had been killed in the war, and to make ends meet the two women took in boarders. And so we became their boarders for a time.

Now, a *Freundin* can simply mean a "female friend" or it can signify something more. Did Papa know Irene before the war, or did they just meet in Voitsdorf? How would they have known each other before, living 300 miles apart? I had more questions than my brother could answer. When I expressed disbelief at what Klaus was telling me, he protested that he was certain.

He said, "When you're nine years old, like I was then, you can sense these things. I knew that Irene was his girlfriend. They liked each other, and the two of them took little trips into the surrounding countryside. Sometimes they took me with them. I'm not sure that they were lovers, but they were certainly very good friends." On hearing this, I fumed at my horrible Papa and felt sorry for my devoted Mutti, both long dead. But Klaus continued on to add that Mutti knew and that my parents had heated discussions during which Mutti let Papa know that she didn't appreciate whatever was going on between the two "friends."

Of course, this drama sailed right past Doris and me, but Irene's name stuck in my memory because as I was growing up and becoming aware of relationships, I heard family members including Mutti kid my Papa about Irene. He was good-natured about it. He would say, "Don't be *doof* (silly)." Was that a quick smile dancing around his eyes but then gone in a blink?

My brother had fun in this pretty Czech place, Voitsdorf, where the hills were covered with timber and foot trails would take walkers from one village to another. Klaus went to school there and did the normal things kids do, unafraid once again and not running for his life at the sound of sirens. Doris and I played with our dolls, and went on little outings. Doris had a doll carriage with a long handle and a pillow inside for the doll. I heard that I tried to get in it so she could push me around, but she absolutely refused to do so. Her doll wasn't going to have to share the carriage with me.

We didn't have a care in the world. In one picture, we stand hand in hand in a meadow, gazing at each other. With flowered dresses and woven flower wreaths in our hair, we look adorable, very much like little girls inhabiting a normal world. In another photo, we seem to have been atop a rock-covered hill where we are sorting through rocks with our brother. In yet another black-and-white photo, Mutti and Papa are standing beside us three children. Papa has a full head of hair and a mustache too. He is wearing pants and suspenders and a short-sleeved shirt. It looks a pleasant day. Still, I wonder who snapped the shot, because my entire family is in it. Mutti looks pretty in an off-white dress, with her black hair fashioned around combs into a roll at the nape of her neck. She is smiling, I imagine with happiness at having escaped Hamburg and the daily worries about keeping her family and herself alive.

We didn't stay in Voitsdorf very long, because Mutti made her wish known that she wanted to move away from the little village as soon as possible. Papa worked mainly in *Tetschen-Bodenbach* (now Decin in the Czech Republic), and there he met a pharmacist who owned a house on the Schneeberg, a mountain 2372 feet in elevation, the highest in the Elbsandsteingebirge, a range southeast of Dresden and about six miles from *Tetschen-Bodenbach*, a big city of about twenty thousand people. The whole area between 1919 and 1938 belonged to Czechoslovakia, but in 1938 it was annexed to Germany under the name of the *Sudetenland*.

The pharmacist let us rent the partially furnished house and we moved in with the few belongings we had brought from Hamburg. I will only remember this house from photographs. When I was older, I felt like an outsider listening again and again to the stories about Schneeberg, straining to see if there weren't some small moment that was my very own to remember. But no, everything in my past thus far had to be recreated for me verbally and pictorially by my parents and brother. As I listened to the stories about our life on the mountain, I pieced together a story in my mind of what life was like.

◆   ◆   ◆

The village of *Schneeberg*—houses nestled around a narrow road that wound its way from *Tetschen-Bodenbach*—had about five hundred people, some of whom had lived there for generations. For the next two years this village became a safe haven for us, far away from the devastation, the hunger, and despair of our Hamburg.

We were the newcomers in *Tetschen-Bodenbach* and, along with thousands of other Germans mere occupiers of a region that really belonged to Czechoslovakia. But because I never heard any stories otherwise, I have to assume that we were treated civilly. We lived on top of a mountain, which to me meant living very, very high up above everybody else, but as mountains went (2372 feet), this was no Mont Blanc (a 15892 feet-high mountain range in the Alps).

In photographs, the house looked cozy and especially the front yard. In order to get to the front door, we had to walk up four or five concrete stairs, and pass under a lattice-work archway that in the summer was covered with roses. Sometimes we had company from Hamburg. In one picture Doris and I, all bundled up, stand on the stairs beneath the archway in front of my grandmother Emma and grandfather Ernst. My Oma is wearing a black winter coat with a big black fur collar, and my Opa wears a hat and a buttoned-up long black coat. There are lots of pictures with our relatives and us in various combinations in front of this archway. It made a pretty background, especially in the summer. The house had a gabled roof and was two stories high, and we had the whole of it to ourselves.

In the winter, *Schneeberg* (snow mountain) endured howling, blinding snow-storms. Snow drifted and piled up against the back door of the house, as high as the top of the door. We used the front door to get out (the front of the house was slightly elevated), grabbed the shovel leaning against the side of the house, and started shoveling. Not me, though. I was too little.

But not too little to get on skis. The whole family skied, or tried to. My brother was the best, my brother says. He was at the ideal age to get on skis, learning quickly and fearing nothing. Mutti and Papa went down the slopes in a fashion which can only be described as unusual and even hilarious. Doris never developed the knack, which surprised me, because later in life she became an enthusiastic cross-country skier, the outdoor type who never tired of the cold. With rosy cheeks and a smile on her face, she was outside for hours, sledding, throwing snow balls, skating. But skiing down a mountain at age four was not for her.

I was two years old and learning to ski on boards that were thirty-two inches long. From all the stories I heard, I can picture the descent—my brother half-way down the slopes, my parents crossing their own skis, falling, getting up, traversing the slopes, doing the snowplow all the way to slow themselves down. And me? I probably went straight down, ignoring Mutti's plea to snowplow, discovered that I couldn't stop, toppled over and landed in the snow, and then broke out in sobs, all of which no doubt made Mutti nervous because she wanted to pick me up but couldn't get to me immediately for her snowplowing. By the time she reached me, I was more than likely in a very bad mood for having fallen again. But soon I was ready to return to it. There weren't any gondolas to take us back up, so how-ever far we had come down we had to walk back up.

Fortunately, the house could also be reached by a bus that came up from *Tetschen-Bodenbach*, the town where Mutti did most of her shopping. The village of *Schneeberg* had a general store full of all kinds of items like milk, nails, meat, pencils, band aids, underwear, and stinky cheeses.

Besides being a place of meeting and gossiping for villagers, it was also a place to acknowledge the esteemed leader of the current regime. *Guten Morgen* had been a perfectly good German greeting until Hitler came to power. Mutti, who was no fan of Hitler's, preferred *Guten Morgen,* and who could blame her? The storekeeper, it seems. The scene went like this: Mutti would enter the store and say a friendly *Guten Morgen* to the storekeeper's displeasure. "It's not *Guten Morgen,* Frau Behnke, it's *Heil Hitler.*" Mutti would reply cheerfully, "For me it's *Guten Morgen,* because it's morning." Case closed. Mutti never relented, for her mind was made up that she would never use the despised words that included the dictator's name. She was, however, playing a dangerous game, because she could have been reported or at least scrutinized more closely.

There was another incident involving Mutti's failure to play along with the authorities. She had the dubious honor of having been born on the same day as Hitler, April 20, and on his birthday flags flew everywhere. On April 20, 1944, Mutti had "forgotten" to display the flag at the front door, bringing the party group leader of the region by our house to admonish her. He said, "Frau Behnke, why isn't your flag flying? Could you possibly not know why all these flags are flying everywhere?" "Oh, yes," she replied, "I know why, it's my birthday!" The *Ortsgruppenleiter,* a local party leader, had no reply. Speechless at such flippancy, he turned on his heels and left.

Aside from these run-ins with Hitler-supporters, we spent two relatively quiet years in *Schneeberg,* two normal childhood years in the middle of a monstrous war raging throughout the rest of the world. Papa worked in or near Görlitz or *Tetschen-Bodenbach,* and now and then he had business in Dresden. He would take a bus or a train to Görlitz or Dresden, then return to *Schneeberg* for the weekends.

Klaus went to school in *Schneeberg,* where he studied and played with his buddies. Doris and I made friends with another German family that lived in the house next to us. Their daughter Ingrun and son Ulf were about the same age as Doris and I, and we played with them every day. My only remembrance of them comes from a black and white photo I have of them: they were both blond, curly-haired children. Their father didn't live with them as he was away being part of the war machine. There seemed always to be something mysterious about the father, and I heard him talked about more than once after the war when these stories became so much a part of my life. He was a highly-placed officer, but something apparently had happened to him because after the war ended the mother took Ingrun and Ulf to New Zealand where they remained for at least ten years.

In my teen years, I found that family fascinating, so much more interesting than mine. When the family returned to Germany in the late fifties, Ingrun visited me once and she and I read my diaries and giggled. Then my towheaded playmate from so many years previous became Miss Germany in 1960 and Miss Europe 1961. I never saw her again. She survived the war only to die in a car accident while still in her twenties. I remember feeling awed by the fact that she had had the courage to walk down a runway and endure everyone's stares.

While Doris and I played with Ingrun and Ulf, my brother made friends elsewhere. About a year before the end of the war, when he was ten, he had joined the Hitler-Youth movement because it had sponsored camping trips and other fun stuff. Later, when I saw pictures of young German boys saluting the flag, I thought that the whole Hitler youth movement was built around kids going on camping trips. The group would take a big tent, big enough to hold twenty-four male bodies, and along with other camping equipment transport it to some spot by a lake or a river where they would proceed to have a good old time singing patriotic songs and kicking a soccer ball around. Sort of boy-scoutish it was, but with the sinister twist that the boys would get hooked on the good times and end up all too soon as fodder for the war machine. When I told my brother I was astonished at his having joined this group and expressed further wonderment about why my parents ever allowed him to join, he said that it would have been impossible for them to voice their opinion about this group without fear of reprisal. (In fact, the group's big tent served a good purpose in our eventual flight from *Schneeberg*).

In scraping together a mental picture of my life during these war years, its dailyness often faded because of the lack of detail, but the stories I heard of the horrendous, the humorous, the sad and the ugly stood out enough to leave me wondering what a normal routine was like and the few pictures I have can't tell anything approaching the complete story. The smiles on our faces speak of happiness, not anxiety, so I have to let it be.

◆   ◆   ◆

Another horrendous event took place on February 13, 1945: Papa made a near-fatal decision. He journeyed to Dresden on business, just as he had done many times before. His job was to buy steel for his company, and he needed government permits to do so. That day, the city was filled with hundreds of thousands of refugees fleeing westward to escape the advancing Soviet Army. Trains overflowing with people and their belongings had wound their way south and west from Riga, Gdansk, and Berlin to, finally, Dresden. The people then took refuge in schools, hospitals, and railway stations, confident that Dresden would not be bombarded since it had no industrial sites or military installations. Why would the Allies bomb this beautiful city?

Because of all the throngs, Papa found it difficult to get around in the city. Many of the men, women, and children were dragging their few belongings on rough, wooden carts. Or, in some cases, their carts were piled high with sticks of furniture and pots and pans, with children pressed tightly up to the belongings to keep an eye on them while the parents pulled or pushed. They tried to keep the river in their sight to jump in if bombs began to fall, but the congestion was so great that often they had to take streets that only shunted them away from it. The air was cool on this February afternoon, and people were hurrying to get to a school or a hospital where they might find shelter for the night.

Papa moved quickly through the crowd, weaving in and out of the carts crowding the streets. He was hoping to finish his business with the government, but by the time he reached the appropriate office for official approval of his undertaking the place was closed. At first he thought to stay overnight in a room he had reserved by the central train station and return to the government office the next morning, but he decided at last to take a bus home to *Schneeberg*. When he arrived home that night, all of us were overjoyed to see him because we weren't expecting him till the next day. Our Papa was home, Mutti was happy, hugs and kisses all around. Love here, hatred about to be unleashed there.

The night Papa returned to us, February 13, 1945, was the first night of Dresden's firebombing. It continued the next night and eventually killed at least 35,000 people, most of them burned to death from incendiary bombs that rained from the sky. Air-raid sirens were wailing, people were running through the streets like live torches, burning, burning, dropping, dying. Thousands were wounded, maimed, went insane with terror. Their bodies afire, people threw themselves into the river Elbe, but as soon as they surfaced they continued burning. The city burned for eight days, with fire winds reaching between 125–180 miles an hour. The whole center of Dresden, an area of eleven square miles, was destroyed while military airfields, factories, and railways were scarcely touched.

Of course, I wasn't there when Dresden was firebombed, but the stories—oh, the stories!—and the pictures!—are with me forever. I try to make the images go away, but there pops up Dresden, a moon-like landscape, smoldering, stinking of burnt flesh and boiled bodies. By happenstance, several hundred thousand people converged, thinking themselves safe, only to experience hell instead. Some lived, more died. My Papa was spared, because of his decision, or random selection? Surely he was meant to live for Mutti and us. Thank God, others say. What God, I ask? Who let the horrors of Dresden happen? I don't know. When I learn about

Dresden later, I am not really shocked. This story is like so many others, and yet while other stories fade in time, the images of burning bodies and smoldering buildings will never quite go away.

I am thankful that my Papa's life was spared every time I hear the story. The pre-bombed city becomes more beautiful each time my parents talk about it. A gem, a jewel, they say. A model of inspired architecture. Buildings filled with sculptures, paintings, golden objects of history. I don't visit Dresden until 1994, almost fifty years after it was destroyed. Its landmarks, like the baroque Semper opera, the cathedral, the Zwinger, and numerous other churches have been rebuilt. The Frauenkirche is in the process of being pieced together again. I see the buildings but my mind is elsewhere. I can't imagine what went through the minds of the men at the moment they dropped the bombs. Or later, when they shoveled the boiled bodies into holes dug especially for the nameless. Nothing then would make the stink go away. The brutality of war remains in my mind forever.

Toward the end of the war in the spring of 1945 Vlasov's Army paid us a visit in *Schneeberg.* Andrei Andreyevich Vlasov was a Russian general who had joined up with the German forces out of opposition to Stalin and the Bolsheviks. First he had distinguished himself in fighting for Russia in the Battle for Moscow, but in a later battle in which his forces ended up surrounded by Germans he surrendered. Stalin had twice told him to keep fighting, but Vlasov surrendered and decided to fight with the Germans against Stalin. He felt that Stalin was the chief enemy of the Russian people. The Germans wouldn't let him fight for them again until close to war's end when Hitler was desperate for more cannon fodder.

In the meantime, Vlasov put together an army of Russian POWs and was ready to return to battle. I knew nothing about Vlasov or Stalin, but my parents were upset when this army of Russians in German uniforms showed up. They were actually fleeing from the Russians, their countrymen, because the word got out that any "real Russian" who captured a member of Vlasov's army could shoot that Russian/German without giving him the benefit of a trial. So there they were, Russians in German uniforms fighting for Germany!

Apparently, some of Vlasov's fighters decided to "live" with us, though that's not the right choice of words, because instead of living with us they were wreaking havoc. They had brought with them panje horses, a cross between a horse and a pony, industrious creatures, and these horses were now idling in our front hall. Apparently, nobody had told Vlasov's men that horses belonged outside. My parents appealed to the air force support station in *Schneeberg* for help in keeping the Russians and their horses under control, and airmen stayed with us around the clock and kept a watchful eye on us.

Soon enough, though, another army appeared, this time the real Russian Army, at which Vlasov's men and their panje horses left in a hurry. We thought we were now safe, but the real Russian army was made up of men from all parts of the country, some of them White Russians but others trigger-happy, women-defiling Mongolian cowboys who shot at everything that moved. My family and the rest of *Schneeberg's* villagers hid in our houses, though this didn't help many of the women who got raped anyway. Conveniently, being available to be raped seemed to be yet one more contribution women made to war, aside from scrounging for food and keeping their families fed and alive.

My Mutti was in the prime of her life and must have been eyed by the Russian soldiers, so much so that she decided to play sick. In her youth, she had been an amateur actress and now her acting ability came in handy. She took to her bed and pretended to be deathly ill with something.

Two Russians were standing by her bed, as was my Papa, in his pocket a knife he was ready to use if the soldiers had so much as touched my Mutti. The Russians had taken off their pistols and put them on the nightstand, in preparation for their crime. My Papa stood ready to kill them and be killed in turn. This is how one version of the story went. Another version involved a large knife kept in the bedside table drawer that Papa would have attempted to use but which, years later and back in Hamburg, ended up slicing bread.

Nobody ever recounted how this rape crisis was resolved. Perhaps Papa bribed the soldiers with his watch; maybe they didn't want to rape a sick woman although they raped countless pregnant and post-partum women. Maybe the Russians had a heart and recognized my Papa's good nature, his way of connecting with people. In the end, I want to believe that my Mutti wasn't raped.

Although we lived in fear most of the time, not everything that happened during this time was heart-stopping. Humor surfaced now and then as a kind of much-needed relief. White Russians, also called European Russians, were supposedly a very friendly but also fearful people. Some of them, as it happened, were filling our house as "guests." But one day, two more Russian soldiers knocked on the door, heavily armed with machine guns and hand grenades, asking for lodging. Since they knew a little German, Papa explained to them that a brand new house was being built on a nearby hill and they should stay there. Though the house was not yet quite finished, he persuaded them to stay there and they left. Fifteen minutes later, after dark, there was a commotion at our front door, and the two Russians were standing there, obviously spooked. They all but hugged Papa and told him that they didn't want to sleep in that house because they were all alone and they were afraid! So they joined us as well, making themselves right at home, snooping through everything, opening drawers, cupboards, and closets. Even locked cupboards didn't keep them from breaking the locks and taking inventory.

What they found in one of the cupboards in my brother's room was potentially dangerous for Papa. Klaus, a typical boy, found the swirl of wartime activity around him to be quite exciting. This was true adventure but with an edge of danger to it. In the midst of real soldiers, guns, grenades, and ammo belts, my brother was playing war. He had been collecting the rank badges of soldiers and officers, keeping them in a box that the Russians discovered during one of their snooping expeditions. The interlopers held a machine gun on Papa and accused him of being a militarist and a Nazi to boot, which was far from the truth. Papa talked to them, and in one way or another, they took the old kitchen clock instead of taking Papa because more than anything they liked watches and clocks. "Uhri, Uhri," that's all they wanted. They went around with watches running up one arm and down the other, like watch salesmen at a carnival, constantly asking each other what time it was.

Another incident gave away the fact that back home the Russians didn't have toilets that flushed when a chain was pulled. They saw our toilet and exclaimed, "Ah, good bowl to wash potatoes in." And so they put their potatoes in the toilet bowl and pulled the chain to see what it would do, and when the potatoes disappeared they yelled, "Sabotage!" and then ran in the basement to see if the potatoes were somewhere there! When I was little, this was the story I wanted to hear again and again. I think that the Russians' naivete made them more human to me, years later of course, because if they could be laughed at they couldn't have been all bad.

Besides being fascinated by clocks and watches, they also fancied faucets. Just imagine—turn a faucet screwed into a wall and water came out. This magic they wanted badly for Mother Russia. So they ripped the faucets out of the walls, stacked them with their—or, rather, our—belongings, and carried them all the way back home where they planned to screw them into the walls of their homes after which, like magic, they would have running water too.

◆   ◆   ◆

But one day our life in this nearly idyllic place came to an abrupt halt when the mayor of *Schneeberg* came to our house with a demand from the Czech government to leave the country by noon the following day. This was bad news, considering all the work that had to be done in one day, not to mention the pain of being uprooted. It was made that much worse by the fact that my Papa was working about two hours away. He had learned what the Czech government was up to and decided to leave work immediately, grabbing a bike that wasn't his and pedaling all the way to *Schneeberg* where my mother greeted him with tears streaming down her face. My Papa was her rock.

And here our trek began. Hamburgers on the move, we. The gruesome, backbreaking labor of this return journey to Hamburg came home to me every time I heard the story of the fear of what might have happened next. I take solace only in the fact that we were not alone.

But first the packing, or what not to pack. The mayor had given Mutti a list of what we were allowed to take per person, one suitcase weighing no more than 130 pounds plus one piece of hand luggage weighing no more than twenty pounds. We crammed everything we could into these cases, pots and pans as well as clothes. Big household items such as lamps, mirrors, rugs, and bedding had to stay behind, and by order of the mayor the beds had to be freshly made before we left. Someone in the village had a wagon consisting of a piece of wood 6'x 3', four wheels, and a shaft, and onto this wagon my parents and brother lifted the belongings that we were allowed to take, and covered them with the large Hitler-Youth tarpaulin that had been stored in our house since my brother's glorious but short-lived Hitler-Youth days. I thank my brother for helping our parents either push or pull the wagon, in which Doris and I sat either on or under the tent. We left by noon as we had been ordered to do.

The first part of the journey took us through a Russian-occupied zone where our meager belongings became more meager still because the Russians took whatever they pleased. And, of course, my parents were on their feet the whole time, about 110 miles, until we reached the American zone. For some reason, the Americans didn't want to give us passage and we were allowed through only after my Papa had spoken to them in his broken English. The border patrol soldier knew Hamburg, so they chatted for a while until the soldier said, "I'll take Hamburgers any day," and he let us pass.

The next portion of the trip could very well explain my aversion to driving on the German Autobahn today. When someone passes me at two hundred 200 miles per hour, I say to myself, "What happened to the good old days?" We "drove" the Autobahn with our wagon, but at a safe speed of four mph and probably only somewhat faster when we barreled downhill for a spell. My parents sat on the front of the wagon, with Papa holding the handle, my brother sitting in the back, and Doris and I atop of our belongings, charging down the hill, laughing and having a good time. No doubt, my parents and brother enjoyed those moments most, because as soon as the road went uphill, Klaus had to push and my parents pulled while Doris and I relaxed on the wagon. We were the princesses Doris and Christel, leading charmed lives on top of a wagon that moved as if pulled and pushed by magic powers. I wonder what we did when it rained. Did we all crawl under the tarpaulin? Where did we sleep? I know sometimes a farmer would take pity on us and let us sleep in his hayloft. Other times we slept on the ground or on the floor of unoccupied or bombed-out buildings.

The next day was no different than the day before. We trudged on. There were thousands of people just like us, on the move. The old and the young, the homeless, tired, and hungry, out of their minds with fear for the future.

At times, we were able to get on a freight train. There was an informal network of people telling others which train was going where and at what time. At this particular time, we had arrived in Chemnitz (west of Dresden) and someone told us about a train that would take us thirty miles further. What a relief that must have been for my parents and my brother, and even for the princesses Doris and Christel who, after all, were exposed to all kinds of weather. So our wagon was hoisted onto the freight train with the help of willing strangers' arms. And for the next thirty miles we sat among wagons, maybe on blankets and maybe on a hard freight train floor, but always with our parents and brother and never alone. This trek was not made in isolation; on the road were hundreds of wagons and other homemade contraptions on wheels going everywhere where home had once been, masses of people criss-crossing in every direction.

Their common goal of getting home brought these people closer, and they talked and encouraged each other when they could. They also shared food when they stopped at farms along the way and were lucky enough to receive some bread or a few potatoes.

In Chemnitz, one of the boys in a group of several wagons traveling together had a bicycle that was relatively new but that crucially lacked a chain. A Russian soldier on a bike with a flat tire saw this new bike, walked up to the boy, and demanded it. "Here, give me bike, you take mine," he said, just like that, no questions asked or money offered. He took off on a bike with no chain and, after feeling the earth spin he probably never got on another bike again as long as he lived.

In Lüneburg, about twenty-eight miles south of Hamburg, my brother remembers having another chance to get on a train headed toward Hamburg. The cars on this train didn't have doors. It was an open freight train, filled with gravel. No luxury train, this one. Several men helped us heave our wagon, including all our belongings, atop this mass of gravel and there it sat, my parents watching it anxiously. They couldn't afford to lose any more than they had already lost, unable to bring along everything they had owned in Schneeberg. But this was not their only worry. We had to get through the small town of Bardowick, north of Lüneburg, that was occupied by a large number of Poles who also happened to be kleptomaniacs. They made their day's work out of stealing anything and everything in sight, including robbing trains. Fortunately, the train we were on made no stops but crawled on through this kleptomaniac-country at moderate speed, fast enough so that the Polish Wild West brigade couldn't ambush it. We made it through Bardowick with our few belongings intact.

South of Hamburg in the suburb of Harburg, though, we had to stay in a refugee camp for three days before we were allowed to proceed, mainly because our papers had to be filled out and signed. Our hometown was within our grasp, but we had to wait to reclaim it. Over the three tedious days, we contracted lice and other parasites. However, after three whole days of filling out forms and scratching our heads, we were allowed to leave, lice and all.

So far, we had been on the road for twenty-three days, most of them on foot (except for Doris and me), which meant that my parents walked an average of twenty miles per day while pulling and pushing a loaded wagon. I wonder what my parents' shoes looked like. Were they walking on cardboard by this time? If I had been able to look into their souls, what would I have found? How were they able to hold up? What gave them the courage and strength to do this hard physical labor that they had never before had to do? What helped them rise to the occasion? But if I had been able to ask them then, they probably would have simply said, "We just did it. Everybody else did." Part of the will to carry on was the fact that their fate was shared with others, that they were not alone.

But it wasn't over yet. This slow flight home to safety had to go through one last test—our arrival in Hamburg. From Harburg, my parents pulled the wagon through the suburbs of Wilhelmsburg and Hammerbrook that looked identical with their leveled piles of stone until we finally reached Barmbek, our home suburb. No trees, no bushes, no flowers, just mountains of rubble, streets piled high with heaps of bricks, broken glass, houses burnt to the ground, and bombed-out shells of apartment buildings. They looked like dark ghosts with holes for eyes watching us pick our way. A moonscape with aliens—dust-covered people like us. It was not the Hamburg that we had left; it was as though we were on a different planet where living things were alien to the landscape. To walk on against this bleakness took so much courage, because my parents knew not if their house was still standing or if it had been leveled. Miraculously, though, Hartzloh 38 had survived! Not so the apartment building at the end of our street. I have always looked at the reconstruction of that apartment building as symbolic of my growing up.

My mother, Klaus, Doris, and I in 1943

The house we rented in Schneeberg, Sudetenland

My mother, brother, sister,
and I in Schneeberg,
Sudetenland, 1943

Doris and I
in Schneeberg, 1943

Moonscape Barmbek, ca. 1945

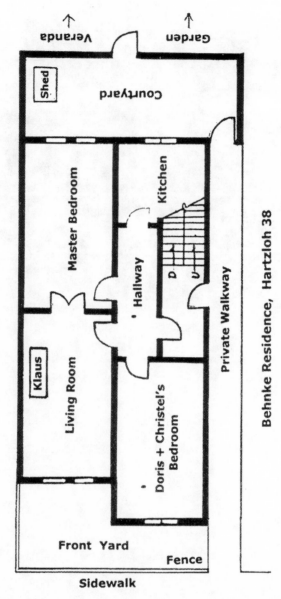

Floorplan of our apartment in Hamburg—614 square feet

3

Childhood years in post-war Hamburg

✦

1945–1948

We arrived at our house in Hartzloh on a warm day in May, 1945. Our wagon stopped in front of the gate leading into the front yard. Doris and I sat on the edge of the wagon, waiting for what was going to happen next and probably wondering what we were doing here. I'm not sure she remembered this place, since she was less than four years old when we left to live in the Sudetenland. I am certain that I had no recollection that this structure was the house in which I was born.

There we were—tired, hungry, dirty, and badly in need of soap and water. Lice crawled through our hair. Our shoes were tied to our feet by strings. Our clothes were dusty and raggedy. My uncle and aunt came running out of the house to welcome back their bedraggled relatives. Since phones weren't working and mail service had stopped, there had been no way to notify them of our return.

When we left Hamburg in 1943, my parents suggested that Tante Klara, Onkel Heini and their only child, my cousin Inge, move into our house from a hut in a *Schrebergarten* where they had sought refuge when their apartment building was reduced to rubble. A *Schrebergarten* was a small plot of land where Germans who lived chiefly in apartments spent their weekends planting vegetables, tending flowers, and sometimes staying overnight in their huts. There was a Schrebergarten at the end of our street, and in 1945 many families were able to make these one-room huts their emergency homes. Their apartment buildings had been bombed, leaving them homeless except for this small plot of land with a hut built of wood. Some huts were big enough for a couple of chairs, a mattress, and a table big enough to hold a few utensils.

When we returned from *Schneeberg,* our home of 614 square feet was now shared by eight people, six of them adults. Each of us thus had seventy-six square feet—about as much space as a normal bathroom—to call our own. But then again, we couldn't call any space our own because there were just too many of us. We couldn't even fit around the table at the same time to eat together. Our family ate in the living room, which also served as a dining room, and Tante Klara and her family ate in the kitchen. We were lucky to have tables to gather around.

The same family that lived upstairs before we left Hamburg was still living there, and my brother was happy to be playing with his friend Ernst again. Our long and narrow backyard had been converted into a vegetable garden, but it also became a haven to which to escape when things got too crowded in our four rooms. The primitive basement bathroom that had no tub became a sanctuary of sorts, although with eight of us using it, nobody could claim it for too long. Any personal cleansing had to be done in the kitchen sink and once a week in a tub hauled into the kitchen for bathing.

Although living together with relatives in such a cramped space was not easy, all of us found solace in being together in our shared misery. Not too long after we returned, Tante Klara and her family moved back to their patched-up and expanded Schrebergarten hut, where they lived until they were later eligible for an apartment. Now we were able to "spread out." My parents had their bedroom back, and my sister and I slept together in the *Kinderzimmer,* the children's room. The wagon, with its wheels removed and crude pieces of wood added for legs, became a makeshift bed for my brother. It stood in the living room for years, barely disguised as a couch during the day, a grey Army-issue blanket covering the straw mattress and a lumpy pillow giving it a lounge look.

Finally it was summertime and my sister and I could play outside. We wore cotton dresses that were quickly becoming too small at every critical point: our arms hung like sticks out of sleeves that were too short. The memory I have of that summer and those too-small dresses comes from snapshots. I am almost four years old and I'm still not aware of myself.

The big event that summer was my cousin Inge's wedding. Tante Klara's daughter had met a man from a well-to-do family. At least I think he or his parents were well to-do, because how else would this wedding have been possible? The bride wore a long white dress with a gauzy veil that was gathered in a circle around her head so it looked like a crown. In my eyes, she was a princess holding a big bouquet of flowers that her somber-looking groom took from her as he helped her out of the carriage when it arrived in front of the church. The groom wore tails, no less, and a black top hat. Doris and I were flower girls along with two other girls who were a few years older. They wore long dresses and so also looked like princesses. Oh, to have a long dress with gathered lace trimming! It was every girl child's dream. Even as a child I pored over the photo of the four of us. Envy filled my heart. The older girls' flower baskets were lined with fabric and featured lace on the outside, whereas our baskets were woven and bare except for a big bow on the handle and a flower stuck on the outside.

By the time the bride and groom emerged from the church, word had spread around the neighborhood that a wedding was taking place, and adults and children gathered in front of the church to gaze in awe at the bride and groom. In another photo, my sister and I are in front of the bride and groom, and Doris is grabbing my arm because it looks like I'm ready to take off. The wedding's over, let's go. Our hair is cut short in identical styles with some hair gathered on top in big white bows. Our dresses are short-sleeved and short-hemmed, made of white muslin with little circles embroidered around the hem and the top of the dresses. I wonder if these dresses were made from curtains. Where else would we get such fancy dresses, so unwarlike? Only our plain brown shoes, which somehow don't match the dresses, speak of the destitution of the times.

Inge and her aristocratic, emaciated-looking husband Werner left in a carriage pulled by two horses, and the reception was held somewhere where tables were laid with flowers and fancy china. And there was food. It remains a puzzle to me how this abundance of food had been acquired. Maybe an oriental carpet or two had been bartered for it.

Most of the time we had little protein to fuel our bodies, and wood and coal for the cooking stove was hard to come by if at all. When there was coal to be had and when we had money to pay for it, it was just enough coal to keep one stove heated. Enough to keep the kitchen warm for a few hours every day. When we had food, it was cooked on this stove. Papa and Klaus took turns replenishing the coal. They did so by taking a bucket to the basement coal cellar and filling it, then feeding the stove. But many times there wasn't enough coal to fill the bucket. If we were lucky, there might be five briquettes stacked against the wall, more precious than bars of gold. Sometimes, a small pile of egg-shaped pieces looked so inviting that my Papa was tempted to grab a handful, and then another and another to fill his bucket, but in order to make it last longer, he had to stop himself from being too greedy. His dream was to fill the stoves in the *Kinderzim-mer* and living room to overflowing so that his family could wake up to warm rooms in the morning. For now, Papa counted the pieces he placed in the bucket, their egg-shapes reminding him of a food he hadn't tasted in months. The living room stove and the one in the *Kinderzimmer* remained cold and smelled of left-over ashes from fires long past. It wasn't until years later that we were able to afford a gas stove for cooking.

Meanwhile, as summer was coming to an end, my parents were busy gathering fuel for the winter, which was to be one of the coldest in memory. Gathering wood meant chopping down any remaining trees that had survived the bombs. Down the street from our house along the sidewalk by the hospital, one huge and magnificent maple tree still stood, against all the odds, and then one day it stood no more. Somebody had taken the axe to it in the night, and all that was left were the roots which my industrious Papa and Onkel Heini attacked with a wedge and a hammer to extract the splinters of wood that could be burned.

In the meantime, at the school where I would be a student a few years later, Mutti and some of the neighbors were busy destroying the athletic track. This track was built in layers one of which was slag from the gas company. On top of the slag was a layer of sand. So with shovel in hand, my mother proceeded to dig down to the slag and fill bucket after bucket which Papa and Klaus then carried home and deposited in the basement coal room. The basement was the safest place for storing this fuel, and piling it anywhere else outside would have been foolish given that sharing the precious fuel was not the order of the post-war day. Refugees kept streaming into Hamburg from the East, and they had even less than we did. Since we didn't have much of anything, self-preservation closed our hearts and holding on to the little we had became an obsession. Slag we did not share.

It was also during these first years back in Hamburg that Mutti turned into something of a coal miner. She had heard that there was a train at the local train station, about fifteen minutes from our house, whose cargo was pressed coal dust that anyone was legally allowed to haul away.

After her job on the local school track, Mutti had become quite expert at mining, all compliments of the war. One day she walked to the train station with two buckets and a hatchet, clambered into a train car, and began hacking away at the pressed coal dust, something she had never before done and had never even dreamed of doing. She got so busy hacking and picking and filling that she failed to notice the train was moving, and when she finally did the train was moving too fast and she couldn't jump off. Outside, the night was now as black as the coal she had been working on.

In Alsterdorf, a suburb a few miles from home, however, the train was stopped by people intent on stealing coal because, unbeknown to Mutti, other train cars were full of the Easter-egg coal. Some kind people helped my Mutti shovel this *Eierkohle* into her two buckets and even gave her train fare back to where she had started. It was midnight when she staggered back into the house, black as a coal miner, to be hugged heartily by Papa in his relief at having regained his Anna. He had already gone to the police to report her missing.

My brother followed in her footsteps and became expert at stealing coal. He would walk to the freight train depot in the nearby *Stadtpark,* quickly determine which cars held coal, fill up a bag, and run. Once the police spotted him and gave chase. It was winter and though the hill he had to climb was icy, he made it without being caught. Still, this "adventure" produced a nightmare in him, vivid and terrifying for years to come.

◆   ◆   ◆

While my parents and brother were busy hauling fuel for the winter, Doris and I kept up our play. We didn't have a playground, but we had the street to play on and bombed-out buildings to explore. I doubt that we were permitted to nose around just any building since unexploded bombs might be lying there. Most of the time we played in our own backyard and in the courtyard in the back of our house, where we had a sandbox filled with plain dirt rather than sand, meaning that we looked a sight at the end of the day. We would drag a chair to the kitchen sink and soak our feet to get the black dirt off. I needed help scrubbing my face and neck, but for some reason my neck usually had a persistent shadow of dirt leftover from the day before and the day before that.

While we played, Papa and Mutti were not only gathering fuel but also much-needed food. Potatoes were nowhere to be had. The national vegetable of the time was the rutabaga, which was available at the produce store now and then. It was prepared in a hundred different ways but hardly ever with meat, so we ate it boiled, mashed, stewed, and raw. A rutabaga is a root with a tough skin which has to be peeled off with a very sharp knife. The inside has the consistency of a turnip, except that it is more orange in color and sweeter. If, for some reason, a minute piece of pork belly could be had, the meal became a feast. Rutabagas are rich in vitamins C and B, but that didn't make them any more palatable when eaten daily for weeks on end. When I tried one again as an adult, I could hardly swallow it for all the memories that were stuck halfway down my throat.

We ate horse meat when word got out that it was available. The main "nutritional" intake was corn in all its forms—corn bread, mashed corn kernels, corn meal made into puddings with the addition of water. Our skin literally took on a yellow cast from eating so much corn! And since we were hungry most of the time, we were tired all the time. When Mutti was lucky enough to get a loaf of bread, clutching her ration card and moving slowly up the line, the bread had to be carried home gingerly for fear that it would crumble because it was made of baked cornmeal and water alone. Still, it was always eaten with delight, if only to quiet the ravenous grumblings of our stomachs. The land behind our house had long been converted into a vegetable garden, so Mutti preserved beans and tomatoes.

◆   ◆   ◆

We also had another supplier of vegetables and, if they felt generous enough, of meat—my paternal grandparents. My Oma and Opa Behnke were vegetable farmers. By the time I knew them, they lived in a thatched-roof house on a farm in Reitbrook, a village in fertile Vierlande, south of Hamburg. Before they bought that property, they had owned and operated a successful produce store in Hamburg-Hamm which they had bought around 1904 and sold thirty years later.

My grandfather, the one with the four first names, was the son of a farm worker, Johann Carl Heinrich and his wife Marie Dorothea Elisabeth Pionetti, my great-grandmother, who died in 1904 when my grandfather was 24. The family lived in Kaarssen, also south of Hamburg, in a rural area dotted with little villages. My grandfather worked as a farm hand until 1902 when he decided to move to Hamburg where he could make more money as a laborer. He lived in an apartment in the inner city until he met my grandmother Emma Maria, the daughter of well-established vegetable farmers in Moorfleet, also south of the Elbe, in an area of fertile land that produced abundant fruits and vegetables.

My paternal great-grandparents had come from Mecklenburg, a state in northeastern Germany, towards the end of the 19th century, and because my maternal great-grandmother had been born there, maybe they had been somehow connected before they all moved to the Hamburg area. Maybe my grandparents had known each other because their parents knew each other. In any case, they were married before grandfather Ernst's mother died, but she never saw her first grandson, my Papa, who was born in 1905. No matter how much I desired it, I could not get any closer to the beginnings of my Papa's life, because either he didn't tell me much about his early years or I never saw the need to ask him the right questions. I suspect the latter. By the time I was old enough to resume being curious about his past, my Papa was dead.

Now, in 1945, he made frequent trips to Reitbrook to help his aging parents work the land and to bring home food for us. During this post-war period, there were many small-time farmers who made their living by taking their vegetables to market once or twice a week. People streamed to the country in search of food, and many farmers in this area became quite well-to-do, because those Hamburgers who still had valuables such as Oriental carpets, china, or jewelry took what items they owned to the farmers in exchange for anything edible. The big problem was that when people returned from exchanging goods for food, they had to pass through a control station jointly set up by the city government and the British occupation authorities, where they had to show proof that they had worked for the food in their possession. Bartering was forbidden, and food was often taken away by the police who were controlling checkpoints. So my Papa carried a letter from my grandparents, saying that the goods he was carrying were given to him in exchange for work and that no other goods (like carpets) were given to them in return for food.

◆   ◆   ◆

Christmas 1945 was coming around, the time of traditional glad tidings, peace, hope, and love. But Germany lay in ruins, people were mourning their dead and missing, families had been torn apart, everyone was hungry. Survivors in their makeshift rooms in bombed-out buildings were cold for lack of coal or wood. There was no glass in the windows and the wind blew desolately through cold rooms unless pieces of cardboard could be gotten for nailing to the window frames to keep out the worst, at least, of the cold.

Daily rations were tiny: five ounces of bread, one ounce of meat, half an ounce of fat of some sort, two ounces of other foodstuffs, probably carbohydrates, one tenth of an ounce of cheese, a little coffee substitute, but no sugar. Just enough food to make us aware of the miserable feeling in our stomachs, but not enough to ever satisfy us. Some areas of Germany had potatoes, others did not. We dreamed about having enough to eat while we lay on our stomachs at night to lessen the hunger pains.

The black market began to thrive. Goods were exchanged for food behind bushes, in quiet side streets or in bunkers, places where people sidled by while whispering, "Bedding," "Yarn," "Bread rations." People who had cigarettes were in business, because cigarettes moved this black market along. Goods were priced according to the price of tobacco. In newspapers, prices were listed like today's commodity prices: butter for 250 Marks per pound (*Reichsmark*), one egg for fifteen Marks, a pound of coffee for 500 Marks. At swapping centers a hammer might be exchanged for a bicycle inner tube, a pair of shoes for a radio.

Beyond the bartering with Reichsmark and cigarettes, there was the plundering. Plundering for survival. Over time warehouses were emptied of stored food by thousands of people. Wheels of cheese were pilfered from warehouses and rolled through the streets. Women performed the backbreaking labor of clearing away debris in exchange for rations. Then, to make things worse, the British occupation authorities lowered the daily caloric intake per adult to 1000 calories per day or even less. The general state of my homeland was grim.

On this first Christmas after the end of the war, we didn't have dreams of sugar plums in our heads because we knew better. All we had was corn bread, some rutabagas, and maybe a few potatoes, enough to silence our hunger pains for a little while. The customs of Christmas, the candles on the tree illuminating glass-blown ornaments and tinsel, the mounds of extravagantly wrapped and beribboned presents, the delicious food, the warm stove—all lived only in people's memories. People were still so numb from the horrors of the war that celebrating Christmas was the last thing on their minds. They felt merely grateful to be alive as they huddled in their cold apartments.

My parents longed to resume the ways of Christmases past, to celebrate Christmas with their children the same way that their own parents had celebrated it with them. But normalcy was quite a few years away. My Tante Else, who was still waiting for her husband to return from a Russian labor camp, had moved in with us. I remember an old flag with the swastika still on it serving as a room divider, since the living room also served as a bedroom. Papa's brother was still missing, held in Russia or maybe even dead. Nobody knew. But despite all that sadness in and around them, my parents rallied themselves to sing Christmas carols, though often they stopped to cry. I didn't know what they were crying about. One minute they smiled and the next they cried, great tears rolling down their faces, for no reason at all or so I thought. Christmas presents would have been homemade and practical—a blanket fashioned into a coat, an old army coat turned inside out and sewn into a jacket.

Twenty-four major war criminals were tried and convicted before the International Military Tribunal in Nuremberg on October 1, 1946. Twelve of them were sentenced to death. Then the second set of trials of lesser war criminals began.

My parents probably followed the trials on the radio. I had no idea what a war criminal was or what a person had to do to become one. I didn't even know what a war was, although I had lived through one and was now experiencing the aftermath of those war criminals' crimes. Mainly, I was thinking of Christmas to come.

◆   ◆   ◆

Christmas 1946 wasn't much better, and it was bitter cold as well, one of the coldest winters in anyone's memory. Temperatures of -4 degrees Fahrenheit were not uncommon. Even the *Alster*, the lake in the middle of Hamburg, froze over. The freezing temperatures wouldn't have mattered so much if times had been normal, but times were not. Rivers and canals were frozen and ships bringing precious food couldn't move. Trains lacked sufficient coal to operate. The population was half-starved. Food was severely rationed, and women stood in line for hours to get what they could. Many apartments lacked windowpanes. Coal or wood were scarce and the stove in our kitchen was fed only for a few hours at a time, just long enough to warm hands and feet. When the stove was cold, it was time to put on another pair of socks, maybe a sweater, and even a woolen hat, and get into bed. Klaus, Doris, and I huddled in one bed to keep each other warm. We had electricity only sporadically. And St. Nikolaus didn't come.

A pre-Christmas festivity—St. Nikolaus—had come and gone without any mention. I imagine that we had celebrated it while living in Schneeberg, but for at least a couple of years after war's end the traditional day of joy for children was suspended for lack of surprises such as nuts, candy, and apples or oranges.

There are many legends about the origin of St. Nikolaus, one of which is that he was the bishop of Myra (in present-day Turkey) and that he died on December 6, in the year 343. He was supposed to have done many good deeds, such as saving ships from capsizing and giving gold coins to desperate people. From the pictures I had seen of him, I knew that he was an old man who wore a long red coat trimmed in white fur, on his head a fur-trimmed hood, in his right hand a long staff for steadying himself as he walked from house to house with a sack-full of presents on his back.

I never actually saw St. Nikolaus because he came through a window or down a chimney while my siblings and I were sleeping. Before we went to bed on December 5th, we placed a clean shoe on a windowsill for St. Nikolaus to fill with chocolate and candy and maybe apples or nuts. The shoe had to be clean or he wouldn't fill it. In the morning, we would rush to the window and see that our shoes had been filled. Oh, the sheer joy of it!

St. Nikolaus' companion was Knecht Ruprecht, and he was the one to watch out for because he punished the children who had behaved badly. This figure, which had different names all over Germany, merged in northern Germany into what we knew as *Weihnachtsmann*.

I was told the story of the Christmas when we heard a knock on the door, and while Papa greeted the *Weihnachtsmann* Doris and I shook with fear, wondering what this figure in red attire and long white beard would do. Would he take his switch to us, or would he put us in his sack and take us away because we had been disobedient. Had we been disobedient? We were to find out: he loomed in the doorway to the living room and in a deep voice said, "*Fröhliche Weihnachten*" (Merry Christmas). There may have followed some chatter which I don't recall. Papa asked him to have a seat and rest, and so he sat down and placed his sack, which had something in it (disobedient children?) on the floor next to him. He beckoned to Doris to come sit on his lap which Doris dutifully did, all the while looking around for someone to save her. Then the *Weihnachtsmann* said in his deep voice, "Doris, have you been a good girl this year?" which she didn't answer right away because she had to think for a minute. But then she said, "Yes, Alfred!" At which everyone burst out laughing and I didn't know why they were all laughing. Why, even the *Weihnachtsmann* was chuckling. (Alfred was the neighborhood watchman who had alerted us to imminent bombing attacks just a few years prior).

Now Christmas 1946 was almost here. St. Nikolaus didn't come, but there was a scraggly Christmas tree leaning tiredly against the shed in the courtyard. Fragrant and green, it was ready to be brought into the house on December 24 and decorated with some candle stubs and a few ornaments. First, though, it had to undergo some cosmetic surgery. Papa cut a branch from the bottom of the tree and drilled a hole in the trunk somewhere in the middle where nature had left a gap. The idea was to make it appear full at those points our eyes first focused. Improvising like this was the order of the day. The back of the tree would face the corner of the living room, so it didn't matter what the back looked like. In any case, we didn't care that the tree wasn't perfect, we were happy just to have one. My brother probably stole it and he and Papa dragged it home in full sight of all the other people who were doing the same thing. My brother, the urchin, had become good at stealing, maybe even begging.

On the morning of *Heilig Abend* (Christmas Eve) my parents had carried the tree from the backyard into the living room, and behind closed doors were busy decorating it. Klaus was helping them, since he was old enough not to get under foot. Doris and I were waiting in our bedroom, cuddled together under blankets, because tonight the coal that my parents had managed to save for this special night was going to be used in the kitchen and in the living room, the two rooms where we would spend the most time celebrating Christmas. With fierce determination, my parents were getting ready to celebrate despite all the adverse circumstances.

We could hear the murmur of voices, laughter, and the rustle of paper from the room next door, and every now and then Mutti running along the corridor to the kitchen. We didn't know why she was doing all the hurrying back and forth. Furniture was being moved around. Were we just imagining the scent of orange peel roasting on top of the stove in the living room, or was it real? Could the scent of orange peel have followed us from Schneeberg? How could that be? We hadn't even seen an orange in two years. Our anticipation made us a little feverish, and I clung to my sister who was slightly more composed than I was. After all, she was seven then, and I was only five.

Finally, it was time. The crystal bell rang and Doris and I were at the living room door in a flash though we still had to wait until the door was opened for us. When it was, we were greeted by Papa's smiling face. He motioned us inside and there we stood, our jaws dropped, trying to take in everything at once. The room was warm, and cold hands and feet were instantly forgotten. There was a momentary hush as we gazed at the Christmas tree, bright with candles, and their light reflected in the few ornaments that must have been saved from better times. The candle light illuminated the table in the middle of the room on which our presents were waiting for us. Presents! But it wasn't time yet to open them; first we had to sing *Stille Nacht, Heilige Nacht* (Silent Night) together, or mercifully only one verse of it. Finally, we were allowed to open our presents, which didn't take much time. There was a *süsser Teller*, except this plate of sweets didn't have any candy. Instead, an apple, a few hazelnuts, and a cookie—all of them little miracles—had made their way from somewhere onto this small plate of goodies. St. Nikolaus had saved them for this moment. No oranges anywhere.

The presents were modest—two dolls were waiting for us, one for Doris and one for me. These dolls didn't move or say anything but were rag dolls, made from leftover fabric, soft and cuddly, and lovable. We clung to them, talked to them, kissed them. The Weihnachtsmann, the equivalent of Santa Claus, had brought them and they were exactly what we had wished for. Little did we know that my mother had made them. In anticipation of things to come and because my parents couldn't afford to buy presents, my brother was given a used razor. That Christmas, he didn't have a single hair on his face that needed shaving. But now he was ready, should one appear. Klaus was barely twelve years old.

Each year after that, Christmas presents became more plentiful, but celebrating Christmas stayed the same. And presents continued to be homemade, such as the crocheted potholders that I showered on relatives and friends. Each year, the Christmas tree got some cosmetic surgery before it was trimmed. My parents always waited until the morning of December 24 to buy a tree at a tree stand, and by this time the remaining trees were mostly rejects. After Papa fitted the tree in the wooden tree stand, he took a saw and removed the branches that were too low for situating the wooden figures of Mary and Joseph and little Jesus lying in a crib under the tree. Each year, a filled water bucket was placed behind the tree because it always stood in the corner next to the sheer curtains that could easily have caught fire. The tree was decorated with real candles, so one person had to be in the room when the candles were lit in case a fire broke out. It never did, however.

For several years, our childless neighbors, Herr and Frau Voss, came over in the evening. When the doorbell rang, we knew it was them and that their arms would be laden with presents for us and even some for my parents. From our neighbors we received our first real dolls, dolls with porcelain faces and soft bodies and, later on, dolls with legs and arms that moved and eyes that opened and closed and hair that we could comb and braid. I can still feel the joy of looking at a doll I received one year—she wore a pink dress and a hat to match. I was in love.

It must have been hard for my parents not to be able to give us the dolls we craved, making Christmas a particularly hard time for them because they wanted to fulfill our wishes but couldn't. My parents' middle-class standing had allowed them to buy things before the war, and with Christmas came a certain expectation of there being presents again and that providing their children with the appropriate gifts would not cause undue stress. For the present, though, this was not so and wouldn't be until a few years after the war. As kids, we didn't think too much about what we didn't have, but our parents were aware of the things they couldn't provide for us. They were always very appreciative of our neighbors' good hearts.

When our neighbors came over on Christmas Eve, Doris, Klaus and I sang Christmas carols for them. *Stille Nacht, heilige Nacht; O Tannenbaum, o Tannen-*

baum, and *Leise rieselt der Schnee* (quietly falls the snow), which we sang in harmony. Our neighbors sat and listened, and for some reason they dabbed their eyes with little white handkerchiefs. We sang and sang until my parents put an end to it, because they feared that the neighbors were too polite to ask us to stop!

As we got older, our presentations became more elaborate and proceeded to poetry recitations. Reciting poems from memory rather than reading them became quite important for it showed that we had put time into preparing. Doris and I curtsied before we began reciting and when we finished. Sometimes, we presented our neighbors with a homemade card.

I saved one of the cards I made for my parents when I was nine years old and in school. I took a piece of letter-sized, cream-colored construction paper and folded it over once. Then I folded a piece of lined writing paper and slid it inside the outer construction paper. The lined paper was the kind we used in school for writing exercises, and the lines were far enough apart to accommodate my gigantic capital letters.

On the front of my card I drew a branch of evergreen, with a hint of brown for the stem and perfectly spaced green needles shooting out from the stems. The upper stem held a red candle with a yellow halo all around it, although a candle holder was nowhere to be seen. Hanging from each of the lower branches were ornaments drawn in the shape of a bell, mostly gold, but with a small red band on the bottom of the bell, and a red circle of a gong, peeking out from the bottom of the bell. I am sure I tried to draw it as lifelike as possible, but if this is what a real bell was like it would never make a sound with the gong it had.

Around the perimeter on the front of my card, I drew a straight line about a ¼ inch wide all around. Within those lines, drawn by pencil and never erased, I placed a yellow dot, then a red, then a blue, alternating these all the way around the edge. Evidently, I was not obsessed with the traditional red, green, and gold Christmas colors. Or maybe the school didn't have enough green pencils. The colors looked like a dash of Easter instead of Christmas! On the inside of my card, on the lined paper, I wrote, "To my dear parents at Christmas 1950" and in the bottom right-hand corner, "Your Christel." This page also got a dotted border in red and blue; another student had perhaps monopolized the yellow! The heart of the card was a poem by the German poet, Eduard Mörike, appropriately called *Weihnachten* (Christmas).

In my best handwriting and staying within the lines with all my determination, the letters standing ramrod straight and filling out the entire space between the lines, I copied twenty lines of poetry which began with, "Blessed be the holy night which brought us the redeemer of the world," and then went on about angels and heaven, shepherds, wise men, kings, lambs, and whatnot. I memorized this poem and recited it for my parents, siblings, and any neighbor who happened to come over around Christmas. On the flip side of the poem part I pasted four stars I had cut out from flimsy gold and silver paper. The stars had many more points than normal stars, eight to be exact, and the points were thick and flat as though I was afraid to cut too deeply into the paper. The backside of the card had exactly the same decoration as the front, except for the dots. Maybe the colored pencils were now being used by another class, school materials supplies still being in short supply in 1950. Then I punched two holes into the left side of the card to hold the two pieces of paper together, and into these I threaded pink ribbon, finishing up my art work with a bow.

I made another card a year later, one with more sophisticated decorations, but my favorite colors were still red and blue. Judging by the card, I was obsessed with patterns. The card's decorations had to be symmetrical; no wild, outrageous drawings for me! My parents were thrilled with my effort, needless to say, but I knew even then that I would not become an artist.

Christmas Eve dinner was the same for as long as I can remember. Routinely each year after the war, we had *Würstchen* (hot dogs) and *Kartoffelsalat* (potato salad) for Christmas Eve dinner, served after we had opened presents and sung songs and recited poems. These hot dogs were no ordinary ones, however. On Christmas Eve day, Papa would make a special trip on the streetcar (or walk when the tracks were still torn up and the streets full of rubble) and pay a visit to a cousin who had a butcher shop and made the finest hot dogs imaginable, with skin that made a crackling sound when bitten into. These hot dogs were served with great ceremony on a platter, decorated with parsley when available.

Mutti's potato salad was the best in the whole world, even when the potatoes were soaked in nothing but vinegar. I've tried to imitate her potato salad, and I have come close, but something is still missing. Her potato salad consisted of potatoes, salt and pepper, vinegar, and mayonnaise bought at the fish store in a tub, just enough for one batch of potato salad. So whenever she made this salad, the mayonnaise was always fresh. Even when food became more plentiful and varied, we continued to enjoy this simple meal on Christmas Eve.

For the first few years after the war, if we had managed to get enough potatoes we probably ate the Christmas leftovers at dinner the following night. Later, in the fifties, Mutti roasted a goose or duck for Christmas Day dinner, served with mashed potatoes, gravy, raisin filling (which I despised), and red cabbage.

During those desperate post-war years, my parents somehow got hold of a live goose, enclosed it in the courtyard, and fattened it up for Christmas dinner. Every day the goose waddled around, getting nice and plump. At night, it slept in the shed with the door closed. Shortly before Christmas, my father looked out the bedroom window facing the courtyard and noticed that the door to the shed was open. He ran to the shed and saw what was left of the goose—its head! Our Christmas dinner was gone, its succulent meat on its way into some other family's stomach. We had hot dogs for Christmas dinner that year.

When the story was told and retold, it was always the mailman who was suspected of killing the goose because he was the only person who occasionally came into the courtyard to hand-deliver the mail to my Mutti. He had shooed the goose away when it hissed at him so knew exactly how to handle this ornery bird. Axe in hand, he chopped off its head and our dinner plans changed drastically.

We didn't have any dessert until flour and sugar became more readily available, at which time Mutti made *Sandkuchen* (sand cake), similar to pound cake and served with freshly whipped cream. "Fresh" is the key word, because there was as yet no such thing as cool whip in a tub. Even if there had been, Mutti wouldn't have used it, because she was a purist where food was concerned. I can see her now, sitting on a kitchen chair with her legs spread apart, her skirt or dress and apron hiked up, gripping between her knees a bowl containing the ingredients. With a wooden spoon in her right hand, her left holding on to the bowl, she stirred the batter for at least twenty minutes. Even when she had an electric mixer she insisted on doing it this way because, she said, it made for a moister cake. She stirred and stirred without a break, only straightening her back now and then, until the batter was a creamy yellow. The result was a cake that was light as a feather and when eaten warm could melt all your cares and worries away. Plus make the inside of your mouth sing!

The second Christmas Day, December 26, was a day for visiting or receiving relatives. Tante Else was temporarily staying with us, and Doris and I were on the lookout for her. Whenever she planted her hands on my cheeks, I knew what was coming—one of her wet kisses. Tante Else liked to kiss everyone squarely on the mouth, which was okay, but her lips were so wet that I felt I had just been given a saliva bath. I tried to move my head left and right, up and down, but her hands clasped my cheeks so there was no escape. When I complained to Mutti, she told me just to play along with it, it was an East Prussian custom, and all of Tante Else's relatives were like that. And they were. When Tante Else's husband, Paul, came home from the Russian prisoner-of-war camp, he gave us wet kisses too. The adults said he had "water" and looked worried when they said that. But I associated his "water" with wet kisses. I didn't know what having "water" meant, for to me he looked normal. But the adults thought he looked bloated. He himself was quiet, thinking of things we couldn't even imagine and probably didn't want to know.

Eventually, Tante Else and Onkel Paul moved to their own apartment. He smiled again and talked but never about the war. I can still see him now sitting in a chair, savoring all that was going on in the room: the conversations, the singing, and the laughing. When he came over with Tante Else at Christmas, we showed him our presents and sat on his lap and together we talked a great deal of this and that. He had excellent rapport with children and we always looked forward to his visits. But not to his wet kisses.

When Onkel Heini came over, the first thing my sister and I did was to glide our hands across the short, soft, and at the same time bristly hair atop his head. He was hardly in the door when he picked us up and let us go at the caressing. It was a gesture of love and tenderness on our part, but we always got the giggles too because our hands would get an electric charge from touching his hair.

◆   ◆   ◆

In February of 1947, thousands of people in several German cities, among them Hamburg, protest against the lack of food. It doesn't do much good immediately, but it puts pressure on city administrations to find more sources. At Easter, American soldiers organize Easter hunts for German children. The well-known Hamburg Schauspielhaus is open again.

Art and hunger lived side by side in Hamburg. People craved entertainment, but not as much as they craved food.

For the next several years, life in Germany was notable chiefly for the lack of material necessities and the desperate longing for normalcy. Although we were an intact family, there were thousands of children who lived with their mothers, aunts, or grandmothers. Their fathers had been killed in the war or gone missing or became prisoners of war. Women who stayed at home (unless they had some kind of outside work) made items to sell or barter. American burlap bags that had once held sugar were sewn into warm if somewhat scratchy socks. Curtains and drapes were made into dresses, undergarments, and coats. Coffee was non-existent, but something like it, made from oats and barley and called *Muckefuck*, was available. Mutti thought it was disgusting, but she drank it while never losing her craving for a good cup of coffee more than anything, almost as much as food.

Because of sporadic or non-existent sources of energy, we could only dream of a warm bath. Clothes were washed in cold water with scant soap. Papa and Klaus took a burlap bag or a pillow case and walked (or if snow was on the ground, pulled a sled) to coal dealer Knast whose coal yard was at least a twenty-minute walk away, filled up the bag or pillow case with coal, and paid for it in cash or in installments. A couple of times Papa was refused coal because our account had reached its limit, and he came home empty-handed. When we did get coal, at least we could heat some water to fill a bowl and wash ourselves and maybe some clothes.

◆　　　◆　　　◆

Ironically, we often played outside to stay warm, by running around finding some relief from the chill in the house. Since playgrounds didn't exist, having also been destroyed in the war, the whole street had to be our playground. But in the first few years after the war, there wasn't much traffic to threaten us. An occasional car would tool by, and we would just stop and let it pass before going back to our soccer. Someone had a ball, even if it wasn't a soccer ball. Whatever the round thing was, we kicked it around. It wasn't easy running in our ill-fitting, used shoes that conformed to someone else's feet. Shoes with cardboard soles hitting the cobble stones made us cringe, especially if we hit the edge of a stone. But we were tough little kids, happy to be playing outside. Every now and then a policeman in his dark blue uniform and flat-topped, chin-strapped helmet would walk by on his rounds, heading back to the police station only a couple of blocks from our house. He would always caution us to watch out for cars, but since there were so few we never gave his suggestion the slightest thought and played on. We were completely respectful toward policemen, and they in turn were friendly and helpful.

We often played a game called *Kibbel-Kabbel*. For this we needed to dig a hole in the sidewalk. Only a small hole was needed, but when *Kibbel-Kabbel* was at its most popular, walking on the sidewalk became a bit treacherous. A small piece of wood (like a tongue-depressor) would be put over this hole. Then a makeshift stick would be placed beneath the piece of wood, lifting the wood and flinging it through the air as far as the power of our arms and hands permitted. If we missed hitting the wood we were out, but if we hit it the farthest we were the winner.

This was a fascinating game because it required at least some coordination, but the monotony of it got to us and the game was abandoned for something more exciting, such as *From Tree to Tree*. All we needed were trees, and that's why we couldn't play this game until new trees were planted along both sides of our street. If we had five trees, we needed six players. Standing in a group, at a distance from the trees, one of us would yell: "From tree to tree, who doesn't have a tree?" and then there would be a mad dash to a tree. If we weren't fast enough to secure a tree, we were out. Then the number of eligible trees was reduced by one. We played this until there was one player left, the winner. Running in our makeshift shoes wasn't always easy, so if the day was warm enough, we would just run barefoot.

In the winter, I tired of playing outside long before my sister did. My feet and hands got cold, and the clothes I played in didn't keep me warm enough. If my shoes were made of leather, my feet felt the wet leather and my toes went numb, and if my shoes were plastic my feet felt clammy because the plastic kept them from breathing. The bottom of my pants got soaked if we were playing in the snow, and the wetness crawled slowly down the woolen socks to the shoes. Wet woolen socks smelled like moldy cement. The cold never seemed to bother Doris, though, and she stayed outside for hours. My parents didn't mind my coming in early, although now the clammy clothes had to be hung somewhere near the stove in the kitchen to dry. Drying wet wool made the whole room smell like old cheese.

One day when the neighborhood girls and I were playing in the street, a photographer trying to make a living came by and took a group photo of us which he later sold, and my parents bought one that I still have. I am a slight kid with a smile, more like a squint because the sun is out. I am wearing a plush coat, like a fake fur with sleeves much too short for me. My dress is also much too short for me, being more like a longish top, and in order to stay warm under my dress I am wearing baggy, gray pants with elastic on the bottom and holes at the knees. Everyone in the picture is wearing coats and hats but not pants: I am the only one in those, because I get cold so easily. Certainly, I didn't wear these particular pants because they looked so handsome but because they were my only pair.

Another photo from the year 1948 shows Doris and me sitting on a wall fence. Amazingly, my sister's gray coat has a matching gray hat. Maybe it had once been worn by a little girl in America. We were wearing second-hand and third-hand clothes then. When my neighbor friend Margret, who was a little older than Doris, outgrew her clothes, they went first to Doris to wear for a while before they were handed down to me. That's why I looked like a poverty-stricken ragamuffin. My shoes were laced high tops whereas my friends were wearing more fashionable loafers of plastic. Once a month, an old woman came by our house and picked up clothes that my siblings and I had outgrown. "Poverty-stricken" was a relative term to our minds. There was always someone poorer than us. When I look at the photos of us in the years immediately following the war (it's amazing we even have photos from that period), it strikes me how gray everything is and how the drab rags we wore blended with our surroundings.

It was also during these years immediately after the war when we played in the bombed-out buildings near our house, and especially in the ruins of the apartment house that had once stood at the corner of our street. We sat on the steps leading into the basement or crawled around in spaces that once held people's possessions. I never found any treasures, but Klaus sometimes came home with soap or scraps of cloth. There was a certain tingly excitement to clambering over piles of bricks or jumping from wall to wall. The danger of a wall collapsing, or of bricks crashing down on us, was ever present. But we didn't think about how these ruins came to be as long as we had places to play.

All the neighborhood children played together, regardless of age, and there was no shortage of games we could play without needing a single toy. We played until the sun went down, which in the summer months was around 10:00 p.m.

Since our sidewalks were mostly dirt, they were good places to play marbles. One of us dug a hole the size of a cup (the game became harder only if a circle was drawn in the dirt). Each of us had six marbles of the same size. (How we came to possess them, I'll never know). We lined up around and six feet back from the hole, the turns determined by counting out numbers. The first player rolled or threw three marbles toward the hole. If any of them landed in the hole, she could keep those. Eventually, the space around the hole was covered with marbles, depending on how many people played. Excitement rose when players used their curved index finger to flick the marbles into the hole or hit another marble, in which case it was theirs. We determined the rules we played by, and always our goal was to end up with as many marbles as we could. If we had bad luck that day, we could borrow marbles from someone who was winning to stay in the game, but we had to give them back to the owner at the end. Some of us had sizeable pouches full of colorful marbles which were fun just to hold up to the sun to see their brilliant colors. The marble hole was supposed to be filled with dirt at the end of the game, but that didn't always happen and more than one ankle was twisted on our sidewalks.

Younger kids played *Cat and Mouse*, which required no equipment whatsoever. The players stood in a circle holding hands. The "mouse" stood inside the circle, and the "cat" prowled around the outside trying to break through to get to the mouse. Children in the circle used all their strength not to let the cat in. If the cat made it into the circle anyway, the mouse was allowed to slip through to the outside, and now the cat had to try to break through the circle from within to catch the mouse. Screaming and yelling was a big part of this very noisy game.

Since we all lived within two or three streets of each other, it was easy to run to somebody's house and ask if she or he could come out and play. Or, because we could see or hear that a group was outside already playing, we simply joined them. Sometimes if a group was into its own game and didn't need more players, we were rejected, but that was no big deal as we would just start our own game. I often played with my agemates Ingrid and Barbara or with my sister's friends Hella and Dorle, and even Margret who was older than Doris by two years.

There were two boys who stand out in my memory. Bernhard, who was my age, lived on our street in an apartment house that hadn't been bombed, and he and I grew up as friends until one day when we were teens he made moves to kiss me. I had no interest in him that way and so I rejected outright his tender feelings toward me. After that, we avoided each other for a while until he found somebody else to kiss. Then we were friends again.

Hans was another boy who lived on our street. He and I became knitting buddies when we were around seven years old. We sat at the edge of the sidewalk, facing the street, with our feet out in the street and our knitting project in our laps. I had been taught knitting by my childhood idol Christa, and now I was teaching the eager Hans. Hans and I must have knitted a few long, skinny creations resembling scarves or maybe some simple doll clothes because he also liked to play with dolls. Our knitting repertoire was definitely limited, but we had a good time. Hans thought that knitting was not an inherently female thing, an idea that would be challenged later. But for now, he and I just enjoyed knitting. Growing up with boys as friends was as natural as having girls as friends, an idea that would also be challenged later, especially in America, where having a "boyfriend" took on an entirely different meaning.

Growing up in this community gave me a real sense of neighborhood, the likes of which I've never found again anywhere. Maybe it was the extraordinarily needy time we were in. Maybe we just happened to have the right mix of children of a certain age. The fact was that this wasn't a mobile society and once having been given that longed-for apartment families tended to stay. Whatever the reason for this neighborhood feeling, my playmates and I grew up with each other until it was time to get married or go to a university in another city or get a job away from Hamburg. We knew everything about each other and our families.

There were always kids to play with. We attended each others' birthday parties. When arguments or jealousies arose, we simply had to work them out. I think that playing together on our street gave me the skills to form friendships in the future.

Not all of our childhood activities were benign. And not all of the neighbors liked having us kids play on the street, yelling and shouting and kicking balls into their yards, all of which had wrought-iron fences with flowers behind them. How many roses lost their buds because of us? I cannot even guess.

An old maid down the street, Fräulein Hinn, chased us away from playing in front of her house many times, and as revenge we made up a rhyme, inspired by her last name, which we then chanted directly in front of her house when we knew she was standing behind her living room sheer curtains, watching us. The rhyme went like this:

> *Frau Hinn und Her, Frau Kreuz und Quer,*
> *Frau Hick, Frau Hack, Frau Hühnerkack.*

And then we giggled and ran away. If translated, the rhyme's play on words would lose its kick. The last word means chicken shit.

My friends and I thought of a nasty trick to play on people in the apartment house on the next street, which was also a street we played on and where people knew us. Each floor in the apartment house had apartments directly across from each other. We tied one end of a rope we brought to the doorknob of one apartment and the other end to the one directly across. Then we ran outside and rang the respective doorbells, at which both parties would try to open their doors only to get very frustrated at their inability to open them more than an inch. We would listen and giggle and, after a decent interval, do it again. I wasn't necessarily the leader in the tricks we played on the neighbors, but I went right along with the others. In our defense I have to say that we never did this to neighbors we liked.

◆   ◆   ◆

Most of the neighbors on our street, Hartzloh, lived in the two-flat houses that had been built some forty years before. Others lived in apartment houses. Our next-door neighbors were our Christmas angels, Herr and Frau Voss and Fräulein Sommer. The three of them were not related but were very good friends. When I became aware of Fräulein Sommer, she was probably in her forties, but to my six years-old eyes she appeared old. She had very big, heavy legs, and her swollen feet sometimes poured over her shoes. As a result, she walked slowly and laboriously, leaning a little to one side. She had never been married but once had had a fiancé who died or went missing in the war. When I asked my parents why Fräulein Sommer wasn't married, they said that there were many women like her—millions of men of that generation had gone to war never to come back, and there just weren't any more eligible men. Fräulein Sommer worked for the Cuban embassy, and it must have been a good job because she dressed very smartly. She lived in the downstairs flat and the Vosses lived upstairs.

Frau Voss always said of her husband that he had two faces: one jovial, the other grumpy and nasty. She knew him well, and so did we because we experienced both. When he was in a good mood, he would interrupt his work in the backyard, smile, and talk to me over the fence, even taking an interest in what I was doing. When he was grumpy, he ignored me. It took me a while to learn that he wasn't mad, just grumpy. The good side of him was also the generous side which we experienced at Christmastime when all three of them came over with presents, and he would have a glass of brandy and be all smiles, listening to our poems and talking to my parents while Doris and I played with our new dolls. I was in awe of him because he was so rich. He could afford to buy dolls for us!

Frau Voss was a regal-looking woman with a kindly face. Her hair was always perfectly combed, most of the time in an elegant sort of twist in the back. She had an even temperament, in contrast to her erratic husband. They didn't have any children, and I wondered why because I didn't know any other families that were childless. Both Herr and Frau Voss were in their late fifties and had been married for quite a long time.

The Vosses lived in the upstairs flat. The carpeted stairs leading to their apartment awed me, because our staircase was plain wood. The ridges in the wood from fifty years of wear and tear and scrubbing with steel wool had made our wooden stairs brittle, unsightly, and raw-looking. But when I walked upstairs to deliver the Frau a fly for her frog, I felt the plush pile of the carpet and anticipated what was yet to come because the staircase was not the only space carpeted.

In the hallway and living room, Persian carpets and small rugs covered the space so that very little wood was visible. Even the kitchen had rugs. Oh, the luxury of it! I wanted to stay there forever and be their spoiled child with a room of my own. But I was only there on a mission. In my tightly squeezed hand buzzed an angry fly which I deposited quickly into a jar in which a green frog was lying in wait. It was important that the fly be alive because its frantic buzz gave the frog a little thrill before it seized the fly with its long tongue. Frau Voss needed live flies for her pet frog every day, so I was on the lookout all the time. Five *Pfennige* per fly was my reward, the equivalent of a nickel. I saved it all.

In return for our neighbors' kindness at Christmastime, Mutti reciprocated by giving Frau Voss fresh eggs laid by our stupid chickens. At the time I thought eggs were an unworthy gift. Who would want some dumb chicken eggs? But contrary to my belief, the neighbors always seemed to appreciate fresh eggs. Fresh eggs were actually highly prized because in my Mutti's opinion you couldn't trust the age of store-bought eggs. Though my family always had fresh eggs, I couldn't see the difference between fresh and old eggs until many years later. The yolks of our eggs ran a rich yellow, a color which oozed freshness. Our yolks were runnier, our whites were whiter, and our shells were superior. In sum, our eggs were perfect, especially when compared to the dreadful and disgusting powdered egg stuff we had endured for many years past. I hated eggs because I hated chickens because I had been the one chosen to check for eggs for many years, even until I was in high school.

As soon as Mutti said, "Christelchen, go and collect the eggs," I started itching. "Mutti," I whined, "I have too much homework, I can't do it. Let Klaus do it." That didn't work, for when she needed something, Mutti was persistent. She said, "You'll be back at your homework in five minutes, so go now, I need to sell some eggs." I harrumphed, and then slowly made my way to the backyard, all the while thinking of the fleas lying in wait. Collecting eggs could have been an easy job, satisfying even, holding the fresh warm eggs in my hands and all that, but instead it had become something gross and disgusting. I would have done anything to trade the job with my sister or brother, as I thought we should be taking turns with this job anyway. But no, this was my special job and I had to do my part.

I loved animals, and I helped care for our cat. I fed her most of the time and made sure she had fresh water. More, I liked snuggling with her. Having an animal in the house made living with humans more complete. But I didn't think of hens as pets as my mother did. She had actually named each one of them and even used her own name for one. A chicken named Anna! I don't know how she was able to tell these gray/white chickens apart; they all looked the same to me.

When one of the chickens got sick, when it sneezed and had runny eyes, Mutti scooped it up in her apron and carried it into the house where she let it run around in the kitchen. She'd say to the chicken, who paid no attention to her, "Oh, little Maria, you'll be feeling better soon. Your cold will be gone in no time, and then you can run around again with your friends." When I heard this, I rolled my eyes and looked to heaven for an answer to what made Mutti be so strange. I didn't understand Mutti and her love of chickens, unaware that the chickens and their eggs provided desperately needed additional income for our family. I didn't understand that taking care of them assured us of chicken stew and even a soft-cooked egg now and then, which in any case I refused to eat, probably because of the fleas.

As soon as Mutti had the chicken in the sick bay, she turned the oven on low, and when it was barely warm she put the chicken very carefully into the oven where it sat until it felt good and warm. Then she gripped the chicken firmly in the crook of her arm, pried the beak open with her thumb and forefinger, and dropped a spoonful of oil down its throat. After that, it moved around in a daze and usually shit some runny stuff on the kitchen floor. One day of this special care and the chicken was as good as new. Sometimes, a chicken became constipated (and therefore unproductive), and then Mutti gave it bread soaked in oil so the chicken could shit again. I don't know why the treatment worked or where Mutti had learned to be a chicken doctor. But when the chicken was pronounced well, Mutti re-deposited it in the yard, where it tottered for a moment, mostly from shaking all its feathers since it hadn't been able to do that in the oven or in Mutti's arms before it resumed laying eggs.

Apart from getting sick occasionally, the worst enemies of the hens and the baby chickens were the rats that sometimes roamed the backyard. The baby chicks especially were vulnerable and needed to be protected. After Papa discovered that a rat had devoured two chicks, he took aim at the vermin by throwing at it a two-pound piece of coal out the kitchen window. Even if he didn't hit it, the rat did go elsewhere for food at least for a while.

I hated chickens. They were dirty, boring, and stupid. They were so unlike cats. You couldn't hug them and whisper things to them. If you picked them up, they struggled in your arms. They never looked you straight in the face. The hens and the rooster, Herr Echo, scratched in the dirt yard, their gnarly feet stirring up the ground with a flourish, kicking up their legs a little, like a dance, turning left and then right in case they had missed a bread crumb. With quick, perpetual, almost spastic motions of their heads, their combs flopping from side to side, they pecked away at whatever was spread out in front of them.

When that dreaded time came to collect eggs, I strew some chicken feed around the courtyard to keep the feathered critters busy and out of the henhouse, which occupied half of the shed. While they were busy outside, at least they couldn't peck at me and prolong my agony.

Part of the shed was full of garden tools, pieces of wood, old fencing waiting to be used again someday, and a rusty wheelbarrow. An open door frame led into the chicken coop occupying the other end of the shed. I looked around the straw-filled ledge, where one lone chicken was still trying to squeeze out an egg. The hen was ignoring me, but when it finished producing an egg it jumped off the shelf and ran outside clucking all the way as if to tell the world what it had just accomplished. I would have given anything to leave too, but instead I quickly reached up on the ledge, picked up the brown or white eggs, and placed them gingerly in the bowl. The last egg laid was still warm and I knew that this is what our neighbors craved—fresh eggs from chickens they knew personally.

Sometimes, neighbors called and asked if there were any eggs yet, and I had to run into the shed and look. If the neighbors only knew the agony I went through to assure them the thing called freshness!

From those expeditions I emerged with something that nearly made me drop the egg bowl. My hands and arms were dotted with fleas, jumping and leaping fleas. I was infested! Klaus always joked about starting a flea circus with all the fleas I collected on my daily rounds, obviously choosing to ignore my suffering. So I ran as fast as I could to the kitchen, and placed the bowl with the precious eggs on the kitchen table.

All I wanted to do was flail my arms and jump up and down to get rid of the bloodsucking invaders, but Mutti told me to stand still and then picked the fleas one by one off my arms, neck, and hands, squeezing each flea between her thumb and forefinger thus breaking their backs. Then she checked my hair and the rest of me, telling me matter-of-factly that fleas couldn't hurt me. They could bite but nothing else. But Mutti, what about fleas making me feel disgusted? What about my loss of appetite for eggs? Complaining, though, didn't help me. It seemed that I was stuck with this job for eternity, though in fact it was only until age 14 at which time I asked to be excused from my egg-collecting duty because I was too busy with my homework. Or at least that's the excuse I used, and for some reason Mutti believed me.

Besides Frau Voss, another egg customer was Tante Schütt who with her husband Onkel Schütt lived across the street from us in a house that looked much like ours only prettier. It was white while ours was an ugly concrete gray. They were my parents' friends and, as children of friends, we called them aunt and uncle combined with their last name. My parents called them by their last names as well. When the relationship between the adults was closer and they were on a first-name basis, then the children called them aunt and uncle combined with their first names.

Tante Schütt was very pretty, with regular and delicate features that had been inherited by her two daughters, especially Wilma. Wilma and Ilse were several years older than my brother Klaus. When Ilse did her *Pflichtjahr,* the female equivalent of military service, she was assigned to my family to help with domestic chores and child care. This type of work (state edict of 1938, a four-year plan for the deployment of female workers), done after finishing school but before the beginning of employment, was supposed to prepare females for their roles as housewives and mothers. Perhaps my parents and the Schütts made a deal so that Ilse wouldn't have to work for a family of strangers. Ilse and her older sister Wilma before her, mostly took care of us, played with us, escorted us on walks, and whatever else we wanted to do. Probably military duty would have been easier on Ilse because, though my sister and brother were rather peaceable and gentle beings, I made up for their good natures by being exceptionally ornery. This orneriness was confirmed by my Papa, who often imitated my shrill demanding voice when he talked about me as a child. He always followed these statements with a smile which said he loved me and my ornery ways. Or at least sometimes he did. Papa always brought up my willfulness as a child when as an adult I exhibited the same trait!

After the war, Onkel Schütt bought or leased a gas station and the family did very well financially. Ilse began working at the station, pumping gas and fixing cars. She was also the first woman I knew who drove a car! This made an impression on me, because most of the cars I saw were driven by men. How smart she was to move this piece of machinery, I thought.

Onkel Schütt was a handsome man, not very tall, but attractive and charming. He always told his family that *man muss was für gut lassen,* meaning that a German ate special dishes or wore certain outfits only on special days like holidays or Sundays.

But a certain thing he liked to do often. His nickname (which I didn't learn about until I was much older) was *scharfer Zeisig,* a way of saying that he was oversexed. He flirted with women all the time, in a gently seductive way, but if Tante Schütt so much as looked at another man he flew into fits of jealousy. He was sexually demanding, and Tante Schütt went to considerable lengths to make herself available and presentable, doing her hair and applying lipstick, and even wearing nylons when they became available. When her husband came home from work, she would be ready for anything, whether she was in the mood or not. If her husband was in the mood, Tante Schütt went along.

That's the way it was back then. Mutti didn't primp and anyway, my parents never did "it." Or so I thought. When I grew up I wanted to be like Tante Schütt and Ilse and Wilma, dressed in outfits never worn before by anyone else. I didn't want to wear hand-me-downs and I wanted Mutti to have clothes like Tante Schütt's—smart, form-fitting skirts and elegant blouses and shoes with heels. For myself I wanted most of all a pair of shiny new flats.

While I adored Tante Schütt and her family, I found our Catholic neighbors next door despicable. I envied them and disliked them not for their finery but for their religion. The Heinz family stood out in this Lutheran stronghold, but that wasn't their only distinction. They were older than my parents and had grown-up children. Maybe they didn't want to be bothered with young children like us next door to them. They didn't like animals. They threw dirt at cats. Whenever they did something evil, the neighbors would say, "What do you expect, they are Catholic. They go to confession and then they are mean all over again." This is where I got the idea that Catholics would never measure up to perfect Lutheran human beings such as my family members.

Still, I envied Catholics for the ease with which they were forgiven. But I also wondered why they were forgiven so easily, when we Lutherans had to feel guilty for a longer period of time if we had done something bad.

My cousin Inge's wedding, ca. 1946
Christel and Doris in front

Doris, Hella, and Christel (in center of photo) at the puppet show, ca. 1947

Christel and Doris with cherished dolls, ca. 1948

Neighborhood friends—from left: Doris, Dorle, Margret, Hella, Barbara, Christel, ca. 1948

4

Elementary school and family life

◆

1948–1954

It was spring 1948 and time for me to start school. I was six and a half years old when I enrolled in first grade. There was no Kindergarten grade in German schools. I had been looking forward to going to school and doing homework just like my big sister Doris.

In June of that year, German currency reform was introduced, and each German citizen received forty Marks as a starter. Goods were not only easier to pay for but also less difficult to get after that. The black market collapsed, and miraculously stores filled up with goods, but my first day of school fell before June 20 and my parents worried that I wouldn't have a *Tüte*. I nagged them because I simply had to have one. To start school without one was unthinkable.

Luckily, our neighbor Margret had saved her *Tüte* from her first day of school a few years before, and she let me have it. It was a handmade one, made of a sturdy piece of paper rolled into cone form. Glue held the two sides together. Margret had drawn stars, circles, and wiggly lines on the paper with the only colored pencil she owned: green. There was no gold or silver paper to be had yet, no ribbons, no foil paper with which to decorate the *Tüte,* but Margret's mother took a piece of cloth cut from an old flowered dress and glued it on the inside of the cone. There was even enough cloth left at the top to tie into a bow. The cloth had two purposes—it dressed up the otherwise plain-looking *Tüte,* and the bow kept the contents of the cone-shaped item of German tradition in place. Inside were treasures, like a few pieces of paper, a pencil, an eraser.

In normal times, the cone would have been filled with candy and maybe even some pretty hair ribbons or lots of colored pencils, a sharpener, and other school supplies. My *Tüte* was by no means full, even though neighbors had added a few bonbons. It didn't matter so much that it wasn't filled to the top but that I had a *Tüte* to carry.

Both Mutti and Papa walked me to school that morning and picked me up later. The fifteen-minute walk took us along neighborhood streets. I took that same walk thereafter on six days a week for the next six years of elementary school. Yes, there was school on Saturdays; the five-day school week didn't begin until 1970 when Saturday school was dropped. But I didn't really mind going to school on Saturday until I was in high school when, more than likely, I would have preferred to sleep in.

This morning, my *Tüte* was the only thing I carried, cradling it in my arms, as I skipped ahead of my parents, excited about my new adventure. When my parents could afford one, I would carry a *Schulranzen*, a backpack filled with books and paper and pens, because German schools didn't have lockers and all school supplies and books had to be carried around every day.

New school clothes had to wait for more prosperous times. So my army shoes had to last a little while longer. This morning I looked better than my brother Klaus who left for school wearing a jacket our Onkel Max had given him. Onkel Max was very tall and my fourteen-year old brother wasn't, so Onkel Max' jacket served as both jacket and coat. His storm trooper boots reached above his knees. I don't think we cared yet about what we looked like, although I did notice that some of the girls beginning school with me wore shoes that actually looked new. Why could they have new shoes and I couldn't? The thought of not having new things began haunting me later in elementary school and high school.

The school loomed ahead of us now, huge and dark. The four-story brick building had not been hit in the war and its dark red brickwork was intact. Half of the building was for girls, the other half for boys. Long, wide steps led up to a monstrous door with the word *Mädchen* (girls) written in wrought iron across the top. The crest of the City of Hamburg, gateway to the world, loomed above that. This edifice was to be my world for the next six years.

The door remained locked until a bell rang, and when the caretaker came we could hear him unlock both sides of the gate-like door. This ceremony took place every school day morning precisely at 9:00 a.m. Once inside, then, we had to climb another flight of stairs. Sometimes when it rained, he opened the second door early so we could wait on the stairs leading up to the lobby.

Today, we walked with our parents to the auditorium that also served as the gym. I imagine that the principal, probably a woman, welcomed us, gave a short talk, and assigned us to a teacher. After that, our parents left and we were led by our teacher to our classroom. Some of the kids clung crying to their parents as they departed the scene, but I wasn't one of those. I was so ready to begin school.

Forty girls packed the classroom. We had desks, but not enough for each of us to have our own. Sharing a desk was only one of many things we came to share, like books, pencils, colored pencils, and ink pens. The paint on the walls and the ceiling was peeling, and the wooden floor looked dry and splintery. But on a ledge around the room, somebody had placed plants in regular intervals and in various stages of growth from puny to lush, which gave the otherwise bare room a somewhat less severe feeling.

Over the next six years, we sat in that cold, bare room, often shivering when the old furnaces gave out or the coal supply dried up. Now and then, we were asked to bring coal to school to keep the furnaces going. Adding another layer to our clothing was not an option because in many cases we already wore everything we owned and wore it several days in a row.

It was just three years after Hamburg had been almost completely leveled. Still, we had a school, we had limited supplies, and we had teachers! Some of the teachers had been soldiers and had returned to teaching once the war was over. Some of them had been unemployed when school was suspended sometime in 1943. But on a limited basis, some schools managed to reopen in 1945.

Today I remember my first-grade teacher as a serious, middle-aged man who was extraordinarily patient with us children. He never said a sharp word, but there was an air of melancholy about him. We noticed it, but not until years later could we explain it. It had to do with the war: he was teaching many fatherless girls who saw in him the male who was missing from their lives, and he did his best to fulfill their added expectation to be both teacher and father.

From the first day of school until I entered eighth grade, I was totally enamored of education. This encouraged my parents because my school years would not be disrupted by war like my brother's had been. They saw that I seemed to learn easily, much more so than Doris, who wrestled with our native tongue every day of her school life. I remember looking at her notebooks full of dictations and wondering if she weren't learning Russian instead. She even created new letters for the German alphabet. Now I wonder whether she had a disability that nobody was qualified to diagnose back then.

My teacher from second through sixth grades became the most beloved I've ever had. Fräulein Düstersiek was motherly in spite of being an unmarried woman, an old maid as we then called older single women. This state of being manless was often talked about by the adults around me when the Fräulein's name was mentioned. Wasn't it odd that she didn't have a man? Hadn't she had a fiancé? Was he lost in the war, missing in action? Was she single by choice?

But it didn't matter to me whether she was married or not, for I hadn't yet realized that a female was meant to be married by a certain age. Little did I know at the time that a generation of men had been obliterated by the war, and that many women had carried on ably without men—cleaned bricks, rebuilt cities, raised children.

By the time Fräulein Düstersiek became my teacher, she must have been in her late forties, and for the next thirteen years her appearance never changed. She was very tall and thin—even her fingers looked so—and always stood ramrod straight in sensible shoes, even when more fashionable shoes could be had. She never wore jewelry. Her brown hair was pulled back into a bun at the nape of her neck, and not a single hair hung loose. She never wore makeup though her skin was a tired yellow. Her clothes were quite ordinary but not what one could call ugly. I can still see her in a simple black dress and an off-white cardigan, fading into the grayness around her. Still, her wardrobe was no drabber than ours, because we all suffered from a lack of colors.

Fräulein never raised her voice, but in my eyes she was a formidable person for all her kindness and soft-spoken ways. Whenever I did act up in class, meaning talked when I should have been paying attention, and she settled her brown eyes on me I was instantly reminded that inside of me there was a total commitment to pleasing her at all times. I didn't ever want her to be unhappy on account of me. Fortunately, she never had cause to reprimand me except with her eyes.

Fräulein's interest in her pupils also extended to their families. During the war, when school was suspended, she paid close attention to their fate: what exactly did they have to endure and how much had their parents suffered? Many kids in my class had lost their fathers and some had lost their mothers as well and were being raised by their grandparents. She often asked me how my mother was. In my mind, my mother was always fine, of course, or was there something I didn't know?

Being eight, I had no idea what my parents were going through to keep us clothed. All I wanted was a new pair of pants or a pair of shoes or something that made me look more like other girls in my class whose clothes I coveted. Fräulein Düstersiek made it a point never to compliment anyone on their clothing, and if she ever got involved in exterior appearances it was because someone was shivering for lack of warm clothing. At those times she would just happen to have an extra sweater to pull from her desk. Sometimes she would give an extra piece of bread to an overly pale girl. And on our birthdays from grades two through six each of us received a birthday card from her.

Even after I had finished elementary school, my teacher and I kept contact with each other. She lived not too far from us and now and then I paid her a visit. In 1955, when I had just returned from a high school class trip, she sent me my annual birthday card which I have kept all these years. It said, in her beautiful, flowing handwriting, "My dear Christel! You must be back from your trip and here is your birthday card. I was always happy for you when the sun was shining. I send you hearty congratulations and hope that in this new year of your life you will always be healthy and happy. Many greetings, also to your mother and Doris, from your A. Düstersiek." (Her first name was Anna, like my mother's). There were no greetings for my father, probably because he wasn't around much at that time. More about that later.

Walking by our house on Sunday mornings, Fräulein took long purposeful strides, acknowledging the greetings from her pupils who happened also to be on their way to church. Wearing a hat and clutching her black bible and purse in one hand, she made a striking figure walking past our house on her way to St. Gabriel's Lutheran Church. If I was running past her on my way to church, she would stop me abruptly with a friendly "Guten Morgen, Christel," and I had to back up, curtsy, say "Guten Morgen, Fräulein Düstersiek," and then resume my run. Sometimes her solitary figure tugged on me and I felt sorry for her. I attributed loneliness to her, because unlike my mother she didn't have a husband to walk with. I don't remember now what she said to me that made me feel so good, but I always knew that she believed in me and that I could accomplish anything.

Had I kept some mementoes from my elementary school years, I could now recount more details about what and how we were taught. What I do remember is this: our daily lesson plan was always the same. In first grade, we learned reading, writing, and arithmetic in addition to singing, drawing pictures, and taking short dictations. I remember liking everything I did in elementary school, of course including recess.

We had a short recess after each class period but didn't necessarily go outside every time. During our longer break of twenty minutes, we lined up at the classroom door and marched single file toward the backyard door, pressing but not pushing against the girls ahead of us because we were so eager to get outside. Once there, I was reunited with my friends Ingrid and Barbara of my same grade but not class. The boys stayed in the yard behind their side of the school although there were no barriers of any kind between us. We just never mingled. Probably because we thought boys were stupid so why would we want to play with them. But mostly because there was a rule that said the sexes were not to interact.

There was no playground equipment yet, so my girlfriends and I played tag. We also practiced *Handstand*. One girl would squarely plant herself behind another, to receive another girl who pressed her hands onto the hard dirt and lifted her whole body off the ground so she landed against the other girl, all the while trying not to hit her in the face with her shoes. If we wore skirts or dresses, they would now be covering our upper body and head to expose our underwear. But that didn't matter as the boys were far away in a different area. Sometimes we had a *Schiebkarre* or wheelbarrow race. Since I was a slight girl and fairly short compared to my friend Ingrid who was tall and somewhat stocky for her age, I played the wheelbarrow and she grabbed my feet to move me forward to some specified goal. I helped her along by moving my hands as quickly as I could. Barbara, who was smaller than me, also played wheelbarrow. Winning wasn't that important, just having the most fun we could in twenty minutes. Then, when the whistle blew, we had to line up single file in front of the door and march back to our classroom.

I played and learned with equal enthusiasm and my first report card shows it. The original is in my hands, a precious memory. It says, "Christel is a bright student. She participates actively in the classroom, shows much enthusiasm and willingness to work. She learns quickly and works conscientiously. Christel is a lively girl with good behavior." I received grades for reading, writing, and arithmetic. On a one to six scale, my grades were twos, which meant "good." Why not *sehr gut* (very good), I don't know. It further said that I liked singing and drawing and that I wrote short dictations without mistakes. For my parents, the "good behavior" comment was most important, more important than the grades.

◆   ◆   ◆

Being a child well-behaved in all ways meant being obedient, helping others, doing chores (raking in the fall, lawn-mowing, pulling weeds, picking apples, gathering berries), getting homework done on time, not talking back, being considerate to others, demonstrating good table manners.

Besides obedience, being good also meant cleaning my room and the rest of the apartment, carrying groceries for Mutti, feeding the cat, and attending to my grandparents' graves.

Some of this work was not done without argument, especially the cleaning part, but arguing didn't do much good. Talking back made Papa's hair stand on end, particularly when it was done in front of my friends. I can still recall one instance when I was playing in the street in front of our house and Papa came out to ask me to come in and do a job. I replied that I didn't want to come in right now and that I would do the job later. After that, he marched through the front gate, grabbed me by the arm, and pulled me into the house where I got a dressing-down. He said, "Don't you ever talk back to me in front of your friends. Don't be *frech* (fresh)." I had dismissed his request and in a tone that wasn't acceptable. Somehow, there was a difference between arguing and talking back, and I was learning it.

Good table manners were also very important, such as sitting up straight and using a knife and fork (or two forks for fish). Even as young children we used both fork and knife, keeping the implements in our hands throughout the meal. Shoveling food onto a fork with a finger was forbidden. Reaching across the table for food was forbidden. *Schmatzen,* smacking your lips or eating with your mouth open, was forbidden. If we talked too much, talking was forbidden. Sometimes my sister and I would make each other laugh and when we couldn't stop, one of us was sent to stand in the hallway until we could calm down. When guests were present, we children were served last no matter how hungry we were.

Good manners meant getting up for handicapped or elderly people on the streetcar or the subway and never sitting in seats marked for *Schwerbeschädigte* (disabled). If I accidentally sat in one of those reserved seats, a disabled person entering the subway car would flash his identity card at me and I would jump up. There were so many blind and limbless people after the war that as a child I seldom had a seat on public transportation. Consequently, whenever I have used public transportation (say in New York or Chicago) I have always vacated my seat to an older or disabled person while wondering why everyone else wasn't doing the same. The habit goes back so far and has been ingrained so deeply in me that I never even think about it. I jump up automatically and have been turned down occasionally by fellow travelers who may have thought it odd to be offered a seat.

I become more aware of what happens around me.

◆   ◆   ◆

In 1949, German children play in ruins. A generation without fathers. Most families don't have an apartment of their own. On the average, four people share a room. Children fend for themselves while their mothers work. About 385,000 Germans still live in camps. Streetcars are running again and therefore streetcar mailboxes, which before the war were a unique feature of the postal service, are operating again. Street-cars that run by the main train station are emptied of mail every night at 6:00 p.m. Soldiers who have lost limbs maneuver around on home-made "wheelchairs" fabri-cated from a piece of wood large enough to sit on, four wheels, and sticks to shove themselves forward. For the first time in ten years, a shipment of 41,000 crates of Ital-ian oranges and lemons arrives in Hamburg's harbor. A new magazine advertises well-known household products such as Nivea and Dr. Oetker Pudding. The Federal Republic of Germany is created. A fourteen-page catalog shows twenty-two shoe mod-els and a few items of clothing. A model dressed in an evening gown is photographed with a group of young boys behind her, one of whom is shown wearing a key around his neck, indicating that he is a latch-key child whose mother works outside the home. In Hollywood, Rita Hayworth marries the very rich Indian prince Ali Khan.

Well, then.

After the war, when Germany was divided up between the Americans, British, French, and Russians, northern Germany including Hamburg was occupied by the British army. I didn't know what that meant then, except that the Allies pro-vided *Schulspeisung*—meals in school. Often, breakfast at home consisted of a piece of bread, sometimes with margarine and sugar if we were lucky enough to have cornbread. Many kids went to school hungry. The Allies gave each of us a metal army food container and a spoon, and at midmorning when our hunger became too much to bear we would grab our tin containers and line up for deli-cious hot soup. All the ragamuffins in a row, many without shoes! I loved all the soups, which varied every day: chicken noodle, vegetable, and lentil or bean soup. We carried the container home, washed it, and returned it the next day.

It must have been around 1949 when we were finally able to buy good bread again. Bread that didn't fall apart, bread that was solid. Those early days of good bread are still vivid in my memory.

One Saturday morning Mutti, Klaus, Doris, and I were sitting around the kitchen table in our pajamas and sweaters, heavy socks, and shoes. It was warm in this room, the only heated area in the house. So it was our house's only room that didn't frost up. If we had to go get something from another room and tiptoed from the kitchen down the short, linoleum-covered hallway to the living room, our toes went into shock if we weren't wearing socks or shoes. Every day, Papa fed the kitchen stove with coal first thing in the morning so that at least one small space was comfortable. Throughout the day on Saturdays, I had the job of tossing pieces of wood and coal in to keep the fire going, because all of the family's cooking was done on this stove.

Normally, the wooden kitchen table wasn't covered, but today a white table cloth gave it a festive look as though it too, along with five plates and knives, was waiting for something joyful to take place. Mutti had set a small saucer with a thin square of shiny yellow margarine on the table along with a sugar bowl that had seen better days, its once golden rim faded to grayness. It was gray like the world outside was gray, the luster gone. But we didn't care; the bowl was filled with sugar. Bread was on its way, and we would soon have bread with margarine and sugar. It was enough to make my mouth water. We hungered so for real bread.

Klaus leaned back in his wobbly chair and closed his eyes. He was always tired in the morning and so rather quiet. Doris and I liked to sing on just about any occasion, so she and I sang one song after another about fall, harvest, and hunting. It must have been fall. I was eight.

We looked at each other while we harmonized, a habit we had fallen into when we performed for relatives. Doris and I knew a lot of songs. For a few minutes, singing about leaves changing color and the tra-ra-ra of the hunt drowned out the sounds of our growling stomachs, until we began singing a song about potatoes and then there was that nagging empty feeling again. Klaus opened his eyes and shot us a look without a note of appreciation in it, and since we were sitting on either side of him he just stretched his arms sideways and closed our mouths with his hands. Doris mumbled, "Mutti, Klaus doesn't like our singing, say something to him." Sometimes we were able to draw her into our arguments, but today she said, "Maybe that's enough singing for now. Papa should be back any minute."

We waited. I thought about food all the time, mostly about wanting it and craving it, because there was never enough of it. I wet my forefinger and dipped it in sugar. The sweetness made my mouth water instantly, until I heard a sharp "Christel" from Mutti, her brown eyes stern and her eyebrows raised. I never knew about my Mutti. She was unpredictable and flared up easily, especially when it involved food, delivering a short tap on the hands when we reached for food that hadn't yet been divided up. She was the keeper of the food, the custodian, the guard, the allotter of portions. She always served herself last, although she was as hungry as we were.

As we waited for the bread, Doris was playing with one of the knives and my brother yanked it away from her. They squabbled for a few minutes until they heard the front door open. Papa had arrived with the bread. The rumbling in my stomach was deafening, and I felt almost nauseated from it. I wanted to take the whole loaf and devour it, savoring the last crumb under my tongue. *But what about your family?* said that little voice inside me every time I thought about feeding myself alone. I wanted to share but I also wanted the whole loaf.

Papa had just returned from the new bakery at the corner. We heard him walk down the hall toward the kitchen. He was singing! *"Iss dein Brot, iss dein Brot, gute Tage soll man loben ..."* (Eat your bread and praise good days). The bread, the bread, I smelled it before I even saw it. The yeasty fragrance invaded my nostrils, and my taste buds awoke to flood my stomach with a hunger that I knew would be satisfied shortly. If not, I would die! Papa's hands bore a warm loaf of rye bread, wrapped in a thin piece of paper.

He handed the loaf to Mutti, at which she stood up and held the bread to her chest as though she were holding an infant. We looked with wonder and urgency at this piece of food that had been so rare for so many years. I wanted to sink my teeth into it, and this desire made me question why we always had to share. I myself hated, loathed, abhorred sharing. If I were an only child, I wouldn't be so hungry all the time. Mutti would feed me, the only nestling, like a bird mother feeds her baby. Then Papa brought me back to reality when he said, "Anna, please cut the bread, the children are waiting."

Waiting for food, thinking about food, longing for food, hogging food, bartering for food, depending on the kindness of strangers for food. It seemed that life hinged on crumbs.

Mutti nodded, but before she sat down again, still cradling the bread, she took the corner of her apron and wiped her eyes. I wondered why my Mutti was crying when we were all about to be fed. Often I didn't understand Mutti, although most of the time her face betrayed no secrets. Was she crying for herself, for us, for humankind? Her reasons were inscrutable to me then.

Lying on the table in front of her was the blade that was going to cut the bread. It was not a serrated bread knife. The handle was dark brown wood, shiny from all the grease and moisture of hands that had held it over the years. The blade was long and wide, more like a butcher would use. Mutti was still holding onto the bread, though, delaying cutting it. We shifted in our chairs. "Mutti, please, cut the bread," we begged her.

She may have been afraid that the bread she was holding was going to fall apart, like those fragile loaves she had carried home after the war. They had been made of cornmeal and water, and even though she cradled them as if they were pieces of ancient pottery ready to fall apart at the slightest shift of her hands, some of the loaves disintegrated by the time she arrived home from the store. And then the crumbs were so dry, they always got stuck in my throat and seemed to crawl back up through my nose.

There was something about the knife that I remembered from the hundreds of wartime stories I had heard. It was the same knife that my father had grabbed when we were living in the *Sudetenland*, and with which he would have slain a Russian, if necessary. The survival knife, that.

Now my mother held that same knife, the knife that survived the war along with us. The knife that could have cut a man's throat was about to slice bread for us. She made the sign of the cross on the bottom side of the oval loaf.

I noticed Mutti's hands. They were brown and leathery, with green veins she carried with her like a road map of her life. Although she was only forty-eight then, hers were old hands, worn, wrinkled, rough from digging, planting, and scrubbing. Work kept her fingernails short and raggedy. But I liked her hands, for they were always warm, and they breathed love when she held my hand in hers. Sometimes, though, I thought it would be nice if my mother had prettier hands, hands like my friends' younger mothers. Hunger makes the mind wander to trifles.

My mouth was watering. My eyes were focused now on Mutti and the sustenance she was holding. It was time to eat. It seemed that before each meal, there were a few seconds when my stomach became the focal point of my being, when I thought I couldn't live another minute without food in my mouth.

The cross had been made. The knife that threatened the Russian blessed the food. My hunger was as sharp as that knife. I felt angry with the God in whose name this loaf of bread was blessed. I had my doubts about this God, mostly when I was hungry. Oh dear God, could I please have a slice of bread now?

I had been told that my grandmother, whom I had never known, blessed each loaf before she cut it, and Mutti did the same. At the time, the significance of this cultural ritual was probably not apparent to me. Mutti blessed many loaves of bread over the years, in years of hardship as well as years of plenty. I wonder what she thought would happen if she didn't bless each loaf? Would the bread get stuck in our throats, even kill us? Was she seeking forgiveness and salvation by showing her reverence? Was she providing a bite of heaven for her family at this time of hunger and preserving a ritual at the same time? No matter, the ritual was going on too long. I wanted to thank God too for this bread, and most especially not infuriate him with my impatience, but right then I wanted a slice of bread more than I wanted any blessing God could bestow upon me.

Finally, still cradling the bread, and with a quick motion of her wrist, Mutti guided the knife through the crusty top of the bread, made a couple of see-sawing motions, and pulled the knife out of the bottom of the bread, only an inch from her breast. I winced even as she evinced confidence. She held the first slice between the blade and her thumb and handed it to Klaus. Why did he get the first slice, what was so special about him? He was a bony boy, thin as a fence post, his gaunt, handsome face so much like Mutti's. The next slice, thicker, went to Papa, because he needed fuel to keep his family fed; a thinner slice was handed to Doris, and then I held my piece of bread in my hands. Mutti sliced the rest of the bread before she ate. We scraped our ration of margarine on each slice and covered the fat with sugar.

The bread was still warm and the first bite felt solid and chewey in my mouth given that the teeth, tongue, and roof of my mouth were all clamoring for it. The sugar and margarine coated my lips. Nobody talked, but we heard each other's chewing noises as we took bite after careful bite, our teeth cutting through the crust and then working on the doughy, chewy body, not one of us wanting to let go of it, but finally, almost reluctantly swallowing and by doing so gratifying our greatest need. Papa smiled when he crunched down on a grain of rye with its slightly nutty flavor. Then he told us about the long line of people at the bakery, waiting patiently for it to open and then quickly leaving the store with their loaves tucked securely under their arms.

We finished our loaf, and heavenly peace filled the room. We were satisfied for a while, satisfied, that is, until hunger returned and surprised us by stabbing us yet again. Bread was not just sustenance but hope—hope that there would be another slice and another to take the edge off our hunger again and again.

Sometimes candy bars were handed out at school, and these we devoured with a greediness born of years of forced abstinence. Once, my brother came home with a candy bar he had won in a GI drawing contest. Nowadays an unimpressive prize, but then a delicacy, a sensational, rare commodity, to be devoured at once! But not by my brother alone. Klaus carried it home, took a ruler, and measured five equal pieces, so that all five of us could taste this morsel of mouth-watering luxury.

◆   ◆   ◆

The memories of elementary school that have imprinted me the most are not related to academic activities. I loved walking to school with my friends, especially Ingrid and Barbara. Walking home with our school bags on our backs, skipping, running, laughing, singing, and occasionally discussing homework that we were given every day and that had to be done before we could play. Walking home from school we made plans to play later in the afternoon. We couldn't get on the phone to talk to our friends: nobody I knew had a phone.

Barbara had moved to the neighborhood with her mother in 1946, which made us five years old when we met and began a friendship that would last for many years, into adulthood and up to the present day. She was a petite girl with sparkling brown eyes. When I asked Mutti why Barbara didn't have a father like I did, she said, "He is missing." I knew that, but why was he missing? He was missing in the war and was probably dead, a fallen German soldier. I felt sorry that she had only a mother with whom to live. I wouldn't want to live only with Mutti, because I loved my Papa so much and I couldn't imagine not having him around. I have been told that he was exempt from military service because he had three children to support. The fact that he worked for a company that had switched to producing weapons may also have kept him from serving.

Even though Barbara didn't have a Papa, I envied her. She had a seamstress aunt in Copenhagen, so she had an endless supply of new dresses the envy of all the girls on the block. Barbara and I must have had the same bodily measurements, because whenever she got a new dress I got an old one of hers. This is how I came into possession of two dream dresses still vivid in my memory. Their style was identical: long, narrow sleeves, fitted bodice, and a full bell skirt in the *Glockenrock* style. One was green and one was red, and the red one, to top off being already gorgeous, was embroidered as well, with fine white thread. These dresses set me to spinning endlessly, one spin after another until dizziness set in and I was forced to take a break.

The glamour of the fabric swirling around my legs (in the process revealing my underwear!) made me forget that the dresses were secondhand. When I wore those dresses, I felt like a privileged person of higher social standing. Of course, it would have helped my self-esteem, or what I thought was self-esteem, even more had I had a pair of stylish shoes to go with my dresses. All I had were the clunky, sensible ones I wore with everything, day in and day out. How I envied people who had more than we did, especially in the way of clothing and shoes—the beginnings of a critical attitude towards my parents. I often wondered why Papa couldn't make more money so I could have pretty new clothes.

From elementary school on, my best friend was Ingrid Franke. She lived with her parents in an apartment only a minute away. We met in second grade and went to the same school for five years, although we were not in the same room and had different teachers. We did everything together: climbed around on the monkey bars when the playground re-opened, played games in the street, dressed and undressed our dolls, and stayed overnight at each other's homes. She was an only child and her parents were pretty well off, considering post-war German incomes. I envied—here that word envy again!—Ingrid her clothes and her pretty apartment, her bathroom and the pretty bedroom that was hers alone. Not to have to share a room with my sister—oh, what a wicked wish!

At our house, we still cleaned ourselves using the kitchen sink and cold water. It wasn't until the fifties that we had an "on-demand" gas-fired hot water unit installed above the sink. When the new hot water faucet was turned on, the pilot light in the unit ignited the gas that heated the water. It was such a relief to take a sponge-bath with hot water.

As small children, though, Ingrid and I didn't care whether we cleaned ourselves with hot or cold water. Although Ingrid had more luxuries than we did, she was at our house more than she was at her own. She stayed with us more often than I stayed in her apartment. In the room Doris and I shared, Ingrid and I put make-up on each other, using tiny sample tubes of lipstick that were given out at drugstores and which served both as lip and cheek color. Never mind that we looked like clowns, we loved how we looked.

Despite the relatively impoverished conditions of our house, Ingrid liked being around our family and especially Mutti. I think there were times when she loved my Mutti more than I did. I wanted a young mother like Frau Franke, somebody vibrant and fun-loving. Mutti had a ready smile, true, but she was old now that she was in her late forties! Frau Franke was a tall woman with striking chestnut hair that fell to her shoulders in curls. Oh to have hair like hers! She seemed always to be in a good mood, laughed freely, and spoke her mind in a loud and clear manner. She volunteered at school and accompanied our class on field trips. All the kids liked Frau Franke, all except Ingrid who felt perturbed by her hyperactive mother. Neighbors gossiped about how loud Frau Franke was. Shouldn't she tune it down a little, wasn't she embarrassing sometimes, what with Herr Franke being such a gentleman and having such an important job? And weren't the Frankes somehow mismatched?

Well, the gentleman eventually divorced the full-of-life woman at a time when divorce was still extremely uncommon. My mother would say, "Frau Franke shouldn't give him a divorce. He's just having an affair, but he'll come back to her," and our neighbors all agreed.

It made me wonder even then why she couldn't have an affair of her own, or why a woman would want to wait for a man to come back to her. How could she ever forgive him his trespasses and live happily ever after with him? Mutti's attitude really confused me, but I figured she knew more about these things than I did. So I didn't really dwell on the Frankes too long. In the end, Herr Franke never returned to his wife.

It was a small world for us still, walking to school, roaming around the neighborhood within limits set by our parents, but we were becoming more aware of what was going on around us. We still took the same route every day, no matter whether rain, sun, snow, winds, or occasional hail, and we were by no means dressed for the occasion all the time, still walking on cardboard-soled shoes, lacking warm winter coats, and wearing hats that were too small and squeezed our heads.

A tall hedge grew next to the sidewalk along the main street leading to school, and the attraction of this hedge was that at certain times of the year it grew small white berries that popped when they were squeezed. This we were doing one day when we heard a noise from the bushes. As we peered into the greenery, we saw the blurry outline of a man wearing a coat he was holding wide open for all of us, exposing his manhood. When we saw this organ (and we hadn't seen too many of these), we screamed and ran to the safety of the school in record time. He never appeared again. When I told Mutti about it as soon as I got home and asked her what was wrong with him, she said that it was the war. War damaged people.

I thought of the young man I had seen walking up and down the main shopping street by our house who persisted in looking up at the sky every few seconds and then down again, over and over, all the while mumbling words to himself and waving his arms. We called him the *Sternengucker*, star gazer, just because he was always looking up, perhaps looking toward heaven but seeing something other than the sky. Shoppers in the neighborhood knew him and stepped out of his way, because he paid no attention to what was going on right in front of his eyes. He may have been expecting a bomb to drop down on him, because at times he became quite agitated. Had he, a helpless observer of death shooting out of the sky, seen a bomb drop or explode? Maybe he had watched bombed people die. Maybe right then he was still running to a shelter, in his head hearing the hissing sound of bombs that wouldn't leave him alone.

Mutti had seen him too, and said, "It's the war, it made him crazy." It had crazed many people, in truth. The flasher was crazy, too, according to Mutti. The war was over, and yet it was ever-present. How could that be? My family and I were normal, weren't we? Why wasn't I crazy? Or was I crazy? I had to find out about the war from another perspective, beyond the personal stories I had heard so often. I had a child's curiosity about the war. Maybe in school I would learn about it, in history class. Then I would get answers! But I didn't know then that the war would not be officially taught for the eleven years I was schooled in Germany. Instead, everyone lived the post-war life for many years to come. I was not to learn details about the war until years later and only when I went to England at age nineteen.

What war did to people was driven home to me one day when I must have been seven or eight. Those who were bombed out scrounged for living space for themselves and their families. Some lived in mere shells of apartment houses, in apartments without glass in the windows and walls that threatened to crash momentarily. Some lived in basements of bombed-out buildings and claimed a room as their own there.

Doris and I and our friends were so used to playing in the basements of bombed-out buildings where nothing was left standing but the basement walls and maybe a stretch of ceiling. We were accustomed to exploring these buildings, but one day we got a scary surprise. I can still see the staircase going into this basement. At least fifteen stairs led down to a door, which was odd because doors were now rare. If there were any left and they were wood, they would have become firewood long ago. Maybe this door was one of those metal doors, an air raid door, guaranteed to save lives in case a bomb dropped and a fire broke out. However, a door had never kept us from exploring, and so we pushed it open. We saw immediately that this was somebody's home: a mattress on the floor and assorted sticks of furniture around it.

Standing by the mattress was the man who lived there. We nervously looked at each other. The man looked unkempt and angry and we were instantly frightened. We turned on our heels and ran up the stairs, thinking that he would close the door, our adventure now over, but then we heard footsteps behind us. The man was chasing us. We ran over cobblestone streets for blocks and blocks until our house came in view; we opened the wrought-iron gate and saw Mutti's shadow behind a sheet she was hanging up in the courtyard. It was wash day. Whew, we were safe! We almost knocked Mutti over, then stood behind her and closed our eyes, sure that the man was standing right in front of us all. But he was nowhere to be seen. He had given up chasing us, probably when he saw us opening our gate. We were then given an earful about not bothering people, respecting their privacy. How would we like it if somebody knocked on our door and then ran away? We had opened the door for nothing and felt like fools besides, and then Mutti made us hang up the laundry as punishment.

Since then, I have played this scene over and over again in my dreams. I related it to my sister, but she doesn't remember any of it. Sometimes I wondered if it really happened, but in the end I know it did. I think this man had grown tired of children disturbing him in the makeshift home he had made for himself and wanted to put a stop to these incursions once and for all. Generally, privacy was and is highly valued by Germans. Rooms with doors that are shut each time you enter or leave, yards with fences that keep strangers out, are indications of this desire for privacy.

To this moment, even though I know the outcome as I'm dreaming the dream, the terror of being followed is so real and so powerful that my heart beats hard and my chest cannot seem to contain it. But it also makes the sight of Mutti even sweeter.

Since our return to Hamburg, Papa had worked hard at making a living for us. Whether the company he had worked for before and during the war was not up and running yet, or whether he didn't want to go back to his old job, I don't know.

I always heard that his first love was music. He had been trained at a conservatory and played the double bass, violin, and trombone. Maybe he thought that in these post-war years, people craved entertainment and so performance work would be easy to find. Thus Papa became a freelance musician to a segment of society financially able to attend dances. He also played in a band at the pleasure of the British Allies. He liked the British, even though they had just bombed his city. Very odd, a combination of forgiving them and needing them. They paid well, and money badly needed by our family.

The band members had to look presentable, so Papa dressed up for the job. He had one white shirt which Mutti washed daily by hand, starched, and hung up to dry overnight in the basement or outside on the clothesline. The next day she ironed it so it was ready for him to wear again if he had a job that night. He had one pair of black pants. Holes in the knee area Mutti had darned again and again using very fine thread so the darning wouldn't be too conspicuous or look as though he was wearing pants with knee pads. But standing behind his double bass, he was able to hide his darned knees.

The patrons of the dances sent alcoholic drinks, mostly beer, to the band members throughout the evening, which the musicians gratefully accepted and consumed between numbers. One night Papa drank too much liquor, and after he had taken a toilet break and was walking down a hallway he opened a door that he thought led back to the ballroom and fell to the ground floor, breaking his elbow. Such was the condition of that building—a room for dancing with a door to nowhere.

We laughed whenever we heard the story, but a musician without a working elbow was not able to perform, and money became scarcer. Freelancing, the lack of a dependable income, made it very difficult for my parents to get back on their feet, and they struggled on for many years after the war.

When Papa did have work, some of the money was used to pay off the debts incurred when he was jobless. Sometimes my parents had to rely on government unemployment money that Mutti parceled out at the various stores where she had credit. All the merchants had known her and my Papa for many years, and they gave her credit no questions asked because they knew she would pay off her debt. I hated it when Mutti asked me to go to the dairy store to get some milk and "ask them to add it to the tab." I could hardly look Herr Scholten in the eye and ask for credit, because I was embarrassed about not having money. There I was, mad at Mutti for making me ask and mad at my parents for not having any money to pay for groceries up front.

Though Mutti had admonished me to carry the metal milk container carefully, I still managed to spill some of the "blue" milk just by skipping and making waves in the can. The milk was transparent, because it contained very little fat. When I was really mad about having to get milk on credit, I would do the "experiment," grabbing the handle of the can and swinging the filled can in a big circle, round and round, hoping that some of it would fly out. My Onkel Heini had shown me this physical science phenomenon by using water in a milk can for the big swing. Something to do with gravity, but I thought that with milk the result would be different. But it never was. The milk stayed in the can and I handed it over to Mutti, refusing myself to drink a drop of the disgusting liquid.

◆   ◆   ◆

Gradually, the neighborhood opened up for us kids when we took different streets to and from school, sometimes taking a longer way on purpose to procrastinate when it came to doing homework. Looking at different ruins and piles of rubble only made the walk more interesting. Sometimes we stopped and watched trucks getting piled high with bricks and pieces of twisted metal, and what was once an apartment house would be carted away before our eyes. We balanced on still-standing basement walls and gathered every salvageable thing, like anything aluminum, which we then took to a collection place where we received a few pennies for our find. At a time when a bread roll cost six pennies, our income from salvaging made a small contribution to the family.

The world opened a little more on the field trips we took around Hamburg. When trains again ran, our class took monthly field trips. Bombs had not fallen on the woods around Hamburg, and there were plenty of destinations for us. A train took us part of the way there, since not all tracks had yet been repaired. Then the real work began. Serious hiking for miles in miserable shoes, but singing all the way. Singing as a group was a way to make time go by faster and more joyfully than just marching along silently. When we came to a spot that Fräulein Düstersiek particularly liked, we sat on the woodsy ground and ate our lunch—a couple of slices of bread spread with margarine and sugar and then maybe an apple. On these outings, we never drank anything with our meals.

For the rest of the day we hiked, stopping sometimes to look at creepy things on the forest floor, insects and such, or to listen to birds, examine leaves, and figure out the names of trees. We had never seen so many trees all at once, since most of our neighborhood trees had been chopped down for firewood. The moss beneath my bare feet felt soft and silky. Lying on the forest floor and looking at leaves against a clear sky made me feel optimistic. I came home from these outings happy from singing and being with my friends, tired from walking, and happy for having been away for a day from home where the aftermath of the war and issues such as chronic lack of money suffused the air. Money earned from selling eggs paid for my field trip. Nature warmed my heart.

Some of the field trips acquainted us with museums and other places of interest such as bombed-out churches, the remainder of Hamburg's harbor, and the famous *Hagenbeck Zoo* that stood unbombed and full of monkeys.

◆   ◆   ◆

I have a few memories of family life during this time. Occasionally while I was still in elementary school, my family and I would go on outings, usually on Sundays. Most of the time, we walked to a lake near our house. When the trains were running again and we could afford tickets, we went to a bigger lake. I learned to swim at the bigger lake, the *Bredenbeker Teich* in Ahrensburg which was at least half an hour away from our house. Knowing how to swim was a very important, life-saving skill stressed by my parents: to be able to swim meant you wouldn't drown, you would live. Therefore, to swim meant life. Some day we would spend vacations at the Baltic Sea, like my parents had before the war, and we would need to know how to swim. Thus, learning to swim became the focus of these Sunday excursions for my sister and me. I was probably eight then.

Early on these Sunday mornings, we packed what we wanted to take along for the whole day. To make the journey worthwhile, we had to stay for that length of time, which meant taking food, forks, a blanket, towels, and anything that fit into bags which we all had to carry to the train, hold onto on the train, and lug on the long walk from the train to the lake.

The lake was surrounded by a grassy area on which we spread our one and only old blanket. I wore a bikini, a knitted, woolen one that scratched me, wet or dry. Doris and I wore little head kerchiefs that we removed before we got into the water. Papa and Klaus wore minimal bathing suits, like Speedos, and I knew what the bumps in their bathing suits were. Mutti wore a one-piece bathing suit suitable for a matronly figure in her forties.

The serious business of learning to swim began. I held Papa's hand, and together we waded into the sort of silty and slimy edge of the lake. I couldn't walk through the repulsive water grasses quickly enough to get to the sandy part of the lake bottom, which was fairly deep and where I could barely stand up without swallowing water. Papa or Klaus picked me up, held me high over their heads, and then dropped me—splash—into the lake. I kept my eyes closed and tried to hold my breath until I came up, my arms paddling and my legs thrashing, to the sound of my Papa's reassuring voice telling me to swim to him. Somehow I made it over to him but in a fashion that could hardly be called swimming. Then he scooped me up and proceeded to do the whole thing over again. I was like a dog doing tricks. Paddle here—splash—hold your breath—paddle there—splash. Then it was my sister's turn who, though already ten at the time was also just learning to swim.

Eventually my movements became less frantic and I learned the breaststroke. Mutti did the same breaststroke that I was trying to learn, and she looked so very smooth and calm. That's how I wanted to swim, just glide across the lake and back. I imagined that my body would never get tired. That was my dream, to get to the opposite shore, moving, always moving toward it. I don't know with absolute certainty, but learning to swim may have been the beginning of the urge to move to another shore later in my life.

In the meantime, my family had worked up an appetite from all that splashing and thrashing and near-drowning, and we plunked ourselves down on the blanket and dug into a lunch consisting of bread and margarine and sometimes potato salad all of which had been sitting out in the sun since the morning. We didn't have any coolers then. It was years before I knew that bad things could grow in potato salad, but none of us ever got sick from our warm mayonnaise. We enjoyed Mutti's delicious concoction, taking a few bites and then passing the container on to the next person. Paper plates were unheard of then. Sometimes we even had hot dogs that Papa had bought from my uncle twice removed, the butcher. These *Würstchen* we would eat cold, holding them firmly in our hands until every scrap was gone. There were no cold drinks or even warm drinks, no concession stands, and no drinking fountains. We washed our hands in the lake, and then lay in the sun until it was time to go home. I didn't learn to swim in one lesson, but in my recollection it didn't take too many times at the lake until I felt that I could stay afloat.

Other outings of sorts were periodic visits to see my Tante Gretchen. Doris and I usually went along when Mutti decided to see her sister. Mutti's relationship with her sister was a little tense, Mutti being the underdog for having married a husband who didn't make much money. Tante Gretchen had married into money in the form of tall, debonair, and rich Onkel Max who either owned or operated a rice mill near Hamburg. Tante Gretchen had moved from lower middle-class Barmbek where we lived to upper class Klein-Flottbek, not too far from Blankenese, where rich captains lived on hills overlooking the Elbe river and where wives were believed to sight their husbands' ships coming in, giving them time to say a hasty good-bye to their lovers. I always found that story amusing, thinking to myself that rich people were not so different from middle class people like Herr Franke, who had also deceived his wife. Sitting on the subway across from Mutti I was trying to think of anything other than the imminent visit with Tante Gretchen. Mutti was already wringing her hands. I was actually a little nervous myself, gnawing the inside of my mouth, a nervous habit that continues to the present.

Before we left our house, Doris and I had undergone a rigid inspection by Mutti for our hair, ears, fingernails, toenails, and clothes before *Fox Eyes*, (Mutti's "affectionate" name for my aunt) laid eyes on us. If Mutti overlooked a missing button, Tante Gretchen wouldn't. She would espy any irregularities about her nieces and promptly inform Mutti, who would hastily acknowledge the fact of the missing button as her neck began to turn a spotty pink. Mutti was already aggravated, and we had only just arrived. It was not unusual for both Mutti and my aunt to be exhibiting bright red necks by the time their visit came to a merciful conclusion. They may have loved each other, but in their relations anymore they operated below the belt most of the time, flinging the most mundane accusations at each other, as about the missing button. Mutti would only occasionally retort that Gretchen had just one child to take care of whereas she, Mutti, had three, and would Gretchen like to be the one to sew on the button. It was a strange sort of caring when I think of it now.

My aunt's lifestyle had improved considerably since she had married Onkel Max. The house in Klein-Flottbek was large and tastefully furnished. I remember Persian rugs everywhere on polished wooden floors. Doris and I spent long intervals of time in the bathroom, which actually boasted a bathtub. This was a wondrous thing to us because we had to spend Saturday nights in a gray aluminum tub dragged up from the basement where it usually sat full of wet clothes needing to be hung up. Other times it was used to wash massive amounts of spinach. Our aluminum tub held no magic for us. Here in front of us, however, was the perfect porcelain bathtub with fixtures out of which flowed hot and cold water. But we couldn't use it, because we weren't visiting my aunt to take baths.

At home on Saturday nights, Mutti would fill a kettle and a big pan with water and heat it on the stove. First she dumped the hot water in the tub and then followed it with cold until the right temperature was reached. We had to take turns being the first or last to be washed, and of course nobody wanted to be last because who wants to get into "used" water? If I was second, Doris had to skim the tub, before Mutti added a kettle of hot water and I could have my turn. With shiny faces, wet hair, and bodies slightly pink from vigorous scrubbing, we sat towel-wrapped in the kitchen to stay warm. My cousin Renate, Tante Gretchen's daughter, ten years older than I, probably took a daily bath in her glorious tub. Oh, I wanted to be an only child, a rich only child!

Our visit wasn't over yet and the most horrifying time was yet to come. Dinner. Pushing up the chairs to the table was probably the last sound to be heard for the next hour, unless it was a request to pass the food. A "no-speaking-at-the-dinner-table" rule was strictly enforced. The lack of background noise motivated us girls to find a way of swallowing without that vulgar gulping sound in our throats. Needless to say, we never ate our fill out of politeness (and because Mutti said so) and usually had to have a hearty snack when we got home that night.

In the subway, Mutti's neck would gradually return to its normal flesh color. She didn't say much about the visit, except to say that we had behaved well. When we entered our modest apartment, she sighed. It wasn't in Mutti's nature to be envious. But she must have had a complicated relationship with her sister, considering that we were living in a house owned by that same sibling. My parents paid a minimum amount of rent, and Papa did all the repairs, which were considerable and for which Gretchen may have been grateful. Maybe she was just playing older sister when she criticized Mutti.

Balancing my aunt's critical nature was a generosity she showed us when on several occasions she had her seamstress make matching dresses and coats for Doris and me. These we wore for a long time, until the hems couldn't be let out another centimeter. They were by far the best clothes Doris and I had ever had up till then, not a second-hand stitch anywhere on them. We even had to go for fittings!

◆   ◆   ◆

By the time my siblings and I were all in school, a routine emerged that didn't differ much for many years. When we came home from school around noon or one o'clock, we sat down to eat. *Mittagessen* was the big meal of the day. Big was a relative concept, especially in the early post-war years. Sometimes our big meal consisted of white bread broken into pieces supplemented with sugar and hot "blue" milk. Or if not eating a slice of bread with sugar and margarine, we would have *Schmalz,* similar to bacon fat, with salt. Hot, nutritious meals we could only imagine. Cheese, meat, and potatoes were often non-existent or rare unless they were exchanged for cigarettes, but how to get our hands on cigarettes? Sometimes my brother stole them, brought them home proudly, and later exchanged them for food.

Sometimes we had a fried egg, vegetables from the backyard, and some fruit or berries. A couple of sayings come to mind when I think of this time of food scarcity and hunger: "no salt to put in the soup" and "mornings, eat like an emperor, at mid-day like a king, and evenings like a beggar." Later, when food became plentiful, it made sense to eat like a beggar at night: sparingly. But in the late forties, we ate like beggars so much of the time, except when our grandparents shared some of their slaughtered hog with us. How a king or an emperor would eat, we had no idea.

We took all our meals together, sitting mostly in the kitchen which would be cozy warm if we had gotten any wood or coal to burn. When coal was scarce there would be no fire in the living room stove, so we would stay in the kitchen all day except when we went out to play. The room Doris and I shared was seldom heated because heating three or even two rooms would have been a luxury only to be dreamt about. On the other hand, sleeping in a warm room was popularly thought to be unhealthy. Even so, when I beheld frost clinging to the walls of our room, damp with potassium nitrate, I would have given anything to have slept in boiling hot conditions. Often we went to bed early, fully dressed. If we spent any time in the living room, which would most likely have been in the summertime, we had to be out of that room by the time my brother went to bed because he slept there on a makeshift bed. And in the years between 1945–1948, we had so many relatives living off and on with us that virtually every square foot of living space could turn into sleeping space at night.

Nevertheless, we were lucky to have an apartment (sometimes I call it a house) because it was a house, even if a duplex. It had windows with glass panes, wooden not cardboard floors, stoves, and assorted sticks of furniture.

The house my paternal grandfather, Johannes Schmidt, had built in 1901 was located in Hamburg-Barmbek. The village Bernebeke (as Barmbek was once called) became part of Hamburg in 1355. Around the turn of the 20th century, apartments were built in such a way that they had limited access to sunlight, and cross-ventilation from the back of an apartment to the front was impossible, because each floor was crowded with three or more apartments. By 1910, only fourteen percent of the apartments had a bathroom, although building codes specified a *water closet* (toilet) for each apartment. Most people lived in apartment houses of four to five stories, and most exteriors were of brick or stucco. Apartment houses on shopping streets usually had stores with large windows on the ground floor and apartments above them. The stores supplied many of the items for daily life: bread and cakes, fish, vegetables, dairy products, but also hats, shoes, stationery, and hardware. Window-shopping was then a favorite pastime.

When Hamburg was fire-bombed in July 1943, Barmbek was the hardest-hit district. About 7,000 of its 9,000 large apartment complexes were destroyed. Compared to the living conditions of most people in Barmbek, our semi-detached house built by my grandfather was more of a middle-class dwelling than most apartments in Barmbek, although still it had only a water closet rather than a bathroom with a tub.

All the houses on our street were semi-detached duplexes and each building was occupied by two families, one upstairs and one down. A common main door led into a small hallway, with the door to the downstairs apartment straight ahead and a staircase on the right rising to the upstairs apartment. A third door led into the basement, where the upstairs family used one room as storage. The rest of the basement belonged to the downstairs family. Generally, the downstairs family owned the building and the upstairs family rented, except soon after the house was built when Mutti's extended family, including my Oma's sisters, occupied the whole house. Oma Julie's sister Ottilie was supposed to have kept a bottle of schnaps on a string in the downspout to keep the schnaps cold and available. Then, whenever she felt like it, from her bedroom window she would pull the bottle up to her and enjoy a secret drink.

Around 1930, and after the death of my maternal grandparents, Onkel Max bought the house from their estate. Onkel Max was the only one in the family (he was then already married to my Tante Gretchen) who had enough money to make such a purchase. He bought out Mutti and Tante Klara, and my parents became caretakers. Luckily, Papa was very good at making repairs, so that over the years Onkel Max more or less relied on him to fix things without necessarily reimbursing him. The war years had taken their toll on the structure, because there was no material available with which to make repairs or paint. The house looked a sad thing on the outside.

◆   ◆   ◆

For the downstairs family, the toilet was in the basement as were three other rooms used for storage. The basement had taken on a life of its own for me, and I was deathly afraid of it. If only we could have lived upstairs because of its toilet room at the top of the stairs off a small landing. Use of the toilet required leaving the apartment, which was perhaps inconvenient, but so what? I was about nine years old and my basement phobia had started developing as soon as we arrived back in Hamburg in 1945.

The construction of bathrooms had not been a priority when our house was built at the turn of the century. I had to go to the basement to pee, but I would have gladly peed in my pants in order to avoid that toilet. I tried to put off the call of nature. I crossed my legs or went outside to play where sometimes I would do an embarrassing thing and pee in the backyard hidden from view by a big cherry tree. Most of the time, though, when I couldn't hold it any longer, I asked Mutti to descend the stairs ahead of me and I would follow, holding onto her housedress. The monsters rattling around in my head wouldn't hurt Mutti, they only wanted me and my young blood!

Sometimes at night, before falling asleep with my *Federbett* (feather comforter) tucked in around me, images of frozen soldiers lying in stacks on fields of snow would flash across my eyes. Blinking hard, I'd attempt to scramble the images somewhat, and sometimes I was even successful. I knew that my Onkel Werner, Papa's brother, had gone missing in Russia. Probably frozen to death in Russia, wherever that was. I didn't know its exact location, only that it was freezing cold there. Maybe one of the monsters was my uncle, missing after all these years and trying to get home. Maybe they were all soldiers, reaching out for me, for help, transfused blood, life. Maybe they wanted me to help them find their way home. I pulled my *Federbett* up over my cold nose. Sleep cradled me eventually, and the monsters faded until the following night.

Our basement bathroom did not have a tub, pretty curtains on the windows, fragrant bath oils and soaps in a basket, a rug on the floor, or fluffy towels on the rack. The room was only big enough for a stool and a sink. A metal chain hung from the water tank well above my head and little me had to pull hard on it to release the water. The cast-iron sink was just big enough for washing my hands with the biting cold water.

This bathroom didn't look anything like the ones I had seen in my friends' newly-built, post-war apartments, which had new toilets with a lever to push instead of a rusty chain to pull. I prayed that when my friends came over to play, they wouldn't have to use our bathroom. A faint odor of urine permeated the room. I had seen Mutti scrub the gray, cold concrete floor on her hands and knees with a *Feudel*, a square piece of heavy cloth. But the foul smell of wet cement wouldn't go away. The stucco walls had once been white, but that was a long time ago and there was no money now for paint. The little room was sunless, almost lightless, except for a dim haze that came from a bulb screwed into the ceiling.

Now I was on the toilet, alone in the room. Except I had Mutti stand in front of the door of this indoor outhouse. "Stay right there, Mutti, don't go away, please."

Mutti was usually kind about helping me, but sometimes she got impatient with my reluctance to overcome my fear. When Mutti's face hardened and her mouth took on a determined look that made slivers of her lips, I knew that the "nothing-is-as-bad-as-war" lecture was coming. She would say, "When you are starving and freezing, and when bombs are falling on you, that's bad. This isn't. You know what's in every room in this basement and there is nothing down here to hurt you. I'll stand at the top of the stairs, and I won't leave until you are done, but I'm not going down there with you. Isn't it about time you were a big girl and did this alone?"

Nevertheless, every time I had to pee it was a guessing game as to how Mutti would react to my request. Obviously, Mutti didn't know about the monsters in my head, and I wasn't about to tell her or anyone else, not even my sister. Doris too had an issue with the basement and she, older by two years, would beg me to accompany her. We teamed up, one deathly-afraid girl protecting the other, cramming into the little room, doing our business in utter silence, rushing through cleaning up or skipping the hand washing altogether, pushing the door open and racing up the stairs, breath held until we reached the top where at last we saw relief in each other's faces. But I never told Doris about my monsters.

The monsters really clattered around in my head when Mutti was away. I was sure that they knew I was alone in the house and that sooner or later I would have to go downstairs. And now it was time again. Creak! If my foot touched the front of the step, it crackled like brittle wood that might splinter momentarily. Whether I tiptoed or flew down the stairs, each of the ten steps had its own tortured strain. By the time I reached the seventh step, just at the bend of the staircase where I could see the closed rooms of the basement ahead, I was ready to turn around and run upstairs.

The toilet was only ten feet from the bottom of the stairs now, and none of the doors to the other rooms had yet opened. Sliding door hook into eye took only seconds, and for now I was safe. The moment after flushing, though, was the most frightsome, because the monsters were lying in wait in the next room over and in the room beyond that. Yes, that's where they lived.

One of the other rooms, the coal room, was deeply black from all the coal that had been stored there over the years. In these hard times, when coal was difficult to come by let alone pay for, my parents would fetch a few pieces from the coal dealer when they could afford it. No more credit, he said. In better times, coal had been delivered in burlap bags, the bags slit, and the opening pushed through the window to deposit into our basement the chunky egg-shaped pieces and briquette ovals in the shape of gold pieces. Black dust flew madly around and eventually settled everywhere—on the floor, the ceiling, the walls. Only a light bulb dangled from the ceiling, throwing shadows on the black pile of potential warmth.

The lock on this room kept the monsters from coming out, but whenever I flushed the toilet I knew that they lay in wait just outside the bathroom door, having lurched from the darkness of the coals and squeezed through the cracks of the coal room door to wait for my passage. Soot-covered monsters, their eyes glowing like pieces of burning coal, they would reach for me, grab my hands, and pull me deep, deep into an even scarier basement in one of those bombed-out buildings that my friends and I sometimes played in. And from there I would never, ever get back to see my family again. I would lie there with all the bodies that had been killed in the war, piteously crying for Mutti.

At last, I was done with my business and ready to leave. With trembling hands I reached for the lever on the door, pushed it open, and ran up the ten stairs with lightning speed. Mercifully, my legs didn't let me down. As soon as I reached the door upstairs, for now safely out of the monsters' reach, I peeked down to see … nothing and nobody.

Then the next time came, probably even the same day, when I had to go down the stairs without Mutti. And if the monsters in the coal room weren't up and about, it was something else astir in the next room, the former air-raid shelter. Before I darted into the bathroom, I always threw a quick glance at the shelter door to be sure it was tightly closed.

This shelter room held the memory of that night when the whole family assembled there, including me as a baby. Hearing different versions of the story about the bomb that landed only a few feet away from me and the subsequent mayhem, screaming, and sickening fear in everyone in the room filled me with extreme trepidation every time I so much as looked at the door to that room.

I tried to rationalize this seemingly unreasonable fear of the basement. On the surface, I wanted nothing more than to have a shiny, new bathroom with plenty of light, pretty soaps in baskets, and fluffy towels. I think I wanted a new bathroom that wasn't in the basement even more than I wanted new clothes. The ugly bathroom represented the unsettled post-war conditions generally, and the opposite of my desires. I wanted to be normal, meaning less poor, less hungry, and less cold. I wanted things. Material things, I thought then, would replace my obsession with not having them, and having things would help drive out the fears I harbored, especially when I heard fire truck sirens. Without knowing how it was even possible, I believed that the sound of sirens during the war had permanently settled in my mind and body. I was never fearful of losing my parents.

I did fear the feeling of hunger that spread over me, even when I was no longer starving. I did fear the cold and its numbness, even when I was no longer freezing. I did fear the basement as long as I lived in that house, and if I had to go back there today I would still shake.

The first floor of the house had its challenges as well, but it wasn't scary. Except for the toilets, the upstairs and downstairs flats were laid out exactly the same. The living room and bedroom were next to each other. The kitchen next to the bedroom and the Kinderzimmer next to the living room faced each other across a long, hallway. The big window of the Kinderzimmer looked out on our street, Hartzloh. The living room was directly across from the entrance to the apartment. Next to the living room was my parents' bedroom with two windows looking out into the courtyard, and with French doors connecting the living room and bedroom. Next to the bedroom and across from the Kinderzimmer, separated by the hallway, were the kitchen and its big window looking out over the courtyard.

The hallway was always dark because the doors to all the rooms were always kept closed. Each time we entered a room, we would close the door behind us. There was no central heat, so keeping the doors closed helped retain the heat from the room's stoves. Sitting in a room whose door was closed also gave a feeling of coziness. Coats were hung on a rack in the hallway, and hats were placed on a shelf above the rack. The floor in the hallway and the kitchen was covered with linoleum of a faded pattern, but the other rooms had wooden floors. A fake Persian rug that was purchased sometime in the fifties covered most of the living room floor.

The smell of dampness and mold was ever-present in the *Kinderzimmer*, because potassium nitrate had set in on one corner, and no matter what my parents tried in order to get rid of it they never could. It would reappear through coat after coat of paint, growing some kind of fungus on part of the wall, especially in the corner by the window, and all because the room directly above our *Kinderzimmer* had a leaking balcony. At its worst, the fungus looked like lacy white cotton candy, growing straight out from the wall. When touched, it would disappear like a ghost. The paint was discolored there, black spots appearing gradually, until the whole mess was scraped off and painted again. The problem required some basic work, like the tearing down of a wall or the fixing of the balcony, but Onkel Max never saw fit to spend the money so my parents coped the best they could. When we had enough money for coal and maintained fires in the stove every day, the problem lessened a little.

The kitchen had the same problem, though, and sometimes it looked pretty gruesome. A coat of paint wouldn't have made a bit of difference, because there was some residual wetness in the wall that had been there for years and years. There was heat in the kitchen, too, so even fires in the stove wouldn't have eliminated it but just lessened it a little. The kitchen was tiled half way up the walls with tiles in the blue and white of the Dutch style, depicting bonneted little girls carrying water buckets. The windows had two panes which came together in the middle and hooked onto each other by their grooves. There was a steel rod that went up into the window frame to lock the window. The panes opened outward and lacked screens, and so there was the occasional fly. A fly trap hung from the ceiling and caught these innocents in the glue and refused to release them until they gave up and expired.

When Mutti had a handful of bread gone moldy, she'd open the window and with a deft motion throw the crumbs to the chickens that suddenly came running from wherever they were pecking. Many times I jumped from that window down into the courtyard, too lazy to walk from the front door to the gate which led into the courtyard that in turn led into the backyard.

The fungus problem in our house wasn't helped by the weather. It rains a lot in Hamburg and even when it doesn't, there is a fine mist in the air, a dampness chilling down to the bone. I felt this chilliness more acutely as an adult; as a child, though, I was in perpetual motion and the weather didn't bother me in the least. I was aware of the gray skies and the continuous breeze that made it to us from the distant North Sea. Occasionally, we would have warm and balmy days in the summer, days when the sun shone all day, and daylight kept us playing until 10:00 p.m. It was hard falling asleep on those long summer nights when it was still light outside. On occasional humid days we would take off our clothes and play naked in the backyard. Or we would jump into the old, cast-iron bathtub under the downspout that always filled with soft, silky rainwater. There we would splash and dunk each other, Doris and I, afterwards running around in the yard until we dried off.

The bathtub had another, darker purpose. When our cat Muschi had another litter of kittens, Mutti drowned them all when they were only moments old. My siblings and I failed to get upset by this natural method of population control. The kittens were too new to be cute yet and they looked like little rats. And who is going to take care of them, said Mutti, when there isn't even enough to go around for the people? Why was she always so logical, so tough, when on the other hand she loved nothing better than to sit with our family cat in her lap. Nobody thought of neutering cats, although everybody knew cats had to go outside to accomplish their reproduction and other business. Keeping a cat indoors was thought to be torture for the cat, but when they went outside they bore at least three litters a year. Each litter usually had four kittens, so there were at least twelve deaths in the family every year. It didn't make sense to me to keep going on like that, but it was nature, supposedly, and Mutti took care of it in her own way.

Since we only had 614 square feet of living space, we learned early that in order to keep things neat we couldn't leave our stuff lying around. Besides learning to be neat, my siblings and I learned cleanliness an early age. A clean house was important on principle, but especially because we couldn't do anything about the ruins all around us, the piles of dirt, bricks, and twisted metal. Thus keeping our apartment clean meant that inside our own walls we enjoyed some measure of normalcy.

On Saturdays, the apartment was cleaned from front to back and top to bottom. Windows were opened so the bedding could be hung over the windowsill to air. Before the *Federbetten* were put back on the beds, they were shaken vigorously to rearrange the feathers, making for even warmth of coverage.

When I picture those Saturdays I don't see my father, but he was probably fixing something or working in his basement workshop, one of the three storage rooms. He wasn't one to sit around. Upstairs, Mutti and my siblings cleaned, dusted, swept, and washed the floors with cleaning rags and buckets of water containing a few shavings of soap.

Washing the wooden floors was dangerous, because the wood had splintered over the years. The splinters were big enough to be used for kindling in the stove, so rough had the floor boards become. They were fifty years old by then.

A few times a year, and before and even after the purchase of the fake Persian rug, Mutti would take a steel pad, put on a sturdy pair of shoes (as if she had any other kind), step on the steel wool pad, and with a forward-backward dancelike motion of her leg sand the boards starting in the living room. Afterwards, the steel wool would be full of splinters. After that she swept up the wood dust and threw it into the cold stove. Next, she washed the floor, moving the furniture around so she could get into the corners. When a section dried, she got down on her hands and knees and applied a coat of wax to the wood which then was allowed to soak in. Finally, with a clean rag and back-and-forth arm movements, she shined the wax. Sweat would run down her face, even in the dead of winter, even with the windows open. Finally, she repeated the process in the *Kinderzimmer* and the bedroom. The rooms smelled clean and looked pretty when Mutti was done, but these floor-cleaning days were dreaded by us kids because even though she waxed one room at a time the room in the process of being cleaned was a mess until it was all done. Until then, the dining-size table in the living room couldn't be used for homework, the room being off-limits until the floor was done. The whole apartment felt *ungemütlich,* uncomfortable. Even the fire in the stove wouldn't be started until the room was clean.

I always thought that our house was ideally located. Hartzloh was a quiet cobblestoned street with semi-detached houses on both sides. All of them were built in the same style, each with a small front yard and each yard configured and landscaped differently. Ours had a small fir tree planted in the middle, and in the spring my parents planted snapdragons when they could afford them. Without those flowers, the front yard was just dirt raked periodically to make things look prettier, showing off the lines the rake made.

Our neighbors across the street had grapevines climbing up the front of their house and when the grapes were ripe, we filched a few when we knew nobody was watching. Grapes were an exotic fruit to grow in this damp climate, and they were pretty sour. But we had to try them anyway.

One end of our street intersected with the Fuhlsbüttlerstrasse, the main shopping street, and just before our street ended on the other end stood a block-long apartment house. Across from the apartment house was a block full of miniature houses, the Schrebergärten. These tiny structures surrounded by small garden plots were meant for people who lived in apartments to have a weekend retreat where they could grow vegetables, talk to their neighbors about what to plant, or just relax and sit in the sun.

I always felt sorry for people who had to make do with such a tiny piece of land, when behind our house we had more than enough land to cultivate. Our fruit trees, for instance, gave us everything from pears to apples, cherries, and plums. We, Doris and I had only to walk a few steps from our front door to the backyard to have our pick of whatever fruit was in season. We could pick an apple, or climb a tree and sit in it and eat one apple after another until the effect of so much fruit made us clamber down to squat in a convenient spot, afterwards wiping our behinds with enormous rhubarb leaves. Then we wiped our hands in the grass or splashed them around in the tub full of rain water. We didn't want to go inside, because the toilet was in the basement and the basement was still a scary place.

Where our street ended, the *Rosengarten* (Rose Park) began. Like other city parks, it was a block-long, walk-through garden surrounded by tall hedges. You could either walk through the garden or walk on the other side of the hedges along the sidewalk. Inside the park, there were wooden benches every thirty feet or so on which housewives would sit and rest their feet from carrying heavy bags full of groceries. For some others, it afforded a cigarette break. But for young couples, mostly at dusk, the park was a place for kissing and groping, looking into each others' eyes and sighing.

My friend Ingrid and I at about nine or ten years of age got a good look at these goings-on from behind the hedges tall enough to hide us but not dense enough to hide the activity on the benches. We were fascinated by what we saw but couldn't imagine wanting to be that close to a boy or to keep our lips glued to his for such a long time. How disgusting, and then what was all the groping? We giggled mostly, or imitated kissing noises, smacking our lips together and sometimes concluding with a loud pop. Occasionally, a couple would get fed up with our juvenile behavior and leave, but most of them stayed and ignored us until we lost interest. Even though we never wanted to indulge in this kind of thing with boys, there was something about watching lovers that created an unexplainable yearning for things to come. Those nights, I hugged myself in bed or kissed my hand. Oh, the warm feeling!

Eventually, a sandbox and monkey bars appeared in the park. I liked to hang upside down on the bars, and overall I was very good at climbing and hanging. I would hang over a bar that was close to the ground, grab my feet with my hands so that now I was wrapped around the bar, and then I just went round and round until I got dizzy, in the process rubbing the plush pile off my second-hand coat.

Besides cleaning the apartment on Saturdays, Mutti also did the grocery shopping. It was really a daily task, requiring going from store to store, and since stores closed at 2:00 p.m. on Saturdays and were not open on Sundays, Mutti shopped for a two-day supply of food on Saturdays. Sometimes Doris or I, or occasionally Klaus, went with her to carry her leather shopping bag and nets. The street with the shops, Fuhlsbüttlerstrasse (Fuhle, for short), intersected our residential street. Taking up one whole corner stood the old *Wirtshaus*, a tavern where my grandfather had done his singing and drinking so many years earlier. Next to the Wirtshaus was the shoe repair shop owned by Frau Bures, who lived in the flat above us with her two children. She was a war widow and a refugee from Silesia who had received money from the German government to open her shop, where she toiled long hours. Next to her was the Scholten dairy store. For many years my parents were friends with Herr and Frau Scholten, but custom demanded they call each other by their last names. Still, even though they used last names, they were informal with each other.

Mutti was well-liked by all the shop keepers, even though she often had to resort to something called *anschreiben* (credit). When I was instructed to fetch milk by myself and had to ask Herr Scholten to *bitte anschreiben* (please put it on the account), I cringed out of fear that he would say no because he needed the money too, didn't he? But he always nodded and said okay. For a while it seemed that very little cash was exchanged for goods between the shopkeepers and Mutti. Then Mutti would make a payment to reduce the amount owed, but soon it was back to *anschreiben* again. Nonetheless the shopkeepers trusted her because they had known her for a long time, had known her parents, and knew our family's situation.

Besides the dairy store, the Fuhle had food stores of every kind that Mutti visited almost daily: the produce shop, the fish store, the bakery. Weighted down with nets and canvas or leather shopping bags, I couldn't wait to get home and taste some of the goodies, although this covetousness over the food was quickly stopped by Mutti because she had bought just enough to make a meal or two and also because with food having to be divided equally nobody was allowed to just dig in and help themselves. I recall that once when Papa had garnered a cauliflower from his parents' farm, Doris was so excited at seeing a whole cauliflower in front of her that she broke off a couple of tiny pieces, only to be severely reprimanded by Papa who wanted everyone to have an equal share. He was more lenient when food stuffs became more plentiful.

I liked going shopping with Mutti most of the time, because besides getting milk and later cheese and butter and herring and gooseberries, we also got the latest gossip or news. We heard nothing mean-spirited but rather news about people who had just come home from the war, who like my parents, were having a tough time. Other topics were the job situation in general and the reconstruction of buildings. I pretended not to listen to most of it but perked up when the talk turned to Tante Lene.

Tante Lene lived across the street from us and besides Tante Klara was Mutti's best friend. She and Mutti were about the same age, in their late forties. At this advanced age she had become pregnant (tsk, tsk) with a change-of-life baby, that is, an accidental pregnancy. And a first child, no less. I didn't understand any of this until much later. At the time Tante Lene was the subject of gossip, she had grown from a heavy-set, big-busted woman into an enormous figure. Lene's size baffled me, and I asked Mutti, "Mutti, what's wrong with Tante Lene?" She replied, "Lene is going to have a baby," in a tone that declined to invite further discussion. I was nine then, not old enough to be told much about or be interested in the subject of procreation. I fantasized that maybe Onkel Albert, Tante Lene's husband, had touched a chimney sweep for luck and now the stork was set to bring them a baby.

Although Lene was getting very big, she continued to walk to the neighborhood stores and I continued to be in awe of her big stomach. One day, I watched a neighbor cross to the other side of the street just as she saw Lene approaching her. Did this behavior have something to do with Lene's stomach? Another time, a group of women chatting on the sidewalk by the neighborhood pub simply ignored her as she walked past them. A few days after that, while I was shopping with Mutti and walking from store to store, we ran into two of Mutti's friends. Hilde said indignantly, "I just don't understand, how did this happen? She's fifty years old, why is she having a baby at fifty? She's old enough to be a grandmother and here she is having her first child. It must be a *Wechseljahre* (menopause) baby!

How ridiculous." It sounded like Tante Lene had done something really awful. Literally, *Wechseljahre* means "change years," and I was very worried that she was not only going to have a baby but in the process actually change into something else. Tante Lene was the first pregnant woman I had ever seen, and from then on I understood what was going on when I saw other women with protruding stomachs. Listening to the gossip was a roundabout way of learning certain things. Though I still didn't know how babies were made, I knew now what a pregnant woman looked like. And I had an idea that malicious gossip and small talk were not the same.

◆　　◆　　◆

1950—The lack of apartments is acute. There are ten million apartments for sixteen million people. Every day, 15,000 refugees from the East, many of them from East Germany, stream to the West looking for places to stay. They resort to refugee camps, because not only do they not have a place to live, but they haven't any money. In Hamburg, a search service is established for parents looking for missing children and missing parents. American nylon stockings can be had for 6,95 Marks (an average paycheck per month is 250 Marks) so only some women can afford to buy a pair. Cities begin rebuilding brick by brick; many women clean old bricks lying in huge heaps everywhere one looked. People want clothing, shoes. For all that, the populace is full of hope and energy.

One day in 1950, my brother brought home an emaciated female German shepherd puppy and sweet-talked Mutti into keeping her. From then on, the puppy followed Klaus around, and when he went out playing with his buddies she stayed by his side even without a leash. When she was old enough to stay outside, my Papa and Klaus built a dog house for her which they placed by the shed in the courtyard next to the henhouse. Nobody was ever going to steal a chicken from us, oh no, because Nelli barked at anybody and anything unfamiliar to her. She protected vegetables and berry bushes as well as us, becoming a guard dog with house privileges. Nelli came in the house for all her meals and for nap-on-lap times. That dog became a member of the family and was treated as such. Still, she had to spend nights in her dog house except when it was really cold or when Klaus begged Mutti to let him bring her in. Then she slept on the floor by his makeshift bed in the living room.

In the house Nelli sometimes helped herself to things she shouldn't have eaten. One day, my parents thought that Nelli had hemorrhoids because something was sticking out of her behind. Fingering the strange, rubbery substance, they realized that Nelli had swallowed a balloon which now appeared in a semi-blown up state at her tail end!

Nelli had us and we had her for four years. Most of the time she looked straggly, scrawny, and thin, but we loved her with all our hearts. I remember romping in the backyard with her, putting my arms around her and whispering in her ear, especially when I was sad about something. She sat perfectly still and listened, never repeating a word to anyone. Long afternoons she slept in the yard, only to interrupt her naps by barking periodically at something we couldn't see but she could.

Then one day, she started foaming at the mouth and having convulsions. Whenever Nelli had been sick in any way, Mutti healed her like she healed her chickens and cat or, at that, any injured bird or living creature—with tender, loving care. We couldn't afford to take her to a vet, but Mutti's ministrations wouldn't help this time, because our dog was sick with something Mutti hadn't seen before. So she fastened the leash to Nelli's collar and rode the streetcar for a seemingly endless fifteen minutes, sitting on a hard bench with a sick dog on her lap. I imagine that my Mutti whispered into Nelli's ear that she was a good dog and that we all loved her and that she would find out what caused her to be so sick and that everything would be all right. The vet examined Nelli and concluded that she must have eaten something poisonous. He advised Mutti to put her to sleep. My poor Mutti! She loved animals, and to make the decision to euthanize our beloved dog was heartbreaking for her. She stayed with Nelli until the end, she told me when I came home from school that day and asked where Nelli was, her eyes still red from crying as she pulled me into her arms and sobbed, "Nelli is in dog heaven."

I cried for Nelli for months and swore revenge on our neighbors. Papa, suspecting the Catholic Heinz family was behind the poisoning, told them that we had eaten a couple of our chickens the night Nelli died. They grew worried and admitted that they had thrown a piece of poisoned meat over the fence because Nelli's barking was bothering them. Fearing the law, they thought that the chickens we ate that night had also consumed some of their poison. Our family and the chickens were fine, but poor Nelli was dead. Klaus was heartbroken.

I have never been able to forgive those neighbors for hurting our dog. Later in my life, I had occasion to make the decision to put beloved pets to sleep, and the memory of Nelli and Mutti was always with me up to the last minute when the gates of pet heaven again opened. My love for animals will always be tinged with memories of Mutti and her pets.

While I missed Nelli and all the fun times we had with her, I continued play-ing with my friends on the neighborhood streets. And on Saturday afternoons, I would often go for walks with my parents and Doris in the big city park, or Klaus would take Doris and me to the public pool there. It wasn't really a pool but a sectioned-off part of the lake, all mucky and murky and made even less transpar-ent by the hundreds of people who would show up on a sunny day. If only I could have had a bathing suit that wasn't knitted and scratchy. Mine was knitted of wool! After a few washes, it turned all fuzzy looking, and it felt like something foul was growing on it that was squeezing the life out of me. I tried to remain invisible, staying submerged in the water up to my shoulders, then sprinting to the blanket lying on the grass and covering myself with a towel that had also seen better days.

Part of the park wasn't available to me, and the fact that I couldn't partake created a great deal of envy in me. At one of the entrances to the park, hardly vis-ible behind a solid line of bushes, lay tennis courts of reddish clay. I would stand behind the bushes and peer through gaps in them, staring at the girls and boys in white swinging their racquets and chasing balls. Every now and then they would disappear into a club house and others would come out to replace them. I couldn't understand why I wasn't allowed to play there, but the sign said, "Mem-bers only." I felt like an outcast, and if anyone had caught me watching them, they probably would have chased me away. Tennis was for rich people only.

On snowy, cold winter days we walked to the part of the city park that was hilly, dragging our sled behind us and, once there, walking up the hills, sledding down, and walking back up until our energy was spent. All our clothing would be wet, our mittens soaked with snow, and our feet icy cold because we wore rubber boots made for rain not snow.

My elementary school days were filled with another activity which opened up my world to music in an even more active way than before. Up to now, music had been part of my life because of Papa's profession. Every day he would rehearse one or more of his instruments for a couple of hours in the afternoon, whether he had a job that night or not. Sounds of trombone drifted out of our house and could be heard by anyone walking by the house. I remember standing behind the lace curtains in the living room and turning the pages of music for Papa at his music stand. Some people outside would stop and listen, mostly the same people every day walking home from work or on their way to shop or to visit neighbors down the street. They knew my Papa was a musician. For the passers-by, it was like getting a mini-concert for free.

Other music memories involved the whole family, all five of us singing German folk songs of which we knew many, like *Auf der Lüneburger Heide,* or *Muss I denn, muss I denn ...* (later sung by Elvis). I sang alto, Doris soprano, Klaus tenor, Papa bass, and Mutti melody, either on-key or off. She didn't have much of an ear for music when it came to carrying a tune, but she was an enthusiastic singer and loved listening to music and especially to Papa playing the violin for her.

One song she liked especially well was the "Barcarolle" from Hoffmann's Tales. When he played it for her on the violin, she looked straight at him, her brown eyes shining. *Schöne Nacht, o Liebesnacht* (Beautiful night, oh night of love) was so special to my parents that they would actually forget their children were in the room! Another song Mutti liked that all of us sang for her was *Ännchen von Tharau,* a song about a strong love that conquers all and gets stronger through sickness and pain. She loved it when my father sang it to her because she truly was his Ännchen. Their love, like the love in the song, had been tested through all the pain of war.

◆   ◆   ◆

1951—300,000 women are waiting for their husbands to return from the war. Almost fourteen percent of German women are either widowed or divorced. The economy is slowly improving. The knife sharpener came around and he sharpened knives until they were good as new, and he made his living that way for many years. Cornelia Froboess, eight years old, sings "Pack die Badehose ein" which becomes a big national hit. A German-Iranian woman named Soraya marries the Shah of Iran. Her dress sparkled with 6000 diamonds.

◆   ◆   ◆

1952—The island Helgoland is German again. Long distance telephone calls can be made without an operator. The Compensation Law goes into effect, helping refugees and other war victims who have lost their belongings in the war. The national anthem's third stanza becomes the official hymn again. Unity, Justice, and Freedom. There are 4664 television sets in Germany, and on Christmas Day this year the entire television program consists of a movie called "Silent Night, Holy Night." When it's over, the program for the evening is done. Most people can't afford a TV, since it costs the equivalent of three months' salary. A VW Bug can be had for a sixteen months' salary. Eva Peron dies.

Evita is firmly entrenched in my mind as a saint. She had cancer. Oh, why did she have to die in the flower of her life? What a tragic romantic figure! I want to be like her, I want to be adored by millions of my country people. I had to be daydreaming.

My parents had gotten some money as compensation for having lost household furnishings, and the money helped to buy a much-needed couch for the living room. We could finally get rid of the rickety, makeshift couch that used to double as my brother's bed. He still didn't have his own bed, but now he could sleep on the new couch. Klaus was eighteen and not home that much, so when he did come home from seeing his girlfriend the living room was his and he didn't have to worry about chasing anyone from it because we were already asleep, Doris and I, on our new sleeper couch also bought with the compensation money.

The Christmas when I was eleven, Doris and I received our first musical instruments: recorders. Hers was a used one, made of rosewood, dark and shiny, given to my parents by a neighbor whose child had outgrown it. That meant they only had to buy one recorder, an inexpensive one of light-colored wood. I still have it, all these years later. Yet I coveted Doris' recorder and played it whenever she wasn't around. That Christmas Day, Doris and I practiced around the clock, or so it seemed, until we drove Klaus mad. He dashed from the house in pain, his ears assaulted beyond belief. Eventually, though, Doris and I became quite good at our instruments. We learned the scale quickly, our fingers were nimble, and our breath got more controlled as time went on. For my parents, who wanted us to learn an instrument, the recorder must have seemed a poor substitute for what they really wanted for us—a piano. We never did get a piano, though.

When I was old enough to read music sometime in elementary school, I asked to be taught the violin, and Papa agreed to teach me. "How to hold the violin and the bow" was the first lesson in what would stretch to several. "But Papa, let me hold it this way," I would say and soon we were arguing. The first few notes I managed to squeeze from the instrument were unbearably shrill to me (Klaus made a point of leaving the house even before his ears were traumatized). I never went beyond knowing how to hold the instrument and bow, and very poorly at that. It was apparent that, although Papa had taught other people the violin and was a patient, encouraging type of teacher, he simply couldn't teach me. Or maybe I didn't really want to be taught by him, because I was intimidated by his mastery. My attitude, nonetheless, was "I know it all." I did have a good ear for music, but I wasn't willing to yield to the master and put in the time that practice took. I went from instrument to instrument without mastering any except the recorder and even tried the accordion that Papa had borrowed from a colleague because it most resembled a piano. I wanted to play the piano but there was no way to have one in our flat, no money to buy one, no money for lessons, no place to put it. So I learned to play a few songs on the accordion, manipulating the keys easily but not sticking with it either. Instead, my voice was my instrument of choice.

When I was in fifth grade, my sister and I joined a community choir made up of girls from all over the city of Hamburg. Our music teacher in elementary school had recommended us—we didn't have to audition. My sister was in her own group because she was two years older. Both of us read music by that time and went to rehearsal once a week at the elementary school. We never met with children from other parts of the city until we rehearsed together a few times before a concert. We had been taught songs by our elementary school music teacher, but the combined choir rehearsal was led by the Herr Director.

The concerts took place at least twice a year at the *Musikhalle* in the heart of the city, a baroque-style concert hall that had miraculously escaped the war's bombs. Herr Director Dietrich was a man in his forties who gesticulated wildly with his arms and periodically wielded his right hand palm up to make sharp jab-bing movements toward his neck, meaning that he wanted us to project more. We thought he wanted to kill himself. But he would just keep going, jabbing, jabbing, as we tried our best. We were cooperative and mostly serious, but burst-ing with an excess of energy as only fifth graders are.

I remember one concert in particular. Each age group had been told by their teachers where to meet. We had to assemble at a building nearby, warm up, and leave there together to walk over to the *Musikhalle*. I hadn't listened carefully enough to the instructions, which was then and for many years a particular prob-lem of mine. When we (Mutti, Doris and I) got to the meeting point, I looked for my group and learned that they were already singing at the *Musikhalle,* having their turn before the older girls. I was crushed. I wanted to be on stage, I wanted to sing for everybody (meaning parents) in the audience, to sing with an orches-tra, to be seen as a member of this chosen group of girls. But it was not to be. First I cried, then I blamed Mutti for getting us there late and then I conferred with Doris. She said I could go with her group and stand in the back while sing-ing quietly with the altos. After all, I knew all her songs. And so that's what tran-spired. But the whole time I was on stage, I was deathly afraid that Herr Dietrich would suddenly notice this face that didn't belong in the choir, strike his direc-tor's stick on the podium, stop the music, and demand to know what I was doing there. Still, nothing dire like that happened, and afterwards we gloated over the fact that we had fooled him and that I had been able to sing for the masses after all. It didn't even matter that I was wearing ugly second-hand clothes.

In eighth grade, I decided that I couldn't afford the time it took to rehearse my music because by that time I had mountains of homework every day. I quit the choir, but I never stopped singing. Looking back, I am impressed with the community leaders who conceived this idea for a choir and made it happen. Within just a few years after the war it was giving Hamburg's children an outlet for their singing abilities and a break from the dreary reality of our lives.

◆   ◆   ◆

By 1953, more and more television sets were appearing in German homes, but my family wasn't able to get one and wouldn't be until sometime in the sixties. Our family had to look for our entertainment elsewhere.

A few years after the war, a movie theater opened on the *Fuhle,* the shopping street, showing Laurel and Hardy movies on Sundays at noon. If we went when it was cold, each of us had to bring a piece of coal to keep the theater furnace warming us in our rags.

A ticket only cost fifty *Pfennige,* but even that was sometimes hard to come by and often our neighbors the Vosses would buy tickets for us or take us. If one of us knew a retired older person, we would ask for their *Rentenausweis* (social security I.D.), go to the movie theater ostensibly to buy a ticket for that friend and then use it ourselves for a later performance. We were in cahoots with a number of older people who didn't mind helping us out with their senior discounts. Sometimes, my tickets were paid for with money earned from selling eggs, but I didn't care where the money came from as long as I could laugh at Laurel and Hardy. I was obsessed with seeing those goofiest, funniest guys and I couldn't get enough of them. To this day I like slapstick comedy, laughing at others because they are doing what we are all capable of doing: getting into a jam, sliding on a banana peel, socking it to someone and then getting socked back. Life is like that, or is it? So for two hours on Sundays we laughed and screamed and clapped and forgot all about what life was really like.

I have a photo that shows my sister, her girlfriend Hella, some other kids, and me sitting in a theater and watching puppets perform on stage. Doris and I were about nine and seven and we were sitting on either side of Hella who as far as we were concerned was the luckiest child in the world because she was an *only* child. She didn't have to share *anything!* In the photo, Doris looked like she was saying "Oh no!" Hella was laughing, but I stared with complete concentration at the stage. In a theater I was in another world. My favorite plots featured princes and princesses, swords, bad guys and castles—everything that I adored. When a bad guy was about to do something behind the prince's back, the whole group of kids would yell, "Watch out! There's somebody with a sword behind you, and he's going to strike you." Thus pandemonium would break out in the audience while silence prevailed on stage. The prince couldn't hear us warning him that disaster was going to strike, but of course he was miraculously saved and went on to wed the princess.

Wanting to be a princess and a ballerina often blended in my mind. My friend Christa told me that in order to become a ballerina, I would have to take classes and practice a lot in slippers that would let me stand on my toes. But my parents couldn't afford to send me to ballet school. I stood on my toes anyway and pretended that I was a ballerina, arms outstretched to the sides, reaching upward. I couldn't reach far enough and soon I realized that the dream was too far-fetched, and it faded. I would never be a ballerina, but I could learn ballroom dancing and turn it into a lifelong hobby.

After watching puppet theater shows featuring princesses in sparkly gowns, I was obsessed with the desire to be a pretend-princess and wear a pretty dress and a tiara! I had read the Cinderella story and talked to my girlfriends about performing Cinderella for the neighborhood adults and children. Of course, I would be Cinderella. A neighbor had given me a dress of pink taffeta and organza that she had outgrown. I couldn't understand how some people could have fancy taffeta dresses while I had to wear the same ugly outfit every day of the week.

The dress was the catalyst; I was going to build the fairy tale around the dress. My friends and I wrote part of the play, the biggest part belonging to me, of course. We assembled a cast and rehearsed lines. I wore the dress at home, whirled and twirled near to wearing out the old mirror hanging in the hallway. I couldn't wait to have everybody in the neighborhood behold me in that dress. I wanted to perform for other people, to be on stage, to be applauded, to be in the limelight, to be famous! Then where did the throbbing heart and the fear come from, late at night when I tried to get to sleep but couldn't? We even had a prince, my old knitting buddy Hans, though he declined to kiss me. That was only one snag of many, and slowly everyone including me lost interest and never performed a single line for any of the neighbors. At first I felt morose because I had failed but soon got over it because I still had the dress. And I had managed to rally my friends even if for a short time.

I am twelve and in sixth grade. The world is not at peace. But there are people working for peace, like Albert Schweitzer, and Bertrand Russell. I read about them.

1953—Uprising in East Germany on June 17. Dissatisfaction with the dictator-ship and circumstances of daily life. Soviet troops stationed in East Germany brutally suppress the demonstrations. Many people end up in prison or dead, shot by Russians and their East-German helpers. Albert Schweitzer receives the Nobel Prize for Peace. There is a widespread shortage of apartments. Quonset huts on the outskirts of German cities hold many families still waiting for better living quarters. The first two million care packages arrive from the U.S., mostly intended for people living in refu-gee camps. A care package contained rice, shortening, raisins, prunes, peas, legumes, sugar, powdered milk, even a can of beef. Young German women, the Fräuleins, socialize with American soldiers stationed in Germany. American soldiers are warned by their superiors to "stay away from Gretchen." It's considered unpatriotic for Ger-man women to date Americans. Many of their fellow Germans term the young women "Ami-Flittchen," floozies, and they call the soldiers the disrespectful, derogatory "Ami."

Now I want to live in west central Africa's Lambarene and help Albert Schweitzer take care of people with leprosy. I talk myself out of it because I'm too young to leave Germany plus I would miss my parents much too much if I did.

◆   ◆   ◆

During these grade school years, between 1948–1954 and beyond, we visited my grandparents several times a year, whenever we had the cash to pay for train rides into the country. I loved my grandfather Ernst because he was fun, and he had some habits that I couldn't wait to see in action. One was the ever-present cigar in his mouth, which he could shift around without ever touching or pro-ducing smoke. Eventually, I figured out that his cigar wasn't lit most of the time. My grandmother Emma was a kind but serious person who tended to get us kids involved in work projects when all we wanted to do was play with the neighbor-ing farmer's kids. I noticed that she called my Opa "Ernst" when she needed something done and he was slow to react but "Ernie" when he was in her good graces.

The trip from our house to *Reitbrook,* where my grandparents had a farm of about eight acres, took at least three hours. When the streetcars were running again, we took one to the main train station in the center of Hamburg, along the way passing one bombed-out building after another. Our next mode of transportation was a coal-driven train that had wooden benches and mostly glassless windows. Some windows, though, were covered with cardboard. So in the winter we wore any piece of woolen clothing we had to stay warm on that train. Arriving in *Bergedorf,* a suburb of Hamburg, we had a good hour of walking ahead of us along rural roads until busses were running again between the city of Bergedorf and the village of *Reitbrook.* Whenever the whole family went to see my grandparents, the walk was almost enjoyable because Klaus would chase us or carry us on his back for short stretches at a time. We sang folk songs with a marching beat to make the walk seem shorter. As soon as one of us had spied the windmill (built in 1870), we knew we had arrived, because my grandparents lived just a few houses away.

For several summers in a row, Mutti took me to my grandparents' to stay for a couple of weeks. The purpose was for me to get a good dose of fresh air, hearty food, and exposure to my Opa's old jokes. Many times I had heard that I looked pale and my parents had tried to get me into a camp for sickly children where I could recuperate. Because I looked pale, it was thought that I had worms, and so I was checked for the parasites several times. But when worms were in fact found, there weren't enough of them to get me admitted to a camp. My brother also was pale, but he was too old to be sent to a *Kinderheim,* and my sister's rosy cheeks made her the picture of health that no *Kinderheim* would have taken.

Because my grandparents breathed the fresh air all around them, and I looked pale, I was the natural choice for an extended stay with them. My sister threw a fit if Mutti even mentioned sending her to my grandparents. She liked being around Mutti and would have suffered homesickness without her. My teenaged brother was no longer interested in living in the country where the pigsty had to be cleaned, the lawn mowed, and the vegetables picked. It sounded too much like work to him. My parents wanted rosy cheeks and plainly, I needed them the most.

Just before Mutti and I approached Reitbrook, with the windmill immediately ahead of us, there was an obstacle we had to cross—a bridge that crossed an arm of the river Elbe. I was old enough to know that arms were arms and water was water, but for the preceding hour I had worked myself into a frenzy imagining arms reaching out of the river and grabbing at me. As soon as we stepped on the bridge I gripped Mutti's hand, closed my eyes, and incredulously dragged her across the bridge. For the next two weeks, I never once crossed that bridge until it was time to go back home, although the bridge was close to a house that had been made into a makeshift store where my cousin and I could buy candy for ourselves. I often gazed at the Elbe, I even played in the Elbe, but having to cross a bridge over the Elbe frightened me.

The last five minutes to my grandparents' house we walked along the dyke. On our left and below the level of the dyke and protected by it stood the farmhouses. All of them were squat, one-level structures with thatched roofs, except my grandparents' neighbor's house that was a more modern, two-story home. On the Elbe side of the dyke stood apple orchards which gave the river at the edge of the orchards some resistance to overflowing the dyke should the river top the banks. In my memory it never did: it was just a tributary of the Elbe and so flowed along placidly.

We had to descend a steep walk to my grandparent's house. Instead of beds of flowers, vegetable plants covered every inch of the front yard. The front door of their house opened into a large room which in my memory served no purpose except to hold muddy shoes and boots and several thick coats that my grandparents wore when they went outside. A door on the left led to the living room/kitchen combination which in turn led into their bedroom, where the wooden bed with the big feather comforter made quite an impression on me. A child could be swallowed up by this mountain of feathers, never again to be found. In her last years of life when she suffered dementia, my Oma would hide butter under the feather-filled comforter. For the geese?

The whole back end of the house was rented to a young couple. Therefore, the house had two kitchens. I think my grandparents moved into the front half of the house and rented out the other when the whole house got too much to take care of. They added a stove to the living room and ended up with a kitchen/living-dining room combination. It was a room stuffed with furniture—a green velvet couch where my Opa took naps, a rocking chair, a combination dining/couch table, and two chests that held their dishes. Pots and pans were kept on a shelf over the stove that was fed with wood and coal. When my Oma cooked, the whole room became so hot that the door to the adjoining bedroom was opened, to warm up this space that otherwise would have been ice-cold in the winter. In the summer the bedrooms stayed cool because the house was built of bricks, with a roof of straw.

I slept in a separate bedroom off the big hallway, also under an enormous feather comforter that once it was shaken vigorously looked like a marshmallow sitting on top the mattress. I didn't spend much time in that room. Except for meals, I played or worked outside most of the day.

One year I wrote a letter to my friend Christa who lived a few houses down from ours in Hamburg. Christa was at least nine years older, so she was probably nineteen when I wrote this letter to her. She was tall, slim, and long-limbed and that's how I wanted to look. Klaus, who was two years younger than Christa, always spoke of her with a certain disdain, saying "She's too skinny, there's nothing to hold on to," which didn't make sense to me at the time. What would he want to hold on to other than maybe her arm or her hand? I was so naïve.

Christa always talked to me when we saw each other on the street, and I adored her for taking the time. In newly-learned cursive I now told her about my activities, and I can almost see her smile at my childish letter. "The weather is good here. I like playing with my cousin Hans Jürgen. I like looking at the pig. When it eats potatoes and pears and bonemeal, I like to watch. And on the meadow, I do my handstands and practice the backbends and then I combine the two. One day passes and then the next. One day we pick peas and another we pick beans, and sometimes we pull weeds for the animals." I think the animals consisted of the one and only pig in addition to the chickens and roosters.

◆   ◆   ◆

Every year, a pink piglet came, and Johnny was his name. Under the mud that would start clinging to his coarse hair, he was pink all over. When his ears stood perky and straight up, they looked like leaves on a redbud tree, pointed at the top. When they flopped around his face, tops turned over, they gave him a bookish look. Whenever he snuffed around in his pen his pink ears hung floppy and relaxed. He had a wet, pink snout which was always engaged in an up-and-down-and-sideways motion.

I fed him leftovers and weeds and stroked his head and ears, which he loved, and even wiped his snout when it was crusty with muck. He rubbed against me in his pen, and when I walked by the pen he would come running to the fence and stick his head through the wooden slats. I loved that pig.

And then came the day he was slaughtered. Our family went to the farm that day, but Doris and I were not allowed to see the pig's artery cut before a rope was wrapped around his hind legs and he was hung from a tree with his head down to bleed out into a pot. His blood would become blood soup that the adults all raved about, though I myself wouldn't touch it. We were spared seeing Johnny being pulled out of his pen, dehaired, scraped, and gutted. But later we saw the bloody knives, hammers, cleavers, and saws.

My parents and brother, and even neighbors helped with the processing of the pig's parts, a process that took all day. Everybody worked hard while Doris and I played with our friends next door. I was in tears off and on all day, because Johnny had become my friend and now he was gone. The adults were matter-of-fact about slaughtering him; to them he was just food, a notion which was not something I understood then. I was, however, acquiring a better understanding of where food came from while living on my grandparents' farm.

We kids were allowed back into the kitchen while some of the cutting, cooking, and canning was underway. The blood soup bubbled on the stove while the liver was being cooked and made into *Leberwurst* (liver sausage). Hams were cut, set aside, and later hung from the rafters in the attic of the house. *Sülze* (headcheese) was being cooked from the snout and other parts of the pig's head and meats along with onions, carrots, pickles, salt, vinegar, and sugar later added. The sweet-sour flavor of *Sülze* makes my mouth water as I'm writing this. The entrails had been washed and washed again, then scraped and washed again. Red meat was ground up for sausage, cooked and seasoned, and then stuffed into the intestines. I vaguely remember a press with a spout doing that work, and when an intestine was full it was tied into links.

The kitchen was hot. It smelled of boiling blood, a rich iron smell which made me gag. This was the year's busiest day of cooking. When dinner time came around, the adults assembled around the table and slurped blood soup. I ate a freshly made sausage which I forced down my throat, tears in my eyes. After dinner, the kitchen work continued mostly in the form of clean-up work. Overalls and aprons worn by family and friends had to be washed by hand and their boots scraped, washed, and put on a shelf to dry.

We left late to go home, lugging parts of cut-up Johnny down the road to the train station. My grandparents gave us some meat, but some hadn't been processed completely and most of the latter stayed on the farm to feed my grandparents for an entire year until the next Johnny met his fate. Mutti carried home some bacon rind with a layer of fat on it which she would rub all over her face, arms, and legs to keep her skin moisturized. I can fuzzily remember words my parents exchanged on the train, on how stingy my grandparents were about sharing the pig with their children's families, some of whom, like my siblings and I and my cousins were undernourished at times. The truth lies somewhere in between, because I can also remember bringing home more than a few farm-produced items from our visits throughout the year, such as vegetables and fruit and a can or two of liverwurst which we forthwith devoured, slathering it thickly on black bread. Oh, the deeply satisfying smell and taste of freshly made liverwurst!

In my memory, I'm sitting on a wooden bench with my grandparents at the back of their house. Around us are piles of vegetables in tubs—carrots, parsley, radishes—all of which had to be assembled into bundles. That was my job and I loved it. I savored the smell and felt the dirt before I dipped the vegetables into the water to clean them. Dirt-free, the carrots were vivid orange and the radishes bright red. I tied strings around the bundles of vegetables and placed them in another tub. Then all the vegetables were piled into a wheelbarrow that my Opa pushed up the walk (no steps) to the dyke and then down the walk to our next-door neighbor's. This neighbor then took my grandparents' vegetables in a horse-drawn carriage to the market in Bergedorf about thirty minutes away (an hour on foot) where they were sold to housewives anxious for fresh produce. In the early morning hours we had picked beans, peas, and dug up potatoes, and these too were transported to the market in wooden crates. My Opa and fresh-from-the-earth potatoes will always be intertwined in my memory, along with Opa's sense of humor.

My grandparents liked us kids to visit around harvest time to help with the chores in the fields, particularly with pulling potatoes. One day, Klaus and Opa walked to the potato field behind the house, carrying buckets into which they placed the small new potatoes. Opa said to my brother, "Klaus, why don't you start with that row over there—that looks like a good one." My brother said, "Okay," and Opa chose another, a few rows behind my brother. Klaus gathered the green stalks of the first potato plant in his hands, twisted them, and pulled up. In the groove left by the plant lay three enormous potatoes, each as big as a navel orange. He pulled the next plant, eager to see what this one would have to offer, and there in the earth lay a few small potatoes. Now he was really curious. Was the first plant just a fluke? Faster and faster he went down the row, excited about the giant potatoes he discovered under every other plant, until he had the whole row done.

Then he turned around to show Opa, who was standing a few rows behind him and shaking with laughter from head to toe. Opa couldn't stop laughing, delighted that his little trick had worked. It seems he had gone out earlier in the morning and placed huge potatoes under every other plant just to see how his grandson would react. Klaus laughed too. Opa had played another trick on him.

When I stayed with my Oma and Opa, I was allowed to eat all I wanted. I must have eaten all day long, because I was surrounded by food everywhere. Over here raspberries, gooseberries, strawberries, over there black and red currants. Cherries and apples, pears, carrots and young sweet peas.

But the best part of the day was dinner, when my grandparents and I and other family members who happened to be there sat down in the kitchen/dining-living room, tantalized well in advance by the aromas emanating from the pots on the big stove. But the very best part was yet to come.

My Opa is sitting across the table from me with such clarity that I think he is there and I can touch him. He leans over his plate, his fork in the left hand, his knife in the right, and takes his first bite. I can't take my eyes off him. He is the one and only person I have ever seen chew at a pace truly remarkable. How could anyone grind and chew, chomp and gulp so fast? It is as though he has captured a tornado in his mouth.

I try to imitate him, but there is no way I can move my mouth that fast. I ask him if he could eat more slowly, but he replies that he couldn't, having been made to eat this way. He lets me put my hands on his cheeks to see if he can slow down, but he just can't. I never ever saw another person chew like this again.

Most of the summers I spent on the farm were happy ones. Mutti delivered me, and straightway I was off playing. I never missed her or felt homesickness in any way, except once, possibly the last year of my visits when I was around ten.

Christel doesn't get homesick, not like Doris, or so my parents agree. In fact, I had a vague feeling of contempt for homesick people. If they were homesick, they could never stay with other people or be comfortable anywhere other than in their home. I teased my sister about her refusal to stay on the farm. She was being such a sissy! But in the summer of my tenth year, I was to eat crow!

Mutti and I made the same trek we had made for years, except maybe now there was a bus running from Bergedorf to Reitbrook, and the bus carried us across the bridge where my bridge-crossing drama had previously occurred on a yearly basis. I sat next to Mutti on the bus, silent and chewing my cheeks as was my nervous habit even then. Mutti, though, was oblivious to my anxiety; she was delivering me to a place I had always loved coming to.

As long as Mutti was at the farm that day I was fine, although I was watching the clock and dreading her leaving. I clung to her when she left to go home alone and hugged her extra hard. Her encircling arms were soft and round, and I felt so sad to see her go. She wished me fun, and I just couldn't tell her I wanted her to take me home. I couldn't hurt my grandparents' feelings by saying that I wanted to go back to Hamburg. So I stayed.

The next day I started crying, first when nobody was around. But even my playmates couldn't make me feel better. Games with them had always been so much fun, but now even playing *Fussball* couldn't coax any excitement out of me. At the pigsty I talked to Johnny and dropped tears on his hairy snout. His pink eyes looked at me, and he snorted as if he might have understood me but soon he went about his business.

I decided that I had to look for a reason to feel badly enough to go home. I ate green gooseberries that were so tart, I had a hard time swallowing them. They were so far from being ripe that I felt badly for picking them because they wouldn't have a chance to grow to the point of sweetness that I loved about them.

That night I came down with a stomachache. Maybe not that much of a stomachache, but enough to moan and groan and hold my hands over my stomach until I got a reaction out of my Opa. He said something like, "What did you do, eat some green apples?" I denied having done any such thing but informed him that something was wrong with my stomach and I was in pain. I lay down on the couch and passed up dinner. I so wanted to go home that I was becoming unhinged. Then the berries worked and I had to run to the outhouse.

I ran out the front door, around the side of the house, to the back where the outhouse stood. I was almost sorry I had eaten the berries, because now I had to go into the dreaded place. I pulled the wooden stop through the loop in the door and didn't bother to lock it, ripped off my shorts, and crashed onto the wooden platform that was the equivalent of the toilet seat at home.

The unripe berries had done their job, but my grandparents wouldn't be too concerned about a little diarrhea. I had to convince them that my stomachache involved something mysterious, something serious, something that needed attending by a doctor. I continued ripping green gooseberries off the bushes and adding a green apple for good measure. Walking around hunched over, unable to straighten out for the excruciating pain, I finally convinced them to call Mutti and have her come get me. This she did and I went home with her, cutting this last summer visit with my grandparents short by several days.

Mutti, Papa, Oma, and Opa had bought my dramatics! I had put on a convincing performance! Or did they see through my subterfuge but decide not to say anything? I'll never know. The subject never came up again. I had saved face without hurting anyone's feelings, which had been my intention to begin with. One nagging thought remained, though. Why had I not been able to admit that I was homesick? What was so contemptible about being homesick? Did I sense then that I wanted to go places that would take me away from my roots? Or would I be too homesick hereafter to go anywhere alone?

◆   ◆   ◆

Since the time I had learned to read, I had read many books, but none has stayed with me more than a series of "girls" books (at least I never knew a boy who had read them). *Nesthäkchen,* written by Else Ury, is the story of a girl growing up in Berlin at the outbreak of World War I. The series followed her and her family until she became a great-grandmother. I probably began reading these ten pre-teen books when I was around twelve years old. In volume eight, the main character's seventeen-year-old daughter falls in love with a young Brazilian man. She marries him and leaves Berlin to live with him in Sao Paulo. I was enchanted by the idea of living in a foreign country with the man I loved. Even better, the characters lived a life of luxury in a tropical paradise. The reality of life in Germany around 1953 was so different from the life of opulence the characters lived that I could only drool with envy and resort to marathon daydreaming.

Owning books was not a given at this post-war time. Books were expensive and only the very rich could afford to buy them. I recall that in order to buy books at a discount and at the same time make some extra money, Papa had joined the *Lesering Gutenberg* a couple of years prior. This meant that in his "sales territory," he would sign people up for buying a book a month and/or selected magazines which he would then deliver to them and collect the money. His book customers were responsible and paid promptly. Not so the people he had signed up for magazines. I remember helping Papa deliver magazines in his territory which would constitute blocks and blocks of walking to neighborhoods far away from our own. The magazines were heavy, and when it rained they weren't all that well protected in our canvas bags (usually Doris and I worked together). The worst part of this job was collecting the money once a month. Although the customers loved it when we delivered their fresh new gossip magazines such as *Der Stern*, they were often absent on the day of collection or they didn't have change or they wouldn't be paid for another two days and would we please come back. We heard all sorts of excuses and I often cursed Papa who had recruited us for this job. The good thing was that we were able to buy books at a discount and that the Lesering Gutenberg gave a Christmas party for children of booksellers and magazine distributors at which we received candy and presents. We did love presents!

My time in elementary school was drawing to an end. I was in sixth grade and twelve years old in the fall of that year, 1953. Eight years after the end of World War II—that is how we measured time then. My grades had continued to be good throughout elementary school. I liked my teachers, including my music teacher who taught us folk songs that I still sing.

Now I was about to take a step that would decide my academic future for a long time to come. An earthshaking event was about to take place, and the memory of it is still sharp.

Sixth-graders who had consistently shown good grades were going through the process of being sorted out as to who would proceed on to the *Oberschule* (high school). We were being tested, and, as determined by my teacher Fräulein Düstersiek and my parents, I was academically ready to take this step. In German schools at that time, the test results would decide if children were to stay in basic education at the *Volksschule* (grades one to nine) until the end of the ninth grade, at which time they would be done with school unless they went into a trade and then had to do three more years of combined trade school/practical experience. For instance, if their goal was to be a hairdresser upon completing the nine grades, they then attended a trade school once or twice a week and the rest of time practiced hairdressing at a salon. If they were deemed academically superior but didn't want a college education, then they attended *Mittelschule* (middle school) which meant that they actually switched to another school building and followed a different curriculum for the next four years. Students enrolled in a Mittelschule completed ten grades and became skilled tradesmen, draftsmen, or workers in a technical field. Armed with a Mittelschule certificate, a *Mittlere Reife*, and additional training, they could enter a skilled profession.

But if they were deemed more advanced academically and their test results were superior, students went on to attend an Oberschule, and on completing the seven years there they then qualified to enter a university and study whatever they desired.

The day of the test came. I knew that a group of administrators and/or teachers from a high school were going to come into our elementary school and administer the tests in all subjects, but I only remember the arithmetic part. I wasn't worried about any of the proceedings and was my usual jovial self, probably cracking jokes and causing laughter among my classmates who were also academically superior. I felt confident, even superior to the classmates who wouldn't be taking this test, because they simply weren't academic material. But I was, and so I was better than them. It didn't matter if they wore new shoes, I was more intelligent. In retrospect, I don't know how my parents and siblings tolerated my obnoxious airs, even before let alone during and after the testing.

In math, a group of high school teachers set about teaching us the new concept of percentages. The question asked on the oral part of the test was: if you loaned someone one hundred Marks and asked for an interest of twenty percent, how much money would you get back? I wanted to be the first one to answer, so eager was I to show them that I had grasped the new concept, that they wouldn't make a mistake by allowing me to attend academic high school, that I was worthy of advancement. My hand shot up in the air, I was given the nod, and I replied, "Twenty Marks." No, they said and asked again, at which one of my classmates answered correctly, "one hundred twenty Marks." I wanted to die, I felt so humiliated, not believing that I had made that stupid mistake. In hindsight I know that they could tell I had a grasp of the concept but hadn't thought it out completely.

My last report card from elementary school read like a dream. I had three As, in singing and music, artistic expression in speaking and reading, and swimming, and Bs in German, English, handwriting, needlework, math, and physical education. I wouldn't see good grades like those ever again. I only missed one day of school that year.

My time in elementary school was completed on April 6, 1954, when I was promoted to the seventh grade. The hardest thing about leaving elementary school behind was that I would no longer be seeing my beloved Fräulein Düstersiek on a daily basis. I was now going to be a student at the *Oberschule*.

My paternal grandparents' house in Reitbrook, 1950s

My paternal grandparents, Ernst and Emma Behnke, 1950s

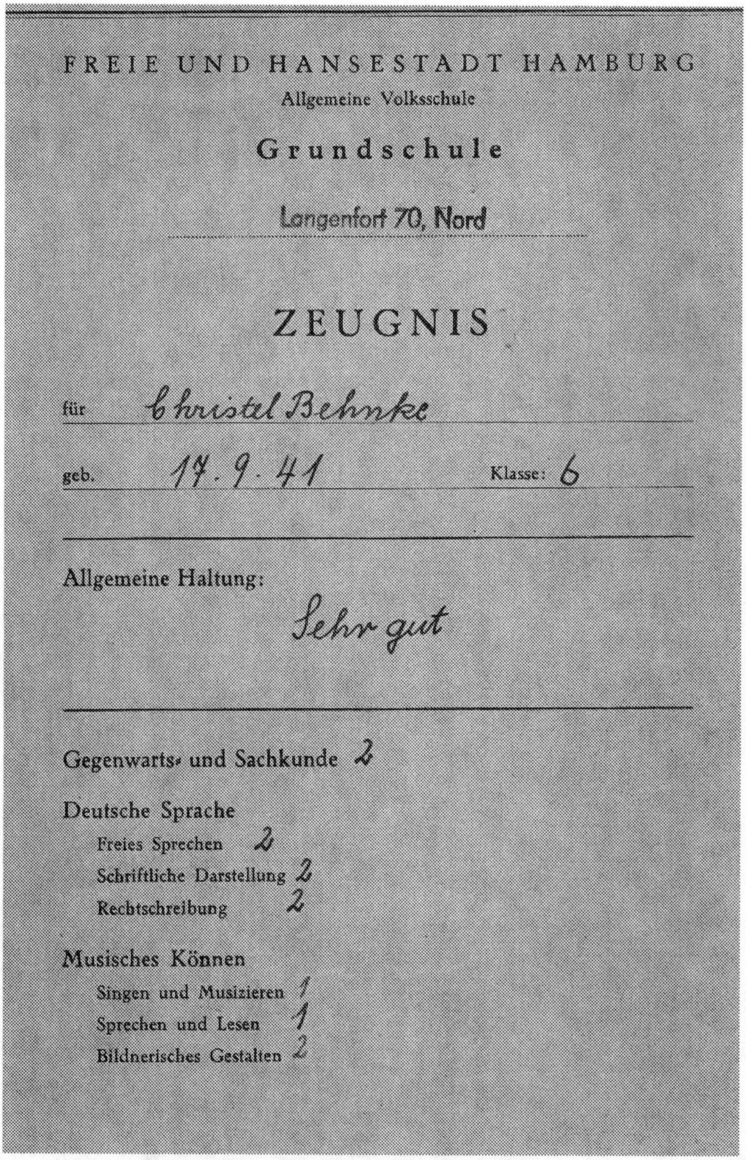

FREIE UND HANSESTADT HAMBURG

Allgemeine Volksschule

Grundschule

Langenfort 70, Nord

ZEUGNIS

für   *Christel Behnke*

geb.   *17. 9. 41*   Klasse: *6*

Allgemeine Haltung:

Sehr gut

Gegenwarts- und Sachkunde *2*

Deutsche Sprache

Freies Sprechen   *2*
Schriftliche Darstellung *2*
Rechtschreibung   *2*

Musisches Können

Singen und Musizieren   *1*
Sprechen und Lesen   *1*
Bildnerisches Gestalten *2*

My sixth grade report card, 1954

Schreiben 2

Werken und Nadelarbeit 2

Rechnen und Raumlehre
  Rechenfertigkeit 2
  Sachrechnen 2

Religion *nahm teil*

Englisch 2

Leibeserziehung
  Schwimmen 1
  Gymnastik
  Leichtathletik 2
  Spiele
  Gerätturnen 2

Bemerkungen *Versetzt nach Kl. 7*

Versäumte Tage: 1

Hamburg, den 6 · 4 ·   1954

Schulleiter: Klassenlehrerin: *Diesterweg*

Gesehen (Erziehungsberechtigter oder gesetzl. Vertreter):

Abstufung der Zeugnisse:
1 — sehr gut; 2 — gut; 3 — befriedigend; 4 — ausreichend; 5 — nicht ausreichend

My sixth grade report card, page 2, 1954

The "musicians" Doris and Christel, 1952

5

High school
Class trip to Sylt

✦

1954–1955

1954—The Bundestag (German Parliament) allows conscription to establish military service over the objections of the Socialist Party of Germany. June 17 becomes the Day of German Unity. One Saturday a month stores are now allowed to stay open until 6:00 p.m. instead of closing at 2:00 p.m., and store clerks and unions riot in Munich. One wage-earner per family working nine-hour days can now support a family of four. Alfred Kinsey's Sexual Behavior in the Human Female *is published in German and creates indignation. Petticoats are in. First self-service shoe store opens in Hamburg. The Supreme Court of the U.S. orders racial desegregation.*

By the time I got to high school, my brother Klaus had graduated with a *Mittlere Reife* certificate, meaning that he'd completed ten years of school. His education had started only to be interrupted by the war, and he spent the remainder of it in the chaotic post-war years. When he graduated, he was at least two years older than he would have been given normal times.

So where was my brother now? On a freighter going around Africa. I don't know how much the chaos of the war contributed to his decision to become a sea captain, but I can well imagine that he wanted to leave behind all the devastation he had been through as much as to see the world. Living in Hamburg, so close to the sea, must have encouraged his dream as well. I can envision him seeing himself in a smart uniform, in charge of a ship. But what did Klaus have to do before he would wear that smart uniform? On his first voyage to Africa, his assignment was to take charge of scrubbing the deck! He must have heaved with the rolling soapy waters and thrown up a lot, I imagine. Then, as the ship crossed the equator, his shipmates and the captain in good maritime fashion delivered him and others who had never before crossed the equator a ritual bath by dunking him into a pool of foul liquids and semi-solids, including kitchen wastes that had been collected from around the ship. Through this dunking he supposedly would discover the mysteries of the deep and become a real sailor all compliments of His Majesty, King Neptune.

Just before Klaus left Hamburg, he had met Anne, the girl who would become his wife. All this "fun" he was having on the high seas surely did not keep him from thinking about her, so much so that the merchant marine lost a future captain after just one trip around the Cape. In his absence, I looked forward to the postcards he sent from mysterious places on the "dark continent," as we called it—Mombasa, the Cape of Good Hope, Dakar, and Mozambique. I looked up each port on a world map and then studied his postcards, astounded by the palm trees, jungles, and exotic animals.

As for my travels, I began a stamp collection and continued it for many years, carefully removing stamps from letters and cards and organizing them in a stamp book. Then, by looking at the stamps I could imagine the places of origin. German stamps were boring compared to the cheerful ones from Central and South America, Bermuda, and other faraway places. I must have bought some of the stamps with my meager funds because I didn't know anyone who lived in places so far away.

For a long time I couldn't understand why my brother would trade the exciting life of a captain for a mere girl, but home he came and home he stayed. The good thing was that after a few months of depriving us, he was finally back and ready to begin a land-locked career as an accounting apprentice with a company called Sunlight. His position paid well enough to give Doris and me an allowance.

Then began the battle between Mutti and Klaus over Anne. Mutti didn't think that she was worthy of Klaus. When he came home late, Mutti would confront him and they would begin arguing. And then there was the matter of handkerchiefs that Mutti fished from his pants, hankies that to her had a certain incriminating texture not unlike hardened glue. I had no idea what the big fuss was about, as what could possibly be in handkerchiefs other than snot?

I was too preoccupied with the changes in my own life to pay too much attention to the troubles between Mutti and Klaus, although I did occasionally come to his defense which further enraged Mutti. But for all that ado, Klaus was twenty and going steady. He still slept on the couch in the living room, so I imagine he and Anne conducted a lot of their dates in the park, because privacy was a hard thing to come by in our house.

◆   ◆   ◆

In the spring of 1954, at almost thirteen years of age, I entered high school. Rather than walk to school, I now took a twenty-minute streetcar ride past the ruins of houses and stores. In my memory, the ruin of Karstadt had not yet been razed and every day I stared quizzically at steel beams and heaps of bricks. Karstadt had been an elegant, six-story department store in the lively Hamburger Strasse, where before the war Mutti did her shopping. But on the night of July 30, 1943, 370 people died in the bunker beneath the department store. Ghosts of the war were still all around, everywhere.

Using public transportation had always been part of my life, but now I had to make sure I was at the streetcar stop on time to catch the one that would drop me off just before school started, at 9:00 a.m. At several stops, school friends would board and sometimes we could hastily compare our homework. I was hardly ever tardy, but I had to sprint to the streetcar stop a few times with my bag bull of books because the next streetcar would get me to school late. I couldn't run back home and ask Mutti to drive me, because we didn't have a car. And, anyway, she didn't drive.

I don't know how I came to be enrolled in this particular school, the *Wissenschaftliche Oberschule für Mädchen am Lerchenfeld* (Academic High School for Girls at Lerchenfeld, Lerchenfeld was the street name). My class was full of girls—yes, girls only—from all parts of Hamburg.

Rewind.

The school had originally opened in 1910. In July 1942, bombs destroyed the auditorium, tower, and music room. Teachers who that night had done duty watching the school used fire extinguishers to keep the blaze confined until the one fire engine in the area could arrive on the scene. This first strike did not stop classes, but as the air raids increased there was increasingly less instruction. Students and teachers would spend hours in their own cellars or bunkers, waiting for the all-clear signal. In the beginning, when the air war hadn't yet gotten so "serious," students would look at the clock to see if they would miss a class. Daytime alarms also cut into this or that unpopular class. But disturbed sleep, interrupted work, and attacks of fear, even when nothing serious was happening, took their toll on students' health and performance.

In 1943, air raids did extensive damage to the school and orderly instruction became out of the question. On the last day before summer vacation in 1943, students and teachers gathered for the last time not knowing that they wouldn't meet again until October 1945. Instead, students and teachers would help harvest potatoes, collect wood and berries, and work threshing machines. A group of Polish workers came in to repair the school's roof so that French prisoners of war could at least have a roof over their heads. Another part of the school was given over to bombed-out civilians for shelter, and the gym became a storage facility. I didn't know the history of the school until years later, when I read a 75th anniversary commemorative booklet.

Between 1940 and 1945, some children were evacuated to safer surroundings in southern Bavaria, where classes continued to be held and where students and teachers also helped with community work needful of doing. One such camp was in upper Bavaria, in a cloister where the children helped in the gardens and fields, fed the animals, and for recreation sang with the nuns and performed dances for them. Teachers and students alike were happy to be in this sunny environment while at home their school was being bombarded.

School restarted on October 3, 1945, with 193 girls happy to be back and eager to learn. Because Hamburg was under British occupation, the British determined the curriculum. At first, the subjects were religion, math, drawing, physical education, needlework, gardening, and writing. One subject was added at a time, with history and geography getting tacked on at long last. Any instruction about Germany's borders was forbidden, so much so that the teacher would carefully cover the German (red) borders on maps with green and brown paint. The British came in on inspections and everything had to be in political order.

My brother, who had returned to school in 1945, encountered some peculiar practices enforced by the British occupation forces. Any physical education class on the way to the track was not allowed to walk in unison for fear that it could call up the "ghost of militarism." One directive given to teachers said that "sharp commands in gym class are undesirable!" Approved textbooks covered song books, catechisms, and math tables. German classics were only admissible if the edition didn't have prefaces or comments, and teachers had to search students' bags to make sure they didn't contain banned books. The fairy tale favorite "Hänsel and Gretel" was even banned because it dealt with "crimes against humanity!" Teachers were always walking a tightrope, never knowing what was allowed and what wasn't with their students. They and the administrators were subject to dismissal if a forbidden subject or text was discovered on the premises.

In 1945, Lerchenfeld was indescribably filthy. The most recent occupants, the French, had left whatever they didn't want to take including their dirty underwear. Walls were covered with their "dirty" pictures and graffiti. Now glassless windows had to be covered with paper and each room disinfected to eliminate insects. Teachers, parents, and students helped restore, sand, and glue the furniture that for two years had been rained on through gaping holes in the roof. Holes in the walls were covered with cardboard. The school secretary had found a typewriter in a heap of rubble and happily hammered out letters without the letter "w".

Teachers improvised, working without curricula from the fall of 1945 to the spring of 1946. Books were in scarce supply and so were other teaching materials such as paper, ink, and chalk. Teaching was done in semi-ruins, with fire-blackened hallways that turned into dripping caves on rainy days. Even worse was the undernourished state of health of both students and teachers.

Then came the winter of 1946–1947 with freezing conditions lasting for weeks at a stretch. Students sat in unheated classrooms wearing hats, gloves, long pants, and scarves, all these "outfits" then covered with old army blankets.

Extremely helpful in these dire conditions was the school food provided by the Americans and Danes. Students only had to pay a small amount for its preparation and transportation to the schools. Shoes and clothing, though, were in short supply. So a shoe exchange was started. If students brought in a pair that they had outgrown, they would receive a ration card entitling them to a pair that fit. The principal's room was piled high with shoes, and she took time from her duties to help with the fitting. Other clothing was handed down too, and second-hand sweaters and coats once worn by the older students were seen on younger students in the following years.

Because public transportation was not yet back to regular service, students and teachers had to walk to school, sometimes an hour or more on an empty stomach or on a few slices of rutabaga. More depressing was the walk home through streets that were cold and dark and rubble-strewn. Older students wrote their tests in between sessions of stretching and jumping jacks performed in order to warm freezing hands and feet, which in turn led to the burning of more calories and then the onset once more of hunger.

The outer turmoil mirrored the inner distress that teachers and students felt. Kids had had to endure misery, poverty, and, much worse, cruelty and atrocities. Many fathers would never come home, and many families had not yet been reunited. Bombs had torn families apart, and families who had managed to stay together now broke apart because they couldn't cope with the war's aftermath.

Many fathers lost their jobs because of their previous political affiliation. Refugee children had to cope with losing their homes and trying to adjust to their new surroundings. The psychological consequences of the war had only just begun to scab over, although lofty goals had been established for students, among them the "training for proper work and performance of one's duty; independent thinking; courage to develop one's own opinions and defend them; respect for another's opinion; political sense of responsibility; voluntary and enthusiastic integration in the community; social sensitivity and action; respect for all life and for the mysteries of the unknown." (Gymnasium Lerchenfeld, 1910–1985, 75th Anniversary Commemorative Booklet).

◆   ◆   ◆

Before I joined this school with the lofty goals, Easter was just around the corner and I am reminded of it because it was probably the last time we colored Easter eggs. On this Easter Sunday in 1954, when I was almost thirteen, Doris (fifteen) and I went to church. The bells of St. Gabriel rang around 9:30 a.m. and tolled for five minutes. My sister and I put on our best blouses, skirts, and shoes, our "Sunday clothes." These clothes weren't worn at any other time but Sunday, unless we were close to outgrowing them and then they became everyday clothes. My skirt had blue and white stripes and underneath I wore a stiff petticoat. With a white, short-sleeved blouse that Mutti had starched and ironed, the outfit showed off my slim waist and gave me a clean, smart look. Just the way I liked it. Doris also wore a petticoat and together we bounced into the backyard where Papa and Mutti were sitting on the veranda drinking their morning coffee. They couldn't have cared less about going to church on such a glorious day, and even Easter couldn't compel them to leave their comfortable corner in the backyard. It was bright and sunny and already quite warm at this hour. With Klaus' help, my parents were going to hide the eggs while we were gone. "Get going," they said, shooing us off, "we can't hide the eggs while you are hanging around here."

If we walked quickly, we could make it to church in five minutes. Down to the end of our street, a short left and past the police station, then a right on Hartzlohplatz, at the end of which stood St. Gabriel. We were just rounding the corner at the police station when the bells began to ring again. Ten minutes to ten, plenty of time to be seated by 10:00 a.m. when the service began. The church was always packed for Easter and other holidays, because the regular churchgoers were joined by those that came to worship sporadically. I liked the deep, vibrating sound of the organ, and the rousing singing of the congregation, belting out resurrection songs, like *Christ ist erstanden* (Christ has risen), and songs about spring, like *Grüss Gott, du schöner Maien* (welcoming May, although it was only April). The songs were full of hope and the renewal of the seasons. According to them the month of May was a joyful one, notwithstanding that school would begin in a few days.

Pastor Wendt gave the sermon this morning and as usual, he droned on and on, his monotonous voice wafting me away from him and the rest of the congregation into places in my head that had nothing to do with Jesus or the resurrection.

The backyard came into my head and I scanned it for eggs. Over here in the apple tree, down there by the raspberry bushes, by the compost heap (it would be my brother's idea to hide an egg there), or even somewhere in the veranda rose trellis. I thought of last night when Papa and Mutti, Klaus, Doris, and I sat around the big table in the living room, coloring Easter eggs. The trickiest thing about doing Easter eggs was the removal of the yolk and the egg whites. With a knitting needle, I carefully poked a hole in the top and bottom of the egg by tapping repeatedly but lightly on the shell. If, in the process, the shell didn't crack in any other place, I proceeded to the next step which was to blow short puffs of breath into the hole on one side until the egg white emerged from the other hole, followed by a glob of egg yolk and then some air bubbles. The whites and the yolk merged in the bowl, ready to be made into scrambled eggs for breakfast on Easter morning. Mutti brought out the egg cups into which I placed the empty shells ever so carefully.

Now the creative part of this Easter tradition could begin. We had a set of watercolors in a container and each of us had a thin, pointy brush. We dipped the brush into a bowl of water, chose a color, and then swirled the brush around in the water color until the bristles were saturated. Holding the egg with one hand, the brush in the other, I decorated my egg in my most favorite way—alternating straight and zigzag lines about a centimeter apart all around the egg. Each zig and zag received its dot of green. My egg was done in no time while Klaus, who was very artistic, was drawing on his a mother bunny and baby bunnies encircling. I thought, "Why can't I be like my brother and paint a more interesting design on my egg?" I took another egg and tried to paint a tree with an Easter bunny sitting underneath it beside a basked filled with colored eggs, but the bunny looked like a dog, a deranged one at that, and so I just took my brush and dipped it into the different colors and covered the whole egg yellow, green, red, orange, blue, brown, pink, and purple. It was a very loud Easter egg, but I quite liked it. It looked like it had been painted by a three-year-old. I said, "Klaus, you can paint all the Easter eggs next year," but he looked very unimpressed with his effort. He never did make a big deal of his talents. When we were all done, we placed our eggs in a basket where we looked at them for a few days, after which we threw them out. I wanted gooey chocolate eggs in brightly colored paper, and ... *may the Lord bless you and keep you* ... Pastor Wendt was now sending us on our way. I had missed most of his sermon!

Instead of running home afterwards, Doris and I decided to make one stop. Just a short block away from the church, on the fourth and top floor of an apartment house that had been rebuilt in typical red-brick post-war fashion, lived an aunt of ours. Tante Möller wasn't really a relative but we called her *aunt*. Tante Möller was about seventy years old at the time and in pretty good health. But her legs were bad, and they were wrapped in bandages so they resembled the legs on mannequins in store windows, pale and stiff. She had difficulty managing four flights of stairs, and so she didn't get out very often. We thought we'd surprise her.

"*Fröhliche Ostern,* Tante Möller, just stopped by to say hello." She smiled, "Come in, come in, I'm glad to see you, I might even have something for you." I looked at Doris and knew what she was thinking. Secretly, we had both hoped that she would have something for us, an Easter egg or maybe a couple of coins. She said, "Sit down and tell me about church. Did Pastor Wendt give a good sermon or was he boring a usual?" Not waiting for our reply, she continued, "How are your mother and father?" We were very polite and answered her questions, but we were also getting a little hot sitting in our Easter finery in her stuffy living room that had so much furniture covering every inch of space. The sun shining into the windows made the room even stuffier. It was getting hot out there and we were feeling the urge to get home, to shed our Sunday clothes and to look for Easter eggs. "Tante Möller, I said, "our parents wanted us to come straight home after church and I think we had better get going because they planned to hide eggs outside." We shook hands and that's when she gave each of us one Mark to do with whatever we wanted. This was more than we had hoped for and we shouted a quiet hallelujah. A bag of gummibears or maybe a chocolate bar would cost less than that. A ticket to the movies, perhaps, to see *Laurel and Hardy* and laugh my eyes out. Oh, the possibilities. I was rich!

Doris and I ran home hand in hand, taking turns pulling each other along until we arrived home sweat-soaked. "Where have you been, we've been waiting for you, let's go," Mutti said hurrying us into the backyard. "Now look for your Easter eggs and be quick about it, the eggs are melting. You can change your clothes later." We ran around the yard and couldn't find anything under the trees, but when we looked up we saw several colorfully wrapped goodies nesting in the crook of gnarly branches in several trees. Without regard for my Sunday clothes, which were damp and clinging to me, I clasped my arms around my favorite apple tree, the one I knew really well, and climbed, freeing one hand then the other and digging my shoes into the bark. I reached the first fork in the tree and there they lay—several melted Easter eggs, their flatness bearing no resemblance to their normal oval shape. I grabbed the sodden mass and with one hand holding onto the tree and my legs wrapped around it inched down until it was safe to jump. Quickly I tore open the foil and licked the melted chocolate until there wasn't a trace left on the paper. I swore to myself that next Easter I wouldn't go to church. That way I could have perfect Easter eggs.

◆   ◆   ◆

By the time I entered *Lerchenfeld* (field of larks) at Easter of 1954, the school enrolled seven hundred students. The gym had been repaired, and the rebuilding of the school was continuing apace. First the ruined walls were torn down, creating a lot of dirt and noise. After the foundation stone was laid in November of that year, the building of the addition to the school began. The temporary roof of the old building was torn down and parts of it clattered down a chute past our classroom windows. When it rained, big puddles formed in the hallways, and when it snowed there was the melting snow to contend with. But we had windows with glass!

The schoolyard that had finally been fixed had to be torn up again in order to bury cables. There were only three toilets for the seven hundred of us and our teachers. On field days, we often went to museums or just hiked near the school because instruction was nearly impossible in our noisy, dirty school. When walls were torn down between floors to accommodate a new heating system, we couldn't help eavesdropping on classes above or below. This was the perfect opportunity to send notes on strings to the classroom below.

In German schools, a class stayed together through all the grades, in our case from grade seven through thirteen. We had an assigned classroom, and the teachers came to us. There were no lockers and no congestion in the hallways. But in 1954, my first year in high school, we still didn't have a classroom to call our own; new rooms hadn't been built yet and old ones were in the process of being torn down. We would use any room that fell empty because another class might have left it to go on a field trip. Sometimes we even gathered on a staircase for a class. The following year, 1955, was labeled by the principal the most disruptive that teachers and students had ever endured. The noise from the various machines, cement mixers, drills, and electric sanders virtually drowned out the teachers, the recitals of poetry, and even the dictations!

In sewing class, thirty-five students were forced to share six sewing machines, all of which had been found in the ruins of apartment houses. So we had to take turns, and I learned enough so that I was able to make my own simple dresses. Mutti had her mother's old, manual Singer machine with a big foot peddle. When there was money to buy fabric, I used it to work on dresses or skirts for myself.

The first musical instrument that the school received was a grand piano lacking legs (they had probably gone the way of all firewood). New legs were constructed, and other instruments followed slowly. Sheet music was needed badly, though.

In art, there was a need for paint brushes, paints, visual aids, and art objects. Maps had to be acquired for teaching geography, religion, and history.

Natural science collections had been destroyed, and a range of stuffed animals, skeletons, and bugs on pins needed replacement. By the spring of 1956, we were in new physics and chemistry rooms. At least we didn't have to be in basement rooms like some of the students before us, rooms in which there was no natural light and no ventilation to get rid of the foul-smelling odors, especially the hydrogen sulfide that reminded us of rotten eggs. Nevertheless, I didn't really care where we had chemistry or physics because those two subjects were without doubt my most hated ones, mostly because I failed to find meaning in either.

Every subject was compulsory, even English. For our second foreign language, we had a choice of either French or Latin, and I chose Latin, partly because my friend Ingrid was taking Latin in her school and my parents urged me to take it. It would help me later, they said. Shortly after we began our Latin studies, Ingrid and I renamed each other "Dickus," using the German word for "fat" and putting a Latin ending on it. It made no sense at all, but we called each other "Dickus" from then on.

Well, then. The physical and emotional state of my school was in disarray when I entered. And who was I? I was smart and had proven that with my excellent grades. I was quick-witted and never at a loss for words. I clowned around a lot. I was funny, and my fellow students thought so, too. My teachers didn't always appreciate my humor, however, and sometimes I was called on the carpet for appearing disrespectful. I was energetic, but the downside of this was that often I didn't bother to slow down enough to concentrate such that instructions sailed right past me. Early into the school year I had had a big surprise—I actually needed to study to keep up with all those classmates from other elementary schools. Had my beloved Fräulein Düstersiek been too easy on me? Some of my fellow students seemed to know rather more than I did, and it unnerved me that I had catching-up to do. I laughed and joked about school, but I was very disappointed in myself and even embarrassed when my first report card did not match those of my earlier years. Doubts about my abilities surfaced. Should I have been selected to attend this school, or had a mistake been made? Was I really smart enough to make it? How could I fulfill my parents' expectations that I go to college?

I also felt intimidated by some of the girls whose parents had more money than mine. I didn't have a different outfit for each day of the week, and many times I wore the same dress two or three days in a row. And then there were the hand-me-downs from my sister. And my family didn't go on vacations from which those who did returned with glorious tans. My family's lack of money was very frustrating to me, and I felt inferior because of it.

Although there were a few girls in my class whose parents were not well off, there were always families who were worse off than mine, and anyway, the school's goal to instill in us a call to social action became a bigger part of school life than did wealth. Around harvest time, we were asked in the spirit of giving to bring in staples such as bread, flour, and margarine or shortening. All our donations were piled high on the temporary stage in the gym before we assembled a variety of food into laundry baskets, nets, or bags. Two younger girls were paired with two older ones for the walk to deliver this food to old people and poor families who sometimes lived in bunkers if not in corrugated steel huts surrounding our school. We had to be sensitive about giving these "free" things to people so they didn't feel they were getting a handout. I was also sensitized to the fact that Mutti found it truly difficult to part with food for school drives because we didn't have much to spare ourselves.

We also collected books, shoes, socks, coats, sweaters, dresses, and toys for the *Durchgangslager Friedland,* a transit camp for refugees from the east. The thank-you notes the school would later receive made us feel that we were doing a good thing.

Then we signed up to collect for the *Müttergenesungswerk,* a charity for mothers who needed a break from the grim reality of being the sole parent for their children after their husbands died in the war. We received a can with a slit in the top and went around neighborhood streets, asking people to donate money. By the time we were in ninth grade, however, we didn't volunteer anymore or at least not willingly.

Members of the *Schulverein,* the equivalent of a PTA, helped with class trips and field days as well as paid for milk and chocolate milk for undernourished students. There were still plenty of them, even in 1954.

Although I was busy with these activities that I enjoyed, I missed my special relationship with my former teacher who had always taken such a motherly interest in me. I wished all teachers had been like Fräulein Düstersiek.

Instead, I had teachers who had titles, which elevated them and their education to a degree that was nowhere to be found in my immediate family that boasted no Ph.D.s anywhere. The brain power of two of them in particular intimidated me. One was Frau Dr. von Beyn who taught biology and Herr Dr. Bargstaedt who was the Latin teacher. They were both formidable persons in intellect and bearing. Frau Dr. von Beyn looked down on us as if from the heights. She must have been over six feet tall, or so it seemed, with her erect posture and eyes that could take in all thirty-five of us at once.

She was as serious as Herr Dr. Bargstaedt for whom we held some degree of sympathy for the leg he had lost to the war. We could hear him coming down the hall, because his prosthetic leg made quite an unnerving noise on the concrete floor. He opened the door, and by that time all of us were standing at our desks, and after a brief *Guten Morgen,* he sat down before us. He would place his briefcase on the desk, open it, and begin to teach in a strict and unsmiling manner. I thought he and Dr. von Beyn were only interested in teaching their subject. Why didn't they care about us? And what did they know about adolescent girls? They scared me so much that I lost my sense of humor in their presence. Clearly I wasn't the only one who thought this way, because when we were informed at the beginning of ninth grade that Dr. Bargstaedt had transferred to an all-boys school, the whole class of girls cheered.

Every morning when we entered the school, we had to stop and curtsy to the teacher standing at the top of the first flight of stairs, and if we forgot because we were talking to a girlfriend or were in a hurry we were called back to stand before the teacher, curtsy, and recite *"Guten Morgen."* Then we were free to go to our classroom. I hated it when Frau Dr. von Beyn was the greeter, because she never smiled.

I became somewhat of a *"Pennaeler,"* making remarks about what the teacher had just said in class under my breath, but loud enough for my desk neighbors to hear and start laughing. It was a way of getting support from my classmates while feeling vindicated in my dislike for my teachers. I felt that they were not willing to help me, and so I distrusted them. At the same time, I was not afraid to make my views known, even in a confrontational way.

Each class was assigned a "class teacher," who was the main contact person for students and parents. Dr. Bargstaedt was our class teacher. Whenever parents needed to speak to a teacher about a problem (even with another teacher), it was the class teacher they first spoke to. Then there was the class speaker. My class voted me class speaker for two years in a row, meaning that whenever the class had a problem I was the one to speak to the teacher. If my grades in Latin had been better, I might have had an easier time speaking with him, but as it was I always felt he wondered why I was selected the class speaker when I was such a poor student in the subject so dear to his heart.

I can even now feel the trepidation with which I approached him, although approach him I did. The only way I knew how to speak to him was to be straight-forward. I had no diplomacy in me, being only twelve years old at the time. I would raise my hand and say, "The class would like you to postpone tomorrow's test, because we don't feel that we are prepared well enough," but often I felt that he had heard me say, "Christel Behnke wants me to postpone the test because she is not prepared." Most of the time, an issue like test postponement fell on deaf ears, but once in a while he would relent and give us a little more time to prepare.

◆   ◆   ◆

Outside of school, I had to deal with changes as well. My best friend Dickus went to a different high school and inevitably made new friends. As did I. We saw less and less of each other. I was jealous of her new friends, and she on her side didn't want me to make new friends. But she spent more and more time with her new friends which made me mad. She came to my house less often, and once in a while she still stayed overnight. I think she agreed to stay because she liked my Mutti's maternal ways. Secretly, I wanted Dickus to give up all of her new friends so that I wouldn't have to feel jealous any more, because jealousy drove me to nastiness. I would not speak to her. "So there, that's what you get for having new friends!"

Though our contacts grew irregular, we never lost touch completely. It was sometime during these high school years that Dickus' mother died at a relatively young age. Frau Franke was the first person I knew who'd had cancer. In the fifties, many patients weren't informed that they were cancerous. *Krebs* was a terrible word, and no one wanted it to cross their lips lest they themselves ended up with it. Relatives and neighbors of Frau Franke knew, but the patient herself didn't. Cancer was a truly deadly disease and virtually nobody survived it. The German word *Krebs* also means "crab", and so I thought of cancer as a crab or maybe a maggot eating its way through the body until there was nothing left. It was unthinkable that fun-loving Frau Franke should have cancer and that Dickus would lose her mother. Dickus came to our house often during the time her mother was ill, but I don't think we ever talked about her. Mutti treated Dickus as one of her own, and so my friend became increasingly a part of our family until she moved away to live with her father and his second wife whom she naturally hated.

Dickus and I didn't become close again until we had both graduated, worked in the city, met at a fountain downtown to eat the lunch we had brought from home, and began talking again.

My new friends lived in other parts of the city so I needed to take public transportation to meet up with them. I had a monthly pass for all forms of transportation and rode streetcars, trains, and subways all over the city, growing quite independent for the experience.

Extracurricular activities were not part of the German school curriculum. After school was out, our time was our own. Only in theory, though, because homework severely limited any time I might otherwise have spent with friends.

When school dismissed at 1:00 or 2:00 p.m. five days a week and around 11:30 a.m. on Saturdays, I went straight home to have the main meal of the day with Mutti and sometimes my sister, who was apprenticing in a neighborhood cosmetic store. Doris was going to trade school three times a week to become a trained saleswoman.

After lunch I had at least three hours worth of homework. At the beginning of seventh grade, I did my homework conscientiously but nonetheless began sliding into daydreaming as my grades slipped. Mutti would check to make sure I was on task, and with papers and books spread out all over the living room table I would reply, "Ja, ja," which meant that of course I was studying, what did it look like? ("Ja, ja" can mean a lot of things, depending on the tone in which it is uttered).

The one person who could have helped me, especially with Latin and physics, was my Papa. But he was touring with a band and mostly unavailable. Nor could I do homework on the phone with him, because it was too expensive to make long-distance phone calls. I missed him, not only because he could have helped me but also because he was calmer than Mutti, whose temper flared up more easily at my youthful failures.

Papa was a trained musician who had been playing in the same band in and around Hamburg for many years. Occasionally, he played in other bands when they needed a violin, bass, or trombone. But the Walter Lucke Band was his "home" band. In the early fifties, when the need for entertainment coupled with people's ability to pay for it became greater, new bands with younger musicians started forming. The members of these new bands played for less compensation and asked for fewer breaks. And so the Walter Lucke Band found itself competing with musicians who could have been their sons.

A decision was made to accept jobs outside of Hamburg, and Papa went on the road wherever jobs were available. These engagements seemed to be mostly in and around the Rhineland in cities such as Düsseldorf and Cologne. Papa might come home once a month, or maybe not for a couple of months. Sometimes my mother got on a train and went to see him where he boarded, in a *Pension* or the equivalent of today's bed and breakfast. For long periods, though, their only communication was by phone. When a gig was up, he came home and freelanced locally.

Neither of my parents liked the situation, but our standard of living increased slightly during this time, and the constant worry about money consequently eased a little. With my brother's and sister's contribution to the family income, we were able to buy more clothing and household furnishings.

Without Papa's steady presence, with Mutti on edge from lack of her husband's help in handling Klaus and his drive for independence, with my chaotic school in disrepair, with new friends yet to make and old friends lost, and with academic demands on me that I was finding difficult to manage, I rapidly fell into distraction, irritability, and moodiness.

So, I turned to Jesus. I joined a church group. I was thirteen now, and thus far in my life my relationship with anything religious had been sporadic and superficial at best. As a young child, I had memorized a rhyme that I repeated every night before going to sleep, not on my knees but abed with my hands in the praying position. It went like this:

> *Müde bin ich, geh zur Ruh*
> *Schliesse beide Äuglein zu.*
> *Vater, lass die Augen dein*
> *Über meinem Bette sein.*

(I am tired and going to rest. I close my eyes. Father, please watch over me). The Father in the prayer wore flowing robes and had a long beard. The words didn't mean that much to me and I had no special relationship with Him.

My parents went to church only on special occasions such as Christmas and Easter. I went along then, and I especially came to like the midnight service on December 24th . When candles became available again after the war, their glow made our plain Lutheran church so rich-looking and warm. Singing *Stille Nacht, Heilige Nacht* was always the high point of the service for me. I don't know who promulgated the rule, but I grew up thinking that that particular song could only be sung on December 24th and preferably after dark. Even now I don't like hearing it played in the malls throughout the entire month of December.

Other church visits were purely accidental. When the church bells rang on a Saturday afternoon, I knew that a wedding was about to take place, and my friends and I would interrupt our play and run to see the bride. Other neighbors would come to gawk, and soon a crowd would be waiting in front of the church for the bride and groom to arrive together. After the wedding guests were seated in their respective rows, the bride and groom walked down the isle together, the onlookers following to take seats in the back of the church. It mattered not that we didn't know the bride or the groom or any of the guests; we were simply enchanted by the bride all in white.

So I decided that I wanted to be more connected to St. Gabriel, our neighborhood church. For that reason, I joined a youth group of eight neighbor girls who would meet once or twice a month in one of the church's back rooms. Sitting on folding chairs in a circle, we talked about school, sang folk songs, and played board games such as "Aggravation." We also read the Bible and discussed what we read. I believed every word I read, no questions asked. The Bible was the word of God, and who was I to question His word?

We also read other books, and because we didn't have a leader we took turns preparing short talks about a favorite book or piece of music. The church had a record player, and we listened to music. The Bible discussions became sporadic over time, but the fellowship with the girls and the fact that we attended the same church brought with it a sense of belonging. This was *my* church, and reinforcing this feeling of being a member of a group were the once-weekly catechism classes I took with the pastor who would eventually confirm me. I was a Lutheran, baptized in the faith, and therefore I would be confirmed in a couple of years. My class studied the Ten Commandments, the Apostles' Creed, the Lord's Prayer, Baptism, the Sacrament of the Altar, and the Forgiveness of Sins. Plus I fell in love with the pastor, who unfortunately was married with a family.

I became totally absorbed in my Bible studies, and the words Jesus and God crossed my lips easily and often. My being so wrapped up in the catechism and the Bible led me to proselytize at home, but my family in turn made fun of me. On Sunday mornings when I left the house for church, Klaus would yell, "Say hello to Jesus for me!" My face burned with fury at my brother, which of course was not a Christian reaction. My parents told him to let me be, but why didn't they make him go with me or for that matter tell Doris to get some religion? In my view, the whole family could have used some spirituality, by God! Going to church on Sunday would make them feel good and inspire them to be better people. I asked my parents, "Why will you let me be confirmed if you don't believe in God?" and they replied that they believed in God but they didn't want to go to church because they could worship anywhere, not requiring an edifice to do it in. They wanted me to be confirmed because that's what Lutherans did and somehow our family was Lutheran although most of us declined to go to church. My parents and siblings were Lutherans only by way of history and custom and not necessarily by belief, and there was nothing more to be said about the matter.

What I didn't realize then was that Mutti was already a saint without even having to attend church. She was what people called *"eine einfache Frau,"* a plain woman not in any derogatory sense as one might label someone lacking a higher education, but with a much-admired good heart. Anna Behnke was famous in the neighborhood for her kindness and good works. From my Papa I learned (among other things) how to cut a proper edge on a flower bed; from Mutti I learned compassion and the meaning of Love Thy Neighbor. She was a role model of what a good Christian should be and do. But I rejected her as my role model because she didn't go to church! There was I, a dogmatic teenager with her head full of the gospels but inflexible and self-righteous in quite an un-Christian way. To me, going to church equaled being a good Christian. I accepted Jesus as my savior and I tried to be non-judgmental, but I remained critical of my family.

Well then. My catechism classes and Sunday services kept me on the Christian track. Leaving church on Sunday mornings to talk to the many fellow worshippers I knew by now made me feel at home, so much so that the social part of church, the meetings with my friends, the trips to the church library, and the secret adulation for my pastor became more intensely important than learning about God, Jesus, and the Bible. I was a fraud! Why couldn't I just be a good student, concentrate, and not get so distracted by social doings?

The year is 1955, and ten years after war's end the last prisoners of war return to Germany from camps in Russia. Ten thousand of them. Some are fathers who have never seen their children.

My Onkel Werner, Papa's brother who had gone missing in Russia, was not one of those destined to return, and my Tante Gretchen declared him dead. Her declaration put an end to his life. For all purposes, he dissolved, leaving only a photograph of himself in uniform. His return, something she desired so much, wasn't going to happen. Maybe he died the way I envisioned it in my nightmares—frozen to death on Mother Russia's ice, giving his life for the Fatherland. Tante Gretchen cried each and every time she visited us, both before and after the declaration of death, but life went on and what else was there to do? She had to raise my cousin by herself. I, on the other hand, had Mutti and Papa and absolutely no idea of what it was like to lose someone dear.

Princess Ira of Fürstenberg, fifteen, marries Prince Alfonso of Hohenlohe-Langenburg, thirty-one. He buys her emeralds worth 1,2 million Marks. James Dean dies in a car crash on September 30.

Doris and I cried for days over James Dean, luxuriating in our grief. Although I was only fourteen, I dreamed of marrying him at a young age. If the princess could do it at fifteen, then I could at fourteen. Klaus thought we were stupid to cry for James Dean; after all, whose fault was it that he died? His own. Together Doris and I assaulted our brother (something I couldn't do on my own because he was stronger than I was), punching him while he was lying on the couch and then jumping on him, at which point he wrestled both of us to the floor and it was all over in a second. At that point we really had something to cry about because he had given us "a thousand needles," twisting our wrists until they burned.

James Dean's last movie, "Rebel without a Cause," had not yet been released in Germany and so we had to wait. We didn't have a television to follow stories about him and had to rely on magazine photos we cut out and taped to the wall in our room.

◆   ◆   ◆

I was in eighth grade now and my parents' dream of college for me was slipping away ever further because my grades were not good or at least improving. I don't remember ever getting a helping hand from my teachers to get me back on track. Parents didn't participate much in the life of the school then, unless they came to a special occasion like a school play or to see about a child who had gotten into trouble. Maybe my teachers talked to my parents, but I can't be sure now. If Papa and Mutti had been consulted, they would automatically have taken the teacher's side. The outcome of a "conference" would have been close parental supervision of homework time.

What I do remember is that I liked only one subject: English. Instead of going home right after school, I took the subway to the *Amerika Haus* located in downtown Hamburg. The building was modern (now I would call it square concrete), with many huge glass windows just as I imagined the look of buildings in America. Modern and clean. No bombed-out buildings in the United States! When I stepped through the door of the *Amerika Haus*, I felt like I had traveled through time and space. I left the agonizing rebuilding process that was going on all around me behind at the door and walked into a carefree atmosphere where I was welcome and where it didn't matter that I was a poor student. I chose the books I wanted to read and spent many hours at this American information center, reading magazines and newspapers, watching movies, listening to lectures about America, and borrowing books from the library. So my love affair with America had its beginning about that time when I was fourteen. The seed had been planted: some day I would go to America.

◆　　　◆　　　◆

Because my parents couldn't afford to take us on vacations, I had to make do with trips in and around Hamburg and to the Baltic Sea. I remember riding bikes (Doris had her own, bought with money she had earned as an apprentice; I had to borrow one) from Hamburg through Lübeck to Grömitz, at least six hours of hard pedaling. We didn't take much in the way of clothes—a bathing suit, shorts and shirts, and maybe a sweater.

Grömitz was an up-and-coming resort. When Papa had engagements in Grömitz and had to stay there for a month or so, Doris and I visited him a couple of times. We were put up in the same *Pension* (bed and breakfast) where he stayed, sleeping on cots in his room and earning our room and board by doing dishes for the *Pension*. We did dishes in the backyard, in two deep ceramic bowls sitting on a wooden table. One bowl had cold water with dish soap, the other cold, clean water for rinsing. I always found it odd that the mother and daughter, who owned the *Pension,* should ask us to do the dishes in cold water (Mutti always used hot water). Greasy breakfast dishes weren't easy to clean in cold water, but saving money on fuel was more important.

When done with the chores, we spent time on the beach with our Papa. One day, he put us on a boat that spent half an hour undulating on the surface of the Baltic during which time both my sister and I got sick, thus putting an end to our seafaring days for the time being.

From the promenade, a walkway by the beach, we watched the people sitting on the terraces of the restaurants—elegantly dressed women wearing hats and men in smart suits. Those were the well-heeled people Papa and the band were entertaining. I often thought of Mutti at home, in her flowery smocks that looked like big aprons to me, and wished that she could be sitting on this terrace with someone serving her coffee and cake.

The disparity in German people's standard of living was quite apparent, and I felt envy of these "rich" people, anger at my parents for not being part of this group, and sadness and even pity for how hard they had to work just to get by day to day. But I was just a kid, and while on the beach with my Papa and Doris I pushed these thoughts out of my head and threw myself into alternately jumping around in the Baltic and stretching out on the warm sand.

Recollecting these visits with my Papa also brought back a vague memory of my first fleeting thoughts of someday becoming a stewardess. I don't know why exactly I thought of this there in Grömitz—maybe the smartly dressed men and women sitting on terraces while sipping coffee reminded me of pictures I had seen of people mindful of their finery as they stepped from airplanes.

I was not doing well academically. In fact, I was just squeaking by in most subjects, especially physics, chemistry, and math. My parents' desire for me to study music was falling on deaf ears, and it just so happened that in 1955 the first Lufthansa propeller plane took off from Munich, flying on to Frankfurt and then Hamburg. Pictures in the newspaper showed young women in navy-blue suits and jaunty caps serving passengers whose legs stretched comfortably all the way out in front of them. I now wanted to be a stewardess, mostly because I would have a chance to see the world. Yes, my sense of adventure would be well-served by this career choice. I just wasn't crazy about the flying part.

My cousin Wolfgang, who wanted to be a pilot, had been tested in a drum to see if he could tolerate air turbulence. He was rotated in this drum until he threw up, a sure sign that he was unsuitable for navigating a plane. Although I had never flown, I remembered getting sick on a boat and I imagined the same thing would happen to me on a plane.

I and my friend Sabine, who also wanted to be a stewardess, went to the Hamburg airport several times just to soak up this glamorous atmosphere of pilots and planes and stewardesses as pretty as their pictures and so self-assured, not at all green around the gills. The airport was such a novelty that it soon became a regular sightseeing destination, a place where one would take out-of-town guests. The whole notion gives me the giggles now. But back then this dream of flying, speaking several languages, and maybe falling in love with a passenger or pilot lasted for about a year. Finally, I gave up the dream, mostly because the in-air part scared me.

Other memories of 1955 were captured in photographs: my parents' 25th wedding anniversary and my sister's confirmation, two events which brought the whole family and neighbors together. In one photo, Mutti's sisters Klara and Gretchen, her cousins, and my Onkel Heini were in the living room crowding around an extended table laden with food and china. The china was new and bought on credit for this occasion. Mutti wore a silver crown in her hair hovering above a black dress with a large, lacy white collar tacked on, not permanently attached. All my aunts wore black dresses as well and smiled profusely for Papa's camera.

At one point in the evening, I saw my parents standing in the kitchen, kissing, his hands on her breasts. She was giggling and saying, "Oh, Henry," and glancing at me as I stood grinning at the other end of the hall. I liked seeing them stand close together, so intimate, their affection obvious to all after all these years of marriage. I wanted a tender, loving husband just like my Papa was.

In a momentary flash I can see Mutti standing in front of a mirror with one hand on her stomach, sucking it in, and then standing sideways to see if her profile had improved any. And yet her roundness, which could not be denied, made her desirable in Papa's eyes, I imagine.

The anniversary celebration continued all day. Photos show a living room that had changed over the post-war years. Now there were lamps and sheer curtains, although we still had black-out shades at the windows because there wasn't enough money to buy drapes that could be drawn for privacy. The drapery panels at either end of the windows covered the uneven edges of the sheers.

My parents were still struggling ten years after the end of the war. Mutti may have had to use her creditworthy standing in the community to buy the food for this celebration, but it would be paid for by and by. If she was worried about the expense, she didn't show it. Instead, there was genuine happiness on her face as she smiled and talked with her guests. My uncles smoked cigars and told jokes, and even if we had heard the jokes before we still laughed. It seemed that my ancestors were present too, watching from their photos hanging on the walls.

Everybody stayed not only for coffee and cake, but also for the evening meal. Mutti had a talent for creating eye-catching dinner platters. Generous plates of cold cuts, cheeses, fish, and tomatoes and radishes cut and carved to resemble flowers. Several baskets containing black and white bread, as well as butter dishes were spread out across the table.

Ten years after the war, when butter was available again, Mutti made butter roses for her company. She would fill a crystal bowl about the size of an individual custard dish with unsalted butter and smooth it out with a knife. Then she would dip a teaspoon into a bowl of very hot water and, starting at the edge of the dish, push the warm spoon into the butter about half an inch deep. Then she moved the spoon toward the center and repeated the process, each time pushing a small amount of butter forward which then looked like a petal when it reached the center of the dish. She repeated this process around the entire bowl, leaving petals which formed a "rose." Guests were usually reluctant to be the first to dig into this butter rose. But everybody loved butter, and so sooner or later someone extended their knife to it to make an open-faced sandwich with cold cuts and cheese. An open-faced sandwich would always be eaten using a knife and fork (as opposed to a sandwich made of two pieces of bread, which was eaten without the use of implements). Hot tea would be served with dinner.

I was already thinking about the dishes that I would have to help wash by hand because we didn't have a dishwasher, an unheard-of appliance at that date. Doris and I had to do the dishes twice, after coffee and after dinner, because we didn't have enough china to go around for both meals. Using paper plates, even when they were available, would not have been considered proper. They would have been all wrong, and my parents insisted on doing things "right," in the time-honored manner, the way things had always been done. Unless, of course, there was a war going on. In that case, celebrations would have been more makeshift.

Another big celebration in 1955 was Doris's confirmation. While I continued with my religious studies, Doris had finished hers, and on the day of her confirmation she was having a big party. Again relatives, friends, and neighbors came to our house bearing presents. My parents' bedroom furniture was moved somewhere and the French doors between the bedroom and living room opened so that guests could eat in one room and dance or talk in the other.

The confirmation party was and wasn't a solemn occasion. Doris had now been accepted in the community of the faithful. To honor this momentous occasion, she wore a black taffeta dress and black pumps, looking as though the cross has been passed to her and she alone was to bear it from then on. My sister, a sorrowful black lamb of Christ. Her guests were smiling, but Doris wasn't, although her expression soon enough changed to delight when she opened her presents—slips, pajamas, chocolate, and hosiery bag for the stockings she was going to start wearing one day (hosiery, another sign of growing up!) Then too, she received money whose glint caught my eye, and I later tried to talk her out of some of it but she wouldn't let go of a cent.

Doris was sixteen and my trailblazer. She achieved the milestones before I did and showed me what they were all about. Ahead of me by two years, she modeled for me what I was still anticipating for my future teenage years.

In the meantime, my misery at school continued. The eighth grade is mostly a blur, but I recall feeling anxious many mornings as I boarded the streetcar knowing that I wasn't prepared for the day's tests. I was no longer motivated to put in hour after hour studying physics, chemistry, and math when all I was interested in was English. Not even German tugged on me, and in Latin I had lost the thread that would make sense of all the rules. Latin was supposed to give me a good basis for learning all Western languages, (according to my parents who had urged me to take it rather than French). Certainly my thinking processes would strengthen by my analyzing the connection between syntax and meaning, and daily exercises would, per my school, lead to perseverance, precision, and conscientiousness. Then again, translation of Latin into German would lead to better understanding and manipulation of the mother tongue. Little did I know back then that in my life the benefits of Latin would prove to be true!

In my confusion-riddled eighth-grade brain, I saw no other way than to cheat on tests when necessary, mostly by glancing at the paper of the girl next to me. My teachers had multiple eyes that swept the entire room, and now and then I would get caught and then had to step up on the platform to the teacher's desk for a whispered conversation about the offense that I had just been caught in. If the teacher gave me a second chance, I was sent to another room to finish the test all by myself. Such embarrassment! How humiliating! So in childish fashion I swore that I would get better at not getting caught!

◆   ◆   ◆

What I remember most about the eighth grade was our class trip to Sylt, a Frisian island in the North Atlantic off the coast of Germany. Class trips were a staple of German school life, and a great deal of preparation went into their planning and organization. We were supposed to come away knowing more about the geography, biology, culture, economy, and sociological makeup of the area we were visiting. And to assure that this trip would be a success, lots of playtime, fun, and recreation were included. The teacher was a pivotal figure in this huge endeavor. Leading thirty adolescent girls was our class teacher, Herr Dr. Bargstaedt.

On Saturday, September 3, 1955, I stood on Track 4 of the *Hauptbahnhof,* Hamburg's main train station. The place was buzzing with the chatter of all the eighth-grade girls, their mothers and fathers, and other family members as they waited for the train to the first class trip. I really wanted to get away from my parents and school, and my friends and I agreed that we needed this break from the daily routine of classes and homework. So the trip meant blessed freedom from reports and tests. As we stood on the platform amidst our luggage (one suitcase and one bag for each girl) getting last-minute instructions from our parents, we weren't thinking about the written report that would be due shortly after our return to Hamburg. But "What I learned from my trip to Sylt," would be the subject, I was pretty sure. Maybe I should take notes. Alas, just a fleeting thought.

Mutti was seeing me off, and now she said with some concern in her voice, "Christelchen, make sure that you dry your bathing suit completely before you wear it again the next day. You don't want to catch cold."

"Mutti, I know, I know, I'm fourteen and old enough to know how to deal with wet bathing suits, but if I had two it wouldn't be such a hassle."

This was a sore point between us because I had asked for a second bathing suit to bring along. But there hadn't been enough money to buy another one, so now I had to do with one. There I was on the train platform, arguing with her, feeling indignant and guilty about feeling indignant. I knew full well that it took a major effort on my parents' part to raise the money for this trip. They wanted me to go, of course, but money was still tight and clothing and trips were low on the list of priorities.

The permission slip hung around the house like an uninvited guest. But finally I returned it to my teacher relieved and a little annoyed and apologetic for returning it at the last minute. I worried about how my clothes would measure up. There were girls in my class whose parents were better off than mine, and I was envious of the clothes they seemed to wear with such ease and assurance. Their shirts and skirts always matched, and they had at least six different outfits, one for each school day, and more than one pair of shoes.

I should have been more grateful, because I know my parents were doing the best they could. Ten years after the end of the war, life was not yet back to normal, and travel was not commonplace. In my mind, only rich people could afford to travel, especially by air as was again possible within Germany after Lufthansa began service in April of that year, 1955. Passenger trains were once more running and so were freight trains, not only to deliver goods but to transport German prisoners of war home from Russia.

Now I was about to go on my first long trip, and in my head I was repeatedly going over the contents of the suitcase Mutti and I packed. A bathing suit was just one of a list of required pieces of clothing; others were pants, shorts, two pairs of shoes, socks, tops, underwear, sweaters, and if possible raingear. I took along my old, dark blue raincoat with white stitching on the pockets for those inevitable rainy days, but I told myself that I wouldn't really need the protection because I could only see myself on the beach with the sun shining on me and giving me that longed-for hazelnut tan.

For the trip, the school had sent home lists of things to bring and not to bring. Sheets, pillowcases, and towels were required. We couldn't bring any clothing not on the "To Bring" list and no jewelry or makeup whatsoever. God forbid we should bring an extra pair of underpants! The list had the following notation: "Bed wetters have to be identified in strictest confidence. They have to bring a waterproof mattress cover and at least two sheets." I was very relieved that I wasn't a bed wetter because to confide the fact to someone if I had been would have ruined the trip before it began. And then to actually be a bed wetter on a trip would have been mortifying. Of course, we all started wondering who the bed wetters were.

The train was pulling into the station, and it was time to say farewell. Mutti and I hugged, and instantly I felt such shame over the way I had spoken to her that I could barely look at her because the love in her eyes never diminished no matter what outrageous things I said. "I promise to write cards," I assured her, and then everybody began pushing and shoving to board the train.

I wanted to be in a compartment with my friends, so I hurried along the narrow corridor checking each compartment for those seats, holding my suitcase in front of me at times in order to leave some room between me and the girl in front of me. I felt panicky in this narrow corridor with all these girls (some relying on their parents' help) intent on locating just the right seat. Finally, six of us settled in a compartment for the five-hour ride. I had been on trains before, having gone to my grandparents' house just outside of Hamburg, but this train was meant for long-distance travel. Instead of wooden benches, there were seats upholstered in dark, floral prints. There were even pleated drapes on the windows, open now and hooked with brass rings onto each corner of the window.

I was excited to be going to an island and especially to see the Atlantic Ocean, having read about how we could walk on the ocean floor when the tide was out. My best friend Sabine, who was sitting next to me, turned to me and said, "What happens when the water comes back and you are still out there somewhere and all around you there is water coming in, and your feet are heavy with mud and they get stuck? It'd be like walking in slow motion. How would you ever make it back to shore?" I didn't want to consider this disastrous scenario at the moment, so I told her to imagine lying on the beach. She said, "I don't really like lying in the sun," and at that point I ordered her to shut up.

I had my own worry that I wasn't prepared to share with anyone because, after all, it might not happen: I was worried about getting homesick, like I did once when I stayed at my grandparents'. I had bamboozled them into thinking that I had eaten a bunch of very green, unripe, sour gooseberries from one of the many berry bushes around the farm and had moaned and groaned that I was having a bad stomach ache rather than tell them I was homesick. Later, I came to be known as Miss Independence, the "I'll-go-anywhere-for-any-length-of-time girl." So what if I got homesick on this trip and what would I use as an excuse for my misery? I told myself that in that case my friends would help cheer me up, and staying busy would keep my mind off Mutti. Was it Mutti or the familiar surroundings I thought I would miss?

As the train inched out of the station, we pulled the top part of the window down so we could look out and wave a handkerchief or a scarf at our families standing there on the platform. I sighted Mutti in her beige rain coat and small, black hat that used to have a net to cover her face until the netting fell apart. Without that touch, the hat looked like the shell of a turtle. Mutti was smiling, but was she feeling sad or relieved at my departure? I wanted to know if I would miss or be missed.

Eventually, we girls settled in for some talking, joke-telling, and singing. After entertaining ourselves with those activities for a while, Anke read aloud the opening chapter of the romance novel she had brought along, *Regina's Secret Love*. We were feeling a little jittery, apprehensive about this Schulheim (school home) we were traveling to. How were we all going to get along twenty-four hours a day for two whole weeks?

And I was also wondering about how I was going to relate to Dr. Bargstaedt, my Latin teacher, in this more relaxed setting compared to the strict one at school. I think he disliked me because I didn't always do my work, and I disliked him because I felt he didn't appreciate my work habits (such as they were). He scared me, this mostly gentle man who always took time to listen but who could be very tough and curt in the classroom. He didn't excuse laziness, and now would he be able to see past my careless attitude at school to the girl with a sense of humor that I was? Would this insecurity-ridden shell I had wrapped around myself finally break so that I could accept this teacher? Maybe I was on a journey that would teach me something about my teachers as people. About our chaperone, the assistant Latin teacher Fräulein Bormann, everyone was in agreement: she was terrific and well-suited to deal with teenagers.

The train took us through Schleswig-Holstein, the northernmost state in Germany. Miles and miles of wheat had been harvested and the fields looked stubby and cold under a heavy, rain-laden sky. The monotonous landscape had a dulling effect on us, and we slept until we reached the coast. A narrow causeway was the only land connection between us and our destination: the island of Sylt. The narrow strip of land was just wide enough for a train, and as far as we could see there was water surrounding us. We had thought of lying on sandy beaches under a bright sun, but after almost five hours on the train we arrived at *Westerland,* the main city on the island, under rainy skies. An ominous beginning to this long-awaited trip. There were no busses to get us, so we trudged the thirty-minute walk to the *Schulheim.*

At least our suitcases were being transported by a truck just ahead of us on the quiet island road. Our bedraggled group didn't feel like singing, and the only sounds were the shuffling of our shoes on the gravel road and the whistling of the wind across the waves. Oh, to be in a car now! But there were no cars passing us, even though they were allowed on the island. It seemed that people came here to hike from town to town; in fact, hiking was one of the main activities of vacationers. What's a day without hiking? Not much, as we found out over the next couple of weeks.

"Sabine," I said to my friend, "did you pack enough stuff for cold days, because I might need to borrow a sweater. I don't think I brought enough warm clothes."

"I didn't either," she replied, "I never thought it would be this cold." How were we going to stay warm in our beds that probably lacked feather comforters?

Sylt is an island that is best visited in June, July, or August when there is a slight chance that the sun will shine and the North Sea will warm up to a tolerable sixty degrees Fahrenheit. A temperature just warm enough for Germans to frolic in the waves, throw themselves into the foam of the breaking water, and exclaim over and over how *erfrischend* the water was, how very refreshing.

We had visions of sunny days on the beach, but at the moment we were traipsing along on a country road as the cold rain drenched us to the bone, until our bodies shivered and our teeth chattered. The wind blew constantly, and the salt from the sea clung stubbornly to our lips and even tongues. The talking had virtually stopped.

Finally we reached the school home in Wenningstedt. It felt good to be out of the wind and inside a dry building. When our rooms were assigned, at least the guessing was over and we knew at last who was going to be in which room. There was nothing more important than being in the same room with our friends; it could make or break the entire trip. Sabine and I hugged, overjoyed to be in the same dorm.

There were some long faces, though, because two of the girls didn't want to be in *our* room. Irmgard, whose best friend ended up in another dorm, was now sitting on the edge of her bed and sobbing into her hands. Still, we knew that our teachers wouldn't budge and nobody wanted to complain to them, least of all Irmgard who was quite a shy girl. After two days in our room she had quietly accepted her fate and even played along with our goofy fashion shows and storytelling.

And then there was Konstanze who didn't want to be in our room because she thought she was intellectually superior to us. She accepted her fate too, but she never joined in with us.

The rooms were spartan, the floors wooden with no rugs to cushion our steps. My room had nine beds, nine chairs, and one big, rectangular table. My bed was by a big window through which I could see the ocean, which lifted my spirits in giving me a view of the dark water in the distance. I loved the Baltic as well as the North Sea, their endlessness being somehow soothing.

Each girl was assigned a tiny space in a pine wardrobe (comparable to the size of an American school locker). As I unpacked and put my things away, I realized that the clothes on the "To Bring" list fit exactly into this locker space with not an inch to spare. Woe to the girl who brought that extra pair of underpants!

After we made our beds with the sheets we'd brought along from home, we changed into dry clothes, combed our hair, and made our way to the dining room. It was 6:00 p.m. by now, and we were famished. We sat on wooden benches at long tables across from each other as delicious *Leberkäse*-sandwiches (meatloaf) and chewy black bread slices spread with *Schmalz* (cold bacon grease) were set on platters before us.

I wolfed down two of the *Schmalz* sandwiches and they reminded me of home, except Mutti sometimes added apple pieces and onions and let it all simmer before she cooled it and we put it atop the bread. I didn't eat much Leberkäse at home, but tonight I was too hungry to be particular and I devoured at least one of them with great gusto. When the platters were empty, a woman with a smiling face brought out more, announcing, "Eat as much as you want, we are used to big appetites here. The ocean air makes you hungry." We didn't know yet how true that was. We were thirsty too, and until we were water-logged drank hot black tea from thick, oatmeal-colored mugs.

Before we returned to our rooms, Dr. Bargstaedt read the rules of the home from a manual, but the only ones I now recall are: keep rooms tidy, make beds, put away clothes, and discard junk. It had been a long day. We should have been tired but talked on and on while lying beneath our blankets. Ulla said, "I wonder why Bargstaedt brought his wife and child along? Do they usually go on these class trips? I've never heard of it. Is she a chaperone? Do we talk to her when we have a problem? She doesn't know any of us and we don't know her. I'd rather talk to *Schrubber*" (our nickname for Fräulein Bormann who had hair like a *Schrubber,* or brush).

I agreed with Ulla, "I like Schrubber too. She listens and she's a girl." As it turned out, we talked to Schrubber all the time about things like how to dry our wet clothes, how we could get out of taking yet another hike, would she tell the kitchen staff please not to put so many onions in the potatoes? Important things like that. Soon, on our first night there, we finally exhaled and I could hear some of the girls breathe deeply in and out as the rhythm of the water lapping at the shore gently rocked me to sleep.

For the next day and all the days to come our activities were thoroughly planned out. We visited every corner of the island, all ninety-nine square kilometers of it. Sylt, one of the North Frisian Islands in the North Sea, almost touches Denmark at its northernmost point. Settled around 1430 A.D., some of the prehistoric mounds or hills indicate that the island was first inhabited around 3000 B.C. by Jutes, a Germanic tribe, and later, around 850 A.D., by Frisians, another Germanic tribe from the islands off the coast of the Netherlands. Fishing for haddock and herring was their main occupation. It wasn't until the 1880s that Sylt was "discovered" as a vacation place.

Nestled in the dunes were whitewashed cottages covered by reed roofs, some of them owned by the descendants of those fishermen. The lucky Germans who could afford to take vacations here rented these cottages or perhaps just a room in one of them. The fresh air, the bracing North Sea wind, the miles of dunes that made hiking a challenge were all considered to be healthy for a person. By 1895, ten thousand people from all over Europe were visiting Sylt every year. After

World War II, tourism kept increasing, especially in the summer, but in 1955 the island hadn't yet seen the tourism explosion that was to start in the sixties.

In 1955, Sylt was a sleepy, beautiful island with white sandy beaches, tall dune grasses, and purple heather. By the time we arrived in September, most of the tourists had gone back home. We were to crisscross the island several times, always on foot or on rare occasions by taking the slow little train, nicknamed the *Rasende Emma* (speeding Emma) because it gave us time to hop off, pick a few flowers for making wreaths to put in our hair later, and then jump back on. It was also known as *Käseschieber*—or a wheel of cheese being slowly pushed by the train.

Eighth graders from Lerchenfeld had been coming here for years because Sylt was close to Hamburg, and the trip was affordable for most parents, some of whom were still struggling financially ten years after the end of the war. We were here to develop camaraderie, to have fun as a group, to play, to get some rest, and to learn something about geography, biology, oceanography, and island life in general. In these we were continuing a long-standing tradition. Looking out the window on this first morning on the island, I could see that the ocean was only a few minutes away from the school home, but I couldn't see the beach because we were on a cliff and the drop was steep at the end of the walk from the home. I could see white dunes and tall sea grass weaving and bending in the breeze. The air smelled musty from the marine life decaying on the bottom of the ocean. Nothing, not even the gray clouds hanging overhead, could diminish my happiness at being here. The anticipation of getting to know this whole island made me want to round up everyone and say, "Let's go! We've got things to do today." Our chaperones only wanted us to get our feet wet on this first day, to get used slowly to the water temperature, to the cold and salty air, and to the wind whipping around us. I was awed by the huge ocean and the white caps of the waves crashing toward the shore. How much fun it would be to throw myself into those waves!

After spending the first morning outdoors, we had worked up an appetite and we couldn't wait for lunch. We took just enough time to change into dry pants and then devoured whatever was set in front of us, most likely boiled or fried potatoes, meat or fish, and vegetables. All this was served family style, each dish passed around and bowls filled again and again until we were almost bursting and couldn't eat another bite.

Quiet time, from 1:00 p.m. to 2:30 p.m. seemed endless but welcome at first. Then, as we got used to life on the island and developed a certain toughness, we didn't sleep as much and quiet time turned into an opportunity to talk, clown around, and amuse ourselves with fashion shows featuring beach clothing. As long as we didn't get too noisy, our teachers let us be.

At 3:30 p.m. we had a quick snack, usually coffee with milk and cake or some other sweet. After that, it was time for another hike, long enough to have us return with our tongues practically hanging out but with energy yet to dive into mountains of sandwiches stacked up in front of us. As was the custom, dinner consisted of bread and cold cuts like salami, ham, and pork as well as cheese, smoked fish, and tomatoes or cucumber slices. I liked all of it and even better because the kitchen staff had made the sandwiches ahead of time, so we didn't have to make them ourselves and spend time passing around platters of cold cuts and cheese with bread and butter. Hot black tea was served with the evening meal, and several times the kitchen staff even made us hot chocolate.

Sometimes there was dessert, like raisin soup with lots of raisins swimming around in some kind of sweet, soupy liquid, and when it was set in front of me my face told exactly what I thought of it. I couldn't hold back the disgust I felt—"*Igitt!*" But then I ate it anyway, because waking during the night with a growling stomach was worse.

The daily routine didn't vary. We got up at 7:00 a.m. and made our beds, swept the wooden floor, swept part of the hallway, assembled at 8:15 a.m. in front of the "goodweather" or "badweather" door, marched into the dining room, ate, then went on a hike or to the beach, after which we had lunch, then quiet time, and another hike in the late afternoon. Dinner followed at around 7:30 p.m. after which we took another hike in the dunes when it wasn't raining.

Judging by the numerous hikes we took, we saw the entire island several times. I think our teachers were trying to tire us out so that we would be quiet at night, and their strategy worked. Most nights we fell into our beds and off to deep sleep without further singing, talking, or joking.

Sometimes we took turns reading a few pages from the romance novel we had started on the train, but mostly our eyes were too heavy from the wind, salty water, and fresh air to concentrate. Still, we had to get through *Regina's Secret Love* and find out the ending, knowing that all these romance novels we had seen our mothers reading ended happily, but still we wanted to know what Peter and Regina would do when at last he told her that he loved her. Would there be more than kisses, and how much more? We were all Reginas-in-waiting, instantly vaguely aroused and yet often disgusted by anything to do with sex.

There was much to discover yet. The list of the "must see" places was lengthy, and so we trudged off to Westerland, the main town on the island. It was raining at lunchtime so we were hopeful that we wouldn't have to go, but no such luck. Mere rain was no deterrent.

Among the old churches we had to see was a small church in *Alt-Westerland* (Old Westerland). It wasn't the church so much as the cemetery that was the must-see because here were buried people who were part of the history of the island, such as Dirk Meinerts Hahn who in 1838 had taken some locals to Australia on his sailboat. Those islanders who had wanted to escape this harsh place, so constantly cold and windy and offering only fishing for a living took a big chance with Meinerts Hahn, who subsequently delivered them safely to Australian soil and even managed to get some land for them to farm. To show their gratitude, the immigrants named the new place in Australia, Hahndorf. Dr. Bargstaedt pointed out another notable name carved on a gravestone. There lay Merret Lassen, who had had the distinction of having given birth to twenty-one children. One woman responsible for producing nearly enough offspring to make up a whole class like ours! I pretended to be Merret for a moment and asked my classmates, "And what would you children of mine like to eat today? Herring or herring?" They all yelled in unison, "Herring, please, and lots of it!" At this, did I see a little smile flicker across Herr Bargstaedt's face?

Another cemetery was on the list, this one for the nameless dead that had washed up on the beach. Maybe they had been sleeping on the beach and were surprised by the high tide. Maybe they had been drunk and lost their wits. Maybe they had been sailors who had washed overboard. The sea was all-powerful.

It was late in the afternoon, still raining, and all we cared about was getting back to the home as quickly as we could. We ran across meadows of heather and clover, while one of our classmates breathlessly told a love story about a rich landowner and his romantic adventures. Who cared about the rain when there was a love story to listen to?

It now appears obvious that we were completely preoccupied with relationships between men and women though we wouldn't have admitted it. Women in the romance stories we read and recited were always waiting for men to make the first move, at which they revealed themselves as being willing to do virtually anything the men wanted. It never occurred to us to question this scheme of things; in fact, we loved it! We, too, wanted to look into a lover's eyes and straightway be taken, devoured, ravished.

As we ran and talked, every now and then we would glance back at our teachers who were having a difficult time keeping up with us. Dr. Bargstaedt walked fast enough using his walking stick but having only one real leg slowed him down. His wife and their one-year-old daughter usually stayed with him, while our other teacher, Fräulein Bormann, tried to keep us from getting too far ahead of everyone else. They gave us just enough freedom to let off steam.

The next morning Germany's northernmost point, List, awaited us. Although the little Käseschieber train took us almost all the way there, several hours of hiking through the dunes still lay ahead of us. The old Germanic name for List, Lista, means *edge*, and here we were at the northern tip of the island first mentioned in a document from 1292 in which the Danish king turned the administration of List over to the Danish city of Ripen, making List a Danish possession up until 1864. That year in the Peace Agreement of Vienna, Denmark gave up the Duchies of Schleswig, Holstein, and Lauenburg to Prussia and Austria. From then on List belonged to Germany, as did Sylt.

Now, in 1955, we walked every inch of these magnificent dunes. They were *Wanderdünen,* wandering dunes, because their sand masses shifted several feet every year, from west to east. Some of them were more than ninety feet high and 5000-plus years old. The famous author Thomas Mann exclaimed on his first visit to List, "Multiply them [the dunes] by five and you think you are in the Sahara." Small wonder we thought of ourselves as a herd of camels being driven over the sand.

I ran up and down the dunes, kicking up the sand and rolling in it, and later dragging myself through the dunes, calves heavy with the effort of running through shifting stuff. I imagine we were allowed to rest for a short while and watch some of the hundreds of different birds, such as the swallows, storks, and larks that made their nesting grounds around the island.

The goal of this trip was to learn something about Sylt, and our teachers made sure we did because on every hike we visited churches, museums, and even burial mounds, the most famous of which were not very far from the school home. This particular mound, the *Denghoog,* had probably been built by the Jutes around 4500 B.C. (the Stone Age!), though the burial chamber had only been uncovered in 1868. A twenty-foot long walk opened into the burial chamber held up by twelve huge boulders; the walls were six feet high in the west, and almost five feet high in the east. A human skeleton had been found here along with many bones from several other burials. Amber jewelry, carved clay dishes, and flint weapons were also found in this burial site. I remember going into the burial chamber and having the urge to turn around immediately and plead, "Please let me out of here!" So dark and old and musty it was. I don't think I had the proper respect for what had been discovered here. Vaguely I remember comparing the chamber to my musty, old post-war Germany. Was I even then thinking of leaving my country?

Sometimes after quiet time in the afternoon, we wandered along the cliff not too far from the school home, skipping and singing, arms wrapped around each other's waists in our favorite style of walking. We thought any distance we had to cover would fly by if we sang folk songs. The marching rhythm of *Auf der Lüneburger Heide* (On the Lüneburg Heath) or *Das Wandern ist des Müllers Lust* (A Miller Likes to Travel) made the hiking go so much more easily.

Strolling close to the edge of the cliff gave us a thrill in more ways than one, because at the bottom of this stretch of steep cliff not far from the home happened to be a nudist beach, the FKK (*Freikörperkultur*), and we couldn't help but see that a few brave nudist souls were still there taking in the last warm rays of the autumn sun. Dr. Bargstaedt ahead of us on his bike must also have been taking in the sights, and we laughed because he couldn't fool us—we knew what he too was doing. Just a glance or two at the nude flesh told us girls that we would never do that, we who hid our budding breasts in bras we still didn't need.

At other times, we hiked in the dunes at night. I stayed close to my friends then, because who knew what might lurk in the shadows behind the tall grass or in the valleys of the dunes? I recall one night in particular, when we were huddled in the shallow of a dune while a thunderstorm revealed some magnificent sights to us. On top of the dunes the wind picked up the sand and swirled it around, the lightning illuminating every blade of grass, and for a second each blade looked like a shining sword ready to strike at the sound of thunder. I shivered with fear and longed for the safety of the home. Even now as an adult I feel so much better when I am inside a building looking out during a thunderstorm.

For a brief moment I picture my Mutti sitting in her easy chair by the living room window while a thunderstorm is rumbling outside. Every time a thunder booms, she grabs the pillow she is holding in her lap, covering her face with it and making muffled sounds of dread. Why she didn't move away from the window, I don't know. Maybe the lightning gave her a charge. In any case, I have inherited her fear of thunderstorms.

We had hiked hither and yon every day for a week. Since the weather wasn't good enough for stretching out on the beach, we hiked instead. There were no stores and no movie theaters to keep us occupied. There was, however, another building next to ours which housed boys, and although we made some small attempts at contacting them, such as by passing notes back and forth, nothing really happened except for some heartbreaking crushes. It so happened that a few of the girls (I was one of them) fell in love with the same sun-tanned, blue-eyed, golden-haired boy. My friend Karin lay in bed, lovesick and weeping. In a way, our flirtations by note and glance were entertainment far superior to any movie, more exciting even than listening to music or dancing with a girl.

One activity I will always remember was the *Wattwanderung*. There was a *Wattenmeer*, resembling mud flats, around the eastern coast of the island and when the tide was out we walked for miles in the direction of Denmark. Once we were on the flats, we realized that unless we carried them we would lose our shoes in the mud of the ocean floor, and so we took them off (just as my friend Sabine had envisioned) and carried them. Our feet sank into the mud and were immediately covered, with our legs looking like sticks firmly rooted in the ocean floor. Each step we took was a slow, deliberate motion, except in places where the mud was packed down more, solid with the mosaic of hundreds of organisms. The Watt was the breeding ground and nursery for herring, plaice, and sole, among other food fish.

For this Wattwanderung we had a guide who would tell us when to turn back, well ahead of the incoming tide. Every six hours, the floor of the ocean showed off its treasures, although we didn't see it quite that way when we tried to step over the hundreds of piles of sickening excretions of some creature or other. The guide told us that lug worms ate through the ground, making openings for other organisms and in the process letting water seep through. In less than six hours, this entire, endless bottom of the ocean would be flooded with salty water once again. I really disliked the way the slimy mud felt under my feet. Even so, we flung mud at each other until Schrubber shot a warning evil eye at us. If we got too wild with our ways, our free time was cancelled and we would have to spend quiet time in our rooms.

Most of the time we were dutiful and well-behaved girls. However, I do remember one time when we had simply had it with the interminable hiking. Another little town, Keitum, was on the list of must-see places that day. It had charming, whitewashed farmhouses with thick reed roofs. All around grew oaks, elms, alders, and hedges of hazelnut and whitehorn bushes. Keitum looked over the *Wattenmeer*, and it had a *Heimatmuseum* which depicted the history of the seafaring people of this island. Full of historic clothing, paintings, and pottery it was.

But we weren't for seeing any of it! Revolt was in our hearts, revolt well-planned out the night before. On this particular morning Dr. Bargstaedt's voice boomed, "Be downstairs in ten minutes." We didn't follow his command but instead we closed the drapes, jumped into our beds, and covered ourselves completely to pretend to be asleep even as we listened for the footsteps we knew we would soon hear. His angry voice, shouting at the girls in the room next to us to get out of bed, reached us and we moved not a muscle. Then he stood red-faced in our doorway, his big, solid frame filling the opening. "Get out of bed now. Get ready to hike," he thundered, not used to having his orders ignored. Still, his anger had the opposite effect on us. As soon as he left the room, we laughed until we almost burst. Of course, we hiked to Keitum that day.

When the sun was out and the sea was relatively calm we finally went to the beach. At last I got to submit myself to the waves, the force of the water lifting and pushing me forward until it threw me back on the beach. The receding water then joined the next wave on and on and on in a display of endless energy. For a moment I felt light-headed from the waves hitting my face, but when the next wave came I was ready to dive under or jump over, arms raised, my whole body expecting the wash-over. Our youthful energy seemed inexhaustible, and even when we were forced to swallow great gulps of salt water we would just spit out the brine and continue our water play until our bodies couldn't take any more pummeling.

The only girls who didn't brave the waves were the ones who were having their periods. Our teachers automatically excused us when we told them we had "our days." "*Dr. Bargstaedt, ich habe meine Tage,*" we would say, and he would reply, "Okay then just stay on the beach." The blessed event that perpetuated the human race incapacitated us and one by one made outcasts of us. In 1955, swimming in a pool or even the ocean was still taboo when the female body was discharging such a heinous substance as menstrual blood.

Out of the water and still in our wet bathing suits, we set out to work on our *Burg.* There were no cabins or bath houses for slipping out of our suits. Instead, we all learned how to change clothes quickly and efficiently by using a towel that we first draped around our waists, wiggling off the top part of the bathing suit with our backs turned to our teachers, pulling on a shirt (forget the bra), and then waggling out of the bottom of the bathing suit, dropping it in the sand and pulling on underpants and shorts. It only took a minute to do all this, but most of the time we just let the sun dry our bathing suits on us. My only bathing suit, a light pink one, had the disadvantage of being smocked all over, creating puffy little pockets that held the water longer than smooth-surfaced fabrics. Another unfortunate effect of smocking was that is made me look bigger than I actually was at age fourteen, and even at this young age I was already self-conscious of my plump bottom.

The work ahead of us was time-honored, handed down through generations and carried on without questions. Didn't everyone in the world make burgs or sand castles, spaces of their own on the beach? Germans might have liked to spend whole days on the beach, but they couldn't just lie around—they needed something constructive to do. So "Let's make a Burg," would come the cry, and out came the shovels and rakes for the fun to begin. The size of the Burg depended on the builders' level of ambition.

When our group started digging, (each dorm group made a Burg), we knew we wanted ours to be big enough to seat eight to ten people in case we had visitors in the form of our classmates. The hole was dug, and the resulting rim was pounded with shovels, hands, and feet to compact the sand in place. Thus the sand on the Burg's bottom was cool and firm. We created a small "doorway" into our sand fortress so we wouldn't have to jump in over the rim. The hand-smoothed rim was now ready for decorating, and for this purpose we had gathered shells of different sizes which we pressed into the damp sand to create sea horses, starfish, and sea urchins. Then, as the crowning touch, we spelled the name of our Burg, "Poseidon." I don't recall how we made that leap from Poseidon, the Greek god of the sea, to Dr. Bargstaedt, the Greek scholar, but it seemed appropriate and was innocently intended to please him. And indeed, he beamed with pleasure. Now we had to maintain our fortress, and so we repaired it every time we were on the beach, patching the rim because the high tide always reached out for our Burg while we hoofed it over the dunes on the next hike.

Other vacationers on the beach would never dream of using our Burg or mutilating it in any way. It was an unwritten law that a Burg was a private space, and unless the people who created it had not used it in a couple of days or had perhaps left the island, it wasn't to be touched.

There is a photo of me sitting in our Burg, surrounded by my girlfriends. They all have a look of anticipation on their faces, as if saying, "Come on, Chrille [my nickname], open it up now." I had a package on my lap, sent by my Mutti for my fourteenth birthday, and I was about to pull out whatever was in it. I removed the underwear first, and everybody grabbed for it because at this point we were all a little short of clean undergarments. We washed our cotton undies every night, but nothing dried in the clammy Sylt air and there were no electric dryers. So pieces of our very unsexy-looking lingerie lay dripping and air-drying for days at a stretch on the windowsills. When we were desperate, we were forced to wear our freshly-washed panties still slightly damp.

As I reached into the package again, I found the gummi bears, those chewy, red, yellow, green, and white pieces of candy shaped like their namesake. Squeezing the bear in half with the teeth made a satisfying squish as flavored sugar exploded in the mouth. Naturally I had to hand the bag around to everyone, because even at this distance I could hear Mutti's voice telling me, "Always share what you have and it will be returned to you twofold." She didn't say that sometimes it might take time to get favors back, but sharing was polite and so I did.

Now I got to the bottom of the package, and there I saw the best present of all—money! I can't say how much Mutti sent, but I do recall wishing in my typically ungrateful fashion that I had received it earlier because I had been chronically short of spending money on this trip. There were souvenirs that I wanted to buy! Things like pottery made on the island, woven napkins, and a soft, square shawl in rich, natural colors. How I envied the girls who had enough money so they didn't have to think about whether to buy this or that while I fretted all the time. And yet at the same time I knew that Mutti had done her utmost to send me any money at all. Over the years since then, silently or at times sobbing at the memory of my ungratefulness, I have thanked her a thousand times for this precious package.

Our time on the island was coming to an end, and there was only one more thing to do—take another hike! The day before we left was blustery, the sea churning and foaming and the waves rolling in as though they couldn't wait to break. They stole our Burgs, and instead of lying on the beach one last time we chased each other through the dunes, up and down, tumbling like gymnasts, doing cartwheels and rolling in the dune grass until we had spent our energy and Dr. Bargstaedt commanded us to return to the home for the big clean-up.

We pulled the blankets from our beds and dragged the bundles outside. Two girls grabbed each end of a blanket and shook it up and down until all the sand fell out. Had we really slept for two weeks under all this gritty sand? Then lockers had to be emptied, wiped down, and readied for inspection. Dr. Bargstaedt swiped his index finger over the shelves, and if he found any grains of sand the slovenly culprit had to wipe the shelves again, this time properly. Packing took very little time because every piece of clothing I had brought was dirty, so I simply jammed it all into the suitcase. But in between the items of clothing I carefully placed the few small pieces of pottery I had bought for my parents: an ashtray for Papa and a light brown sugar bowl etched with the outlines of shells for Mutti. I bought a woven napkin for myself to use as a doily on the chest of drawers in my room at home.

I slept fitfully, waking up several times during the night because I felt so chilled that even a dozen blankets were not enough to absorb the heavy, misty dampness that inhabited the room. It was barely dawn when I woke up to the sound of *Es tagt der Sonne Morgenstrahl* (The sun's morning rays are breaking), *Geburtstag ist heute* (a birthday song), and *Hoch soll sie leben* (a congratulatory

cheer), sung by my classmates in a semi-circle around my bed. Even Dr. Bargstaedt and Fräulein Bormann sang along. It was September 17 and my fourteenth
birthday. After breakfast, the whole class gifted me with a stuffed raven, which I
called *Schnacki*. (A raven makes a lot of noise, and *schnacken,* a northern German
colloquialism, means "to talk.") "Whose idea was this?" I asked, but nobody
would take credit for it. Still how wonderful it was that they remembered. And
that my teachers cared enough to join in the singing!

We had to hurry this morning, because—oh, the luxury of them—busses were
waiting to take us to the train station in Westerland. "Auf Wiedersehen, auf
Wiedersehen," cried the staff, waving handkerchiefs as we pulled away from the
school home. Were the cooks, the servers, and the dishwashers crying or laughing? Hard telling. If another group came in after we left, they would be here at
noon, so the staff disappeared inside as soon as we were at the end of the street
and turning onto the main road that would take us back to Westerland.

On the train back to Hamburg we talked about Dr. Bargstaedt, and my friend
Sabine said, "I think he's really a pretty good guy." "I don't disagree with you," I
replied, "but he's so reserved. I don't think I know him any better now than I did
before, except that I liked seeing him hold his baby daughter. Somehow it makes
him more human." "And another thing," I added, "I didn't like the way he
planned out every minute of every day," though this wasn't quite true because we
did have free time. "The next time I see this island, it'll be on my own terms. I'll
go there in the summer, and I'm going to lie on the beach all day." "But Chrille,"
she argued, "you know that he had to plan something for us every day. We were
supposed to learn something on this trip—about the island and history and culture and language and whatnot. Think about that." Sabine was right. A class trip
was supposed to be a mixture of fun and learning, and in hindsight this trip
accomplished both.

Smelling the North Sea, feeling the sand under my feet, and tasting the salt on
my lips, I had experienced calm. On some of our many walks, when the wind
whipped across the island, I had to push my body forward to get ahead. Or I
walked backwards at times against the force of nature. But most of all, the power
of the water awoke in me a life-long love for the sea. This first long trip had
opened up my world, and I now found myself wanting to see more of Germany.

Oberschule Lerchenfeld, Seventh grade, 1954
Christel front row, third from right

Class trip to Sylt in 1955—Student home in Wenningstedt

We named our burg "Poseidon"

Christel, Klaus, and Doris on Klaus' makeshift bed—early 1950s

Papa, Doris and I at the Baltic Sea, 1950s

My mother and her chickens, 1950s

6

Last year of high school and dance lessons

◆

1956–1957

In 1956, refrigerators are available for 600 Marks and are the dream of every woman, although some would rather have a washing machine. Self-serve stores are becoming more popular. West Germans eat 3000 calories per day, partly because they now eat more sugar, more white bread, and more candy. Germany has a standing army once again. The Soviet Union crushes an uprising in Hungary against the communist regime and 2700 people die. Marilyn Monroe marries Arthur Miller, and a dream wedding takes place in Monaco when Prince Rainier marries a commoner, Grace Kelly the film star.

In 1956, Doris and I were glued to a neighbor's television set (our family didn't have one yet) to watch every detail of this glamorous royal wedding. How romantic to arrive on a boat at your new kingdom (or princedom) and be met by your prince! Of course, they would live happily ever after, and every day would be a holiday. The sun would never cease to shine on them in their Mediterranean paradise, and they would never have to look at the ugly ruins of buildings. They would wear beautiful clothes every day, washed for them by their maids.

In our home Mutti washed all our clothes by hand because we couldn't yet afford a washing machine. On washday, the whole house got involved. Washday could be smelled as soon as one stepped in the door—the odor of detergent mixed with hot water, the steam from the water boiling on the stove in the kitchen flowing through the rooms and making them clammy and yet comforting at the same time, especially in the winter.

The washtub was the same one we used for our baths, and for rinsing sand off great quantities of *Grünkohl* (kale), a prized winter dish. For washday, the tub was set on a table in front of the kitchen window, so when Mutti looked out over the courtyard she could see the crisscrossing clothes lines awaiting her. She picked up the heavy pot with the hot water and carried it to the tub, spilling some on the floor.

Bent slightly, her stomach pressing against the metal of the tub, Mutti stood there for hours, scrubbing clothes against a washboard with a rectangular wooden frame and a corrugated metal surface. The water in the tub covered clothes which were about to be rubbed on the washboard. While they were soaking, some of the white cotton items like sheets were slowly boiled in a big pot on the stove. They had to be boiled before they could be washed just because that was how it was always done, period. Cotton items had to be boiled.

Now Mutti grabbed an item of clothing from the tub and placed it on the washboard, rubbing the piece up and down until it appeared clean to her seasoned eyes. Clean clothes were dropped into another tub for later rinsing.

Mutti was wearing one of her floral-patterned house dresses. All her dresses were flowered, but that didn't necessarily mean they were cheerful to the eye. Some were dark, with vines and grapes intermixed with undefined, fuzzy shapes, and I hated the way they looked on her. Over these short-sleeved shifts she wore an apron with an oversized pocket full of clothes pins. For now, she was determined to get everything that was soaking in the tub scrubbed and rubbed and all the dirt and grime removed.

Mutti worked at a steady strong pace. Although her hair was pulled back in a bun, a few strands came loose at which she lifted her arm to push them away from her face. Her hands were already red and puffy, but they were deft for having done laundry for so many years. She didn't waste any time eating or drinking while working.

Where was everybody? Why wasn't anybody helping her? It was a weekday, probably Monday, and Doris and Klaus were at work while I was busy with school. In my memory, I don't see Papa helping her, although he would have been at home because he worked at night. He might have been fixing something in the house; he was very good at that. Laundry, though, was woman's work, and that's why he wasn't there for her. My friends' mothers did the laundry for their families, so I didn't dwell on why it should be woman's work.

Mutti worked and worked. When one load was done, she put all the washed underwear, bras, shirts, and pants into another tub of clean water and rinsed everything several times, in the process wringing each item several times. Her arms and hands worked furiously, her back was bent. The rinsed clothes went into a basket that she picked up, and in hurrying down the hallway she left a trail of water because the basket was only wicker and the clothes were still somewhat dripping. Passing through our apartment door and the small hallway, through the house door, down three steps, alongside the house to the gate and into the courtyard, she finally put the heavy basket to rest. Another quick wringing of a blouse, a pillow case, or a sheet, and the pins began emerging in rapid file from her pocket as the clotheslines filled up. When washday included sheets, their weight dragged down the lines, so she grabbed a long stick which Papa had fashioned from a piece of wood. It featured a groove on the top which she positioned under the line, pulling it as she grunted with the effort and planting the other end of the stick in the dirt. Now the sheets could flutter.

When all the laundry was done, Mutti wiped the tubs and the floors and checked on the clothes every now and then to see if they were drying properly, repositioning a piece when it needed more flutter. When things were almost dry for easier ironing, the pins came off and clothes were folded and placed in the basket. Next day was ironing day and all the wash was pressed, from the bedding to underwear to towels. My father's work shirts had to be starched before they could be pressed. I helped iron towels because they were easy, whereas a tuxedo shirt seemed too complicated to do.

When I was first married and living in America, I ironed everything too. But not for long. It seemed that my American girlfriends had given up ironing towels and their husbands' underwear long ago and so I simply followed their example.

But back in Germany circa 1958, my parents finally bought a washing machine with an attached wringer though Mutti didn't take to it right away: the wringer had to be cranked, the water from the washing machine collected in a tub, the tub emptied into the kitchen sink, and after all that the clothes still needed hanging up on lines to dry. Electric dryers were not yet available, and even if they had been most apartments were not big enough to accommodate one. If it rained on washday, Mutti carried the baskets filled with wet clothes to the basement and hung them up to dry in our former air raid shelter where they would remain for days at a time because it was so damp down there. When not in use, the washer sat behind the door in my parents' bedroom, covered with a colorful scarf to hide the fact that it was a big machine.

◆   ◆   ◆

While Mutti worked very hard to keep up our home, I was continuing to slip at school. I was in the ninth grade now and my marks had not improved. At almost fifteen, my mind was elsewhere, away from my forbidding school. While improvements had been made, our classroom remained in the old building. Our chairs and desks slid all over the stone floor, helped along by us when we played "Bump the Desk" resulting in complaints from the class below us. The floor was not the only unfortunate feature of this room. There was something creepy about the old, decaying walls, a constant reminder that there had been a war and that all was still not well.

To date, I hadn't learned anything about World War II in any history class, though we kids knew we were living the aftermath of it. Of course, what with the Greeks and Romans and everything before and in between and after them, who needed to study recent history anyway? Maybe nobody knew yet how to teach it. My lack of formal knowledge about World War II came to embarrass me more than once when I lived in England as a nineteen-year old.

Our class stayed in one room for all periods. In this "home room," the blackboard didn't work the way it should have and at the end of each the day the eraser left lines of heavy chalk until at last the blackboard gave up the ghost and turned white. The device to hang up maps was broken, so we had to use a free-standing, metal map-holder that came crashing down every time one of us gave it the slightest touch (which happened fairly often), bringing the Roman Empire down with it.

The number of subjects we were taught hadn't changed from the seventh grade, only their level of difficulty. Some of my teachers were new, and I took a liking to my needlework teacher because she reminded me of my beloved Fräulein Düstersiek from grade school. I disliked physics the most because the subject didn't speak to me and I usually didn't understand what was going on. Plus anything with numbers failed to interest me even a little. My mind—or was it my body?—was elsewhere.

The bombed-out apartment house on the corner of our street was being rebuilt and I walked by it every day, sometimes several times a day. Frequently I walked to the corner and turned around, which gave me another chance to look at the site. I had my eyes on one of the construction workers. He was probably all of nineteen, but in my eyes he was an adult. And sexy. In warm weather he didn't wear a shirt, and his tanned upper body made me quiver. As soon as I got home from my "encounter" with this boy, I lay down on my bed and daydreamed about him, my hands roaming all over my body. I had known him for a few years because he was the son of friends of my parents'. But I had never paid any special attention to him before until that night when, it seemed, he became flesh and blood. He made my heart pound and my nether region tingle. I would stroll by the construction site, seemingly paying no attention but all the time knowing exactly where he was working, and when I would look up he was there with his legs spread over a beam, pounding nails into wood or whatever it was that construction workers did. When he saw me walk by, he would smile and my day would be complete. But sometimes he paid me no attention, and when that happened I had to find another reason to stroll by the site again because I had come to need his smile. I needed so to be acknowledged by the opposite sex.

And then one day the apartment house was roofed, and a wreath with streamers flew from its rafters. Reason for a celebration! The head carpenter recited a verse to bless the structure and the people who would live in it. Then, finally, he downed a shot of schnaps and smashed the glass on the beams. At this, the *Richtfest,* the topping-out celebration could begin. (Nowadays, there is less drinking because the workers drive instead of walk home, and the no-drink-and-drive laws are strict).

The Richtfest meant that the building would be finished soon and along with it my infatuation with Gerhard, because it needed to be fueled by my daily sightings. But Gerhard's disappearance from my life wouldn't put an end to my need to be infatuated. If I couldn't be smitten with a real live person, a dead movie star would do. In fact, being obsessed with an unreachable person made my obsession so much more delicious. Because what would I do if a real live boy were to try and kiss me? I wasn't thrilled at the thought of it.

James Dean wouldn't ever try to kiss me, but I was in love with him all the same. His picture, newspaper cutouts, posters, and any other mementoes that Doris and I could lay our hands on were up on the walls in the bedroom we shared (she was in love with him too and so were thousands of teenagers the world over). It didn't matter—from the poster he gazed only at me. Coming home from school one day on the streetcar, I saw that the Roxi theater was showing the last film he had made, *Rebel without a Cause,* translated into *Denn sie wissen nicht, was sie tun,* meaning, "And they don't know what they are doing." This was a movie about me, my age group!

My friend Sabine and I decided to go but we had to butter up our mothers, because we had to be sixteen (I was not yet fifteen) to get in. Our mothers gave their permission if we could figure out how to get past the ticket taker. I had a problem—I looked younger than sixteen: with my short hair and barely budding breasts, I looked more like twelve.

What to do? Get glasses! I would wear a pair of glasses to appear older. With a pair of my Mamuschka's (what I sometimes called my mother) reading glasses perched on my nose, I stood in front of the mirror and looked instantly older. Mutti, normally wiser than I, thought I could get by without the glasses, but I took them with me anyway. Just in case.

The day arrived. I didn't pay any attention in school that day. How could I, knowing I was going to see my love tonight even if only on the screen? At half past six I was on a streetcar, headed for the Roxi. I was going to try getting in without wearing glasses because I felt uneasy about deceiving the ticket taker. However, my apprehension could be overcome if only I could lay my eyes on James Dean! The glasses were in my coat pocket for now because if I had worn them on the streetcar, I would have thrown up! When I practiced walking with them, they distorted my vision, making me lightheaded and queasy.

Sabine and I handed our tickets to the ticket taker. He said to me, "How old are you?" and I said, with emphasis and indignation, "Sixteen!!!!" But he wasn't fooled. "Do you have an I.D.?" Of course I had an I.D., but showing it to him was not in my best interest. He said, "Then get one and I'll believe you." I could have killed. The man was keeping me from gazing at the one I loved. And then something humiliating happened. He let Sabine through even though she was three weeks younger than I! It was time to activate plan B.

I left the theater lobby and walked outside, pretending to be looking for some-one. Intently I studied the movie pictures posted outside in little window boxes. Next, I squinted, pretending that I couldn't see anything. Then I whipped out Mutti's glasses. Now everything got really blurry.

At most, five minutes had gone by since I was told to get my I.D. when I turned around and went back to the ticket person. He took my ticket, no ques-tions this time. I was in! But I couldn't see Sabine for wearing the glasses. When I finally took them off and saw where Sabine was sitting, I told her the story. We giggled. Later that night I cried, not because I had been deceitful and was ashamed but because my James Dean was dead.

In any case, my obsession with being infatuated continued. I felt like a spider ensnaring its victims, although the subjects of my infatuation were unavailable and the ensnaring transpired only in my head. I made up possible "ensnarios" without end.

At last, in October of 1956, my fantasies were energized by real live boys. I was fifteen years old. On Tuesday nights, our girls' class would be taking dance lessons at a local dance studio. What luxury to receive dance lessons, only eleven years after the end of the war. Our partners were tenth graders from my brother's former school, the *Oberschule für Jungen Uhlenhorst-Barmbek* (high school for boys).

On the first Tuesday night Herr Bender, the owner of the studio, gave a short speech on the importance of knowing how to dance as we sat in chairs, glancing around the room and making mental notes about the boys. More like judgments, they were. Based only on looks. Blond was good, modern haircuts helped. Some wore hideous glasses, while another guy was glowing red like a Christmas apple. Some had pimples, others were tall, short, cute, stupid (how could I possibly decide instantly who was stupid?) So I made a wish. I wished that a cute boy would ask me to dance, or else. Or else dancing wouldn't be any fun. Life would lose its meaning if the objects of my desire didn't ask me.

Was anybody actually there for the dancing? I asked myself this much later in life when I thought about what really happened during these dance lessons. Dancing the waltz or the rumba, swinging the hips, holding hands, and sideway glancing all signaling invitation or rejection and sometimes both simultaneously.

Just as I was thinking how confusing this dance of life was, and how many promises it held, the girls whispered and shifted in their seats. The boys were asked to form two circles and were now practicing some kind of basic step while starting to look awkward already. Next, the girls formed circles and practiced the same thing. The boys were looking at us, but they were not whispering. Lesson one was introductory and short. Before I went to sleep that night, I picked the boys I wanted to dance with and wrote their names in my diary.

LESSON TWO—A pimply boy stood in front of me, ready to practice our elementary waltz steps. His face was peppered with red spots. Pimples! Some had pus crests that were threatening to explode. Next to his left ear, there was a blemish the size of a boil, promising that dancing cheek to cheek would take on a whole new meaning. Cheek to boil! I was ready to burst at the thought of it. Revolting!

My partner was the one whose face always got red with exertion. The one whose hands got so sweaty that he had to keep wiping them on his pants. The one who had forgotten the ironclad rule to always bring a white handkerchief for shielding a partner's back (sometimes, ugh, her bare back) from the sweat of a drippingly overanxious palm. The handkerchief was supposed to be white, but of course my pimply partner's would have to be a deep, dour purple which clashed with the soft paisley print dress Mutti had let me buy for these dance lessons. She advised me that, "You'll be the belle of any dance if you know how to follow the man." Papa added, for good measure that, *if* I liked dancing, this class could be a stepping stone to my becoming a competitive dancer some day. Of course, I liked dancing; hadn't I on many occasions waltzed around the living room with Papa and Klaus or even my brother's friends? But to dance with boys I didn't know, total strangers? Ugh! Apprehension ruled the day of the second lesson.

Oh, many times I had watched this boy and his buddies talk at the dance studio. From far off, he looked a little like James Dean. James Dean, as everybody knew, was so-o-o-handsome and I was in love with him as was every other teenage girl. But James Dean was dead. All the love of all the girls hadn't saved him from killing himself in 1955 in that stupid sports car. A year later we were still in love with him, fantasizing about him—*Oh Jimmy, my Jimmy. Had I been there, I would have made you slow down, and you would still be alive and we could dance cheek-to-cheek.*

When the music started and the James Dean look-alike asked me to waltz, his face turned bright red and his hands felt as slick as a skinless mango. A mango is really hard to hold onto, it wants to just launch itself from the hands around it. Now how was I supposed to grip his fingers when they felt like a slippery fruit?

With one arm around my back, pulling me toward him, and his other hand clasped firmly in mine, he held our arms as high as if he were announcing the winner of a wrestling match. I nudged his arm down a bit, but that only worked for a while. Somehow over the course of the dance our arms would become airborne again and again, leaving my shoulders sore and my arms heavy and fatigued. That wasn't all. The guy had two left feet. He reduced the one-two-three beat of a waltz to a heavy marching beat, with considerable strength and even force steering me around the room. I told myself that this second lesson was only an illusion. It couldn't get any worse!

LESSON THREE—I was wrong. The third lesson was again devoted to the waltz, with an introduction to the foxtrot at the end of the two hours. Then, after a few rounds with several boys who didn't know the meaning of rhythm, Pimply Face asked me again. If I had to do another turn, I would barf. I felt clammy, my armpits wet. For heaven's sake!

Of all nights, I was wearing a sweater. It was another of Mutti's ideas, talking me into wearing a sweater because it was going to be a cool night. So there I was twirling around the room getting stickier by the minute with my full, mid-calf, navy-blue skirt bobbing left and right and up and down, my obligatory starched-to-perfection petticoat giving the whole thing that extra bounce. If the petticoat had been starched too stiffly, it would have been scratchy and ruined my one and only pair of nylons. But to my relief Mutti had actually used the right amount of starch. But in my two-skirts-and-a-sweater outfit, I was getting hotter by the minute. So was the pimply partner holding me closely.

Herr Fallen had told us that men and women dancing the waltz kept plenty of room between them until about the year 1800, when a man held the woman close to his body, embracing her so to speak. Shock waves at the impropriety vibrated through Europe. Vulgar, sinful, indecorous, wicked, as they called it.

I fantasized about what it would be like to be twirled around the room, outrageously intertwined with a man who knew how to lead. I made up a man, gave him the name Hugo, dressed him in black and white, dressed myself in shimmering green taffeta with cleavage and shoes to match my dress. I had us waltzing around a big ballroom, smiling at each other, turning this way and that, never faltering. It was heavenly, and then..... .

I saw Pimply Boy's face glowing red as usual, his hands feeling more slippery with each turn. Out of the corner of my eye I saw his eyes wandering over my shoulders, up my neck to my face where they rested for a few seconds before darting to the floor. Was he trying to make eye contact? Not on my life, I was not about to glance at him. Although I never looked at him directly, I knew that he was looking even though I never gave him even one encouraging smile. Nor did I ever say anything to him. More, I never stepped on his feet, and when he stepped on mine I didn't let on that it hurt although I wanted to let out a blood-boiling yell. Whenever his eyes wandered, he lost the little rhythm he had and took me with him on his stumbling spree until at last he got us back, sort of, on the one-two-three.

When my eyes alighted on some of the wallflowers, they rolled their eyes and smirked sympathetically as we waltzed by. Why couldn't I be sitting with them instead of dancing with this peasant? Why, his black pants were two inches too short, stopping at his ankles and showing his gauche white socks. Even his shoes were an ugly brown. The higher he raised our arms, the more his blue, short-sleeved shirt pulled out of his pants. In short, he looked a mess, a rumpled James Dean sprayed with pimples and boils.

Herr Fallen had said, "Don't think of anything while you are dancing; just let the music and the rhythm carry you away. The waltz is meant to be a light, joyful dance." Yet this waltz was more like torture, not at all what I was hoping for. The boy had no rhythm. This was a bad Tuesday indeed.

LESSON FOUR—Before this lesson, my girlfriends and I compared nightmares about the dance lessons. We weren't flattering, either, we wanted our money back. How hard was it for a boy to go one-two-three around the room, especially if he could count that far? How could I ever be the belle that Mutti wanted me to be if the beau couldn't lead me? But although I didn't want to follow most of these guys, I couldn't make myself stay away from the lessons either. There was something exhilarating about being around so many boys.

So I kept dancing and complaining. Commiserating with my friends made me feel better, since they felt the same frustrations. They understood.

One week I was griping about the guy who reeked of sweat from lack of deodorant (the use of which hadn't really caught on yet in post-war Germany); the next week I grumbled about a guy whose hair was all gleaming bristliness. Worse, these boys couldn't lead.

Herr Fallen must have been able to read our minds, because tonight he worked with the guys on leading—the subtle movements of the male wrist or shoulders that let the girl know what she was supposed to do.

I had no idea how hard it was for the guys both to do the steps correctly and to lead. I only wanted to glide over the floor with ease and elegance. I didn't want much!

During practice, Pimply Paul (we had introduced ourselves, as part of the protocol) had been digging his wrist into my back and twisting my frame every which way until the teacher stepped in and separated us. Herr Fallen then assumed the dance position with me and showed my partner how little he had to do to get me to go in a certain direction. Herr Fallen also asked me several times to wait for him to signal which step I was to take. I guess I had gotten used to doing some of the leading, but only because *somebody* had to with this type of boy, particularly Pimply Paul. Oh, how heavenly to be led by Herr Fallen. I didn't want to let go of him, but he connected me back with Paul and we continued practicing the foxtrot. If there was an improvement in his lead, it was too imperceptible for me to notice.

LESSON FIVE and SIX—During the next two lessons, when we were finishing the elementary steps for the foxtrot as well as beginning to learn the tango, I perceived that Pimply Paul's lead was beginning to improve. No longer was he bullying me around the way most of the other guys were still doing with their partners. He had acquired a solid touch and I told him so.

I said, "I like dancing with boys who know how to lead." He smiled and returned the compliment.

"You are such a good dancer." At that, I turned red.

James Dean eyes, long lashes, I thought, and for a brief moment a James Dean-and-Christel tango fantasy flashed across my mind, though I was quickly brought back by the tango music and Paul.

We danced in close position, not looking directly at each other. My heart hammered against the same rumpled blue shirt he had worn at each lesson. I had never been that close to a boy's thighs before and I teetered a bit on my heels, unsettled by being so close to this maleness.

When the dance was over and we untangled, I felt a lingering tingle. It was as if I had shed all my defenses. My obsessions with things that didn't really matter, like his clothes and his skin, fell away as we stood around for a few minutes and he told me that he liked the tango best of all the smooth dances. It had so much character, he said, and there was so much room for expression. I agreed. Sometimes, the dance would resemble a fight, with quick back-and-forth head movements; sometimes it expressed longing and tenderness. We had only just begun to learn the intricacies of the tango. Or maybe of life?

I had noticed that at the end of a lesson, some of my girlfriends were leaving with boys in tow. I learned the following day that some were escorted to the subway or streetcar stop and others all the way home. But no boy ever asked to take me home. Instead, a group of us, boys and girls, would jump on a streetcar and then get off at our respective stops. I was much more comfortable with the group than I would have been with the one-on-one. Thinking about what could have happened if a boy had taken me home, things like kissing, turned me off. But then what was the tingling all about?

LESSON SEVEN—With three lessons to go, we had reached the Latin phase of dancing in which we were introduced to the rumba, cha cha, and jive. I looked forward to learning these dances, because except for the jive I hadn't ever danced them.

I was no longer grumbling to my girlfriends about the guy who reeked of sweat from lack of deodorant or about the guy who had smeared one dab too many of some kind of cream into his hair. When I wasn't asked to dance, I watched the couples on the floor intently. Especially the guys.

I zeroed in on a few that I wanted to dance with because they looked like they could lead, and when they didn't ask me I felt disappointed. But there was nothing I could do—no way could girls ask boys to dance. We had to wait to be asked and we had to accept whoever did the asking. If we didn't like them and they were *Blödlinge* (jerks) and smelled and had bad breath—tough, we still had to say yes. My fantasy was that all the boys as one would come rushing toward me, and I would decide who would be my next partner. I knew it wasn't going to happen, but dreaming about it was fun.

Now the guys stood in a circle, waiting for Herr Fallen to give them directions. Some fidgeted with their hands, gliding them over their pimples and sweaty foreheads and making me shudder briefly at the thought of touching the hands that had just come from those places. Of course, the handkerchiefs reduced some of the grossness when used in proper fashion. I pinched my cheek to stop my critical thoughts.

The boys were practicing Cuban motion, which is a big part of dancing the rumba. I thought it unnatural for the body to execute this motion. I don't know how to describe it exactly, but only the lower part of the body moved in a strange and, hopefully, rhythmic way. The knees alternated between being extended and flexed, the hips rotated the whole time to the left and then to the right, and the waist got a really good workout given all that below-the-waist activity.

But what a tough dance to do! Only a few of us girls had any notion of Cuban motion. While I was looking at the boys twisting their bodies in a most provocative way (or, at least some of their wiggling was provocative, the rest pitiful), Paul caught my eye. His hips and legs stretched, then relaxed, stretched, then relaxed. The guy had perfect Cuban motion and supreme rhythm! Herr Fallen was playing the girl to Paul's guy to show the other guys how the motion was done. Paul's upper body was perfectly still, which was exactly the way to dance to the Latin beat. Holy cow, was he ever good! I was standing with my mouth open, not unattractively, I hoped, but I just couldn't help myself. From the front or from the back, Paul was Mr. Latin, and I wanted to dance with him right then and there, sway with him in Cuban motion, I his perfect mirror image.

LESSON EIGHT—We had plenty of time to practice Cuban motion by standing in lines, girls facing boys, and rotating partners every few minutes. But first, it was the girls' turn to practice by themselves, and the boys' turn to watch. And did they ever! They whispered, smirked, scrutinized. Our heels clicked as they hit the floor, but otherwise it was quiet in the room. There was no hot rumba music playing, just Herr Fallen's perky directions filling the room: basic slow-quick-quick, slow-quick-quick, open break, underarm turn, fifth position, basic, and again from the beginning.

I wanted to die when Herr Fallen came over, grabbed me by the hips and made me exaggerate the Cuban motion. *Mein Gott,* I was already self-conscious about my behind, oversized as it was, and now the teacher was pulling it way out there. I knew exactly what the guys had gone through, being on display like that, and I couldn't wait to get off the dance floor.

Somehow, over the last eight weeks I had become more aware of how my body could move if given a few steps to follow. Graceful or not, I heard the rhythm and kept the beat, and now and then I even led, even if somewhat surreptitiously. And I loved partnering with Paul. Maybe he would help me with the Cuban motion. We were both obviously consumed by all of the Latin dances.

LESSON NINE—The last lesson came around and all I could think of was to dance with Paul. I was sitting on the girls' side of the room, partially hidden by a pillar, when I heard the rhythmic beat of a rumba. Would Mr. Latin ask me? Did he know how good he was? I had told him several times, and in his usual kind fashion he had returned the compliment. "If you think I'm good, you should see yourself out there with some of the other guys. I watch you, you know. You are good." Now the invitation came, and I turned red, of course: "May I have this dance?"

I put my hand in Paul's hand and followed him onto the dance floor. So what if his hands were still slippery, the pimples still red and shiny, and the boil still lodged behind his left ear. Looking at me was a guy who had learned how to lead and who could dance a romantic rumba.

◆   ◆   ◆

The dance lessons were now over and I wouldn't be seeing Paul again until December—at the *ball!* All of us were buzzing about the ball. What to wear was the single most important question, an agony that was even greater for me because my parents didn't have much money for frilly things like fancy dance dresses. Post-war reality re-descended on me, and I was consumed by my envy of some of the girls whose parents didn't seem to have pressing money problems. For them, shopping for a special occasion dress was no big deal.

Mutti and I went to a dress shop on the *Fuhle*, near our house, because at this shop she could make arrangements for paying off a purchase in installments. On a layaway plan. I was angry and embarrassed because the Behnkes never had enough money to buy pretty things. In the store, I behaved petulantly, my face showing my irritation; I was mean to my Mutti and made a point of fingering dresses I knew were out of our reach. But Mutti was patient with me, and at last we agreed on a dress though even now tears of shame well in my eyes when I think of this incident. I had to leave the dress at the shop until Mutti could pay it off, but I consoled myself with thoughts of how adorable I would look in it. But what would the others think about my dress? The boys wouldn't care less, but what the girls thought was very important. Would the girls think it adorable? I had to pass inspection, I just had to.

The all-important dress was antique blue and shimmered as it moved. The sleeves were short and the neckline high—no décolleté for me, for my Papa had always told me that I had chicken breasts. He didn't mean the size of my breasts, though, just my bony chest. Better to cover it, and the dress did that. The pearls sewn on the fabric even made my chest appear fuller. The skirt was bell-shaped and seemed to flow, especially when I danced the smooth dances like the waltz, foxtrot, Viennese waltz, and tango. Finally, a big bow tied behind my waist. With this creation I would wear black pumps with medium heels.

On a Saturday afternoon in December, we dancers assembled in the big ball-room of a popular restaurant in Hamburg, the *Winterhuder Fährhaus*. Mutti was sitting with the other mothers and a few fathers. The boys had to come to the table and ask properly for the honor of a dance. I danced continuously with Paul and just about every boy from the class. When one boy in particular asked me for a second dance, I immediately started obsessing—did it mean he liked me or liked dancing with me or maybe both? I thought about him all the way home on the subway, and in my imagination we had fallen in love, were married, and lived happily ever after. After all, I had danced with him twice!

My contact with boys continued. Once the opposite sex had invaded my thoughts, it never left. My diary now seemed to be devoted to entries about boys. Whenever there was an affair of the heart of sorts, I wrote about it in great detail.

This particular diary entry had a beginning and an end, but proved not to have much of a middle. It started officially with my friends and I looking at the pictures of the ball later displayed at the dance studio. Horst, a boy from the dance class, showed up. When we were finished looking at the pictures, some of us piled into a streetcar to go home. One by one, my friends said goodbye and got off. Now it was just Ulle, Horst, and me. At my stop, Ulle bid me a hasty farewell.

I said, "Why are you leaving?" (She was supposed to come home with me), and she said, "Stupid, don't you know Horst is taking you home?"

I had no idea, and now I felt weird. He had heard this exchange, so what could he be thinking? Still, Ulle stayed and walked with us. Then we stood under the street light by my house and talked a little, after which Horst and Ulle moved away because he wanted to ask her something. Ask her what? I started feeling jealous because I liked Horst, but I didn't know who else was in the picture for me to be jealous of. The next day, Ulle told me that she had asked Horst if he liked Gisela. And he had replied, "I can't really comment on that," or something noncommittal like that. And he asked her why she had asked him that particular question in the first place. It all seemed so disconnected, with third parties fading in and out and all dialogue ultra-important.

After all the back and forth, this affair hadn't even gotten started when another event transpired. I received an invitation to a party one of my girlfriends was having, and it requested that I bring a boy. I was dying to ask Horst, but what if he had invited Gisela to the boys' school dance that was coming up? It would be too humiliating to be turned down. Then when Gisela told me that Horst would probably ask her to the school dance, I wanted to scratch her eyes out. He had asked for her address and wasn't that proof enough? Now I wouldn't ask him, not in a million years. I cried, pounding my fist into my pillow.

But the very next day found me happy. Something wonderful had happened: Uwe had met Ulle at the streetcar station and told her that the dance invitations had been sent out. Uwe sent one to Ulle and Horst sent one to me! Victory! And Gisela was with them when he said that, as I heard later from Ulle. It served Gisela right, although I felt momentary pity for her as the loser. I was in high spirits, jubilant, and I buzzed around as if the fairy of frivolity had visited me with chirpiness and that ready-to-burst feeling. Now I could ask Horst at the school dance if he wanted to go with me to the party. I would sew a dress for the occasion, the money for which would come from a small job I had doing grocery-shopping for Tante Möller. I was beside myself when the invitation arrived in the mail.

January 15, 1957, was a bewildering day. Ulle had heard that the boys' teacher thought it a good idea for the boys to introduce themselves to the parents of the girls they were escorting to the dance.

Mutti and I were having our noon meal when the bell rang. My heart started racing even before I opened the door. It was Horst! But why did he have to come at this particular time? How embarrassing to have a boy see you chew and swallow! He introduced himself to Mutti, she asked him to sit down, and we chatted for a few minutes. I was sure he wasn't the least bit interested in anything Mutti had to say, and I was irritated with her because she was asking him questions about his family. After a few uncomfortable minutes, I left with him because I had errands to do and, anyway, I couldn't have eaten another bite. Horst was so cute, and he had asked <u>me</u> to the dance! I was in love!

I read his hand-written invitation over and over again until the day of the *Klassenfest of the Untersekunda (*10th grade) of the Wissenschaftliche Oberschule Uhlenhorst Barmbek. We assembled at the *Gasthof zur Linde* and, after the teacher's remarks and then some coffee and cake, dance cards were circulated. There were sixteen so-called duty dances, and the date was allowed to reserve six of them. To my joy I was assured six dances with Horst. Now my dance card was filled up as was everyone else's and the fun was ready to start. In addition to the duty dances, there were others in-between when the dancers could take a break or dance if they were asked.

We sipped young (not yet mature) wine and my head began to feel a little foggy. Not foggy enough to fail to notice that there was a girl at the table who was staring at Horst as though she wanted to devour him. They danced many times, and after one dance they didn't return to the table. My instinct told me that they were outside even though it was January and cold there in Northern Germany.

She was hanging around when we got ready to leave and then when we got on the subway. She even stayed on the subway for an extra stop. Then, right in front of me, the two made a date to meet at the ice rink! I had barely had him and she had stolen him from me!

My head may have been foggy and my stomach queasy but I was thinking ahead. I should invite this two-timer, or maybe even three-timer, to Uta's party? I had had it! Horst was obliged to take me home even though I could find my own way perfectly well. We talked for a few minutes under the street lamp, and then suddenly he left. The kiss I had imagined (and even practiced on my hand) had not materialized.

For the next few days, I walked around with pretend-daisies in my hand, plucking the petals—I'll invite him, I won't invite him, I'll invite him, no, yes, no, yes, no. Finally, pride won. And, as it happened, Uta decided to invite the boys to her party, taking the asking out of our hands. She had a flower for each of her guests, and the boy and girl with the same kind of flower had to find each other and be dinner partners. (A hostess was born!)

From Uta I learned that she had seen Horst and the other girl at the ice rink, and I knew then that my first affair of the heart was over before it had actually begun. There was a beginning and an end, but nothing of substance in-between. Still, my feelings were hurt and then I was angry at Horst, in whom I had invested more emotions than I cared to admit to.

Subsequent infatuations took on the feeling of a dance of sorts—I want you, I don't want you, go away, come back, I want you. I observed people in love around me. My brother Klaus was in love and I watched him and his Anne hold hands and look deeply into each other's eyes. My parents kissed and hugged each other. Myself, I wanted to hold hands—just hands—with a boy.

◆   ◆   ◆

Unwittingly, our upstairs neighbor fired my romantic imagination. It happened over a period of time, and the phone played a big role. It might even be said that I discovered the phone's hidden uses with this neighbor.

My family had the only telephone on the block. All these years after the end of the war, the phone was still a costly luxury requiring a monthly fee and payment for each outgoing call, including local ones. But Papa, who was still freelancing, needed a phone for professional purposes. The band leader needed to be able to alert him to possible gigs that he would miss if he didn't learn of them in a timely fashion. It was for this reason alone that we had the distinction of having the one and only phone on the block.

My siblings and I didn't use it, though. We didn't see any reason for calling anyone, since Doris and Klaus were not at home most of the day, and I saw my friends in school and on the neighborhood streets after school. Mutti communicated with store owners and neighbors on her daily rounds to the bakery, produce store, and butcher shop. So the black phone with the rotary dial sat mostly idle on a small desk in a corner of the living room, ringing only when Papa received a call or our neighbors had reason to use it.

The news of our phone soon spread down the street. Did you hear that Behnkes have a phone? And they don't mind sharing it, they surely must have added. Indeed, my parents might as well have installed it in a phone booth and collected the coins because the neighbors took to our phone like children to a toy. They liked using ours because they could sit in an armchair and enjoy relative privacy, and so gradually they pooh-poohed the use of a phone booth where they might be asked to hurry up.

When a call came in for our neighbor Frau Ludwig across the street, Mutti sent me to get her. Frau Ludwig, eighty years old and wearing sturdy shoes, stomped across the cobblestone street at the highest speed she could muster because in her mind every call was an emergency. I grabbed her hand; she had so much momentum, I was afraid she was going to stumble and break one of her spindly legs. She mumbled something about whoever was calling her this time and why didn't they just write a note or come by her house.

"Frau Ludwig, it's your sister. She had a little accident, nothing serious, but she needs to talk to you right away."

Once in our living room, Mutti pointed her to the black phone on the desk and Frau Ludwig, who had used a phone before but didn't recall doing it, tried to make the receiver fit both ears. Back and forth, back and forth, saying hello into one end and then shifting to the other end, all the time muttering about not hearing anything. Mutti stepped in to help her while I stood giggling in the doorway. The machine was no mystery to me; its use was so obvious.

Before Frau Ludwig left, she told Mutti, "Well, looks like I have to take some food to my sister. She sprained her ankle and has to stay off her feet. Good thing you have a phone, Frau Behnke." "And Christel, thanks for getting me," at which she pressed a few coins into my hand. Mutti's reward was a little gossip to spread if she chose to.

My parents' house seemed to be open any time of the day, as though they sensed that this machine filled a need for people to connect with each other after the terrible disruption of the war when communication was often so difficult, slow, or non-existent.

In the course of a few months, I guess that every neighbor on that short street came into our living room either to make a call or to receive one. I heard more stories than a fifteen-year-old wanted or needed to hear because the neighbors told my mother about their family problems, and, to all appearances, they didn't care if a teenager was in earshot. Or sometimes they told me when I fetched them and we walked to my house together. Having a phone and sharing it with the neighbors was like having a door to a whole world of information about how to cope with everyday life. I formed opinions about people and decided whether I liked them or not based on the tidbits they revealed about themselves. Often, I made snap judgments. Or I felt sorry for them. And I began cursing the war for what it had done to families, hearing from our neighbors stories that still hadn't made it into Germany's schools. This one phone on the block had enabled me to think past our own family's misfortune in that horrid conflict.

Some of the neighbors ran into Mutti on her daily shopping rounds. "If you're home," they would say, "may I drop by at three o'clock and make a call?" And Mutti welcomed anyone at practically any time, in this way becoming privy to many tales, for after their phone calls, the neighbors would linger and fill her in on their details.

Then one evening, a call came from a man. "*Guten Abend,* Christel Behnke," I said, in the way I had been taught to answer the phone. He said, "*Guten Abend,* my name is Kessler. May I speak to Frau Bures, please?" "Yes, one moment, please," and I put the receiver down. I opened the door to our duplex and yelled up the stairs, "Frau Bures, a Herr Kessler on the phone for you."

Frau Bures came spinning down the stairs, eyes smiling, almost shouting, "*ach, endlich,*" and flying past me into the living room. She was in such a rush that she couldn't stop to talk, but after catching her breath she said, "*Guten Abend,* Herr Kessler. How nice of you to call," with a voice all smooth and soft. This was not the way Frau Bures normally spoke. Plus I had to strain to hear her end of the conversation. Pretending to concentrate on my homework, I listened to every word and wished that I could talk to him, because his voice was so sonorous, vibrant, rich. He was going to call her again, I gathered from her end of the conversation. Never once did she turn around to see if I was listening.

After a few minutes, Frau Bures breezed by me with a thank-you, and bounded back up the stairs. She was not a young woman by any means; in fact, she seemed definitely old. Actually, though, she was middle-aged, which to me meant the same as old. To see her, she was a scrawny little thing, so thin that a light breeze could knock her over. Her face was deeply lined, her lips thin, her eyes unsmiling most of the time. In my eyes she was homely, and who would want to kiss that? But I was getting ahead of myself.

I can see her now. She's coming up the walk to the house. On her feet are heavy, dark, thick-soled shoes, on her legs a pair of sturdy stockings. She's wearing a flowered dress, the kind worn by many German women, with a variety of flowers of different colors on a dark background. Her sparse, brown hair is pulled back into a bun, and her lips are untouched by a lipstick. She's carrying a cloth bag with the day's groceries, having spent almost the whole day in her shoe repair shop mending and re-mending again the soles of used German shoes, often replacing cardboard soles with plastic ones and then eventually with leather when it again became available.

Tonight the phone rang around 6:30 p.m. and Doris answered it. She covered the mouthpiece and told me to get Frau Bures. It was him again, I could tell. Where did she meet him? Was he one of her customers?

She said into the phone, "I didn't see you walk by today, and I was wondering whether I would hear from you. It's nice to hear your voice," in that special tone of hers. "I'll be done by 6:30 tomorrow night. Yes, walking me home would be fine." And on and on they went, caressing the phone with their voices.

My family was in the living room having dinner around the big table. The living room also served as the dining room, and now it had become the *Telefonzimmer*, the telephone room, as well. Mutti and Papa, Doris and Klaus, and I continued talking over the voice of Frau Bures, politely giving her some background noise so her cooing wouldn't permeate a silent room. Forks and knives clanged against plates a little too loudly perhaps. Papa glanced over at Frau Bures with disbelief in his eyes: couldn't she see that we were having dinner? Was I the only one really interested in what was being said on the phone? I pricked up my ears so I could hear every word she said and imagined what Herr Kessler might have been telling her on the other end. I overheard that she was looking forward to seeing him tomorrow, and then I saw her run her fingers over her hair, making me wonder if she would do that to him tomorrow, or he to her. A final kiss was sent into the phone, but no, not a final one, another one, and then another one.... .but Papa had caught on to what I was doing and pulled my ears, which by now were monstrously big from all that straining. Papa asked me something about school, though I didn't want to talk about school because it was a lot less important than what I was witnessing right here in my living room. I had become a voyeur!

Frau Bures thanked us and bounced up the stairs. Something was going on between her and Herr Kessler, I could sense it. Her eyes had become brighter; she had become more light-hearted, friendlier. And the next day I would get to see the cause of her transformation, Herr Kessler, a few minutes after 6:30 p.m.

The duplex upstairs had been assigned to Frau Bures and her two children after she had arrived in Hamburg. Refugees from Silesia, fleeing from the Russian Army, they had spent weeks in a refugee camp and then, having been deloused and certified clean, had been allotted our upstairs. The German government had helped her get her shoe repair business started on the *Fuhle*, where she spent long hours every day and from which she came home tired and smelling of old shoes though occasionally new leather. Now it seemed that she had found one of the few men her age who had survived the war without any visible physical wounds.

No missing limbs, that is. That's as far as I had got with picturing him, a whole man with a rich voice. Tomorrow I would find out if I was right.

A few minutes after 6:30 p.m. the following night, I was watching from behind the curtain in my room that faced the front yard and afforded an excellent view of the gate through which Frau Bures and Herr Kessler would come. There they came, not holding hands but walking close to each other and looking at each other as they talked. Smiles were on their faces. Now they reached the gate and I expected them both to walk through it. But no, she stepped through the gate and closed it, he standing on the sidewalk on the other side of the gate. My good look at him was somewhat obscured by her figure, and I willed her to step aside though of course willing didn't work.

All I can see is that he is middle-aged like her, and thin, and that he is standing on two legs. He's wearing a raincoat. When he smiles at her, his cheekbones form sharp angles. What an interesting face. Now they are shaking hands and he is leaving. They don't kiss. And I had imagined being there, accidentally, when they stepped through the door to go upstairs. I wanted a much closer look at him, but that would have to wait for another time. My stupid homework was waiting. Plus I shouldn't have been hiding behind the curtains to spy on people.

The phone calls came daily now, always around the same time, after 6:30 p.m. They were ten minutes long, then twenty, then thirty. Papa was clearly irritated, but he didn't say anything, at least not yet. As far as the rest of my family went, we usually cleared out of our living/dining room reluctantly, as soon as Frau Bures dove for the phone. I went to my parents' bedroom, which was separated from the living room by a French door, and with my ear to the door I could hear her sighing and murmuring. Every now and then I heard a *"mein Liebling"*, my darling. So this was how far they had come! I imagined his cheekbones lifting and tightening as he smiled at her words. Though I had been told that it was not polite to listen to other people's conversations, I couldn't help myself at this time in my life. Mysterious things were happening here: I wished somebody other than my parents would call me *mein Liebling!* Frau Bures used to be home every night before the love machine started ringing for her, but at least once a week now the phone was silent and she came home late at night.

My parents said, "Looks like Frau Bures and Herr Kessler are in love." What did they mean, looks like? What did "being in love" look like? Had I looked like I was in love when I was enthralled with Horst? Were Frau Bures' eyes brighter because she was in love? Was she wearing skirts and matching blouses because she was in love? Did she go around saying, "I'm in love," "I'm in love?" Was her voice softer, her Silesian accent less harsh? To what extent was the black telephone moving this love affair along?

I had nothing but curiosity. A few few minutes before 6:30 p.m. every day I arranged myself on the couch, languishing and fantasizing, but above all ready to pick up the phone when it rang. Once, when Frau Bures was late coming home from work and the phone rang, he said, "Dear Christel, would you please tell her that I will be over at 8:00 p.m?" In that vibrant voice, the "Dear Christel" might as well have been *mein Liebling,* which I repeated later that night into my pillow until Doris ordered, "Shut up, your Kessler Liebling is in love with Frau Bures. You are just a little kid, he's an old man."

Doris was two years older than me, but what did she know? In my over-stimulated mind, I tried to think of ways to engage Kessler in longer conversations just so that his rich voice would envelop my longings, and he would realize that he should wait for me. As soon as I became a woman, I would unleash my passion on him and his cheekbones would be lifted perpetually because he would be smiling at me all the time. I wanted him to call me *Liebchen,* hold my hands, and kiss me the way I had kissed my own hand. But then again, maybe holding hands would be enough.

At the very least, I wanted to position myself a little closer to him, maybe close enough to touch him, definitely to feast my eyes on him, surreptitiously if need be. He seemed to visit her more frequently now, and on many occasions stayed overnight. The phone conversations had been replaced by an indefinable something else: the phone was no longer needed to connect Frau Bures and Herr Kessler.

I asked Doris, "What do you think they are doing up there?" I knew they were having dinner when the aroma of red cabbage and pork roast wafted through the building along with the classical music on the radio. "Do you think they listen to the radio after dinner?"

"*Dummkopf,*" she said, "they hug and kiss and do other things." She was vague, but I declined to press her for details. The unspeakable needn't be said. Nonetheless I conceived the idea that they had gone way beyond phone calls.

I still hadn't seen him close up and I longed to. In a casual way, as though the answer didn't even matter, I asked Bruni, Frau Bures' seventeen-year-old daughter, if she liked Herr Kessler. She got to be near him, sit next to him, look at him, listen to him. Ach, if I could just be in her place. "Ja," she replied. That was it? Ja?? I knew that the next time I cornered Bruni, I would have to ask questions that would get me more information. What exactly did she like about him, as compared to what I liked about him?

Tonight, when the upstairs doorbell rang, I was ready. Dressed in a skirt with a starched petticoat underneath, my hair carefully gathered in a ponytail, I looked perky and felt irresistible. I didn't wait for Frau Bures to hurry down the steps, but I rushed to beat her in opening the door of our duplex and then the outside door. *"Guten Abend,* Herr Kessler," I smiled politely, and he said, *"Guten Abend,* Christel," shaking my right hand with his left hand. He was old all right, with a deeply lined face, thinning brown hair, but kind blue eyes. Frau Bures was already at the top of the stairs, smiling down on him. She didn't give me a minute with him, and the moment was over, shorter than our phone conversations. How could I feed my infatuation when I wasn't allowed time with Herr Kessler? I hated Frau Bures for dismissing me and flounced back inside to finish my home-work. I was so excited, looking at my shaken hand and caressing my cheek with it. It was only then that I realized Mr. Kessler didn't have a right hand. It had been claimed by Germany.

Eventually, he would give his left hand in marriage to Frau Bures.

Infatuations came and went, and this one diminished quickly. Soon, I couldn't believe I had spent this much time thinking about an old man. The healing that was taking place upstairs, closing the war wounds, bringing love to two people, was not altogether apparent to me then, even though I had a tiny part in their coming-together. And so did the phone.

◆   ◆   ◆

Well, then. Life continued, aided by my religious faith. I was still involved in the youth group and attending church every Sunday, where I prayed for every-body and especially my family. Although my devotion was heart-felt and I couldn't imagine not having God and Jesus in my life, I knew the better part of my contact with religion to be socially motivated.

St. Gabriel, the parish church, owned land in Gudow, a small town south of Hamburg along the river Elbe and approaching the East German border. The church campground was only a short dash away from Lake Gudow, and it was in this pastoral setting of lakes and woods that I spent two weeks in that summer of 1956 sharing a tent with nine girls. We slept on burlap bags filled with straw until 7:30 a.m. when we crawled out of the tent and washed our bodies in the chilly lake. Lake Gudow was our bathtub as well as our dip into spiritual renewal, a cleansing of sorts.

These ablutions were followed with morning prayers at 8:15 followed by 8:30 a.m. breakfast consisting of milk soup and bread with butter and jam. Before lunch at 12:30 p.m., another quick dip into the lake. Lunch followed by quiet time from 1–2:30 p.m. This quiet time got our brains ready for working with the New Testament for half an hour during which we debated a short section. I was quite taken by the idea of debating, although I didn't often say anything for fear of being wrong. Also, Harald was our debate leader, and what would he think of me if I said something stupid. He was a minister-in-training and half the girls were in love with him. Me too. All this debating under Harald's leadership was quite stimulating, mostly for our adolescent bodies. Fortunately, though, we'd have another plunge into cold Lake Gudow sometime between 4:00–6:00 p.m.

Dinner was served at 6:00 p.m. and it just so happened that on this day it was milk soup. Once again. *Milchsuppe* was in fact a dish we ate often, here and at home, especially after the war, provided we had the milk. Or day-old bread. *Milchsuppe,* an inexpensive way to feed a crowd, was made with leftover bread or dough made from flour, eggs and a little milk. This dough was then dropped by the spoonful into the simmering milk. Sugar and cinnamon were added to entice eaters. It was definitely better when not eaten every single day.

After dinner came a short prayer service held outside unless it rained, which it often did. We had a little time at night to sit around a fire (when it didn't rain) and sing German folk songs, a lot of them having to do with ships and seafaring, since we lived in a port city. Many other songs dealt with going out into the world, leaving home, hiking across the land, learning about other countries. *Wir sind jung, die Welt ist offen* (We are young and the world is open to us) was the unifying idea of many of the songs we sang.

Right then, though, our world was confined to camping and a pretty rigid schedule of eating, praying, hiking, swimming, running, jumping, playing badminton, and working. If we wanted a fire at night, we had to drag the tree limbs and branches from the woods to the clearing. We also peeled mountains of potatoes, bathtubs full of them, and went berry-picking, whatever berry was in season. We took turns helping with food preparation, from slicing bread to cleaning carrots.

There were hikes, most of which were taken in the rain. Morning hikes began around 4:00 a.m. when it was still chilly even though it was July. We'd get soaked; chilled to the marrow we'd stare back at deer watching us from the edge of the woods. We'd pick flowers with the rain drizzling down on our windbreakers. There were no complaints because we were regular troopers, we had stamina, we jumped into cold lakes and had fun doing it. We were the young people all our folk songs were about, like *Wer nur den lieben langen Tag,* a song about how only lazy people waste minutes every day doing nothing while we get up early, work as the sun shines above us, and after all the work is done at the close of the day, end up a happy bunch. That was us in Gudow that summer, girls God would have been proud of.

The time spent in Gudow strenghtened my ties to the youth group, and through our shared activities I added a few more friends to my circle. It also turned me off to camping because I couldn't stand being cold or wet.

◆   ◆   ◆

At school, I was slipping more and more and feeling shame for letting my parents down; I felt unsettled whenever I was in school or merely thought of it.

For some unexplainable reason, I was still the class speaker (maybe nobody else wanted the job!) and I had to communicate with the teachers when something was on the class's mind. This was the case late in January of 1957. We had had a math test that day during third hour, and one test a day was the rule. We were assembled in the music room at the beginning of fourth hour, when our teacher announced, "You are taking a music theory test today." The complaints started immediately.

When the teacher was called out for a minute, I took this time to get everybody to agree not to take the test, and just to be sure that nobody would write anything I collected the pencils. Teacher came back and gave us the first item on the test. Everyone remained perfectly quiet, and no one wrote a word. We just stared at her, and she didn't say anything for a long time. Then, "Well, somebody has to say something, otherwise I'll have to get the principal." Now it was my turn to talk. "You know that we've already had one test. It was a difficult one and we would like you to postpone the music test," I said as politely as I could. But she wouldn't bargain with us, forcing me to ask the class, "Do you want to take this test?" And this rotten class actually said, "Yes." So we had to take the test, the traitors and I! Still, I felt I had grown just by speaking up and letting an authority figure know that rules are rules. Of course, I was mad at my classmates, but they tried to cheer me up and told me it wasn't my fault. They just didn't want to get in trouble with the principal. Which meant I was the one in hot water. I was sure my teachers saw me as the bad student with the big mouth.

Before the end of the school year my parents met with the principal, who suggested that I transfer to another school, perhaps a business school. My grades were not satisfactory and my interests didn't seem to be in academia. So, after Easter 1957, at the end of ninth grade, I left my school and began a new chapter of my life at the *Höhere Handelsschule,* a two-year business school.

Instead of getting my *Mittlere Reife* at the end of tenth grade (which was the compulsory grade level for students seeking technically oriented careers), I would get my diploma at the end of the eleventh grade. I had closed the door to a university education.

At this new school, my subjects would be accounting, business correspondence, management theory, typing, German and English shorthand, German, English, Spanish, social studies, geography, and math.

I was so thrilled that I wouldn't have to wrestle with chemistry, physics, and Latin that my feelings of elation somewhat compensated for my nagging sense of failure and the fact that I had let my parents down. I didn't know why, but Papa and Mutti did not appear upset with me. Maybe they were relieved that they wouldn't have to live with my foul moods anymore, and they certainly hoped that the new subjects were more to my liking. I would miss some of my classmates, but one of my best friends, Sabine, was transferring to the same school so I wouldn't be quite so alone. I was in fact entirely optimistic.

The new school was coed!

7

Business school, infatuations and religion

◆

1957

1957—Twelve years after the end of the war, there are still 400,000 refugees in more than 3000 camps. The workweek is shortened to forty-five hours. Next up for discussion is the five-day workweek. Electric typewriters have arrived.

Before my confirmation and transfer to the Höhere Handelsschule in the spring of 1957, Papa was in a serious car accident. He was still traveling with the band, but on a day off he and his band leader drove home to be with their families. They had finished their gig just after midnight and were traveling on a deserted country road when their car hit a tree. Their wounds were such that they would have bled to death had not someone from a nearby village found them and gotten an ambulance to rush them to a hospital. Mutti received a phone call sometime that night, then ran to the train station and jumped on a train to Soltau about an hour south of Hamburg. She found Papa in critical condition. Doris and Klaus were at work and I was home alone and imagining the worst. The most horrific scenes flashed before my eyes and I cried for hours, begging God to save my beloved Papa.

Finally that evening, Klaus and Doris came home and we waited together anxiously for a call from Mutti. When it came, we were relieved to hear that he was alive but in great pain from a jaw broken in three places, a fractured leg, and head wounds. The sight in his left eye was hazy, a condition which would prove to be permanent.

Papa's accident and my confirmation have been forever intertwined in my mind. First I blamed God for the accident and later felt ashamed for blaming

God. On the day of my confirmation, April 7, 1957, Papa lay in bed behind the closed French doors separating the living room from the bedroom. He was recuperating from the car accident which he had survived only by the grace of God. At least I think by the grace of God, for overwhelming doubts about my faith caught me by surprise again and again throughout the day.

Papa was not doing very well on this day of my confirmation. He was home from the hospital where he had spent six long weeks, but he was not yet healed. It was a sight to see him lying on his back, like a corpse. The helmet on his head fed wires to a belt-like apparatus that wrapped around his neck, the wires ending in his mouth. The device was supposed to help heal his jaw, which had been shattered in many places when the car hit the tree. He took his nourishment through a straw.

It was an unusually hot day in April. The room was sticky, smelling of hospital, disinfectant, and sweaty bed sheets. Papa was covered only by a blanket because the feather comforter was far too heavy to rest on his recovering body. His comforter lay on Mutti's side of the bed next to him, where I perched to keep him company. I would read to him until he nodded off or squeezed my hand to say, "Enough, for now, Christelchen." His red hair peeked out from under the helmet and stuck to his forehead, not quite covering the scar that glared red and angry. His eyelids moved, and he moaned. The pressure from the wires bore on his jaw and he moaned in pain even when he slept.

Papa's instruments, his violin and double bass, lovingly cared for since he was a young man, had also been broken and were now splinters of wood hanging together by mere strings.

Now, my brothers, I say be glad for what the Lord has done for you. Philippians 3:1.

I thought to myself, "He has let you live. Here you are, your jaw is barely on the mend, your fractured hips and legs are weak. Your broken nose will never be straight again. You can't talk yet, you can't walk yet, and you will never walk again without a limp. Thank God that he let you live."

God was on my mind this morning of my confirmation. To be confirmed was to be brought into the presence of the Lord, to be accepted into a community of like-minded people, and to become part of a united spiritual family. This Christian rite conferred the gift of the spirit on me, the confirmand. I wanted to be confirmed in my Lutheran faith and to be strengthened by my beliefs. I think I did. I was mad at God, see.

When I sat down by Papa's bed that morning, his eyes managed to open and he tried to smile but the contraption got in the way. The wires only let him open his mouth so far. He wanted to say something, but he couldn't talk very well with his mouth in a grimace. So I bent down and put my ear to his mouth, and what I heard sounded like, "My Christelchen, this is such a big day for you and I have to spoil it all."

He stroked my head, which was to say he loved me. I broke down and cried because I felt so sorry that this accident had befallen him. But there was something else in my tears, another feeling that sneaked in and took hold of me. I was angry at him. I thought, "Oh, Papa, why do you have to be sick on this day of my confirmation? I want this to be a perfect day." Quickly, though, I changed the thought; I should be ashamed of myself. God will strike me dead. Papa is on the mend, isn't he? Thank God, thank God, thank God.

The living room was being set up for a party after the church event. Two white damask table cloths covered a long, rectangular table that was already spilling over with flowers. Mutti and Doris had filled vases with carnations and daisies, set the good china and silverware on the table, added the sugar bowl and creamer and salt and pepper shakers, and folded the napkins so they looked like birds resting on the blue corn flowers of the china. A cheerful living room, in all.

After church, this table would be filled with cakes and glazed tortes with cherries and plums, and our guests would top off these sweet delicacies with whipped cream. Despite all the activity, with Mutti, Klaus, and Doris hurrying back and forth between the kitchen and the living room, there was a stillness about the house, for this was a reflective as well as a festive day. If only my father weren't so sick. How could I be the center of the celebration when my faith was in such shaky condition and I was mad at both my heavenly and my earthly father?

The catechism says that the rite of confirmation is an act that confirms the faith given to me at baptism and is a declaration of intent to remain faithful to the belief I have acquired. Praise the Lord, they had said at my baptism in 1943, praise the Lord, all his works everywhere in his dominion. Did that include the 137 air raids Hamburg had already suffered that year?

Another table on one side of the living room was now brimming with presents covered with another tablecloth such that I couldn't even guess what the presents might be by the shapes of their packages. Slips, hose, pajamas, handkerchiefs, perfume, and billfolds were the popular gifts this year, as they were every year, but I was hoping for another diary. I had things I wanted to say only on paper.

On this Sunday morning I was in my room getting ready for church. My short hair was washed and curled. Mutti had allowed me to wear a trace of lipstick, not too much, for she said only bad girls wore too much makeup. Well, mother, I thought, I may be a bad girl, though not in the way you mean it: I'm mad at my father, and isn't that bad? And I'm mad at God. God has no compassion in my newly-critical eyes. So what's a little lipstick, mother, even if the natural look is much more appealing as you tell me again and again. I applied the lipstick from a sample tube my sister had gotten as a gift at a drugstore.

As I stepped into my black, ankle-length, full taffeta skirt, I thought how perfect it was for dancing. No dancing today, though. The stand-up collar of the black, velvet bodice crawled up my neck and nearly choked me. The short sleeves were a blessing, though, because this day in April was already stifling and it wasn't even noon yet. I slipped on my garter belt and stockings, which felt prickly on my legs. Do I really have to wear them? A nod from Mutti. Yes. I obeyed.

Today I would be initiated into the adult community of the Lutheran church. I had learned that having God by my side would sustain and strengthen me as well as make me a better person. I wanted to be good and I believed what I had learned. Besides, everybody I knew was Lutheran, almost all Northern Germans were Lutheran, and our whole family on both sides had been Lutheran since Luther had rebelled against the Catholic Church nearly five hundred years before. I didn't want to be different. I wanted my relationship with God to last to the end of my days. So why couldn't I just be a good child, like Doris and Klaus?

The church bells rang, calling us to the service. We all blew kisses to the dozing Papa. His face was flushed, and when my mother touched his forehead lightly he moaned. Dear God, make him better now.

I picked up my Bible and my white handkerchief with a sprig of lilies-of-the-valley tucked inside and joined Mutti, Klaus, his fiance Anne, and Doris for the walk to church. We were all in black for this solemn occasion. Doris was wearing her old confirmation dress from two years ago, and my brother's dark suit looked like he had outgrown the pants of this one too. Mutti's black lace dress with the white collar befitted the occasion. It was the same dress she wore for funerals and other more uplifting occasions such as her wedding anniversary. My favorite uncle Paul, the one whose life had hung by a thread in a Russian prisoner-of-war camp and who had been pieced back together again by Tante Else, would meet us at the church.

Now the church bells tolled insistently. We knew everybody in the neighborhood, and soon other confirmands, friends, and neighbors walked together. At the end of our street, our short walk took us past an apartment building of dark red bricks where just fourteen years before a fire bomb had blown away both building and lives. *Thy kingdom come, thy will be done.*

When we arrived at St. Gabriel, my family walked into the chapel, and I joined the other confirmands upstairs in the room where we had been meeting for the last two years of catechism. Pastor Lindemann had asked us not to make comments about each other's outfits because clothes were the least important aspect of this day. We were all children of God, and God loved us all equally even when we were dressed in funereal black with an occasional white collar to brighten the bodice.

The first thing I said to my friend Erika was, "Oh, Erika, I really like your lace collar," and then slammed my hand to my mouth to avoid saying any more nonsense.

As we lined up, Pastor Lindemann reminded us of the order of service, and then we walked downstairs to the back of the chapel. At the sound of the organ's rousing *Ein feste Burg ist unser Gott* (A Mighty Fortress is our God) by Martin Luther, our feet began moving in measured steps. We walked single-file down the center aisle, one little lamb following another, straight into the arms of God. The haunting, sweet scent of the lilies-of-the-valley in the handkerchief wafted up from my hands gripping my Bible, and I looked neither left nor right at a single soul in the congregation. They were all a blur. I was headed for the altar and beyond …

Frau Steinbach, a neighbor and friend, looks in on Papa. He's sleeping, unaware of where I am. She pats his dry lips with a moist washcloth.

St. Gabriel, the parish church, was simple, almost pristine. Wooden pews, stone floor, rectangular windows with clear glass. A wooden cross by the altar reaching to the high ceiling the only adornment.

We arranged ourselves in a semi-circle, three rows deep, the way we had rehearsed it the week before, and faced the altar to see Pastor Lindemann standing in front of us. Everyone had come to see us take our vows. Even God was watching me.

The service began. *Ich glaube an Gott, den allmächtigen* Vater—I believe in God, the Father Almighty, Maker of Heaven and Earth. We recited the Apostles' Creed in unison. My lips moved while I wondered what my Papa was doing right now. Is he awake, sipping chicken broth through a straw? The sucking motion hurts him. He grimaces. The tree was made by God, but why did he put it just there, in the path of the careening car?

Pastor Lindemann asked, *Do you intend to continue steadfast in the confession of the faith you have learned, even in the face of death?* Death, there's that word again. To get ready for this question, I had studied Martin Luther's Small Catechism for the last two years, twice a week for two hours each. We met with Pastor Lindemann at the church, ten girls and a shepherd, and we read and discussed topics like the Ten Commandments, The Apostles' Creed, The Lord's Prayer, Baptism, The Lord's Supper, and the Confession and Forgiveness of Sins. Occasionally we had a test, the answers to which were neatly given in the catechism, passages from the Bible illuminating the answers. For instance, "How does God answer prayer?" "God hears the prayers of all Christians and answers in His own way and at His own time."

But I didn't have time. I prayed for my Papa to get well this instant. Still, in the face of death, I gave God the benefit of the doubt because He let my Papa live, and I will continue steadfast in the confession of the faith I have learned even in the face of death.

Do you desire to become a member of the Evangelical Lutheran Church and of St. Gabriel. Yes.

Do you intend to conform your life to the divine Word, to be faithful in your use of the means of grace and in faith, word, and action remain true to God, Father, Son, and Holy Spirit even to death?

The car, with the driver asleep at the wheel, hit the tree. Papa's forehead split open, leg bones cracked, and skin tore to expose flesh. He and the other man bled, their life slowly seeping into the car and onto the lonely stretch of country road, until someone happened to drive by and called for help.

"Yes, I will conform my life to the divine Word, if you will help my father get well. Dear God, I'm bargaining with you." I felt very hot and uncomfortable in this black velvet top that I had coveted so much. All I wanted was for this cere-mony to be over so I could see how Papa was doing. Is Frau Steinbach fluffing his pillow? Is he awake, motioning to his dry lips? She dips a finger into a bowl of water and taps his lips.

My thoughts meandered to the hospital where Papa lay for six weeks, and I felt disconnected from where I was standing facing the wooden cross. The hospi-tal was sterile white, more hushed even than this church. Papa couldn't speak, so Doris and I sat and chattered and held his hands. Then I had to go to the bath-room. In the hallway, a male figure walked slowly towards me and I looked at him to say hello, but he stared back at me unseeingly. He didn't see the horror in my eyes as they fell on his partially reconstructed face. Blown apart in seconds in the war. Twelve years after the end of the war, surgeons were still piecing together a nose, lips, and ears, and a jaw and cheeks to restore his face. Did he sense me? He grimaced—perhaps a smile of sorts? I was appalled by his visage that first nau-sea and then fear swept over me as though my worst nightmares had materialized. I had seen people with shattered faces in my dreams, but this man was real and he was standing before me. Where did he get the will to live with a face like that? I was trembling now and ran back to Papa's room. I wanted to feel compassion but I was conscious of horror alone. And I hated myself for it, because compassion for all living things was supposed to be present in all of us. My Papa's condition unleashed compassion in me that I didn't know I had, but what about the blind man? Where was my compassion for him? I felt ashamed on this day of my confirmation.

Hallowed be thy name. Why? Why should I say that? And then I said it. Hallowed be thy name.

And the ceremony continued with the confirmands saying the Lord's Prayer in unison. *Vater unser, der du bist im Himmel, geheiligt werde dein Name—Our Father who art in Heaven, hallowed be thy name,* and on and on, I almost in tears because I had been told that God was love and that he loved me. I wanted to love him in return, but I couldn't just now. My Papa needed all my love and compassion and I didn't care if *thy kingdom come and thy will be done.* Finally, the Lord's Prayer was over. I sensed Mutti in the third row fidgeting with her handkerchief. She, too, wanted to go home.

All the questions had been asked and answered, and Pastor Lindemann presented us as communicant members of our spiritual home, the Lutheran church, while we turned around to face family and friends. We had now been confirmed in our faith and had declared our intention to be true to the faith we had embraced. The Pastor gave each of us a booklet with a biblical verse chosen with each of us specifically in mind. The congregation stood and applauded, unaware that there was a fraud among the confirmands: Christel. We moved off the raised altar platform and sat down in the first two rows of the pews reserved for us.

Pastor Lindemann's sermon followed, and while he spoke in his simple and sincere way I opened my booklet to the inside cover where a picture of Jesus faced me, his eyes veiled with weariness and pain, his lips slightly open in disbelief. I see Papa's warm, hazel eyes look for me from his broken face. He is awake, waiting for us.

Then I read the handwritten verse selected for me by my Pastor: *Not as though I had already attained, either were already perfect: but I follow after, that I may apprehend that for which also I am apprehended of Christ Jesus.* Philippians 3:12. I had to read it several times, and even then I couldn't understand it all. The words, "not perfect" stayed with me, though. I understood that I was not perfect, indeed that I was a confused teenager. Still, Pastor Lindemann reminded us that if we sinned, we must go back to God and ask for forgiveness. His mercy is endless. Maybe He will wait for me.

Later that night, Papa's condition worsened and a doctor on duty at the nearby hospital made a house call. Mutti had been by his side since the accident and at the same time had also managed to buy me a confirmation outfit and throw a party for me. Money was tight, because when Papa didn't work he didn't get paid. He was not a salaried man. While Papa was recuperating, my family received disability pay and unemployment from the government, but eventually Mutti was forced to go to work. Since the whole neighborhood knew about Papa's accident, an offer soon came from the local pharmacist who was also a family friend. He needed someone to clean, shop, and cook for him.

At fifty-six years of age, Mutti now had two households to take care of, and she was tired to the bone. Yet she never complained, nor do I recall her asking us for help. She was being her usual saintly self, which made it impossible for me to appreciate the heavy burden she carried.

I would like to say that I helped her, but I probably didn't. My job was to go to school. Maybe I did some grocery shopping for her now and then, but mostly I was wrapped up in my own life and didn't notice when her lips appeared pinched or bluish, at which time she put a little pill under her tongue. She had heart trouble, but she wouldn't go to the doctor for extensive tests because she didn't want to hear any bad news. Mutti was very stubborn that way. She told us, her children, that her heart was weak because she had worked too hard during and after the war. Other than that, her heart was fine, she said. I didn't learn until years later that as a child she had had rheumatic fever, probably caused by a case of scarlet fever that hadn't been properly treated. Since antibiotics hadn't yet been discovered, the rheumatic fever damaged her heart valves. As a child, I didn't know this fact of her life, so blaming the war with all its stress and strain made sense to me.

Papa recovered from the accident but was left with some permanent scars. The one on his forehead eventually became less angry-looking but never completely faded. The scar bisected his forehead vertically, like a straight bolt of lightening across the sky. He had a metal pin in his knee and thereafter walked with a limp. His leg had been broken in several places, but even though the repairs had been made he now found it painful to stand playing the double bass. He continued traveling with the same band again until 1961 when an old colleague of his from pre-war times at the *Vereinigte Deutsche Metallwerke* managed to secure a job for him where he could use his skills as a draftsman. Beginning in late 1961, then, and for the first time in a long time, my parents had income they could count on every month.

◆   ◆   ◆

While my parents coped with the changes in their lives, I got used to my new school and found another interest: politics. On Sunday, September 15, 1957, federal elections were held in the *Bundestag,* the lower house of Germany's government. I don't know where this interest in politics came from so all of a sudden, but I was in a state of frenzy when I couldn't even vote! My new school might have had something to do with my interest, because the election, especially campaign "propaganda," was discussed in several classes. It fell to me to get an absentee ballot for Papa, who was back on the road again. Mutti was completely laid back about the election and told me that she voted only to put an end to my constant sermonizing about the critical importance of each vote. I was angry with her for not knowing the candidates and their platforms. She was apolitical, and there was nothing I could do to change that.

On Election Day, I sat next to the radio (no television in the family yet) and wrote down all the election results until they came with such frequency that I couldn't keep up. Although the Christian Democrats (conservative party) won the national election, Hamburg's voters went with the Social Democrats (liberal party), a trend that continues to the present. Although I tried hard to get my parents to tell me whom they voted for, they never discussed this very private matter.

The next federal election in Germany was held in 1961 when I was still one year short of voting age. When the next vote after that was held, I no longer lived in Germany and had stopped following German politics.

But as I concentrated on my life at my new school, my political interests waned. Being at a new school invited comparison. I had been miserable for the last two years at Lerchenfeld and was ready to have some good experiences. At the high school, the student's ultimate goal was taking the *Abitur,* the culminating exam after thirteen years of schooling, going on to a university, getting a degree, and entering a profession. Some of my fellow classmates were truly brilliant; I was not. For the three years I had been there, subjects such as Latin, geometry, and algebra seemed to have little practical value to me and I considered them a waste of time. I didn't even like studying for my German language classes, especially writing essays in my mother tongue. But since all subjects were compulsory, I had no choice. Only English and music made my mind sing.

The general atmosphere at Lerchenfeld had been strict and restricting and ostensibly unchangeable. Attendance rules were rigid, and any absence had to be fully explained. So I never skipped even an hour!

In contrast, the goal of the Business High School was to train students for a career in the practical world. Students came from several types of high schools. Some had already graduated from technical high schools and were voluntarily subjecting themselves to another two years of business training. Consequently, attendance was more or less up to them, though it turned out to be very regular indeed. I never skipped a day because I wanted to be there, though that didn't mean I loved everything about this school or that I couldn't face its challenges. From the very beginning scholastic competition was much keener than it had been at Lerchenfeld, requiring many hours of homework after a full day of school (3:00 p.m. rather than 1:00 p.m. dismissal). I floundered from time to time, as my report cards revealed. As had been the case all along, if I didn't do well in a subject it was either because I wasn't interested in it or didn't like it because I wasn't doing well. Spanish was one of those subjects, but in the end my Spanish grade proved satisfactory and I was even able to use what I had learned of that language on my first job.

The atmosphere in the classroom was relaxed, and the exchange of ideas was encouraged. Therefore, discussion of business-related matters was routine. Because our class stayed together every hour of every day, we made friendships that extended to life outside of school. It was a time of camaraderie, but one that didn't include dating. Nobody was going out with anyone else exclusively. When we left school at 3:00 p.m., we often walked in groups to the subway station, sometimes stopping at the ice cream parlors, tea rooms, or espresso cafes that were springing up all over the city.

Our teachers were more informal than those at my previous school and invited us to talk freely to them. They treated us as adults, calling us by our last names and titles (*Fräulein* or *Herr*) which in turn encouraged us to act like adults most of the time. There were two teachers whom I remember vividly: our business teacher, Dr. Oelze, and our government teacher, Herr Nielsen. Dr. Oelze was the "my-word-is-the-law" kind of teacher, and I was a little afraid of him. In his class we paid attention for he wouldn't have it otherwise. He might well have served in the military in his past because he had a no-nonsense air about him, holding himself erect and now and then cracking only a bit of a smile. Despite his stern exterior, though, I always felt that he cared about us and wanted us to do well in the business world.

Herr Nielsen was just the opposite—a pudgy man in his thirties, with a pear-shaped face and puffy jowls that had spit gathering in the corners of his mouth, especially when he reprimanded us for our outrageous infractions of the rules. He would say, *"Menschenskinder, nun seien Sie doch endlich mal ruhig!"* ("For goodness sakes, be quiet already"). Here was a teacher whom we had figured out and whose good nature and inability to control us we thus exploited mercilessly. (If it isn't too late, Herr Nielsen, I would like to apologize!) In our defense I had to say that there wasn't much in Herr Nielsen's lectures that couldn't be found in our textbook. When I didn't join in the general mayhem, I would sit quietly reading *Anna Karenina,* holding the book upright on top of my desk and disguised by a textbook. How else was I going to get through eight hundred pages? It wasn't until many years later that I came to regard him as a fellow teacher, as someone who also had had student discipline problems.

Outside of school, activities went on that were typical of sixteen-year olds. I went to the movies with my friends. At this point in our lives we preferred American films because everything American was far more exciting than anything German. I fell in love with every Hollywood actor I saw on the screen—William Holden, Montgomery Clift, Clark Gable, Rock Hudson.

I liked Doris Day movies in particular because her roles allowed her to mix ambition with attractiveness to the opposite sex by means of a kind of flirtiness that was quite appealing to me. Each time I saw a movie of hers, I left the theater thinking that I wanted to be just like her. Indeed, in my mind, I already looked like her. But then, I seemed to take on the looks of any of the leading ladies I saw (Audrey Hepburn, for instance), imagining that when people looked at me they saw Audrey Hepburn. Whenever I left the theater, I felt intensely glamorous, as though one actress or another had entered my body. Here I was with my cotton skirt and petticoat, a white cotton blouse, flat shoes, and a ponytail, and I thought I looked like Audrey Hepburn or Doris Day! Anybody could have seen right through this pretense, this shameful play-acting. Well, by the next morning I would be done with my pretending and back to the Christel I really was—a girl who was vulnerable to romance and glamour in her young life.

America, as depicted in the American movies I attended, fit much better as the backdrop for this romantic feeling than the German movies popular at that time, the *"Heimat"* films. *Heimat* means "home" or "homeland," the place of one's birth, but it meant so much more. It evoked feelings of tradition, of childhood, of the past, of security and family. I liked some of the Heimat films. They showed pretty places, like Lake Constance, a large lake on the Rhine between Germany, Switzerland, and Austria, or majestic imposing ones like the Alps. The landscapes in the movies differed so much from the reality of ruined buildings that we still lived with every day in my 1950's home town. Everyday life in the Heimat films shown against the backdrop of idyllic mountain villages was so unlike the struggles that people had gone through only a few years past. Still, people yearned for the normalcy depicted in the Heimat movies. In them, anger and guilt over the war vanished and the world was whole again. Heimat movies didn't deal with the building boom that was going on in the midst of the ruins but gave people a chance to escape into a fantasy. I liked them for showing places that I wanted to visit, places that were different from the flat Northern German landscape. The movies opened for me the world I wanted to see in and beyond my Germany.

Which brought me back to my fascination with American movies. In America, homes and furnishings and cars were big and pretty, and people were well-dressed in colorful stylish clothes. Americans had washing machines and dryers, television sets and electric can openers. This precisely was the world in which I wanted to live.

◆   ◆   ◆

The movies played another part in my life, because it was through them that I met my first serious boyfriend. On a Sunday in November of 1957, Doris and I had plans to go to the 6:30 p.m. movies with her friend Elke. Because the movie theater was around the corner from our house, Doris had walked there earlier that day to get the tickets for that night's performance. On a walk with her friend Elke that afternoon, they ran into two friends, Lutz and Eberhard, who expressed the desire to go to the movies with us. I had seen Lutz and Eberhard before; we lived in the same neighborhood, and Doris had been to the movies once with Eberhard. He wasn't her boyfriend, just a friend she went out with once in a while, although she teased me later about Eberhard being an *Abgelegter,* a cast-off. His good looks were intriguing, and I had fleeting thoughts about what might be behind those good looks. Did he have a brain, a heart? So far we had only passed on the street now and then, nodded, and said hello.

Doris gave our pre-purchased tickets to Lutz so that he could exchange them in order for the five of us to sit together. I didn't particularly want to go to the movies with boys but at the same time wanted to see *Ferien auf Immenhof,* one of the Heimat films. Doris and Elke said they would pick me up at the house, but when they failed to show up I walked to the theater by myself to find Lutz and Eberhard already waiting there. Lutz introduced himself, shook my hand, and then it was Eberhard's turn. His handshake was extremely firm, and my hand first felt crushed and then tingled like mad. Mutti had always said that a firm hand shake was a sign of character and self-assurance, and if so I had just had an introduction to Eberhard's good character.

When we were all assembled, we went into the theater and sat down in no particular order. The order in which we sat was important. Did this order just happen? I don't know, but I ended up sitting between Lutz and Eberhard, with Doris and Elke sitting on the other side of them. The movie was boring, but sitting between two boys was even more so, as there occurred not even an accidental brushing of hands. Still, I was aware of Eberhard, and my heart was pumping hard. Something must have been happening, but what? I was clueless, or was I? After the movie, we stood around and talked before we all went our separate ways home.

The next day, I ran into Eberhard on the street. He turned around and said, "Hello, Christel." My heart raced again, reacting to this simple and straightforward greeting.

The following day, as I was turning the corner on the street where I lived I saw Eberhard coming toward me. This time we stopped and talked, chit-chat mainly, but I did let him know that I liked to see plays and he said he did too. Wasn't that amazing? I left it at that, but he said, "Maybe we can go together sometime." Actually, he was on his way to get tickets for a performance, whereupon I gave him the money to buy me a ticket. We agreed to meet again at 6:00 p.m., not that I really believed he would be there, because Doris had warned me that he was in the habit of telling small lies. But there he was at my house at 6:00 p.m. with the news that, unfortunately, the performance had sold out. We decided that on Monday he would get tickets for the Thalia Theater, and when we met at 4:00 p.m. on Tuesday he showed me the tickets for the following Sunday.

After that performance, alone with my diary, I assessed the evening as having been wonderful. We had become much closer. I didn't go into details, because Doris might read my diary and tease me. I firmly believed I would never ever forget a single thing that had happened. But I did forget. In retrospect, we probably went so far as to hold hands.

Then in December, Eberhard and I saw *La Boheme* at the rebuilt Opera House in Hamburg. We each paid the 1,10 Marks for a standing place on the fourth tier. There were four small cubicles on the fourth floor, each big enough to allow four people to stand, two in front and two in the back. Because we wanted the two places in the front, we arrived early and were in fact the first two people to enter the building. We removed our shoes, raced up four flights of stairs and claimed our places in the cubicles. From this far up, the performers looked rather small, but we didn't care. We were both students and couldn't afford better.

Walking from the streetcar stop on the way home, Eberhard put his arm around my shoulder and pressed his body to mine. I trembled inside. Hadn't I been wishing for this to happen? Yes—and for more. The sensation of desire was building in me, true enough, but it was still largely in my head.

We met after school sometimes, but only for a few minutes. Long enough for me to watch his lips move as he talked. How often did I think about kissing him? I thought about his lips when they nowhere remotely near mine. Even when I wasn't watching him, my limbs tingled. I wanted to kiss those lips and explore that mouth, but I was also reluctant because I had never done that to a mouth before. How would it feel, would it be disgusting or would I swoon? It couldn't be disgusting, not judging by the delicious feelings I was having just thinking about it. When I ran into him accidentally, I blushed because I feared that my desire was plainly there on my face for him to scrutinize. He took my hand briefly in his, and there I was standing on the street corner with the boy of my dreams. But it wasn't a dream, it was real and internally I jumped for joy, doing cartwheels for the sheer thrill of being in love.

On Sunday, December 15, we attended Verdi's *Masked Ball*. The music was magnificent, and in typical operatic tradition the story line included a love triangle. In this and other operas we had seen, the stories dealt with love, betrayal, mistaken identities, death, and multiple variations thereof. The stuff of life, as we would find out, but also the music thrilled us. Or was it really the music? During the entire performance, we nearly merged along our sides, our sweaty hands intertwined. During the love duets, we gazed into each other's eyes longing for each other's desire. Our eagerness had us breathless for more. Perhaps, dared I think it, a kiss?

I was sixteen years, two months, and twenty-eight days old and I had never been kissed, other than by my family and relatives. This status was about to change, I hoped. As the girl, I couldn't make the first move. When the opera ended, Eberhard and I took the city train home and then walked from the station to my house, arms around each other. I was nervous but he seemed calm. He walked me up to the front door of my house, where my parents had cleverly left the lights on for me. Then we talked for a minute or two until he leaned into me, putting his arms around me. I knew what was coming—my first kiss. Eberhard pressed his body to mine and his warm, searching lips found mine. Delirious, delicious heat surged through me. My heart seemed to leap up towards my lips, exploding into desire that I had never known before. Finally, we separated and Eberhard walked to the gate. I stood and watched him, wanting to call him back first for one kiss and then for another. In this state, I lay sleepless all night, replaying every moment of our encounter.

In school the next day, I sat closed-eyed in class, my breathing almost panting. He was virtually right there with me and his nearness made me lightheaded. Or was I just hyperventilating? He was mine, I thought, forever and ever, and someday I would be Frau B. Eberhard was perfect, so much the man of my dreams that I need not look any further, having found my man so early on. Love was changing me, transforming me, even making me a better person. Yes, I would love everyone in the universe. And even stop arguing with Mutti.

This was our time, Eberhard's and mine. Just like opera had a season, this was our season. Attending the opera every Saturday or Sunday gave us three and a half glorious hours to watch *La Boheme, Fidelio, and Der Rosenkavalier* when we weren't gazing into each other's eyes. Yes, sometimes we even listened to the magnificent music. Standing behind another couple now became our preferred place because it was so much better for kissing and pressing against each other's bodies, while at the same time maintaining some semblance of decorum. Sometimes, music students sat on the floor in the hallway behind the cubes, music sheets spread out over their laps, listening closely to each note or following the libretto. Having these pesky students in back of us kept our groping down, we who had a certain music surging through us, we whose hands were instruments.

Our walks home from the train station were now much longer than ten minutes, sometimes longer than the entire opera. Each park bench invited us to stay. Are those seats still sizzling from the heat of our bodies? We couldn't keep our hands off each other as we kissed, embraced, and he caressed my breasts. Oh, we wanted more, but I had promised Mutti not to have sex. She hadn't asked me right out but had probably said something to the effect of *Mach keine Dumm-heiten*—"Don't do anything stupid." I promised her I wouldn't; I couldn't break that promise because then I wouldn't be able to look her in the eye. Mutti had a way of knowing if I had stepped over a threshold.

Eberhard came to my house and we did homework together, sitting next to each other at the living room table and studying. When our bodies craved contact, we played a slow Elvis song and danced. There wasn't a millimeter between us and I could tell from the bulge in his pants that he wanted me. How much studying we accomplished, I don't know, but at least we had to try to get some work done, though work interrupted frequently by ravenous cross-table looks. Sitting next to each other had been a bad idea because of the heavy groping it allowed. Still, every few minutes we leaned across the table and kissed, each kiss like a period ending a sentence and beginning a new one.

Meanwhile, Mutti was hanging around the kitchen for reasons of propriety. Per her, "The neighbors see Eberhard come over, so I don't want them to think that you are in the house alone with a boy." As far as she was concerned, Eberhard could come over any time, and he was always invited to have meals with us.

For some reason, he never invited me to his apartment. Sometimes I saw his mother walk by our house arm in arm with an older man whom Eberhard called "Uncle." She was a war widow. After the chaos of World War II, people had been forced to make living arrangements that to some extent threw out the old rules. Marriage was not always in the best interests of the two people involved, often as not for financial reasons. Eberhard's mother received a pension from the government because her soldier husband had been killed in the war, and if she remarried the pension would no longer be paid. So she chose to raise Eberhard and his sister with the help of an older man who served as an uncle to Eberhard. Their apartment was only a few minutes away from my house, but I was never invited to step inside. I found that odd, but he and I never talked about it. Instead, he came to my house.

When he was not at my house, and I was in school or meeting with my church youth group for our regular monthly meetings, I would think of him—his blond, short hair, his hazel eyes, his regular facial features, his athletic body, his open mind. I saw him everywhere—in his name that I scrawled in my notebook, in the faces of leading men in the movies. My grades should have been slipping, but somehow they weren't. I wanted to do well for Eberhard and didn't want to disappoint him. Did that make sense? It did then. He told me *Ich liebe dich* and I told him the same, and I meant it. Did he? *Ich liebe dich*, three little words that sounded tempting and terrifying at the same time. Was he saying those words because he wanted more? A sliver of doubt made its way into my worshipful mind. Of course, someday there would be more than kisses and caresses. In the meantime, I saved myself for the promise of more to come.

As suddenly as this liaison began it ended, coming crashing down just as the opera season was winding down sometime in May of 1958. No explanations, no long talks, no harsh words, no confrontations. Very odd. Our dating had come to an end, but I didn't ask why. He simply stopped taking his familiar route past my house, so I could no longer see him or run into him. He was still very much present in my head, and my body remembered and yearned for him, but mostly I was obsessed with needing to find out what had happened. I couldn't just ask him, because then he would know it bothered me that he had dropped me. It was convoluted thinking at its best, and it infuriated me but I couldn't step out of myself and my role which I didn't even recognize as a role yet.

Eventually, with Doris' help, I came to think that he must have another girl-friend. Doris was more astute about relationships; she had horse sense that was born of experience with several more boyfriends than I had had. When I finally saw Eberhard walk by my house with another girl hanging on his arm and talking to him with her face turned up to his (she was shorter), I was nonetheless heart-broken. I stood behind the lace curtains in my room, hidden from view but see-ing Eberhard and the girl quite clearly, while their image imprinted on my soul.

He hadn't just changed routes, he had changed girlfriends. The louse! From Eberhard's sister I learned that his new friend's name was Roswitha. What kind of a name was Roswitha anyway? A despicable, ugly name! Still, this girl had long, chestnut-brown hair cascading down her back through which a boy's fin-gers could weave. I didn't like her and I hated him.

I stood in my room behind the curtains at the same time every day, because I had figured out that he was picking her up from work. It was agony to see them together, and every day I cried for the lost love that I thought would last forever. I would never be Frau B. I continued with this spying for a few weeks, numb with rejection and sadness, until I could bear it no longer and stopped. Still, the misery lingered. Then one day I caught myself looking at a particularly handsome schoolmate and I realized that I was no longer as upset with Eberhard as I had been.

Confirmation 1957—Christel third from left, bottom row

Confirmand Christel with her presents

8

Class trip to the Rhine

✦

1958

1958—German Law granting equal rights to men and women is passed. The Hula-Hoop comes to Germany from the United States and can be bought for 4,95 Marks, about a dollar then. One hundred million of them are sold in the first year. 150,000 people gather in front of City Hall to protest the German government's plan to furnish the armed forces with atomic weaponry. The work week drops to forty-four hours per week in some industries, and work-free Saturdays gradually become the norm. Elvis Presley arrives on board a troop transport ship in Bremerhaven on October 1 and is greeted by thousands. Only a few expressways exist in Germany to date.

In 1958, I traveled again, exploring another part of Germany. And my faith was tested once again on the road to adulthood.

I hadn't traveled much in my seventeen years. So far, I had been to the Baltic Sea, to which Doris and I and our friends rode bicycles, to the island of Sylt in the North Sea on a class trip, and during the war to Czechoslovakia whose beauties I didn't really appreciate until I saw it again as an adult, and assorted places around Hamburg I could reach by public transportation.

Some of my friends, on the other hand, had been all over Germany and even to foreign countries, and I envied them. Their parents could afford to take their families on trips, but my family couldn't. Mutti and Papa couldn't even scrape enough money together to travel, just the two of them. I couldn't help with travel expenses because it wasn't customary for high school students to work after school. It was completely out of the question for me to have a job as well as go to school. Indeed, I had so much homework that it never even occurred to me to look for work, although sometimes I did the grocery shopping for Tante Möller, a family friend. She always gave me list on which she specified in detail what she wanted me to get, such as "good German butter" (by that she meant, NOT Danish butter, only because one of her daughters had married a Dane whom she disliked). After I carried nets and bags full of stuff up the four flights of stairs, she would press a Mark or two into my hands. Just enough to pay for movie tickets.

My parents never gave me an allowance, but they gave me money on a "need" basis. Somehow they scraped up the money for an upcoming class trip, and I added what little I had saved up. Being a typical, normal, self-centered teenager, I doubt that I showed sufficient appreciation for what they must have sacrificed for me.

For ten glorious days in August, I traveled the Rhineland, a part of Germany that played a big role in our legends, songs, and poetry. Our major stops were *Koblenz, Oberwesel, Bacharach, and Idar-Oberstein.*

The train took us from Hamburg to *Koblenz,* and after more than five hours of being cooped up, we finally tumbled from the train to see, high on a hill, the fortress *Ehrenbreitstein,* a massive part of which had been converted into a youth hostel. The only disadvantage to staying in this facility was that a hill had to be climbed and the luggage carried on our backs. The fortress was situated 118 meters above the Rhine, which meant that we had to drag our luggage the length of a steeply-graded American football field. I didn't make that comparison then, but it explained why we had all begun to complain of the physical ordeal.

Our teachers on this trip, Frau Dr. Peeck and Herr Nielsen, didn't waste any time getting us going. Once unpacked in our dorm rooms, we were due for a hike along the river Mosel. Our beloved English teacher, Dr. Peeck, had told us that we would find the area magnificent, and we did. All around us, on every inch of fertile, green hills, we saw vistas of terraced vineyards. Over the next ten days, we would get to know this area very well—hiking, sightseeing, visiting churches and castles and fortresses. The stories read to us as children would come alive for us—stories of chivalry, of brave knights and maidens who loved them. Although I have forgotten many of the Rhine legends of my childhood, one of them still comes to mind. I think I remember it, because the Castle *Pfalzgrafenstein,* where much of the story took place, was located on an island (rather than atop a hill) in the middle of the Rhine River near the village of Kaub. The story began about eight hundred years ago.

Emperor Friedrich Barbarossa and Duke Henry the Lion of Brunswick were cousins and enemies. Count Konrad of Palatine, who lived on Burg Stahleck only a short distance down the river, was a friend of Emperor Barbarossa.

The Count had a beautiful daughter, Agnes. It was time to get her married off. The Count had no sons, so the future husband would have to possess special qualifications because he would be assuming the title of Count when Konrad died.

Agnes, however, had her own ideas, and almost immediately upon learning of her father's special requirements for a husband, she promptly fell in love with Henry, the son of Duke Henry the Lion of Brunswick. Her father was livid. How could she, how dare she fall in love with the son of the Emperor's enemy? Only her mother took her side. The Count tried to no avail to get his wife to change their daughter's mind. He was outnumbered, which was not a state he could accept. So he locked them both up in the tower, thinking that his daughter would be safe there from young Henry's advances.

But Henry wanted Agnes, so he hired a boatman to row him to the island. When mama saw how happy Henry and Agnes were, she gave them her blessing and had a priest ferried to the island to marry them.

Nine months later, the Count's wife (she didn't have a first name, she was simply the "Count's wife") got her husband to come to the island. I don't know how she did that, but I suppose she asked one of the boatmen to contact her husband. The Count thought that the women had come to their senses and wanted to leave the island. Well, he was in for a shock, because not only had he gained a son-in-law but also a grandchild. Of course, the babe was a boy.

This was all well and good, but how was the Count to explain that the son of the Emperor's enemy had joined the Count's family. Would the Emperor ever forgive him? As it turned out, the Emperor was pleased that the Count's daughter had brought the feuding cousins closer together. He became the child's godfather, and the families reunited. You can still see the room where the child's cradle stood.

I always liked this legend, because it had a happy ending and because I liked strong women. Even though I was years away from being a feminist, I understood somewhere deeply in my being that women had the power over life-changing events.

About eight hundred years later, on our first night in *Koblenz,* my classmates and I sat around the ancient courtyards of the fortress *Ehrenbreitstein,* meeting young people from all over Europe. Somebody was playing a guitar and people were singing and drinking wine. A young man sat down next to me and asked me, in German, if I knew French (unfortunately, up to this point, I had only studied German, English, Latin, and Spanish!), and so I said in German, no, I didn't. This moved him to teach me French for "I love you," the most important words in the French language according to him. To which I replied, "Everybody knows those. Je t`aime," taking the wind out of his sails. He was also very impressed and proceeded to move closer. I didn't tell my mother this, but Jacques and I hugged and kissed without being on a date! More, we hadn't even known each other for an hour. Eberhard flashed through my head—why was he still rattling around there? And my mother as well. I heard her say in my mind, "What are you doing, Christel, kissing a boy you don't even know?"

Eventually that evening, Jacques and I had to say adieu. The fortress gates were being closed for the night, and it was lights out for everyone. The next morning our class moved on, this time by boat to *Oberwesel*. I never saw Jacques again, but I never forgot that spontaneous kiss either.

In *Oberwesel* we got a break, because the youth hostel was on the banks of the Rhine so there was no hill to climb. So we had plenty of steam left to let out, which we did at the "Deutsches Haus" drinking wine and dancing and then more drinking, putting some of us in the unfortunate physical state of having to vomit. Certain of my classmates had drunk at four different establishments. Somehow everyone later found their way back to the youth hostel, not only feeling sicker than dogs but also fearful of a stern lecture by Dr. Peeck. Frau Dr. Peeck, however, was in no condition to lecture because she had been overimbibing as well!

The next morning, a group of very subdued, slow-moving teenagers crept to their next hiking destination. So the ruins of a great fortress (probably *Schönberg Castle*, dating back to the twelfth century) didn't get the attention they deserved, because most of the class was in no condition to appreciate anything, let alone ruins. The tour guide warned us not to join the group if we had the slightest heart condition, at which perhaps half the class instantly developed that condition. Those of us who went forward clutched each other's hands, never to let go, and crept through the very dark, slippery, and rocky hallways bent over like hunchbacks because there was no clearance in which to stand up. Finally, we reached the chamber some of whose gruesome instruments of torture were explained to us in agonizing detail. Not civilized people, those. Justice was swift, if it could even be called justice.

We wanted to get out of there and paid as little attention as possible without courting trouble. Creeping back the same way we had entered, we let out a collective sigh when at last we glimpsed blessed daylight. This little experience could truly have attacked a healthy heart. I was terrified, feeling claustrophobic the whole time I was hunched over and fearing to lose contact with the hand I was holding. At least we were able to *play* in *our* ruins in Hamburg. Why were these war ruins tourist attractions, when our war ruins served merely as playgrounds?

At 8:00 p.m. that night, however, we were ready to party again. This time, we started with a wine tasting at *Daubenspeck,* a local winery, where once again we assembled in a cellar to have an educational experience that had been planned for us. Surrounded by monstrous barrels of wine, we learned a few things about wine-making, which also included sampling three different wines from plastic glasses. When we left the winery, we ran into some guys at the next corner who were emerging from a tavern, bottles in hands. They were more than happy to refill our glasses, bottoms up, refill again—hadn't we just learned how to drink wine? We were a bunch of teenagers, ready for another night of silliness, giggling the night away.

The next morning we hiked again for a few hours. To get away from drinking and hiking, my friend Annegret and I spent our free afternoon in the *Deutsches Haus,* this time sipping iced coffee.

By nighttime, class and teachers assembled at the *Goldenen Pfropfenzieher,* the Golden Wine Opener—yet another tavern. There was money in the class account to buy each of us a glass of wine. Then we danced and talked all evening, in sublime harmony with our classmates and teachers.

It was dawning on me that just two glasses of wine took me to my alcohol consumption limit. If I continued drinking beyond that, I would fall terribly sick. This new-found knowledge became a lifelong sobriety guideline for me.

Bacharach was our next stop, and this youth hostel was—yes—atop another mountain! Our bags were driven up to *Burg Stahleck,* the youth hostel (and former home of Count Konrad, he of the legend), but we had to hike. For an hour after dinner, then, everybody in the hostel assembled in the *Rittersaal,* the Hall of Knights, where we all sang German folk songs such as, *Guter Mond, du gehst so stille....,* and *Was noch frisch und jung an Jahren ...* It was a moving experience for me, singing the songs that I had learned in childhood and feeling the shared history. I was surrounded by my fellow Germans and felt pride arise at the thought of my German-ness. It was a new feeling for me and difficult to explain.

Every day, we engaged in a hiking-up-a-mountain-to-see-another-castle marathon. Between Koblenz and Rüdesheim, a narrow gorge of only about thirty-five miles length, there were more castles to be seen than in any other river valley in the world. If it were up to us, we would gaze at the castles from the valley floor, but our teachers insisted that we have an up-close look.

For a couple of days, we actually stayed on fairly level ground. The ferry took us from *Bacharach* to *Lorch,* after which we hiked for about twenty miles through the romantic *Wispertal* or valley of the Wisper, a tributary of the Rhine. I didn't think we quite appreciated the beauty of this valley, for as always we were singing so loudly that our quiet surroundings were lost on us. Then we were anxious to get to our meeting point where our teacher, "Papi" as we had named Herr Nielsen on this trip, would buy us our next glass of wine from the class account.

The next day, our meeting point was *Rüdesheim.* The most famous little lane there was the *Drosselgasse*, which was lined with taverns on both sides of the narrow street. Earlier, the class had broken up into groups in a disorganized fashion, but eventually we all got to our destination. In fact, our group arrived before our teachers. Fueled by the prospect of a glass of wine, we were hiking faster and faster, practically running to *Rüdesheim* while singing, waiving to passing motorists, resting now and then, but always singing. There wasn't a folk song we didn't know.

When we reached the tavern that was our designated rendezvous, the people there were already dancing though it was only 1:30 in the afternoon. In Rüdesheim, obviously, people danced and drank whenever the mood betook them; time of day was of no importance. We were supposed to hike up to the *Niederwalddenkmal,* a huge monument to the Franco-Prussian War of 1870–1871. The central figure of this 125-feet high monument was *Germania,* the symbol of German statehood. She was leaning on a sword in her left hand while in her right hand holding the recovered crown of the emperor. The monument itself was full of details showing the commanders of the armed forces, Emperor Wilhelm I on a horse, and so on. But having spent so much time in the tavern, we never made it up the hill. History was imposing enough for us from below!

At our last stop in *Idar-Oberstein*, the capital of Germany's precious stone industry, we visited jewelry stores and watched the process of jewelry-making. The little money I had left didn't quite suffice to buy even a small souvenir, and I came home empty-handed. That was all right, though; nobody in my family expected me to buy trinkets for them. On this last night, our whole class, all twenty-three of us, slept in one co-ed dorm room, and for once we heard everyone else's jokes!

We had gotten a great taste of wine region hospitality and agreed among ourselves that people in this part of the country were much friendlier than those—meaning us—in the North! When our return train to Hamburg passed the youth hostel in Oberwesel, the so-called hostel "parents" stood on the balcony of the hostel waving at us with bed sheets. Maybe, though, they were just shaking out the sheets from our stay.

The train home was a special student train, and while we had an opportunity to meet and talk to new people we simply didn't have any energy left. Instead, we slept until the train got closer to Hamburg at which time some of my friends wondered if their boyfriends or girlfriends would be there to meet them. I had no boyfriend to look forward to, but that was all right. Doris picked me up, and I was happy to see her. I wondered if our class would stay together after graduation, which was only a few months away, or whether we would drift apart. Reunions were not part of German school life at that time.

Many of my classmates were planning to leave Germany, at least for a while if not forever. I had had my love affair with America for at least the last three years, but at this point I couldn't see leaving this beautiful country that I called home. How could I be happy elsewhere? At this point in my life, my desire was only to see more of Germany as well as to visit neighboring European countries.

Höhere Handelsschule class on a trip down the Rhine, 1958
Christel second row, second from left

Teacher Nielsen with Christel (right) and classmates, 1958

My English pen pal Pauline Steward and I in Hamburg, 1958

9

Graduation from business school, first job and first trip to England

◆

1959

1959—The German "economic miracle" continues. Unemployment is under one percent. Millions of Germans vacation in Italy in their quest for sun. Jets begin service from Frankfurt to New York. There are now 18,000 self-service grocery stores in Germany. The Shah of Iran marries his third wife to produce heirs to the throne.

I wanted to go to Italy too, but it would have to wait until I earned a salary. However, newspaper articles and travel agency posters promoted Germany's neighbor to the south, and pop songs about *Bella Italia* topped the charts. Oh, to glide on the Grand Canal in Venice or sip espresso on the island of Capri. But all of that had to wait until I could make my own living. First I needed to finish school.

I was still attending church and meeting with my youth group of the same girls I had known for many years. But between the time I returned from the class trip in September 1958 and February 1959, my faith was tested again. I had been a member of the Lutheran Church before and after my confirmation, but within less than six months I had virtually defected!

It all began when two young men rang our door bell and introduced themselves as Mormon missionaries from Utah. They were dressed in black suits, white shirts, and ties. Papa, who was always game for something new, asked them to come in. Little did we know then how much I would be affected by their religion.

Papa and I sat with the two men in our living room and listened as they proceeded to tell us about the prophet Joseph Smith who had a vision at the beginning of the 19th century (1827 to be exact). In this vision the angel Moroni appeared and invited him to come along to a mountain, where Joseph Smith promptly found several huge plates of stone, I think. These plates had something written on them which, miraculously, only Joseph Smith and nobody else could decipher.

These hieroglyphs told of a group of white people, maybe a nation that had lived in North America even before the Indians. Joseph Smith translated the writing on the plates into plain English for other folks to read, and eventually this translation became the Book of Mormon. Competition for the Bible, I asked? Wasn't the Bible *the* word of God? Did we really need another book? I was a little irked at this point. It wasn't until later that I learned that Mormons in fact believe in the Bible *and* the Book of Mormon.

When the two young men who spoke almost perfect German pulled out pictures of African and Indian natives in order to illustrate what they had been telling us, Papa tuned out, offended that they thought he couldn't grasp the story through mere words.

And so it was up to me to keep these guys coming back to tell me more. More? I was as incredulous as my father, but these young men were Americans in the flesh, from the land of my dreams! Messrs. Hunshacker (of German descent) and Burn hailed from Salt Lake City, which had been founded when Brigham Young and his Mormons migrated west to escape religious persecution. Probably, American Easterners had thought the story about the beginning of Mormonism, the discovery of the plates, and so on was a little odd, leading them to make life difficult for the Mormons. The bone of contention could have had something to do with the fact that Mormons believed in practicing polygamy. Whatever the reason, I gave all that I learned about official Mormon history my own interpretative twist, and these are the facts I recall.

Very soon after this initial visit Mr. Hunshacker was given a new post in Rendsburg, and in his place appeared Mr. Filchow. I learned from him that Mormons were not allowed to smoke or drink alcohol, coffee, or strong tea. Instead, they drank peppermint tea, fake coffee (what would that be like—Germany's detested wartime substitute?) or milk. Mostly, I thought this very wise given that I was of the opinion then that alcohol or coffee had harmed many human beings. I don't recall how this belief of mine had developed; maybe it was that desperate craving for good coffee that Mutti had endured during and after the war, or the fact that Papa sometimes came home tipsy after an evening playing with the band.

Next I learned that Mormons were baptized when they were about ten years old, making them old enough to decide for themselves whether they wanted to be Mormons in the first place. Mormons, however, believed in an afterlife, and this I couldn't go along with. Apparently, I had forgotten that Lutherans espoused the same belief. What had I learned in all my Lutheran catechism classes?

There was even more Mormonism that seemed unbelievable to me. For instance, the sealing of marriages in Mormon temples. This meant that deceased married couples were guaranteed to meet again in the afterlife, and that children were sealed to their parents so that families could reunite in a celestial life. I kept asking myself how this could be possible and how could anyone be so certain that this would happen? Who had reported back from the hereafter?

My doubts proceeded to go out the window with the appearance of the wonderful David W., yet another American from Salt Lake City. Over a period of a few weeks I became so besotted with him that I believed anything he told me. For instance, that Joseph Smith had divine help when he translated the symbols on the plates because no mere human being could have deciphered them. That was proof enough for me. Then David claimed that Joseph Smith couldn't have made up the story of the people who appeared on these plates. Proof enough for me again. I believed. Whatever he told me, I believed with all my heart.

I couldn't just leave it at that, though. I had to start imagining myself as his lover, his wife, his helpmate. I had become passionately infatuated with this man and by extension with his religion.

Every Thursday evening I went to a meeting held in a German school because the Mormons in Hamburg didn't have their own building. On Thursday nights, I prayed with Mormons, sang divine Mormon songs, of which I recall only "Come, come ye saints," and discussed the Mormon religion with them. It wasn't my religion yet, but listening and immersing myself in Mormon teachings was bringing me closer to it and farther away from my Lutheran beliefs.

Instead of attending St. Gabriel on Sundays, I now went to the school to be with the Mormons. After a hymn, a prayer, and another hymn, someone from the congregation would give a speech. What a democratic church, this! Communion was part of the service, and even children could take it. I found that a little odd, since they probably didn't yet know why they were taking it. Everyone was given a small piece of bread and a drink of water in small, individual cups.

After communion, believers separated into different discussion groups and, lucky for me, David was the discussion leader in mine. My feelings of infatuation were strong, but there was no way I could see to show them. I then asked myself if I was falling for unattainable men on purpose. Did I have to be in love *and* miserable? Apparently so, because in the discussion about marriage I learned that Mormons love children and favor big families, which in my present altered state of mind I now wanted for myself even though I had never before thought much about having children. Still, having many children with David would be all that I could want in life.

When the Hollywood movie *The Ten Commandments* came out, I attended with a whole group of Mormons. It was a movie mighty in scope and I was duly moved to tears not only by the story but also by Yul Brynner who, even without a single hair on his head, was not bad looking! If David had been there, I swear the movie would have been twice as good. Obviously I was a human wreck, a mixed-up fraud, as in my diary I wrote about "God's power over mankind" and "Moses' direct connection to God." God and Moses were pure, but I was impure. Clearly I was on my way to embracing a belief that intimately combined religion and sex. A powerful combination they were!

On November 13, 1958, David called me by my first name for the first time. Oh, the wonderful feeling! Before this special date, he had been in the habit of calling me Miss Behnke to keep a proper distance. Now, with my spoken first name, we were much closer. Or were we?

Two days later occurred another monumental date in the Mormon-Behnke relationship. David and I looked directly at each other! The Mormons had organized a dance fest, and my friend Silvia and I attended. I was longing to dance with David, but to my great disappointment I found out that the missionaries were not allowed to dance. Still, I caught him glancing at me several times. Although I could have been mistaken, I thought there was heat in those looks. A heat that wasn't going anywhere at the time.

When I saw him again a few days later, I asked him why missionaries were not allowed to dance. He explained, "You see, we're in one place for six to eight months and then we have to leave for another city. If we were to go out with a girl and then leave, her mother would be angry with us." Not only the mothers, I thought. I myself would be devastated, cry my eyes out every day, and even imagine that the end of the world had come early. David's was the smart, diplomatic answer, given many times before to girls who would have given anything to dance with handsome American missionaries.

In addition to my daydreams and fantasies of life with David in Utah, I felt growing doubts, especially about the afterlife. According to some of our discussions, we seem to have pre-existed in a spirit world before God embodied us. Our time on earth was only some kind of trial time with the goal of getting back to the ghost plane. I had my doubts about that belief, so much so that I thought it would be a good idea to look at other religions to see what they had to say about the subject. In this way, the Mormons set me free to explore other religions, a venture I had never felt a need for when I was attending the Lutheran church. Years later when my childhood friend, Dickus, joined the Jehovah's Witnesses, I learned of their beliefs, which were also highly suspect in my opinion.

In December, David (that is what I now called him), gave a talk at my old haunt, the *Amerika Haus,* and showed slides of Utah and Salt Lake City. *Come, come ye saints*, a traditional Mormon hymn, was playing in the background. I don't know how much attention I paid to his words and the slides, but because everyone in the audience was looking at him, I was too, though discreetly so as not to draw attention to myself. It was an evening of soaking up David. Utah I could see later.

A few days after that, David and a new missionary named Mr. Edwards came to the house, and along with my girlfriend Sabine who joined us from time to time had a lively discussion during which it began to dawn on me that maybe the Mormon Church was not for me. This was the first time I had made this admission to myself, and I welcomed my brain back to functioning at least some of the time.

By the end of 1958, I realized that I had no desire to become a Mormon and furthermore understood clearly that the sole object of my desire was the unattainable David. His religion I could have, but he was the one I wanted and couldn't have. It was an intolerable position to be in, but being honest with myself proved to be the first step in my rejection of Mormonism.

Sabine and I continued to have weekly meetings with two missionaries, though David was seldom one of them. He had been reassigned to a traveling missionary position and spent his time in one German city after another, speaking to potential converts. The hour or two we spent each week with our missionaries, however, very often turned adversarial, with Sabine and I arguing about Mormon beliefs rather than discussing them with agreement as the goal. In a way, the tables were turning and we became prideful Lutherans making a case for our religion. My ornery, intense nature came through as I argued vehemently. Although the missionaries worked very hard to keep our conversations on track, Sabine and I managed to steer them away from religious talk to items of interest to us, such as life in the United States.

The end of the year 1958 had come, and on Christmas Eve Doris and I attended the Lutheran Church for the midnight service. I wanted only to get away from the turmoil in my heart and head, and listening to Pastor Lindemann was just what I needed. Being back with my fellow Lutherans gave me a feeling of comfort and safety when we sang, prayed, and listened to the Christmas story as we had for so many years.

Compared with Christmas 1946, the Behnke family now reveled in abundance, relatively. Our tree was symmetrical for once and decorated with plenty of tinsel, ornaments, and candles that made the whole living room glitter and glimmer. There were the presents, but now they were less important than the fact that the family was together, that each room in the house was warm, that food was plentiful. The gnawing feelings of hunger of the post-war years, though not totally forgotten, were pushed aside. The traditional *Kartoffelsalat* and *Würstchen* with tongue-biting mustard would be served later in the evening, and we looked forward to savoring this simple meal.

During the day as we had done for so many years, Papa, Doris and I, and sometimes Klaus, took the train to Reitbrook to visit our grandparents, who though always invited to celebrate Christmas with us, preferred to stay at home. In fact, they had never traveled anywhere all the years I had known them. They were now in their late seventies, beyond traveling age.

We sat with Ernst and Emma in their cozy, undecorated kitchen and watched them open presents we had brought. I think the most we ever received from them were chocolate candy bars. But presents didn't matter so much, not as much as did listening to my Opa tell his old jokes. I can still see his eyes dancing as he delivered the punch lines we had already heard from previous Christmases. Then there was all the talking and drinking of Papa's recipe Grog (a teaspoon of sugar, some hot water, and a lot of rum). At last it was time to travel back home feeling pleasantly warm and lightheaded. From the train, we glanced at candlelit Christmas trees in the windows of apartments, telling us it was time to get home for our own *Bescherung*, the exchange of presents.

◆   ◆   ◆

While my heart was still engaged in fantasies that included far-away places like Utah, I was also trying to finish my last year of school. Finals were coming up, and reports had to be written. Predictably, I wrote my English report on Utah! Finals would last five days in February, and there would be one oral final in March.

Feverously cramming for the finals reminded me of all the ignoble times when I cheated on exams, either by using cheat sheets or by glancing at a fellow student's answers. When I think about the cheating, I still feel ashamed after all these years.

The end of my two years at the Höhere Handelsschule, the business school, had come and I thought it would be the last year of school for the rest of my life. Little did I know that later in life I would enter college for many more years of education.

Finals loomed in German, English, Spanish, Spanish shorthand as well as English Literature, German Literature, Business Spanish, Business Administration, and Accounting. Throughout school, we had shared desks with another student, but for the finals we sat at separate desks to minimize the temptation to cheat. We had three hours and fifteen minutes to write an essay, from any one of the following topics: "Discuss several types of today's typical leisure-time activities and state your opinions," or "Discuss the characters of the two women and Thiel's relationship to them in Gerhart Hauptmann's *Bahnwärter Thiel*. I chose the second topic because I liked the novel and was familiar with the characters from our endless discussions with my classmates.

Evidently, I had not done well enough in the written English final and I was notified that I would have to take an oral examination. Our old classroom had been changed into a "courtroom" where four teacher/judges sat at desks in front of me, the defendant. In English, I was questioned about the literature I had read, probably the work of John Steinbeck. Being questioned in a foreign language, even though I loved English, made me hand-wringingly nervous, and tests written or oral would for many years to come arouse in me an extraordinary sensation of fear.

After the oral exam, all the finals were completed, whereupon we were asked to assemble in the classroom where we were told that we had all passed. Off we dashed to *Filippi*, our favorite espresso café at the train station. On the way there, we noted scraps and wads of paper floating in the river running through the park: bookkeeping worksheets, typewriter exercises, folders torn to bits. To that stream I added a few items of my own (that we were polluting didn't even cross our minds). Here and there in the park, we also noted small heaps of ashes—knowledge burnt but hopefully not forgotten. At Filippis we drank coffee, ate cake, and listened to music. We felt so free—unleashed from the constraints of school, done with finals, a whole new and somewhat daunting life passage in front of us.

German schools didn't have proms, but a week after finals the entire graduating class, of which there were perhaps eighty students, celebrated at a local clubhouse. A jazz band played, to which we danced and danced. We had put together a "newspaper" and we all got a copy. I was so impressed with this newspaper that

I told my diary I would keep the paper forever, to remind me of my school and classmates. Searching for it in later years did not bear out that sentimental thought—it was nowhere to be found, and although I recognized the faces of my classmates from photos I had forgotten their names!

When we came together one final time, we received our report cards in a ceremony at which the school choir presented itself at its worst! I was happy with my grades—the mostly Bs and Cs that definitely made me an average student. My overall attitude was judged to be "friendly, easy to motivate; reserved in class (which meant that I didn't contribute much) but attentive and always making an effort; pleasant workmate" (this last judgment would catch the eye of a future employer).

Almost the whole class celebrated afterwards at a local restaurant. The mood was beyond festive, as merriment and hilarity ruled. We were high on life, dancing and drinking non-alcoholic drinks. (For some reason, only the boys drank beer.) For all the good-bye kisses and hugs, a spectator would have thought that these young people would know each other until the end of time. A reunion was in fact planned for the summer, but it never took place. Such was the fleeting nature of forced togetherness.

◆   ◆   ◆

I abandoned my dream of becoming a stewardess in my second year of business school, thinking that I would be better at a land-based job. Although the idea of flying was exhilarating, the actual flying could prove not to be because I got sick on ships and might very well do the same on a plane.

I was qualified to apply for trilingual German, English, Spanish secretarial and clerk jobs. But just because I was qualified didn't mean I was confident in my abilities. Nonetheless, after one interview, the firm of Alexander Petersen and Company found me worthy of employment. Still, I had my doubts, and on my way to the first day on the job on April 1, 1959, I became more fearful the closer the subway from my suburb Barmbek got to downtown Hamburg, where the business was located. Why would they want me to work for them? What could I possibly contribute to their company?

In my desire to let Alexander Petersen and Company find out as soon as possible just how unworthy I was, I arrived at work much too early. After all the important people, chiefly the bosses, had arrived at the office, I and three other newcomers were introduced first to the boss and then to all the other employees. The company was in the export/import business with Central and South America, dealing with a variety of commodities and acting as agents for department stores. There were thousands of import/export firms in Hamburg, and international trade was flourishing again in Germany.

I was hired as a Spanish secretary-beginner, and department head Herr Thomas and I made up the textiles department. Upon meeting Herr Thomas, he launched immediately into Spanish, overestimating what I had learned in two years of school Spanish. So I found out right off how much I didn't know and that I would have to enroll in a Spanish course at the Berlitz School.

Part of my entry-level job was to glue countless fabric samples on index cards, label them, and, if my brain was still functioning when I had completed that task, send the samples to the fabric manufacturers to obtain quotes. It was a repetitive, boring task and I hated it. Once we had cost quotes, Herr Thomas would dictate letters in Spanish which I took down in shorthand, then transcribing them on a manual typewriter and sending them to department stores (after Herr Thomas fine-tuned them and I typed them again!) in Venezuela, Costa Rica, Ecuador, or Peru, among other markets. Fabric departments in those stores would ask for quotes on needles, thread, lace, buttons, and assorted sewing products.

In time I became more familiar with my assignments and, growing more competent, I worked more and more independently, so much so that when Herr Thomas went on vacation later that year he put me in charge of our department. This meant having a daily conference with the big boss, at which time he would tell me what to do, and how to proceed, or I suggested to him what we should do. I liked being in charge and didn't want Herr Thomas to come back!

Work became a big part of my life. My Spanish knowledge improved, and I composed letters myself in German and Spanish. I looked forward to busy days, but when there wasn't enough to do I had to pretend to be busy anyway. I couldn't just grab a book and read. Though that was the way of office life in Germany, it made me miserable knowing that Herr Thomas knew that I was pretending to be occupied. He also had to pretend to busyness, especially since our room was completely open, and our desks faced each other. There were at least twelve people in the room, working away rather quietly.

My beginning salary was 250 Marks, of which 100 Marks went to my parents for household money. The rest was mine to do with as I saw fit, and I bought much-needed clothes, movie tickets, monthly transportation passes, and so on. I had to learn to stretch the money as far as possible because I was paid only once monthly. A nominal amount for health insurance was deducted from my paycheck, and it covered everything from doctors' and dentists' visits to hospitalizations. For one extra Mark I could even get any prescription filled. I became quite good at managing money, knowing that I had to make it last for thirty days. It was only now that I began to realize how difficult it had been (and still was) for Mutti and Papa not to have a steady income on which to get through the month.

There were a number of people my age working for the company, and I made friends easily. Since the office was in downtown Hamburg, I had lunch with friends almost every day. Most of us brought food from home—a *Butterbrot* (two pieces of black bread, with butter and cold cuts or cheese), and perhaps an apple. Although I was almost eighteen years old, Mutti still made this sandwich for me in the morning. Lunch was kept in a drawer of my desk until it was time to eat, and sometimes I would join others congregating around a co-worker's desk for the hour-long lunch. There were no refrigerators at home or work.

Although my colleagues also became friends in my non-work life, it wasn't until my second year at Alexander Petersen & Co. that I began to mix work with romance. In April 1959, I was still driven by thoughts of David, my Mormon heartthrob-at-a-distance. Wasn't he the one who had wanted me to be a good girl, a conscientious worker, a person who would make something of herself? After all, I reasoned, some day in the future I might meet him again and wouldn't he be so pleased that I had become a capable girl, one he could approve of? Of course, David had no way of knowing that he had all this power over me. And my teenage girl's intellect didn't see the pitfalls in this scenario.

◆   ◆   ◆

Working for my employer and for David (in a convoluted way) devoured most of my days, but there were a few activities in which I still participated, one of them being church and religion. In my quest to learn more about religions other than Lutheranism and Mormonism, I attended a lecture on the Jehovah's Witnesses at my church. The speaker was the many-titled Pastor Professor Doctor Engelbrecht, who announced that if a representative of the Witnesses came to his door, he would tell them, "Go on your way, my time is too precious for you." But I thought that another way would be better—let them talk and then announce that they were on the wrong course. In order to do that, however, I would have to know the Bible well because Witnesses religiously quoted passages from it. And I wasn't prepared to do that, having read only parts of the Bible and not being the "proselytizing" kind; I simply wasn't driven to winning converts for Lutheranism.

Instead, I looked at other religions with a bemused eye and a sense of the absurdity of them all, especially the Jehovah's Witnesses. According to those believers, only 144,000 people would be saved at Judgment Day. But they would enjoy the following in Jehovah's Kingdom: a villa, a luxury limousine, a chicken coop, and much more. Sickness and poverty would not exist for these souls, and everyone would live together in peace. So far, I liked what they believed. However, the rest of the members of this sect would not get what the 144,000 chosen ones got. Instead of a limousine, they might get a Volkswagen and instead of twenty chickens perhaps ten? On hearing this, I found it both sad and hilarious that people could actually believe this.

In addition to this promise of opulence in the afterlife, there were various Witness predictions of dates when the world would come to an end. According to the founder of the Society of Serious Bible Researchers, the apocalypse was supposed to take place in 1874; however, when the date came and went he claimed that he forgot to include the forty years between the birth of Christ and the Robbing of the Temple. So though World War I broke out in 1914 after all and Germany went down in flames, the world did not end. I saw that the number of apocalypse dates seemed endless, and Jehovah's Witnesses decided that rather than predicting a year they would forecast that the world would end "soon" and leave it at that. Given all I had heard, I decided that I too, along with the Pastor Professor Doctor, would send them on their way if they came to my door. Maybe I wasn't as open to religions I hadn't been brought up in.

The social side of religion, though, had always appealed to me greatly, with all its sitting with likeminded people, discussing, singing, dancing, and laughing. At one weekend at the Lutheran church's campgrounds in Gudow, about an hour northeast of Hamburg, we sat around the campfire discussing the topic, "How can you trust a church that has changed so little in two thousand years?" The response was mostly silence, which was unusual, because most of the time we talked too much and too long. I have to believe that we were not in the discussion mood and would rather have been regaling ourselves with jokes instead! On the second evening at camp, the Fire Department band came and played everything from marches to waltzes, so everybody danced and we had fun instead of contemplating religious conundrums.

I have found that music in any form furthered togetherness. It was a German tradition that fire departments and the military maintained marching or brass bands. In a small town like Gudow the band would play at the annual town ball and church-related functions such as our camping dance.

Back at the home church St. Gabriel, three boys and I attended a meeting with the goal of putting together a newsletter for the youth group. I volunteered to report on the cinema, opera, and theater. While I was still a high school student, my classmates and I were able to buy discounted theater and opera tickets, and I attended performances regularly, sometimes with the entire class or with just a couple of friends. For the newsletter, culture was my beat in addition to typing and layout.

However, my first report would be on my experience with Mormons. My "Mormon phase" was definitely over and I was back in the Lutheran Mother Church. It felt good being back, and events at the church kept me busy.

◆   ◆   ◆

In the summer of 1959, I was asked by a former school friend of mine if my family and I could take in an exchange student from England who wanted to spend two weeks in Germany with a friend of hers. And that's how I came to meet Pauline and Annette from the town of Peterborough, about an hour north of Cambridge. Pauline was the pen pal of a former school friend of mine who didn't have room in her apartment to put up a guest. We didn't have room to spare either but nonetheless I was quite keen on meeting a girl from England.

So Pauline and Annette arrived by train from Ostende, Belgium. In the afternoon, Pauline proceeded to throw up, which I noted in my diary. Most likely, the rough channel crossing did her in, mixed with her apprehension at being in a foreign country and not knowing her hosts. We were all a little nervous at first, never having met before. At first, I couldn't understand Pauline very well, because she spoke rapidly and my school English was so much slower and deliberate. So I had to search for words constantly from my pitifully small English vocabulary, even after all these years of school English (seven, to be exact).

I worried that Pauline would find the Behnke household wanting in the bathroom department. Since she had to wash herself in the kitchen, I gave strict rules to my whole family to give her as much time as she needed even though it meant that we were restricted in using our own kitchen. Sabine and her parents who were hosting Pauline's friend Annette lived in a new apartment and occasionally Pauline would take a bath there. But we girls were so busy for the next two weeks that worries about accommodations receded to the background. On our pull-out couch, I slept in the middle, with Doris and Pauline on either side of me. It was crowded, but Pauline didn't complain.

It didn't take Annette and Pauline long to loosen up. Everywhere we went, they flirted with each and every German male they met, in restaurants, coffee shops, on the sightseeing boat in the harbor, at the opera, in the movie theater.

I took Pauline to my church group where we played table tennis. She was the star, the engaging British girl with the easy smile that transcended language difficulties. Mutti, for one, didn't know a word of English, except maybe "how do you do," and "good morning," but she and Pauline communicated fairly well with gestures that conveyed what they were saying without ever using German and English words.

Sabine and I took our new friends to a Russian movie dubbed in German, and although they didn't understand a word they got an idea of what a German movie theater looked like and how it was arranged, the seats numbered as were the tickets. Rows in the center of the theater had the most expensive seats, whereas rows closer to the screen and in the very back were the cheapest. Sitting in a center row seat made one feel like a queen, but sitting directly in front of the screen was incredibly cheap and also caused stiff necks. Sabine and I showed our visitors another theater custom: as we moved through the row to our assigned seats, we faced the people who were already seated. Of course, I thought this was the way it was done everywhere, until my face almost collided with behinds in American movie theaters.

Not only did we watch movies, we actually managed to be in one. In 1959, going to the airport was the thing to do, watching planes taking off and landing being so exciting. As was looking at the passengers who emerged from the planes and walked down the steps. They were well-dressed, obviously well-to-do-people, because flying was expensive. Sabine and I took Pauline and Annette to the airport for some serious people-watching, and when we arrived there were cameras all over the place. A movie was being made with Gerhard Riedmann and Eva-Ingeborg Scholz, two very well known German actors. And we were to be extras, standing on a staircase in the terminal, talking to each other, and under strict orders not to look toward the cameras. Asked *not* to act, we ended up as bit players in *Liebe, Luft und lauter Lügen* (Love, Air, and Lies). When Sabine and I later saw it at the theater, only Pauline was visible and then for only a couple of seconds. The rest of us had been edited out.

This experience at the airport, however, did not change my decision not to become a stewardess. I liked the stewardesses' uniforms and hats, their high-heeled shoes, and their leather purses so unlike the plastic model I carried. I liked the fact that they would meet interesting people on board and could converse in several languages, but when I envisioned myself serving meals to passengers I was totally turned off.

On the weekend, Sabine and I took Pauline and Annette to an opera and then to the Botanical Gardens, where an impolite German informed them that their

English dialect was bad, a comment which made me mad enough to retort to him that he was out of line. It was out of character for me to be so forthright with a stranger, but I had a low tolerance for bad manners.

Our nightly jaunts with Annette and Pauline continued, devoted to sightseeing, drinking at cafes, flirting with males of every description. I had never known girls who flirted so much and with such enthusiasm. I was more reserved, tending to observe rather than participate.

These were fun evenings, but one night we just wanted to relax and stay home. Actually, I wanted to stay home and relax but that rest was not to be and consequently I met Bill, my next flame. Annette and Pauline picked me up from work, all excited because they had met two British Merchant Marine officers and made dates with them for 9:00 p.m. The officers would bring along two more, they said, one for each of us. Fine, I thought, I had to do impulsive things while I was young; I could relax when I was older.

So we went home and refreshed our makeup (which probably meant lipstick for me). For Pauline it was a more complicated toilette, because at the time she wore not only makeup, rouge, and mascara, but also took a long time to fix her hair. This attention to "putting on a face" was new to me, something British girls did but no German girls that I knew of. Both Annette and Pauline looked very pretty all made-up, but never having gotten into the habit of it myself and having been very much discouraged by Mutti from enhancing my natural looks, I couldn't quite comprehend why they would waste so much time and money on cosmetics.

The whole process had to be hurried along that night because we had to meet our unknown beaus at a certain time at the Alsterpavillion (a restaurant on the *Alster* Lake in downtown Hamburg). From there we took two cabs to the *Zillertal*, a Bavarian place of entertainment similar to a Hofbräuhaus. The *Zillertal* was a respectable place on the "good end" of the *Reeperbahn*, the red light district, the other end of which also sported countless bars and strip clubs catering to sailors looking for some "action."

We talked, danced, and listened to the Bavarian band, and stayed until 11:30 p.m., a time which deserves mention only because Sabine was supposed to be home a half-hour before that. We were only eighteen years old, after all. Sabine was fuming because Annette disappeared for ten minutes just to say a quick goodbye to the officer she had hooked up with. Finally, we four girls plus two guys hopped on the subway, Sabine and Annette saying a hasty goodbye when they got off. Then Pauline, Harry, Bill and I walked the rest of the way to my house, where we took our time saying goodbye, hugging and kissing our newly acquired boyfriends.

It was 1:15 a.m. when we took our shoes off outside, opened the door and tip-toed into our room. No matter how quiet I was, I could never get past Mutti. She was just emerging from her bedroom, having slept very lightly from entertaining visions of ghastly things happening to us girls. We jumped under the covers, clothes and all, and pretended to be asleep. But it was to no avail because we were laughing too hard to keep pretending and Mutti along with us, relieved that we were alright. I had to be at work at 8:00 a.m., while everyone else could sleep in.

After that, Bill stepped in and out of my life at intervals. He would write letters from exotic places like Indonesia and then suddenly show in Hamburg. Bill was a gentle man, very polite, and he kissed well. What did he do in the other ports he visited if he could be picked up so easily by two British girls in Hamburg? I felt a little twinge of resentment because I assumed that he wasn't saving himself for me. But exactly what did Bill mean to me? Someone who brought a little of the world along with him each time he visited Hamburg and with whom I could speak English.

While I was at work, Pauline and Mutti were home alone busily communicating with hands, feet, eyes, and dictionaries, occasionally raising their voices because they thought that if they spoke louder they would surely be understood. Whatever little German Pauline learned during her two-week stay she used on the squirrels during a visit to the cemetery.

The cemetery in question was similar to the airport, a place to take visitors. *Friedhof Ohlsdorf*, about 20 minutes from my house, was the largest cemetery in Europe. In its park-like setting, it boasted tall trees, thousands of rhododendrons, flowers of every kind, and monuments and tombstones to die for. Graves of famous people abounded here, those of poets and writers, actors and actresses, and composers such as Johannes Brahms not to speak of Carl Hagenbeck of Hamburg's famed Hagenbeck Zoo.

◆   ◆   ◆

As a child, I had visited this cemetery many times, because Mutti went at least six times a year to visit her parents and sister and I accompanied her most of the time. My maternal grandparents and later my Tante Gretchen were buried in one grave, which we regularly tended. The cemetery administration had a standing order to keep the grave free of weeds in the summer, plant only annuals such as begonias, and in the winter cover the gravesite with a blanket made of evergreens.

Mutti and I and sometimes Papa, Klaus, and Doris would set off on foot, loaded down with watering can, bucket, shovels, and rakes. Sometimes we brought pots of impatiens as well, just to make sure that the grave would look attractive. Once we arrived at the cemetery gates, we still had another half hour to walk until we reached the grave, which sometimes led us to stop at a particularly handsome tombstone. We also had to pass the graves of those fallen in World War II. They were marked by identical white crosses. I found it incomprehensible that all these people could have died in the course of just six years. I looked at Mutti, whose sniffling was a sure sign that she was crying though I didn't know for whom. Had she known any of the people who lay beneath those crosses? Or maybe that's where Onkel Werner rested, he who had appeared in my dreams so many times. I couldn't believe that he was just *lost* in Russia and found it more comforting to think that he was buried somewhere close to home. But maybe Mutti was crying because she knew that Onkel Werner wasn't beneath one of those white crosses. In any case, that was only the beginning of a long and tearful day.

Once we arrived at the Schmidt gravesite (Schmidt being Mutti's maiden name), Mutti stood quietly and looked at the double-wide plot that her father Johannes Schmidt had purchased when his wife Julia Jordanski died in 1920. My grandfather joined her in 1929, and both of their names, birth dates, and death dates were carved on their tombstone. A hedge of low-growing evergreens enclosed the grave on three sides. If impatiens were to be planted in the center, Mutti would take a hand shovel and loosen the soil around the flowers. Or she would pull weeds and then rake the dirt on the outside of the hedge to make the dirt look somehow prettier.

When it was time to water the plot, Mutti would ask Doris and me to fill up the watering can at the nearest spigot. Sometimes, she and I would take our time fetching the water, because we wanted to read some of the other headstones. We made sure to walk only on the paths and never ever on the graves since that would have been disrespectful. By the time we got back, Mutti would be crying again and talking under her breath to her beloved parents. I don't know why she mumbled; maybe she was telling them something I shouldn't hear. Whatever she said, I realized as a child that it was all right to talk to the dead.

By the time we left the cemetery, Mutti was all cried-out and in good spirits. She had "spoken" with her parents who had been dead already for at least twenty years. And so I continue the tradition—I don't visit cemeteries but I "talk" to Mutti when I feel that I need her spirit beside me.

In 1959, Mutti was thinking of places to show Pauline, and because the *Ohls-dorfer Friedhof* was such a pretty park, Mutti took Pauline there, this time to walk and look at gravesites rather than to work at the grave. The park was full of squirrels used to being fed by visitors. Pauline tried to lure one such squirrel, and, using the little German she knew she said, "Kommen Sie her," (come here), which in German is quite a formal way of addressing an animal (rather, she should have said, "komm her.") The squirrel got a tidbit, Mutti got a jolly good laugh, and the story will be in my memory forever.

Pauline's visit was winding down, and to celebrate one last time we went to the Espresso Bar even though it was an expensive pleasure. A glass of Fresca cost 1,10 Marks. Since I was only earning 250 Marks a month, one pop from the Espresso Bar constituted a luxury.

On July 9, 1959, Sabine and I took our new friends Annette and Pauline to the train station. Annette started crying as soon as we reached the platform, and then we were all wailing! We proceeded to hug and kiss until the train left exactly at 6:56 p.m.

Before Annette and Pauline left, they invited Sabine and me to spend two weeks with them and their families in England sometime in the fall of 1959. We accepted right away and then began planning the trip, especially the expense part of it. But it was such an exciting opportunity to get to know more English people. Only fifteen years before, Germans and Britons had been bombing each others' cities, but not for a second of their entire visit did we feel any animosity toward Britons Annette and Pauline. Or any ill feelings coming from them. Although we had listened to our parents' stories about the bombardments, we as members of the next generation—Annette, Pauline, Sabine, and I—had not formed any negative thoughts about our respective countries' war-time actions. Other Germans I knew did, but I wasn't going to let the war get in the way and form my opinion until I met an English person for myself. Pauline was generous, fun-loving, polite, and mischievous, just the kind of person I liked.

Before Sabine and I could visit Annette and Pauline, we had to get permission from our parents and our bosses to take this trip. I wasn't eligible for a vacation yet, but I encountered no problems from my boss because as far as he was concerned I would gain personally from a trip to a foreign country while the company would benefit from my improved English.

◆   ◆   ◆

In the fall of 1959, then, Sabine and I took the train from Hamburg to Ostende (Belgium), caught the ferry across the English Channel to Dover, and hopped on another train to Peterborough. All this took hours and hours, sleeping on second-class coach wooden benches and getting sick on the choppy Channel before we finally arrived in Peterborough.

Pauline's family lived in a row house, and the one thing that impressed me the most about it was that Pauline had her own room as did her sister Josephine, a chubby, full-cheeked and cheeky ten-year-old. The house even had a regular bathroom, with a regular tub! I was envious.

Now the tables were turned. Annette and Pauline had to work, and Sabine and I followed them and their families around. I went on shopping errands with Daisy, Pauline's Mum, and was introduced everywhere as Pauline's pen pal from Germany. Nobody gave me an "I-hate-Germans" look, to my great relief. I was not in "enemy territory." The war was over, but I persisted in obsessing about how people would react to me once they learned I was German. Although I was only a baby when the war was raging and the atrocities occurred, I felt guilty.

Pauline's parents had a car and they took the family and me on many outings. I remember one, because I have a photo of us standing around on the side of a road (the car is visible), while Mr. Steward cooked bacon on a little grill. He was probably making fried bacon sandwiches, with a dollop of ketchup on the bread especially for Pauline because that's the way she liked it. We wore short sleeves, so it must have been a nice day in October. It wasn't raining for a change, and I was enjoying myself with my new friends, having my first barbecue ever! When Mrs. Steward made fried bacon sandwiches at home, the bread was fried in the bacon grease as well, as a calorie booster. Nobody was counting calories then, and the bacon grease tasted heavenly. Bacon grease on bread was not new to me because I had eaten German *Schmalz* before, but always it had been slathered onto a slice of black bread. Fried bacon was new to me.

The four of us—Annette, Pauline, Sabine, and I—were so busy that I stopped writing in my diary. Again, I was certain that I would remember everything we did, but again it didn't turn out to be so. I recall that almost every night the four of us went to a local pub, where Annette and Pauline normally hung out and where I met many of her friends. Many nights found us "overserved," meaning that a friend had to drive us home. On the nights we went out, we would stop at a fish and chips place. At this time in England the fish and chips were still sold wrapped in newspaper which we opened as soon as we hit the street. Or we would pick up an order on the way home from the pub, needing to sober up a bit before we made it home. In my memory I drank more than I actually did, because two glasses of ale was probably my limit. Fish and chips, though no longer wrapped in newspaper, are still my favorite English food.

In the two weeks I spent in England, I had spoken mostly English, except when I was alone with Sabine and we spoke German. Slowly it dawned on me that an extended stay in England would rapidly improve my English. Although my attraction to America was still as strong as it had been for a number of years, I had a feeling that my parents would not let me go across the Atlantic at the age of eighteen whereas they might well give their permission to live in England for a year.

I approached the subject as soon as I returned from England and my hunch proved right—my parents would not allow me to visit the U.S. until I was twenty-one years of age. They were fearful of my being so far away, and if something bad happened to me there they couldn't afford to fly to my side. In a couple of years, I would be of age and then, by law, I could visit the U.S., although Papa and Mutti wouldn't be able to come to my rescue because of their limited finances. At the time, I didn't quite understand their reluctance to let me go, but I didn't want to make them unhappy and I had to admit to myself that maybe I wasn't quite ready to go so far afield as America. Going to England definitely felt more comfortable.

On New Year's Eve 1959, Mutti and Papa, Doris and her current boyfriend, Doris' girlfriend and her boyfriend, and I, sans boyfriend, celebrated the New Year by drinking champagne until 4:00 a.m. Klaus was off with Anne and I missed him, especially on this night. When my siblings and I were younger, we jumped off chairs precisely at midnight, champagne glass in hand and yelled *Prost Neujahr* (Happy New Year) to the rest of the world. It had always been the high point of the evening, when we had already ingested a few glasses of grog (sugar, hot water, rum) or champagne, and had eaten a few *Berliners* (sugar-coated, jelly-filled doughnuts). Fortified with sugar, we would jump off the chairs into the New Year, then run outside to watch the fireworks already gloriously booming up and down the street.

I was always afraid of the ear-splitting ratatat of firecrackers and other more sophisticated fireworks, and even in my teenage years I was the one to walk tamely around with a sparkler in my hand (*Wunderkerze*, candle of wonders, in

German). The gently popping sparklers were excitement enough for me, and I could safely observe the rest of the fireworks as they glittered and cascaded from the balconies.

10

Goodbye Germany, hello England

♦

1960

1960—The first Lufthansa jet flies from Hamburg to New York. Germany's unemployment rate is less than one percent. The era of guest workers begins. Germany's economy is number two in the world, behind the United States. The first drive-in theater opens near Frankfurt. Rock-and-Roll fans imitate Elvis Presley's pompadour with ducktail hair, wear leather jackets, checkered shirts and jeans, and dance to American hit music, which many parents call "negro music." Girls wear pony tails. John F. Kennedy wins the election and becomes the youngest president in the history of the U.S. The Israelis capture Adolf Eichmann, Nazi war criminal.

Life in the New Year was not that different from life in the old one: work, youth group, family, friends, English Club—day in and day out all these orbited around each other. I can't say I was waiting for something exciting to happen. Life was that way—normal—unless a person planned for something extraordinary to happen. My biggest plan was to go to England as an au pair in the fall of 1960 and stay for a year. So far, however, I hadn't done much to make it happen, except for joining the English Club. I had a strong desire to speak English whenever and wherever I could.

The English Club was sponsored by the British Council, the cultural section of the British Consulate in Hamburg. It was located close to the *Alster,* Hamburg's downtown lake, in an area of embassies and consulates. Our leader Mr. Clark was a middle-aged gentleman who urged us to speak English at all times. We mostly young Germans sat in comfortable chairs and sofas and discussed a current topic at hand or just engaged in free conversation. Some of us, including me, had to muster the courage to speak. At first, I listened much of the time, not wanting to make mistakes and appear stupid. Speaking English with Pauline and her friends had been easy compared to this more structured approach of speaking on a subject. When the conversation became sluggish, Mr. Clark would jump in and move us along. Now and then someone brought along a bottle of cognac and glasses, and tongues would loosen up so that words would flow. Mr. Clark called me *Miss Peterborough 1959*, because my English had a tinge of the Peterborough dialect. No doubt, Pauline had something to do with my accent because I had imitated her dialect when I had stayed with her. I was beginning to realize that I had a good ear for picking up dialects (German as well), and a formidable tongue for imitating them.

At one of our British Council meetings in February of 1960, I asked Mr. Clark what he thought of my going to England as an au pair. As luck would have it, he knew of a family in London who was looking for one beginning in October 1960. With this query I had taken the first step in the process of making my goal a reality.

As the members of the British Council group became more familiar with each other, we became quite cliquish and failed to properly appreciate new people who joined us. The exception was a young Englishman who came into the room just as one of the members was showing us photographs of what Londoners looked like. He was from London, and I decided to get to know him.

As fate would have it, I ran into him at the *Amerika Haus* where a movie about the USA was showing. We talked without exchanging names, had a cup of coffee, and walked to the train station where we made a date to meet again. Easy, I thought. Two days later, again at the train station, we had a cup of coffee and proceeded to the "Pigalle," a Hamburg nightclub for young people. Then he took me home. I decided I liked him. Two days later, Robin picked me up after work and we had an espresso. The coffee was getting stronger, as was the attraction between us, and when we walked around the botanical garden Planten un Blomen he kissed me. After that we pretended at the English Club not to know each other in a more intimate way, though I didn't know why the charade was necessary. Only my childhood friend Dickus knew, as a member of the Club and my confidante.

Robin and I met almost daily, taking the Alster boat to the Stadtpark station and walking home from there, groping and kissing along the way. Other activities fell by the wayside, including my involvement with the church youth group. I met some of his friends and we would go sightseeing. The need to see him felt more like an addiction and I mentioned to him that we were seeing each other too often. He agreed. Still, those spring walks through the park simply couldn't be passed up and we continued walking. I introduced him to my sister Doris who was home from the hospital after having had her appendix removed. (Recuperation for an appendectomy was then fourteen days!) She liked Robin, but mentioned his grimy raincoat in passing.

Robin and I seemed to walk a lot, have many cups of coffee and glasses of cola, and attend the movies frequently. He always wore the grimy raincoat that had seen better days, or at least had never seen soap and water. After noting this critical aspect about him and linking it to his being English, I told my diary that the outside of a person was not the most important thing. It seemed I wanted to come across as a tolerant person but couldn't always avoid stereotyping on the basis of appearance.

While I dated Robin, I stayed in touch with Bill, my other (sporadic) English heartthrob, via long letters. He wrote that he would be in Hamburg in April, and that, according to a note in my diary, would make me the happiest woman in the world. In any case, I didn't really feel that I was two-timing because one of the guys was out of town most of the time. Then Robin went out of town for four long days, and when I expected him to reappear at the British Council meeting he didn't. What's more, he didn't call. On Thursday, I waited for his call. On Friday, I waited. On Saturday, I took a quick trip to the beauty parlor and then rushed home to wait by the phone. Dickus invited me over to her house, but how could I be in both places, waiting at home for the phone to ring and visiting with Dickus? By 6:00 p.m. I had had enough of waiting, and Dickus and I decamped to the movies. But when I got home, I kept listening for the phone while I distractedly talked with Doris, who was going through withdrawal pains from her most recent boyfriend. She looked like a weeping willow, all watery droopy, compared to my agitated state. On Sunday, Robin finally called and tried to explain his absence, but I preferred to stay in misery a little while longer and asked him to pick me up from work on Monday rather than meet him as soon as possible.

Well, then. On Monday morning, there was a letter from Robin on my desk. I assumed it would be a "Dear John" letter, but upon reading it in the bathroom I realized that he couldn't meet me after work as planned. When we finally got together later that night, we made up. Whatever his explanation was, I accepted it. We talked and kissed and then repeated the sequence.

Robin planned to go to the Rhine over Easter. I went to church and noted in my diary that people should read the Bible more often to learn more about God. I must have been a haughty and self-righteous little twit to invoke God in my love life. I even entered a catty remark about not being able to imagine my girlfriend Sabine with a boyfriend on her having told me she was about to date someone from work. I must have thought I had the monopoly on boyfriends.

On April 20, my mother's 59th birthday, I had to stay home and subject myself to all my uncles' and aunts' hugs and kisses and inquiries about my job, while all I wanted to think of was Robin. The next night I picked him up at the train station and after a walk in the park to get my quota of kisses and caresses, I took him home and introduced him to my parents. This was a fun time, because Robin didn't speak German, Papa spoke a little English, and Mutti spoke none, except to say, *How do you do with a Gummischuh,* a nonsensical rhyme she found humorous. I found her humiliating. Of course, he didn't get the rhyme and why should he? Then followed a polite conversation that I diligently translated. While Robin was talking I could see that my parents were surreptitiously examining the state of his teeth as well as his grimy rain coat. Whatever he said was not as important as his teeth to Mutti, who equated good teeth with a good sense of self. And since she had always worked so hard at keeping our clothes clean, she really couldn't excuse his wearing anything grimy. But if a boyfriend's teeth could pass inspection, the major obstacle would be removed. Afterwards, when I asked my parents how they liked Robin, they pointed out his teeth (too yellow) or his coat (too grimy). But other than that, they liked him well enough and wouldn't try to keep me from seeing him. For his part, Robin thought my parents were *nett,* a nondescript word meaning "nice." He wished he knew more German so that he could have talked directly to them.

Robin and I kept dating, although he had told me that he didn't love me. He had told me he liked me very, very much, but to my mind, liking instead of loving didn't count. I was put off by merely being liked by him, and my mood swings proceeded to go from high to low, from ending the relationship to making it work.

One night when I arrived home from a date, I was greeted with the news that Bill had called twice. This had caused much excitement in the Behnke household because all my family not only knew him but also knew that I was out with another guy. He called a third time and we made a date to meet at our favorite restaurant, the Alsterpavillon, a tasteful place on the lake in downtown Hamburg. After dinner and a stop at the nightclub Pigalle, we kissed in the taxi on the way home. It was only natural that I should kiss Bill too, but should I have? Abed that night I suffered pangs of conscience, but no so deeply that I didn't keep my date with Bill the next day when I took him to the Mensa, the Hamburg University student cafeteria, where I had been with Robin many times. Seemingly, I wasn't afraid that Robin might see me there with Bill, but as my eyes wandered around the room my attention couldn't be on what Bill was saying. Additionally, he spoke with a Manchester dialect and his words had to filter through his full beard, so that I really needed to look directly at him when he spoke. Still, I was impressed with his many travels as a merchant marine, and I envied him for all that he must have seen. From his last trip to Singapore, he had even brought me a musical powder compact which played, "I feel pretty, oh so pretty, I feel pretty and witty and gay" from the musical *West Side Story* when I infrequently powdered my nose.

On Wednesday, a day I usually looked forward to because I would see Robin, I skipped English Club to spend time with Bill. I saw him only one more time after that because, despite our good intentions, we never managed to meet while I was in England. And then, to top that off, the next day turned out to be the last time I ever saw Robin. At the meeting that would be our last we talked again, about everything. He said, "I don't love you," and asked "Do you love me?" to which I replied, "Yes." That might have been a lie. But maybe I just thought I loved him in my confusion of feelings. In any case, I could have spent eternity with him, or so I thought. We cried in duet. Because I hadn't seen many crying men, I fell speechless at the sight of his teary eyes, first thinking, "Why are *you* crying? I'm the one whose love isn't returned." Then I thought he might be crying for himself for not being able to return my love. Most likely he was as clueless as I was. I commented in my diary that he probably didn't know how he felt and that he was unsure of himself because he was so young. I must have been about the same age, or younger, but undoubtedly was much wiser than him. Still, I was also in despair, because I knew that our relationship was over when I wanted a little more time extension.

To keep from obsessing about why I loved him and why he didn't love me, I started going to the movies and spending time with my non-missionary Mormon friends. A few days later to my surprise I received a letter from Robin in which he explained everything once more and said that he wanted to keep writing to me. I replied that he could if he wanted to. So the ball was back in his court. Now all I had to do was look for his letters, which fueled my obsession about the relationship. It was the perfect set-up, as "Did I get any mail?" was always the first thing I asked when I got home from work. Sometimes I would even call from my desk to see if a letter was waiting for me.

Though I could barely stand the thought of not seeing Robin again, in the next few days several things happened that at times kept my mind off him. For one, the new guy at work, D., took me home on his motor scooter, and was I ever thrilled to sit on this powerful machine and have the wind whip my ears until they numbed! I watched the wedding of Princess Margaret of Britain at a neighbor's house as my family didn't yet have a television set and probably never would. They were happy listening to the Grundig radio or reading and didn't seem to have a need for a TV. At least I never heard them lamenting that they didn't have one.

While I was watching the royal wedding on the neighbor's television, I fantasized wedding Robin. I missed him, or maybe just the constant juggling of shifting emotions that accompanied him. When he wrote that he cried upon receiving a letter of mine, my untiring fascination with the state of being in love reached its limit, and so I wrote a note back to him asking him not to write me again. It seemed I needed to suffer in solitude, cry when I wanted to, and let life and future love take their course. And at this point in my life I needed to be getting on with it. The ever-practical side of me said that there would be others, and in the meantime I could mourn this now-dead relationship. Also, it didn't hurt that I had had the last word.

◆   ◆   ◆

I may have been preoccupied with boys, but I was also working many hours. My first-year anniversary at Alexander Petersen & Co. arrived and I felt like an old-timer, especially since there was now an apprentice in our department and I was her trainer. Because she had just graduated from a technical high school and had no prior business experience, I had to teach her everything, from setting up a letter to filing plus everything in between about exporting and importing. I liked being in a position of authority. It gave me a certain standing in our three-person department—I was no longer on the bottom.

At the British Council, Mr. Clark flirted with me every chance he got, calling me *Miss Peterborough* and complimenting my English. I enjoyed his attention, knowing that it would never amount to anything more than that. He had not forgotten about my interest in living with a British family for a year and one day gave me the name and address of a teacher in London who was looking for an au pair. I wrote immediately to Mr. and Mrs. W., telling them of my wish to improve my English language skills in their country. I was hoping for a swift reply. Then too, our neighbor Fräulein Sommer told me about a job working for the consul at the Cuban Embassy that she thought would be good for me, and for a whopping 400 Marks a month! What incredibly bad timing, to be offered such an exciting job prospect just when my sights were set on England.

Although there was a lull in my life that came from being between boy friends, I kept busy by going to the movies with Mutti, my friends, and my sister Doris and her friends. Everybody was crazy about Doris Day, so when *Pillow Talk* came out, we all had to see it. Though to be honest we liked Rock Hudson even better; he was the hunk, the ladies' man, and it wasn't until years later that we learned that he had always preferred gentlemen. Then there was the *Golden Age of Comedy*, featuring Laurel and Hardy. Of them and their pranks I could never see enough.

I helped out at a drugstore where Doris worked and saved the money for a portable typewriter to take to England. Mostly I stocked shelves, which involved heavy work such as hefting big boxes of powdered detergent up from the basement. When I filled in behind the counter, I became easily flustered about adding up a customer's purchases. Doris managed to add items quickly in her head while bantering with the customers, but I had to write everything down on a piece of paper. Then I had to figure out how much money to return to the customer, which really threw me. So whenever the manager asked me to work the counter, I would get almost physically sick. Math had never been my strong point. Neither was relating to customers because I would just thrust their change in their hands, saying *"So, das stimmt,"* which was like saying, "It's the correct amount, you don't need to check it." Doris tried her best to teach me how to properly and politely return money to customers by counting it into their hands, but I soon enough preferred to do the behind the scenes heavy lifting.

Besides working and moviegoing, I was again involved with my youth group at church, but it seemed that our goals of listening to classical music, discussing serious literature, and studying the Bible in earnest had given way to telling jokes and laughing uncontrollably. At one meeting, I was prepared to talk about Brahms, but found "talking" to be out of the question because the attendees never shut up until I turned on Brahm's *Requiem*. Then everyone listened reverently, or as reverently as possible. At a subsequent meeting, I was going to discuss the book *Dr. Zhivago*, which I had checked out at the *Amerika Haus*. (What a curious thing to do, checking out a book by a Russian author in its English translation in a German locale run by the American Information Service!) My presentation never happened, because I wanted to do it all in English but my group was unwilling to make the extra effort it would take to understand the English. Instead, we just adjourned to an ice cream parlor and acted stupid in public. Our youth group mercifully dissolved that summer.

My church attendance was sporadic and on one occasion caused a fight with Mutti. She would criticize my devotion to attending church, but when I skipped Sunday Services she held up the example of my female friends who did go. One day I blew up at her and told her exactly what I thought, hurting her feelings. A couple of days later, though, I apologized, because I loved her and hated being mean to her. Everything was as before, because Mutti never held a grudge.

I myself doubted my dedication to teaching Sunday school to elementary-school age children. Every Friday evening we learned how to organize Bible work, and though I found it interesting and helpful, I skipped many preparations. Not being properly prepared, though, didn't keep me from teaching and one Sunday a little girl hugged me and said, "I really like you." Another child asked me if I was a young lady already. I had never thought about when I would turn into a young lady or even if it was that important to be one.

Judging by my behavior in and out of the youth group, I was years away from being a young lady. Sometimes, Dickus would come over and she, Doris, and I would clown around. Dickus and I were almost nineteen, and Doris was twenty-one, but when we were together, we played little girls dressing up as adult women, laying on the makeup with the samples of lipstick, powder, and eye shadow Doris brought home from the drugstore, so much that we often ended up resembling call girls, albeit virginal ones.

June 17th, the day of German Unity came around. It had been declared a national holiday to commemorate the uprising in the DDR, the German Democratic Republic. Among other discontents, workers were being told to work longer hours for the same pay. The resulting protests were squelched by the Soviet army, and in solidarity with the DDR the day was declared a day of unity in West Germany a few weeks after the uprising. This gave West Germans a day off to sun themselves while East Germans continued to work. This day of commemoration never really resonated in West Germany, including myself. To be honest, I would have to say I celebrated this day off with my friends by going to the Stadtpark and acting goofy, climbing trees, and singing at the top of our lungs. My maturity was in a constant state of flux.

Following my breakup with Robin I stayed home more often in the evenings, and on Saturday nights Mutti, Papa, and I would open a bottle of champagne and talk or listen to the radio. Papa especially had been cross with me for going out with Robin every night, so now he was delighted that at least one of his daughters was home for family time.

I had opened a savings account with seventy Marks, and I figured that if I saved fifty Marks every month I would have 350 Marks by October when I planned to leave for England. It wasn't a lot of money, but vacation pay would be added. I wouldn't be able to take a vacation, but I didn't mind.

◆   ◆   ◆

In the summer of 1960, I took a mini-trip with Mutti and Papa to *Helgoland* to visit Doris while she vacationed there. Helgoland is a triangular-shaped island in the North Sea, about forty-four miles from the German coast. Its main attraction has always been its healthy climate, free of pollen and thus ideal for people with allergies.

I had known the name Helgoland since childhood. My friend Margret hailed from there, and I had heard her say many times that her family wanted to go back. As a young child I didn't know the reason why they couldn't do that until 1952. Not knowing anything about the history of Helgoland, I wondered why they had moved to Hamburg in the first place and why my friend and her family couldn't return to Helgoland if it was in Germany.

It seems that in AD 697 the last Frisian king, *Radbod* retreated to the island after being defeated by the Franks. From then on the island changed ownership several times, from the Danes to the Duchy of Schleswig, to Hamburg, and finally to the British who ceded it to Germany in 1890. In 1945, Allied bombers attacked the island and left nothing standing. The Helgolanders who had been hiding in rock shelters were evacuated the following night. From 1945 to 1952, then, the British Royal Navy used the island as a bombing range, detonating several thousand tons of explosives to effectively wipe it out. Failing in that goal, they instead gave it back to Germany in March 1952 when it became Germany's job to clear away the undetonated ammunition, landscape the main island, and rebuild the houses before it could be reinhabited.

Sometime in the 1950's, Margret and her family began returning to Helgoland, first to check things out and then to have a house built. Each time they came back to Hamburg, they would bring with them precious lobsters caught in the waters around the island. Some of them they would share with my parents, who were overjoyed to receive such a delicacy. Doris and I loathed even the sight of lobster and continued to do so for many years. We had tried it once and disliked the texture as well as the bottom-of-the-ocean smell that made us gag.

So I was hoping that I wouldn't have to eat lobster once we got to Helgoland. Papa, Mutti, and I boarded a boat in Hamburg and most of the time sat and watched the harbor glide by, then the suburb Blankenese with the magnificent houses of the rich, and then the *Altes Land*, old land, the fruit-producing area on the south side of the river Elbe. Eight million fruit trees blooming every spring brought thousands of people into this area, to walk along the dykes and on the narrow cobblestone streets of small, picturesque villages of thatched-roof farm houses. Seeing the small ports and towns south and north along the Elbe gave me a feeling of belonging. I was a Northern German and part of the seafaring traditions of Hamburg, even if I got sick on the water.

At the mouth of the river in Cuxhaven, about sixty-two miles from Hamburg, the boat entered the open sea, which must have been tranquil on that occasion because for once I didn't get sick. The boat was filled with happy young couples, and there I was with just Papa and Mutti. But I shrugged the feeling off because nothing could be done about it. I couldn't just conjure up a boyfriend who would accompany me on a trip to Helgoland. At least I would see my sister for a little while.

Once near Helgoland, passengers had to transfer to smaller boats that would take them to the main island. The transfer was the best part of the trip, exciting and a little dangerous, which was just the way I liked it. We stayed our allotted three hours, visiting with Doris who was chocolaty brown from hours of sunbathing on the beach, whereas we would end up with burned noses from the sun and the wind. One Helgoland landmark is the free-standing red sandstone rock, the *Lange Anna, or* "Tall Anna." Papa had Mutti, who was herself an Anna, stand in front of this 154-foot high rock to take a photo—short Anna standing by the *Lange Anna.* Then we stopped to say hello to our former neighbors, who were by now happily living on their island again. All the inhabitants spoke German but also a Helgoland variety of North Frisian because most of the Helgolanders were in fact ethnic Frisians. I couldn't understand a word of the Helgoland dialect, and not knowing what they were saying was even more frustrating than listening to Mutti and Papa speak *Plattdeutsch* (a Northern German dialect) although I had listened to their conversations with each other and my grandparents often enough that I understood more than I let on. For instance, the word *Donner* (thunder) became *Dunner* in Plattdeutsch; *Abend* (evening) became *Obend.* Since Plattdeutsch contained elements of English, I was able to understand at least the gist of a conversation. Plattdeutsch is now spoken by a few people in villages in Northern Germany.

◆　　◆　　◆

So far in my life I hadn't had any health problems other than the usual childhood scrapes. Mutti had a remedy for most ailments, none of which involved medication. She relied heavily on Nivea crème which she soothed on scrapes, burns, cuts, bumps, and bruises. Nivea was magic, and I use it to this day. Just the familiar scent of it will call up memories, such as the time when I came running home crying after I had fallen on a sharp piece of metal playing in one of the ruins. I had blood pouring from my lower shin and I was sure that my leg would have to be amputated. Mutti stopped the flow of blood, examined the cut, pronounced it curable, and rubbed a little Nivea around the wound.

For a leg that had fallen asleep she had the following remedy: put some spit on the fingers and rub the back of the leg and it will wake up. When I had a sore throat, Mutti wrapped a hot cotton cloth around my neck and then covered it with a woolen scarf to keep the moisture in. The scarf was secured with a safety pin. Then I had to lie in bed under a mountain of blankets and sweat like a pig! If this didn't work and the sore throat turned into a cyst on the tonsils, Herr Dr. Mormann would make a house call and stick what looked like a pair of pliers down my throat, snip the cyst and drain it after which I was allowed to drink sugar water to eliminate the putrid taste from my mouth. When the doctor's big, velvety hands stroked my cheeks to comfort me I felt better instantly.

Once, as a young child, I fell off a swing that Papa had attached to the doorway of our old shed. In it I would swing in and out, in and out of the shed. My neighbor Margret was supposed to watch me, but I fell off the swing anyway and hit my head on the concrete floor. Mutti heard my piercing screams, slapped a towel over the split in my forehead from which the blood flowed profusely, grabbed me by the arm and ran with me to the doctor, Margret flying behind us. The doctor examined the cut and covered it with a band aid, placing that velvety hand on my forehead. He probably should have stitched the wound because the scar is visible to this very day, but back then I thought Dr. Mormann could do no wrong, and I didn't want stitches anyway.

Since I had been so healthy all of my life, I was very concerned when early in 1960, I noticed a constant pain on the right side of my head and face. Mutti took me to several doctors who couldn't find anything wrong with me. Sometimes, the pain would craze me, especially because nothing could be done to treat it. Since the neurologist hadn't found a tumor, I supposed the pain would either go away or I would have to live with it. It wasn't until forty years later that I learned that the condition was called neuralgia, or chronic cluster headaches. Still, nothing in the way of therapy has ever helped and I have lived with the headaches for many years. Sometimes, the pain can be debilitating but most of the time I just gritted my teeth and carried on with my life in good Behnke fashion. I recall Mutti's saying by way of antidote nothing is as bad as war.

◆   ◆   ◆

Sometime in the summer of 1960 I heard from the family in London. I learned that they had three boys aged eighteen, thirteen, and twelve, which was good news mainly because I wouldn't have to change diapers as did many of my friends who lived as au pairs in young English families.

In order to be as well-prepared as I could be for living in England and speaking English, I occupied my time practicing conversational English at the British Club, reading books in English, and watching English-speaking movies. I even answered an ad in the paper from an American male who was looking for a *young lady* he could write to (and undoubtedly for further activities not spelled out in the ad). Feeling that I could pass as a *young lady,* I answered the ad, telling him that I was planning to visit America sometime in the near future. In the meantime, we could write to each other and become pen pals. However, I wasn't quite the correspondent he was looking for, as I discovered when he wrote back. Among other things he said that I could contact him when I made it to America but that in the meantime he wanted to pursue a "man-woman" relationship and that I seemed a bit too young for that. How could I have misread his ad so completely that I thought the man actually wanted a pen pal? How could I have been so naïve in this heterosexual playing field?

Despite my naivete, however, I was ready to plunge into the game yet again, to fill my life with the ups and downs of another on-and-off affair. This time, the player was a real pro, a playboy of sorts, but of course I was rather in the dark, never having dealt with his kind before. D. worked for the same company I did, and we must have been at a party when he tried to kiss me at which I got irritated. The following day we talked about what had happened, and he said that, à la the "game," girls had to resist—resistance heightened the emotional ambiance and physical sensations for both partners. This boy-girl dance was the accepted thinking of the time, normal in all respects. I informed him that if I liked a boy, I would kiss him. And so the comedy began, because a week later I was again in love—with D.

D. and I began our relationship by spending our lunchtimes together every day, mostly by sitting at the *Alster,* the lake in downtown Hamburg, and talking, holding hands, and kissing, again and again, for close to an hour. For the rest of the afternoon, my lips would feel like they were on fire! Then when he asked me to go to a party with him, I was elated. At the party, he drank champagne, which may well have prompted him to tell me he loved me and ask if I loved him. Skeptical about these premature pronouncements, I failed to reply. I had learned from my last affair that the words "I love you" were only supposed to be pronounced after one knew the other person for some time. They were serious words, and when said casually they didn't mean anything. In the same breath, though, D. told me that he had kissed Helga, a girl from the British Council Club. What was I to think of his kissing two girls at the same party? Would I be able to compete, was my first question. And then, why should I have to compete considering that he had just five minutes ago informed me that he loved me? Finally, at 3:00 a.m. he asked me to go home with him. Not on my life, I protested. So we continued the al fresco necking. Several days later, though, I succumbed to his wish to show me his room (what's the big deal, I kept telling myself), only to emerge a half an hour later with a hickey and in dire need of a high-neck blouse. My virginity was still intact, so I promised myself that I would never go to his room again. In the meantime I had told Mutti with a straight face that I had never been to D.'s room, all the while looking like Queen Elizabeth I with my ruff covering my neck up to my chin, and this in the heat of summer! What bothered me greatly was that I had lied to Mutti.

In July of 1960, Mutti and Papa bought their first refrigerator. It was a size which would have served Lilliputians quite well, but as regular-sized people we had to kneel in front of it to remove any item. Now we were able to keep cold cuts, butter, and cheese in the fridge for a few days instead of having to go out to buy just enough for one day. Vegetables and fruits never made it into the fridge because Mutti always said that cold fruit would only upset our stomachs. So when we wanted berries, plums, or apples, we just went in our backyard and picked what we needed at that moment. Tropical fruit such as oranges had more fragrance when not refrigerated, and at room temperature their flavor intensified.

My new love D., the man who said he loved me, informed me that a former girlfriend was coming to town for the weekend and that they were going out together. I didn't know what to make of it but nonetheless didn't want to share him with anyone. Mutti said, "Something isn't right when your boyfriend doesn't have time for you on a Sunday." This was wisdom she had gotten from her mother, and what if they were right? D. and I spent every lunch hour together, but we never had had a weekend date. I believed Mutti's warning but didn't speak to D. about it.

On Monday I gave D. the cold shoulder. Though we walked around the *Alster* at lunch time I rejected all attempts on his part to hug and kiss me. In the elevator on the way back to work, I told him that I didn't want to carry on with him any longer even though at that moment I could easily have thrown my arms around him. The heart is a complex phenomenon and I was a clueless teenager willing to suffer and, most of all, unwilling to offend. Two days later he kissed me in the elevator and I promptly kissed him back, which made me wish for a cure for my amatory indecisiveness! We continued not to date on weekends, and one day the thought occurred to me that D. might have a wife!

Since I wasn't busy on weekends and my brother's wedding was coming up, Klaus picked me up from work one night and we went shopping for my dress. I picked a short, sleeveless dress, belted at the waist with fabric of white and blue flowers cascading in bands down the skirt, under which I planned to wear a petticoat to make the skirt flare and show off the petticoat when I danced. With this dress I would wear white elbow-length gloves and white one-inch heels. I thought it was the perfect outfit. What's more, I paid for it! Doris chose a dress similar in style but with polka dots. We were not exactly bridesmaids, as such personages didn't exist then in German weddings, but we did have certain functions such as holding the bride's bouquet during the ceremony. The wedding was only two weeks away.

In the meantime, D. and I continued to go out together at lunch, and sometimes we ran into Helga. The three of us would greet each other after which D. and I walked on. Sometimes, when he and I didn't have a date, I was sure he was going out with Helga, which seemed okay with me at times though sometimes I hated him for it. Alone in bed at night, I constructed long conversations with him, berating him for his two-timing and telling him how lousy I felt about myself, but I seemed to be unable to muster the courage for a frank, face-to-face conversation with him. My fear was that he would reject me for it, and I didn't want that to happen. Instead, I prepared myself for rejection by rationalizing that in any case this affair would have to end before I left for England, and the departure would put an end to my obsession with this irresistible scoundrel.

I felt that I was developing two personalities. On the one hand I was an indecisive, easily-manipulated fool, in love with a boy who tweaked my chain and kept me in constant turmoil; on the other hand, I was a competent, well-respected employee. When Herr Thomas went on vacation again, I took substituting for him very seriously and would sometimes work until 10:00 p.m. In my daily conferences with the owner of the company, Alexander Petersen, I would lay out plans for how we should proceed on certain items. When he didn't have time to dictate letters in German or Spanish, I myself would write some of them for his signature. If I weren't about to leave for England, I would have expected a promotion as perfectly in order. But my confidence at work was not matched by anything close to it in my private life.

◆   ◆   ◆

At home, a big event was about to take place. After four years of courtship and another four years of being engaged, Klaus and Anne were finally getting married. They were both working and had found an apartment they could almost afford. Mutti and Papa had had misgivings for years about Anne's tendency to spend more money than she and Klaus were making, and they worried that their son, who was a generous and loving man, would not be able to deny his future wife anything she wanted. However, Mutti and Papa suppressed their feelings at this critical moment.

As is German custom, Anne and Klaus went to the *Standesamt*, the registry office, for a civil wedding. A short ceremony took place in front of two witnesses (friends of theirs), appropriate papers were signed, and then with a small group of friends and relatives they lunched at a restaurant. Klaus and Anne were now husband and wife; however, Mutti asked Klaus to spend his wedding night at our house because he wasn't married yet in the eyes of the church. The Lutheran church had never played a big part in her life (at least not outwardly), but for nuptials it did. Even though Klaus and Anne had practically lived together for years, for this one night he was still Mutti's boy, the one she loved with all her heart.

That night, Friday, August 12, 1960, the fun part of the wedding weekend took place—the traditional *Polterabend* (an evening to make a racket). Friends, relatives, and work acquaintances of Anne and Klaus were invited, as were Klaus' long-time soccer buddies. Yummy young men in their prime! Doris and I were elated! The party was being held in the apartment of Anne's aunt and uncle with whom she had chosen to live after her parents divorced. Guests brought pieces of pottery which they smashed at the entrance to the apartment house, supposedly to chase away evil ghosts. For the moment, though, this custom kept the lucky couple busy sweeping up the broken pieces of cups, plates, and saucers and disposing them in a big bin. Until all guests arrived, Klaus and Anne had to leave the party periodically to perform broom duty.

Beer and wine flowed, guests sang and told jokes, and oohed and aahed when Klaus and Anne opened their presents. The buffet consisted of many platters of ham, liverwurst, salami, and cheese; bowls of potato salad, pickled herring and beet salad, and baskets of bread; plates of smoked herring and *Schillerlocken* (strips of meat from the belly of certain sharks) which I always thought of as ideal for the eater who didn't really like fish, given their softness, blandness, and appearance somewhat like the ringlets that graced the poet Schiller's head.

Some of the photos of that festive evening show Doris and me sitting among Klaus' friends, older guys in their mid-twenties who seemed so worldly-wise and sexy to me. We must have played games during the evening, because one photo showed guests raising their hands as though to answer questions. The groom sat in the center of the group with a silly grin on his face, his right hand raising a bottle of beer.

Ever since Doris and I were little, we had entertained relatives and friends with a poem recital here, a song there, and over the years we had added titles to our repertoire. One photo at the *Polterabend* showed me standing in the doorway to the living room, wearing my mother's hat that strongly resembled an upside-down flower pot and singing a song, probably *Kann denn Liebe Sünde sein* (Can love be sin?), made popular by the singing Swedish movie star, Zarah Leander. She had been the controversial Diva of the Third Reich (controversial because she was thought to be backed by the Nazis). The German public still loved her as an actress and a singer for her smoky voice, which I attempted to imitate in my rendition of several of her songs. Another favorite with friends and relatives was *Der Wind hat mir ein Lied erzählt* (The wind has told me a song of great happiness) about the desire for the heart of another to beat only for me. My voice grew smokier and sexier with every beat, because of course that song was really about me. I, Christel, was waiting for that man whose heart beat only for me. After Doris did her rendition of Marlene Dietrich's *Ich bin von Kopf bis Fuss auf Liebe eingestellt* (Falling in love again), we received requests to sing more songs and probably sang our entire repertoire that night.

Around midnight, Doris and I presented the bride with her wreath and veil. We were not really bridesmaids, but as her new sisters we had the privilege of selecting her waist-length veil made of muslin and embroidered with flowers. It was attached to a white wreath of silk flowers which would be pinned to her hair.

The next day, Saturday, August 13, 1960, Mutti, Papa, Doris and I took a cab to Anne's apartment to find Klaus already there. He had dressed at our house and then probably walked to Anne's apartment. Anne's aunt was helping her put on her veil and soon it was time to squeeze into the waiting cabs. Anne's aunt and uncle and her sister went in one cab, my family left in another, and any other relatives went in cabs preceding the bride and groom so that they would arrive first.

A few minutes before 4:00 p.m. church bells were ringing and a group of total strangers were waiting in front for the bride and groom to arrive. I had run to the church many a Saturday afternoon on hearing the bells, knowing there would be a wedding ceremony through which I could sit in complete ignorance of any of the people involved. The attraction for me centered on the brides in their long white dresses, looking so much like fairytale princesses.

The procession down the aisle was led by Klaus and Anne, followed by Doris and me, Anne's aunt and my Papa, Mutti and the bride's uncle, and then relatives and other guests. The Lutheran wedding ceremony was duly performed, the details of which remain foggy. The pastor knew the bride only slightly, and his speech focused on the bride and groom as a couple.

As was the custom, Klaus and Anne had been wearing their engagement rings on their left hand ring fingers. During the ceremony the rings had to be removed from the left hand for transfer to the right hand. (Married men and women in Germany wear their wedding bands on their right hand).

After the ceremony, Klaus and Anne left the church first in a cab at which everyone else followed in cabs to the *Landhaus,* an elegant restaurant situated in the Stadtpark, the city park, where Doris and I had skated on the big pond as young adults and where she and I had necked on the benches with our respective boyfriends.

The wedding reception for fewer than twenty people included a sit-down dinner and dancing. Most likely, the dinner consisted of a soup, followed by a meat course with potatoes and a vegetable. There was no specially decorated wedding cake, just a plain model. Champagne, wine, beer, and liqueur were in abundance. But for me the fun part of the whole evening was the dancing. I had several waltzes with Klaus, who was an excellent dancer, having learned ballroom at the same studio I had attended. Klaus knew that I liked to twirl, and there survives a photo of him and me doing that quite competently. I gather from the photos that Doris and I entertained again, performing the same songs as we had the night before.

Shortly before midnight Klaus and his new wife performed the "veil dance" in which, as the couple danced, the bride put her hands on her head to secure the veil. Then all the guests tried to tear away a piece of it, for good luck. I still have my piece of muslin and embroidery, fragile now after all the years. Soon after the veil dance the reception ended, and the newlyweds made their exit. Their destination was their new apartment, for their wedding night and all the nights to come.

I missed Klaus' presence at home, although he hadn't spent that much time with us in the last few months or even years. It was still his base, and when he was home there was always the chance of a sudden romp that Doris and I so enjoyed given that we were still trying to trounce him. Now he lived in a pretty apartment with Anne, and I wondered how they would include us in their lives. I found out very soon, when I was invited on a Friday night to take a bath (they had a bathtub and we didn't) and watch TV (they had a TV, we didn't). This became a somewhat regular Friday night event. What luxury to have this combination of bathtub/TV. The bliss of it! (In my diary, I noted that I made sure I cleaned the tub thoroughly after my bath). Klaus was happy to have his family over, and Anne was willing to share him with us.

Doris complained in later years that Klaus didn't make enough of an effort to get together with her and blamed Anne for keeping him from our family. Behnke family members have varying recollections of this. I couldn't judge his behavior by how often he visited, because I was absent living in America, but I remember waiting for letters from him and feeling that he had abandoned me because he wasn't taking time to write.

Now that the wedding was over, I could resume my nerve-racking affair with the double-crossing, lying playboy D., and though I knew that I would be gone to England fairly soon we had to play out the farce and bring it to a tidy conclusion. I had only two more weeks at work, and during one of our "lunches" at the Alster I announced to him, "September 16 is my last day at work; then I'm free." On the surface I meant "Free of work," but underneath I was implying "Free of you." It sounded to me like I wanted to be the one ultimately to break if off, but on this day I was just dropping hints to see what his reaction would be. Doing doublespeak so I wouldn't hurt his precious feelings. And what did he do? He asked me if we should take Helga the next time we went to the *Witthues,* the tea café! When I said no, I immediately suspected that I was being jealous. And didn't jealousy come from love? I wasn't so sure about this popular piece of wisdom either but carried on, only partly in charge of my feelings and never truly feeling equal in this relationship.

Doris turned twenty-one on September 4, 1960, and Mutti and Papa threw her a party. Doris saw herself as more mature now than she had ever been before, thus much more serious. But in spite of her self-imaginings she only seemed to get sillier by the day. Along with her great sense of humor came a willingness to make a fool of herself, and she and her many good friends got together all the time and acted goofy, especially when a whole group would meet at the Stadtpark, climb trees, hide in the rhododendron bushes and then jump out roaring, and singing at the top of their lungs.

For her birthday party, Doris invited my childhood friend Bernhard as my date. While everybody else was having a good time, Bernhard and I glared at each other, or rather I glared at him as he threw back looks that intimated he wanted to be more than friends. But I couldn't be bothered. The lights were dimmed, the music played softly, and the four couples were dancing so closely that I thought I saw steam rising from their bodies. Meanwhile, Mutti and Papa sat reading in the kitchen. I watched Bernhard sort records until 1:00 a.m. when I left him at his arduous task and went to bed. In the morning, I cleaned up the house that smelled of cold cigarette butts, leftovers, and beer bottles, while Doris left for a date at 11:00 a.m.

Earlier on the same day of the party, I bought my ticket to England—from Hamburg to Ostende by train, from Ostende to Dover by boat, and then by train to London's Victoria Station. So my trip was becoming reality. I had received a letter from my English host, Mrs. W., in which she told me that the boys liked my photo and that I was now their "pin-up" girl. I wondered if I would get along with my English family, and I worried. Would they like me?

The departure date was set for September 30, 1960. With my last day of work approaching, D. and I were still playing games. One day at lunchtime, my girl-friend and I watched him cross the street with Helga at exactly the same spot where he and I used to cross. The nerve! What did their crossing the street together really mean? With nerves that were tightly wound, I was sad, confused, jealous, and mad, but I never let on. My girlfriend and I continued on our way, effectively preventing me from throwing a fit right then and there. But I didn't understand why I had to control my feelings so tightly. Why the facade when I should have confronted him? The next day, D. and I walked to the *Alster* where he dropped the statement that he liked Helga better than me. That night I told my diary that I felt sad but that I didn't let on to him about my feelings. I didn't know I could be this brave, but what did bravery have to do with hiding one's feelings? At night, I cried in my pillow as usual, but at work I kept up the mask. I felt hurt that a man had pushed me aside for another woman, and yet hadn't I seen it coming? How could I have been so naïve? My bewildered mind wondered what would happen at the party to which both he and I had been invited? I should have seen it coming: I kissed him at the party, and when he took me home we kissed some more. Hot, cold, hot, cold, I was exhausted from dealing with conflicting feelings. I wanted to be in good shape mentally for the round of good-byes to come.

On September 15, Doris and I had to accompany Mutti to Tante Klara's birthday party. She and Onkel Heini had been at all our family gatherings over the years—birthday parties, anniversaries, and confirmations, so it was only fitting that Doris and I should attend their event. Still, we argued with Mutti about having to go. Doris and I thought that time spent with relatives was boring, conflict-free and therefore unstimulating! Two days later I turned nineteen, and Tante Klara and Onkel Heini attended my birthday party, at which I also said my goodbyes to them. I wouldn't see them for a year.

The day before my nineteenth birthday was my last day at work. My co-workers showered me with flowers and a book about London, and my department gave me a ceramic plate depicting the *Alster* and buildings surrounding it. In the afternoon, the whole company (probably about twenty of us) had coffee and cake. D. managed to hand me a piece of paper that carried the message, "It was wonderful with you. Really." What a jerk! To put the relationship to rest, I had to think back to the beginning and admit to myself that I had not wanted this liaison both because of my plans to go to England and my discovery early on that D. was a playboy. I could have played it for what it was worth, but instead I was left with feelings of rejection to deal with. My self-esteem, which was often on shaky grounds, had been attacked by a person not only unworthy of me but who also had issues with self-esteem. My instincts told me that D. was as confused as I was, but knowing this didn't help right away because of my feelings of rejection. At least I had gained some insight which would help me assert myself in my next relationship. Maybe I would make better choices from then on.

The outpouring of affection for me from my co-workers confirmed to me that I was a likeable and well-liked person. Maybe I was better in group interactions than in exclusive relationships. There had in fact been many activities over the eighteen months of employment with Alexander Petersen that seemed to confirm feelings I had about myself and others. For example, a group of us often got together for lunches, dinners, and parties, and even weekend jaunts into the countryside around Hamburg. In November of the previous year, a group of my co-workers and I had had such a good time at the *Hamburger Dom* that we planned to do it again in 1960, but by then I would be in England and so would miss out on this traditional fair. Visiting the Dom had been a group activity that I had unqualifiedly enjoyed.

The *Hamburger Dom* was a fair that had originated in the 14th century. The site where it took place, then as now, was the *Heiligengeistfeld* (Holy Ghost Field), the former site of the Mariendom cathedral. Legend had it that the market vendors on this Holy Ghost Field often were forced to take shelter in the Dom due to Hamburg's unpredictable weather, and so when it rained they began selling their wares in the cathedral. Now spread out over two miles, for a whole month the fair was a giant amusement park with stalls offering food, crafts, and rides of all kinds. Most of the rides proved too daunting for me, but I had a good time on the merry-go-round whose ornately crafted and painted animals fascinated me. If I went on the Ferris wheel, it was only to see the St. Pauli red light district, the river, and the harbor from above. The best thing about the Dom for me was the food—gingerbread hearts with an attached ribbon that could be slipped over the head and other food including chocolate-covered licorice lollipops, sweet popcorn, and roasted almonds. I can still smell and taste it all now.

The farewells continued on to take so much time that Papa got mad because I was gone so much; he felt that I should spend more time with the family since I would be gone for a whole year. But I was caught up in the activities and he let me be. One night I met six girls from work and we headed to St. Pauli where in 1960 there were still a number of places where girls my age could go dancing without risking being accosted. We danced until we were exhausted and couldn't take another step.

The next day, the American evangelist Billy Graham came to Hamburg. To save souls, I imagine. A huge tent was set up in the Stadtpark, and it quickly filled up, mostly with young people. I couldn't explain why so many people turned out unless they were as curious as I was. Here was a flesh and blood American who hammered out short sentences accompanied by stabbing gestures, so unlike the restraint of our ministers in delivering our Sunday morning sermons. When Graham asked us to come forward if we wanted to accept Christ into our hearts, I and a few hundred others leaped toward the stage, where we stood to receive some kind of blessing from this divine motivator, this advance man for Jesus Christ. I myself felt holier than thou from the experience of being completely swept away by the moment. What was the matter with me? I had grown up thinking that religion had a quiet, intensely private quality. You went to a little neighborhood church on Sundays, you listened to the pastor's good words, you sang, you prayed, and you and your fellow churchgoers felt a tinge of righteousness. The subdued feeling I often carried home with me after a Lutheran service was a far cry from the frenzy of the Graham service.

The next day I took communion at my Lutheran church. Maybe listening to an evangelist hadn't been the right thing to do, but there were probably other sins for which I needed forgiveness, like not considering my Papa's feelings about being away from home so much. After church, I said farewell to the parents of my friend Sabine, who was already in England, and then swung by the apartment of my Tante Erika and Onkel Herbert, a local judge, and their children Wolfgang and Ingeborg. Ingeborg had a harelip that I found fascinating to covertly study when she talked.

On Monday night, the church youth group gathered with Coca-Cola and presents to send me off to England. We took the only ashtray in the room, piled it high with paper bags, straws, and anything else flammable in the room, lighted the whole heap, turned off the lights, and sang songs such as *Wir lagen vor Madagaskar und hatten die Pest an Bord* by the "campfire" we lit. Then they walked me home in a *triumphant procession* (as noted in my diary), and my parents poured a small glass of liqueur for everyone.

In the morning, I made the trek to my paternal grandparents' house. In spite of much-improved public transportation in the post-war years, it was still a time-consuming trip. But rather than walking for an hour from the train station, I was now able to take a bus to their village. My Opa was eighty years old and my Oma seventy-eight, both of them in good health that made me certain they'd be around when I returned from England.

Next I visited Onkel Max and his new young wife (his first wife, my Tante Gretchen, Mutti's older sister, had died), and their young son. Since Tante Gretchen's death, we had had little contact with Onkel Max, and I wondered if it really mattered to him that I was going to England. I'm afraid I went to see them because I thought they might want to give me a little something for the trip, maybe a few Marks to sweeten the purse. But no such thing happened, although the visit was pleasant and Onkel Max seemed somehow younger as his eyes danced around his young wife.

There were only three days left before my trip to England, and I was about to have my last contact with Bill. His ship had anchored in Hamburg, and we met for lunch at the *Alsterpavillon*, our favorite place to eat. We sat for a long time and talked as I made mental notes about the British. If they were all like shy Bill, I would have to be somewhat aggressive if I wanted to date any young Englishmen!

◆   ◆   ◆

The day before my departure, I packed and took my suitcase to the train station as, apparently, luggage could be checked the day before. Then, on September 30, 1960, my family assembled at the main train station. I had not wanted Mutti to come along because I knew it would be hard for her to see her youngest child go off by herself even though I would be staying with a very respectable British family. To Mutti, I was still a child even though I was nineteen years old, and her eyes never left me as we waited for the train to arrive. Once I was on the train, I couldn't come back out because it was very full. But all of a sudden, I saw ten people from work running toward my compartment. One of them pushed a pickle into my hand (I don't know why a pickle), and then everything happened very quickly: hands were throwing kisses at me as the train departed from the station. Then I was gone from hometown, from family and friends, from cat and backyard, from workplace, from the beloved German language itself.

After the train ride, on the boat from the port of Ostende to Dover, I felt sick to my stomach, as much from the English channel as from my nerves. A young Englishman sitting next to me kindly took care of me bringing me little sausages and coffee and draping his coat over me. We kept company on the train from Dover to London, and he said he would write to me though he never did. My mind wandered on the long trip to England, and I felt anxious about living with strangers for the next year, people who didn't know me or my mother tongue. What if I couldn't understand what they were saying because they spoke too fast or used unfamiliar words? What if they didn't like me? Then I'd have to return home, never to learn proper English, to become the laughing stock of all my friends, to see my life ruined! These thoughts and more would make anyone queasy.

The day after I left Hamburg, on Saturday, October 1, the train from Dover finally arrived at Victoria Station. I was anxious about this part of the trip too. True, Mr. W. would be there wearing a carnation. But there were several men sporting carnations in their buttonholes, and on my first try I spoke to the wrong man. How embarrassing, especially since the real Mr. W. was probably watching! Where in the world was the real Mr. W.? Did all men in England wear carnations? Was this a custom I hadn't read about? What if I were left standing at Victoria Station? Was I up to this crisis? After agonizing minutes, a middle-aged, medium-sized, balding, bespectacled man approached me and asked, "Are you Christel Behnke?" I said, "Yes," and after introducing himself he motioned to a boy of about thirteen standing next to him, introducing me to Hugh, a chubby boy with rumpled clothes and a round face just like his father's. As we walked to the car with my luggage, they spoke to me in English. This seemed strange to me, but then again I was at my English destination. Arrived!

In a heap called a car we tooled to the northernmost outskirts of London, to an area called Mill Hill. As soon as we pulled up to the curb, Mrs. W. came running out of the house, embraced me, and welcomed me with very warm words.

This embrace, and Hugh's ear-to-ear grin, set the tone for the months to come. I knew that I would like this place and these people and that they would like me. Then I met the other two sons, John (18) and Nigel (11), and altogether they impressed me as being a very nice family. Soon after arriving at their semi-detached home, I went to bed and slept and slept.

The next day was Sunday and nobody was planning to do anything but read the *London Times* strewn all over the drawing room. The walls of the room were greenish, a pretty, translucent green as I remember, and compared to the rest of the house the drawing room looked almost elegant with its two light-colored sofas facing each other. The fire was lit only on Sundays, so the rest of the week this room was cold and clammy and nobody used it. In that way, it stayed relatively untouched by greasy juvenile hands.

Sundays in England were so different from Sundays in Germany that I had a difficult time adjusting at first. A regular Sunday at home had meant sleeping late, except for the few years when I attended church. Services didn't begin until 9:30 a.m., but the church bells chiming at 9:00 a.m. woke me up and I had to get ready in a hurry.

Back at home the highlight of Sunday was coffee and cake in the afternoon. Doris and I would mix our coffee heavily with hot water because we didn't really like the taste of coffee even though we were being groomed for liking it when we were older. Mutti would have made a cake the day before or on Sunday morning. When prune plums were ripe, she would cut them in half, remove the pits and place the halves fleshy sides up on the dough she had pressed onto a type of cookie sheet. Then she sprinkled the prune plums heavily with sugar, and the kitchen started smelling like the juicy meat of a single big plum. Our mouths watered while the cake was baking. When it was time to have coffee and cake, around 4:00 p.m., each square of plum cake would be served with a generous dollop of whipped cream. It was the most amazing taste sensation: the softness of the buttery dough, the sweetness of the plums that hinted of tartness, and the foaminess of the whipped cream barely sweetened so as not to compete with the sweetness of the plums all came together in a delectable way.

In my prior correspondence with Mrs. W., nothing specific had been said about what my household duties would be. I wasn't a guest in this house but was supposed to help with household chores in exchange for a small allowance and the opportunity to take classes that would improve my English skills. I had the feeling that the agenda would be made up as we went along. But on this first day there were no chores for me, and instead we drove to the countryside and picked elderberries. Then I listened to jazz in John's room, and in the evening we sat in the drawing room and read. It was as uneventful a Sunday as many Sundays in England would prove to be.

On Monday, however, I was thrown into the fire. At lunchtime, I fixed fried potatoes, a *Frikadelle* (a pan-fried hamburger, made from a mixture of ground beef, soaked stale bread, egg, chopped onions and salt and pepper), and broiled tomatoes for the man of the house, David W., who was about to go on a trip.

I still didn't know what else I was supposed to do and at what time, so on Tuesday I cleaned the whole house. I knew how to give things a good scrub, and this house certainly needed it! More, it needed organizing and streamlining. It struck me that every inch of space was occupied by books—books on shelves, in book cases, on tables, chairs, and mantles all through the drawing and living rooms. All in all, I was impressed with the house's extreme clutter, and of course I compared it to my Hamburg home where space came at a premium so nothing could be left lying around, ever. Everything had a place, always. Well, I was determined to give every wayward book its proper home and proceeded immediately to do so, not always to the approval of the family members who obviously knew where every book was. Which was where it had been forever before I came along. Needless to say, lots of dust flew for the first few weeks until I had this project under control.

After four days in England, I already had a day off and I took this opportunity to have a look at the city of London. For some reason, I took the bus and not the tube (British for subway) into the city. At the time, the suburb of Mill Hill didn't have its own subway stop, and, given my unfamiliarity with the system I was reluctant to transfer from a bus to the subway. Thus the bus ride from Mill Hill to London took forty-five minutes, plenty of time for me to observe a woman filing her fingernails right in front of my eyes. I had never seen anyone doing that grooming job in public in Germany. It was a job best done in the privacy of one's room, I felt sure.

My sightseeing that day took me to Westminster Cathedral, which I found to be very Catholic and not very interesting. But what other opinion could possibly issue from my very Lutheran heart? On then to Westminster Abbey and Big Ben, through St. James Park and down the Mall to Buckingham Palace. This palace I also found rather unmemorable, but I gave it the benefit of doubt by thinking that it might grow on me after I had seen it two or three times. This first outing was to be the start of a huge sightseeing passion of mine, and thereafter I explored London whenever I could. Having used public transportation all my life, I took the tube, trains, and busses with ease.

London was a sightseer's idea of paradise. On one occasion, Hugh, Nigel, and I spent a whole afternoon at the National Portrait Gallery, a place I found astonishing not only because of the art but also because these two pre-teen boys were actually looking at the paintings. Never mind that they aped some of the expressions of the painted subjects, cracked jokes, and made up stories about the artists and their subjects. I should have known then that the boys would end up being writers!

◆   ◆   ◆

Fairly soon after I moved in with the W. family, I learned to shop for groceries at small stores on the Mill Hill shopping street that was not more than three blocks long. The first few times, Mrs. W. came along and showed me how to select cuts of meat. The butcher produced different cuts than my butcher back home, and at first I was particularly taken aback by the legs of lamb hanging from hooks both inside and outside the store. Once, Mrs. W. pointed to a leg of lamb being examined by a horde of flies in front of the shop. The lamb looked grayish, giving off the appearance of decay. Clearly, though, it looked just fine to Mrs. W., because she bought it and told me that a good soaking in vinegar would eliminate all traces and flies and fly eggs. The following Sunday, everybody including me ate their lamb, though swallowing it proved a bit hard for me because of what I had seen.

After a couple of weeks of shopping with me, Mrs. W. started giving me a list of food items to buy, probably to prevent me from buying German products like head cheese and sliced tongue. Shopping took up a good deal of my daily routine at first, until I got to know the stores and salespeople. The clerks were very nice to me, the foreigner, even if she didn't always understand their English. Often, I had to ask to have a question repeated or spoken more slowly, especially if they spoke a London dialect. Clerks must have viewed me as quite a spectacle given that I always wore my felt hat with a feather in the side. Was this a Bavarian hat, and why did I wear it (especially since I wouldn't have been caught dead wearing it in Hamburg)? I suppose I wore it because when I walked up and down the shopping street everybody would look at me or maybe even talk to me, the foreigner.

Shopping proved to be a daily job just as it had been for Mutti. Mrs. W. was much relieved that I was able to take over this job for the family because she was a busy woman with a full-time job as a college teacher of nursery nurses, among other subjects teaching child development and child psychology. Mr. W. was the principal of a grammar school, the English high school that is public and not private like a public school. Hugh and Nigel attended a public school that required them to wear uniforms. John attended a grammar school, for some reason not a public school as did his brothers. The whole English "public school is private school" idea was confusing to me at first. In any case the parents had busy schedules and needed help in the house, and that's where I came in.

Besides the shopping and cleaning, I was also doing more and more of the cooking, which was the part I hated the most because I didn't know what I was doing. The little cooking I had learned from watching Mutti didn't instill confidence in me given that she had always shooed us children out of the kitchen. The rationale was that it was her domain whereas play was ours. I think now that she simply didn't want us underfoot, because the kitchen was small and we would have been in each other's way. Whatever the reason, here I was in a foreign kitchen, making what I thought I knew how to make. Then why wasn't the red cabbage getting done the way it was supposed to? As I learned the hard way, red cabbage took a long time to cook, and I hadn't scheduled enough time for it to be ready together with the potatoes and the Frikadellen that seemed to be one of my staples. There I was sweating in the kitchen, virtually willing the red cabbage to hurry up and cook at the same time as worrying about whether the boys would like it. They did, and eventually over the course of the year my worries subsided and I cooked with more confidence. But never with any joy. One joy-killer was the fact that what might have taken me two hours or more to cook took the boys ten minutes or less to devour. I found their wolfish behavior offensive and I told them so, but nothing changed and they kept gobbling my carefully prepared food in what to me was a most impolite manner.

As I cleaned and cooked, Mrs. W. was looking for a suitable college where I could take classes in English as a Second Language. We settled on St. Albans College, just north of London, and on October 13 I began my classes. Fortunately it had taken Mrs. W. only about two weeks to get me into school, because the main goal for spending this year in England was to improve my English.

Before I started school, though, I learned the intricacies of the launderette. As a young child, I had watched Mutti bend intently over the washtub full of soapy water and dirty clothes, a washboard leaning against the side of the tub, her hands holding a soap-smeared piece of clothing and moving her arms up and down. From this medieval contraption, she had graduated in 1959 to a washing machine with an attached wringer that was supposed to be an improvement over sheer elbow grease but somehow dribbled water all over the kitchen floor and tied up the sink for hours while the hoses were hooked up to the faucets. Sometimes, in fact, I thought that Mutti missed the old tub and washboard. Back then she had always had the tub positioned for a view out the kitchen window where she could see her beloved back yard. Since the new machine had to be positioned next to the sink, Mutti faced a blank wall.

And now her daughter was in England in front of a washing machine identical to the other machines in the launderette, reading to kill the boredom. Actually, I didn't even have to sit out the laundry, sometimes doing the shopping during the washing cycle. Clever me.

◆   ◆   ◆

It was time for school for several reasons. I had never been in a position of a "mother's helper" before, and though I lived with quite a pleasant family that treated me very well, I still felt like I was a glorified maid. It occurred to me that I had to get over this feeling if I wanted to enjoy the experience and grow from it in a way I couldn't grow from mere housekeeping. I supposed that it was possible to cultivate a feeling of satisfaction for a job well done. Or just done. On the plus side I had the work organized so that the house required dusting only every other day and vacuuming just once a week. The boys were untidy, but I had already figured out that if I picked up after them they would never learn to be tidy. I wanted to teach them a lesson, so I declined to clean their rooms until they had picked up the dirty clothes, books, papers, sweet wrappers, and miscellaneous items they routinely stepped on and over. Mrs. W. supported me in this teaching endeavor, but success was minimal.

In addition to feeling like a glorified maid (not that anyone tried to make me feel that way), I felt inferior intellectually to this family with its passion for reading. I always thought that I had received a good education in German schools and that I was pretty well read for a person my age, having read German and some English literature. Greek and Roman mythology were at my fingertips, and I had dissected and memorized long poems by Goethe, Schiller, and many other German greats. Unfortunately, memorization often outweighed learning about the meaning of a poem. I often hated discussions about poems because I never seemed to "get" their meaning. Why couldn't I just enjoy poems for the beauty of their words, I often asked myself. But here were three boys all younger than I who had read more of the classics than I ever had and they seemed to remember them all. They even knew more of the German writers and of German history than I did. I think this family really liked reading whereas I often thought of reading as a chore. Perhaps going to school in England would make my inferiority complex go away.

I did notice that my English vocabulary was growing rapidly. Apart from speaking German with my girlfriend Sabine, to whom I spoke frequently over the phone, most of the time I spoke English with my family, neighbors, and sales clerks. I felt that I was well prepared to begin college, at least as far as my knowledge of English was concerned.

I had to take the train from Mill Hill to St. Albans, a pleasant ride of about half an hour that gave me time to read or gaze out the window. Tuition costs were reasonable, only one pound for the term, and eleven shillings for three textbooks. I was enrolled in a class that met twice a week from 2:00–4:00 p.m. with a break halfway through. On Tuesdays we had grammar and on Thursdays literature. My classmates represented several nationalities, mostly European—French, German, Spanish, Swedish—all trying like me to learn English.

In addition to the English class, I also enrolled in a once-weekly cooking class in St. Albans, this at Mrs. W's request so that dinner could be started before she got home from her teaching job. And I was rather proud of myself the first time I made puff pastries for the family (they all wanted me to make these little cakes again). I couldn't believe it—this German teenager was enrolled in an advanced French cooking class in England! After cooking class, though, it was back to the cleaning.

Although my life was getting busier by the day, it needed an additional dimension. There was a lack of male companionship in my life, although John W. and I sometimes went to the movies together or took the tube to London there to go our separate ways until we met to return home. But he was like a brother, and I was ready for a boyfriend, not having had one in about two months. Doris wrote that she was through with her Willi and was already in love with someone else who was now proving to be the great love of her life.

A few months back, a theater group from Pembroke College in Cambridge had come to Hamburg's Operettenhaus to perform Shakespeare's *Twelfth Night*. A reception was held afterwards at the English Council Club, where I happened to fall into a conversation with Geoffrey, one of the actors. When I told Geoffrey that I was going to be in England for a year, he offered to show me around Cambridge. It is a truism that one should never extend an idle invitation to Germans, because they'll take the extender up on it. So now that I was in England I contacted him, writing a letter which he answered with an invitation for me to come on up to Cambridge, preferably on a Saturday or Sunday. It was only a ninety-minute trip by bus from London. So I set my wheels in motion, informing Mrs. W., who countered by asking a lot of questions about this young man I was planning to meet. She wasn't all that happy about my going to Cambridge to spend the day with a person neither she nor I knew.

So that I could meet some English people my age, Mrs. W. invited the daughter of a friend of hers to visit us. At the first of many visits from Anna, I noticed immediately that she did not make up her face like other English girls who seemed to have fallen into a pot of paint and smeared the color around, leaving many of them looking grotesque. Anna wasn't like that; she had the "natural" look that Mutti had always told me was "good." Anna usually came calling on Sundays, when only the beds had to be made, and the table didn't require setting for breakfast because everybody just helped themselves. That way, she and I had a lot of time to talk and get acquainted. Usually, however, I had to do the verbal prodding, because she was quite shy and her visits could be rather exhausting.

Our next visitor came to stay for a while. Mrs. W's mother was a tiny woman of eighty-nine, slow-moving, forgetful and maybe a bit senile. Had she been sent expressly to drive us all crazy? I was only nineteen, and I regarded her as an extremely old lady who might have wanted to help but who got in the way given her slowness. In fact, I was too young to appreciate her spunkiness at such an advanced age. All along she had only wanted to help, beginning with doing dishes for the seven of us, a feat that took her all evening. Then she would peel the twenty-five potatoes needed for all of us at the rate of about five potatoes an hour.

Her senility showed most painfully when she would tell me a hundred times that her other son-in-law was stealing her savings. One morning, determined to take a cab to her bank to straighten out the mess that obsessed her mind, Granny departed on foot only to return after wandering the streets for half an hour. The boys and I were relieved to see her because we worried that she had gotten lost. That is, relieved until she picked a fight with Nigel, telling him that he talked too much. He did talk too much, but myself I had learned to tune him out and rejoin him when I was ready, at which time he would in all likelihood still be talking. Then she fought with Hugh, who wouldn't listen to her because he was too busy picking his nose while doing his French homework!

When I needed to get away from Granny, I went to my cozy bedroom. It even had a fireplace which, alas, was never lit, and in cold weather the room was icy cold and damp such that I had to crawl under the covers if I wanted to read. So like everyone else, I did my homework in the living room because on cold days there would be a fire crackling in the fireplace. There was no central heating in the house, a normal state for English homes at that time.

Another escape was to the public library, and I went often. Sometimes I checked out English books in German translation, like *Witness for the Prosecution* by Agatha Christie or *Letter from Peking* by Pearl S. Buck. It was still easier and more relaxing for me to read books in German. Still, everything else I read was in English—all school books, newspapers, magazines, ads, grocery lists, and task lists I wrote for myself.

On my days off, I continued with my sightseeing, at times meeting with my girlfriend Sabine at the German restaurant *Schmidt* (in downtown London) where we ate sauerkraut and sausage followed by whipped cream-filled pastries. I wasn't particularly homesick but periodically I craved some German food. I also continued to feed my love for music by attending Richard Strauss' opera *Der Rosenkavalier* at Covent Garden. Compared to the Opernhaus in Hamburg, where everything was well-appointed and new because it had been destroyed during the war, I found Covent Garden to look quite shabby. There was no carpeting past the first loge, so the rest of the floors looked to be nothing more than a movie theater's. I would sit in the gallery on a small, hard seat, the floor around me strewn with sweet wrappers and other litter, trying to settle in so as to let the music wash my mind of my shabby surroundings. I realized that every time I was confronted with a new locale or customs or food, my first reaction would be to criticize. After a time, though, that cultural criticism would turn into acceptance, as I noted of myself. For instance, one of the first jobs I had to learn was to make a proper English bed. And I asked myself, *Why can't the English make up beds like the Germans?* A German bed had a bottom sheet and a feather comforter in a duvet. An English bed, however, had a bottom sheet, a top sheet, and a blanket, and all of these had to be tucked in. It took me a while to get the knack of it, but I always preferred the German way.

Mrs. W. and I occasionally did errands together, and a month after I arrived I was feeling quite comfortable around her. It was clear that she depended on me for doing the cooking and cleaning, but then again she treated me like a daughter and included me in lunches with her friends as well as on shopping trips when she would frequently ask my opinion about a piece of clothing she wanted to buy.

We also went house-hunting together, because the family wanted to move into a bigger house located closer to where everybody worked or went to school. We looked at two houses one afternoon, but nothing looked good in the rain, of which we were having plenty. Plus the fog could be so dense as to quite unnerve me—I couldn't see beyond my nose! Literally the street in front of me was not visible. So rather than look at more houses, we returned home in the old family car, an Austin Healy convertible whose leaking roof got us wetter than we would have gotten walking in the rain.

It seemed to me that in four short weeks I had acquired skills that would serve me for the rest of my life, whether or not I ever had a family of my own. I learned how to cook, shop, and do the laundry. More, I now knew how to get around in a foreign city, how to keep homesickness at bay, and how to keep learning. Still, I needed to improve my writing skills because so far writing did not come as easily to me as did spoken English or German.

In cooking class I embarked on the big Christmas cake project. I had to weigh fruit, knead dough, chop almonds, and cut paper to fit the cake pan, each week adding various ingredients such as raisins, fruit, and rum until the cake was ready to be baked and served on Christmas Day. I couldn't wait to show off my masterpiece.

◆   ◆   ◆

My Cambridge connection was making progress as well, with Geoffrey suggesting that I visit him the following Sunday. I decided to go by bus, rather than train because the bus ticket was cheaper. Come the day of departure, though, I had a cold, and Mrs. W. advised me to stay home. But I couldn't stop the momentum and simply had to keep the date.

Now I faced getting decked out. On Friday, I had my hair done at the beauty parlor, asking Vivian to do an extra good job. In Germany, when the beautician teased the hair and combed it out smoothly it took at least twenty minutes, but here it was done in ten minutes at most, leaving me to think that I could have done a better job myself.

The next day, I went to central London to buy a dress. London wasn't a place in which fashion could ever originate and take the world by storm (in my considered opinion). Instead, the store racks were filled with ugly apparel. I started to panic, but then found a suit at a reasonable price at C & A (ironically, a German chain): a straight skirt and jacket in a beige jersey fabric. I had gained some weight because the English diet contained much flour and sugar, and my new bulges would have to be controlled by a girdle.

After shopping I had to hurry home to cook that night for the boys, two of their friends, Granny and myself. Who would have thought a month ago that I could successfully cook for seven people? That night I cooked Scotch eggs with peas, carrots, and white potatoes. A feast for the eyes in shades of green, white, and orange. I covered the hard-cooked eggs with ground pork sausage, then fried them in oil. I excelled especially in making the carrot pieces all the same size, this by squaring off the carrot on all sides so that I ended up with a rectangle which I then cut in half, turned, and cut again. I ended up with four rectangular pieces which I could hold together with one hand. With the other hand I proceeded to cut pieces of about ½ inch square. When I followed this rule on carrot dicing learned from my cooking class, I ended up with nearly perfect square pieces of carrots which the boys shoveled in, together with the peas, potatoes, and Scotch eggs. (So much for aesthetics; the boys didn't give a damn!)

The following day, I took one bus to Golders and a second bus to Victoria Station, where I picked up the bus to Cambridge. I was apprehensive the whole time, because I had already dreamed up a full-blown relationship with Geoffrey. Now what if the reality didn't turn out like the dream? What if he didn't like me at all? I had only met him once, fleetingly at best. What if I wasn't pretty enough in my new two-piece jersey suit in which I already felt a little uncomfortable. Was I too dressed up for this little encounter? Besides these doubts I was also having my period, so not only was I wearing a girdle but I had to double up on every-thing in the way of underwear protection lest embarrassing leakages occur. In short, I felt like a sausage.

And then something else went wrong. The bus had a flat tire on the way to Cambridge, and it seemed like a very long time before a repair crew arrived to get us on our way again. Indeed, the bus was 1–1/2 hours late arriving in Cambridge. I fretted that Geoffrey had gotten fed up and left, leaving me in Cambridge alone. But there he was waiting for me, even having brought along his friend John. I could tell that Geoffrey didn't recognize me at first; after all, we had only seen each other once. But I recognized him, having worked hard at keeping his face in my memory. Now my heart was beating as fast as it had when I had first met him.

The three of us spent the day looking at the different colleges, including Pem-broke where both Geoffrey and John were students. We had lunch, after which we walked along the river and across a bridge on the way to Geoffrey's room where we had tea. The beauty and romance of Cambridge was getting to me, or was it Geoffrey I was falling in love with? Why did his friend have to be there? What was the magic in the number three?

Geoffrey had something to do that evening so John took me out for dinner. He was charming and easy to talk to, but my heart for the moment belonged to

Geoffrey. Still, John wrote down my address before taking me to the train station, and by 11:00 p.m. I was home. In bed that night I relived the day a thousand times and wrote a letter to Geoffrey the next day but never again heard from him.

Three days later, however, I had a letter from John who would be in London the following week and wanted to take me out for lunch and to the Royal Festival Hall. This could be the beginning of the relationship I desired, not with the original guy but with his back-up. I was long overdue for a new boyfriend. Besides that, I was thrilled about John's letter.

I was late to John's and my first real date in Trafalgar Square because public transportation in England (busses, trains, and tubes) wasn't as punctual as it was in Germany. (English trains were often just minutes late, but late nonetheless). The date began with lunch followed by some tentative kissing and ended with us being so engrossed with each other that I missed the last bus home.

After lunch, we walked around London and managed to fit in a visit to the National Portrait Gallery, see a movie, listen to Berlioz' *Sinfonie Fantastique* at the Royal Festival Hall, and have dinner at the Chicken Inn. John was incredibly generous, paying for all my tickets and meals. As the day progressed, so did our mutual attraction. My whole being vibrated with all the tender attention it received that day, but finally we had to say goodbye because public transportation in London did not run all night, and around 11:00 p.m. I caught the last tube leaving central London. When I arrived in Hendon, where I would catch a bus to Mill Hill, the last bus had already left and there weren't any cabs. What to do now? I was on an emotional high from which I had to come down quickly in order to figure out what next to do. Outside the Hendon station, I saw a young man standing next to a policeman, so figuring that the policeman would help me I walked over and told them my predicament. The young man said he was waiting for friends and that they would give me a ride. I didn't hesitate for a second to get in the car with three males my age under such circumstances. We talked and laughed, and then they dropped me off in Mill Hill. But I knew I was in trouble the minute I walked in the door, because Mrs. W. was waiting up for me. It was now after midnight, and she had been waiting and worrying that something had happened to me. I was very ashamed, hugging her and asking for forgiveness which thankfully I received. Still, when I told her that I had gotten into a car with three young men, she scolded me all over again and pointed out all the things they could have done to me, none of which had entered my naive mind!

I was already planning my next date. John had invited me to Cambridge for the weekend, and he was waiting for my answer. I had to talk to Mrs. W. but was reluctant to do so because of what happened just a few days before. Finally, I gathered my courage and told her about my Cambridge plans. Her reaction was predictable. I shouldn't go for a weekend, she told me firmly, because it would only lead to indefinable, vague difficulties. Where would I stay? She felt responsible for me, and I felt like a daughter who had to listen and do what she was told. On the one hand, I had already envisioned a wild weekend—a lively romp—in Cambridge. But on the other, my shyness about matters of sex got the better of me, and so when John called on Thursday I told him I'd only be there on Sunday rather than for two days. He sounded disappointed but expressed compassion for the delicate situation I was in, having to comply with the wishes of my host mother.

The following Sunday, John met me at the train station in Cambridge and from there we took a cab to the house where he rented a room while a student in Cambridge. Was I surprised that his landlords were away for the weekend? Anyway, we cuddled up on a comfortable couch and smooched until it was time for lunch which we took at an Indian restaurant, after which we adjourned to Pembroke College for coffee. In the afternoon, we attended a concert and from there went back to his room. He produced tea and crumpets, and we talked, talked, snuggled, kissed, and necked. I told my diary that he had quite good manners and did not attempt anything improper though he was full of fire. Tender fire, if there is such a thing. I wondered would I ever get over this feeling that I was too young for physical love? One minute I was ready to wrestle on the sheet, and the next I wanted to gird myself in armor. So I returned home that day with my virginity intact though very much in love with this caring, romantic Englishman.

Two days later, I had a letter that said he missed me and was longing for me; I read that letter so many times that I learned it by heart. I knew that he would be in London the following Sunday for our fourth date, but after that any time we could spend together would be limited because in four-weeks' time he would go home for the Christmas holidays. Immediately after that he would student-teach for a term in Buckinghamshire, all of which meant that we wouldn't be seeing each other until April. I was at once elated at seeing him within a few short days but also despondent about this impending separation of three months just when we were getting to know each other. Maybe there would be a way to sneak in a visit, because Buckinghamshire wasn't that far away from London. In order to set things right with Mrs. W. about my previous failure to catch the last bus home, John wrote a letter to her, taking the blame and apologizing for detaining me too long. She was impressed with the letter, calling John a "very nice young man." So maybe she would let me go to Cambridge for a weekend in the summer!

My mind was on John constantly. When I fixed breakfast for everybody on Friday, two days before the fourth date, I burnt the toast and made the coffee too strong, and even the bacon too dark, but the important thing was that the boys got to school on time. Then I cleaned the house, went shopping, made lunch, and in the evening fried chips and sausage. The chips were overcooked, but the boys shoveled them in anyway. Granny did the dishes and I rested. At bedtime, Hugh and Nigel did a lot of yelling and pillow-fighting, but eventually they got to sleep. Mrs. W. was at the funeral of an aunt, and I was in charge of getting everybody fed. As was often the case, one of the boys would bring along a friend for supper, or John W. would be out. But by now I was used to cooking for any number of mouths that might be staying for lunch or supper.

In cooking class, my Christmas cake had progressed to the point that I was ready to spread the marzipan on it. In the weeks before, we had added mixed candied fruit peel, candied cherries, raisins, and currants, pulverized almonds, and sherry. Now the marzipan paste had to be mixed with almond extract, salt, corn syrup, and two pounds of confectioner's sugar. The mixture was then beaten with an electric mixer until the beaters couldn't handle any more sugar, at which time I turned to kneading in the remaining sugar with my hands. Eventually, the paste became a pliable ball, though not without difficulties—my hands felt wrung out. But finally the marzipan was ready to be rolled into a circle, about ½-inch thick. I used a plate to cut a paper pattern, then used the pattern to cut a twelve-inch disk out of the circle with a sharp knife. Next I set the disk on top of the cake, and gently pressed it down, after which I cut a 36x3-inch strip of marzipan and wrapped it around the cake, pressing it carefully to secure the marzipan top. Now the cake could rest again for a few days before I applied the final touch—the icing. I couldn't wait until the family saw my masterpiece. There I was feeding any number of people and making a rather complicated cake without thinking that much about how I had grown in two months. It wasn't until much later in my English adventure that I realized how much more competent I had become at taking care of a household, juggling tasks like cooking, shopping, cleaning, and studying.

Sunday, December 4, 1960, arrived and I went to London to see my by-now darling John. He said he loved me, and I returned *Ich liebe Dich.* Finally, the longed-for reciprocity! We walked through the streets of London, hand in hand or arms wrapped around each other's waists, as we window-shopped in Regent

Street. The window displays of Liberty, Wedgwood, and Austin Reed may as well not have been there because we saw only our reflections in the windows. Sometimes, we'd stop and lean against a wall, pressing our bodies into each other such as I could feel his passion. I had to put on the brakes at those moments, which I found difficult to do, and he had to learn to wait! All aflame, we took in the movie *Shadows,* which we didn't see for sitting in the last row and necking, necking, necking.

John called on Monday and Tuesday, and hearing his gentle voice made me wish he were there next to me. Knowing that he loved me made me happy and I sang all day long as I thought only of him. Nonetheless, I wondered why he loved me, considering that I didn't think of myself as particularly attractive and intelligent. Plus I was terribly shy when it came to expressing physical love beyond superficial hugging, kissing, and holding hands.

And what about my studies? I was going to English classes and doing my homework, but I wrote nothing in my diary about how I was progressing. Every five days or so I did mention the most recent letter from John. The mailman came twice a day, in the morning and the afternoon, and as soon as I heard the mail slot clanking and the mail hitting the floor, I was at the door. John was on his way to his parents' home, and student-teaching after that, meaning I wouldn't see him again until February 25. In the meantime, I read his latest letter every night before I went to bed, bringing him closer to me and making the waiting more bearable.

◆   ◆   ◆

Christmas was coming and the whole month metamorphosed into a frenzy of activity. Mrs. W. and I went to see Nigel in the role of a nymph in the school production of Shakespeare's *The Tempest.* Nigel was cute in his role, but I didn't understand any of Shakespeare's language. To buy Christmas presents, I went to downtown London where the streets were gaudily decorated with illuminated angels floating above the streets, electric lights of every color on lampposts, and department store roofs featuring Christmas trees. I was always comparing London with how things were done in Hamburg, where the Christmas trees stood at street level. Angels and Christmas trees don't sound like sensational decorations today, but in 1960 downtown Hamburg must have had even fewer decorations, prompting me to such a harsh comparison with London. In the evening, I met a German friend and co-worker of mine from my job at Alexander Petersen and Company, and we walked through Soho taking frequent breaks from the cold in dark pubs. We saw all types of people in Soho, the artsy section of town. At one of the coffee bars, two boys entered and sang English Christmas carols. In front of a movie theater, a mime dressed in black entertained people waiting in queue by grabbing an invisible rope, pulling on it hard and pretending that the rope was attached to something heavy. It was amazing how the mime used his whole body to create this illusion.

Despite being occupied with all the pre-Christmas activity, I missed another German custom. Advent, the arrival of Christ, began on the Sunday nearest the end of November and was a particularly warm and congenial time at our house. To celebrate this beginning of the Christmas season, Mutti always fashioned a wreath from fir twigs (representing eternal life) that were held together with thread or twine. She then attached special candle holders made to sit securely on the wreath and four candles, one candle to be lit consecutively for each of the four Sundays before Christmas, signifying that the light of God was coming into the world. On Sunday afternoons, we gathered around the living room table, eyes fixed on the fragrant wreath and the candles, singing Advent songs such as *Macht hoch die Tür, die Tor macht weit* (open doors and gates, the savior is coming). We peeled oranges that had come all the way from Spain and threw the rinds into the stove where they sizzled and filled the room with a delicate aroma. We cracked hazelnuts to which we added a slice of orange, making for an instant taste explosion. Sometimes we picked a few needles from the wreath and held them in the flame, their fragrance immediately reminding us of the scent of the coming Christmas tree. I can see my parents and siblings in this time of togetherness as though it were yesterday.

In England, we didn't have a wreath and the *Gemütlichkeit* of the season was missing. On the other hand, I was working on a Christmas cake which I had never done before. In my next cooking class, I made the icing with confectioner's sugar, egg whites, lemon juice, and a little salt, beating the mixture until it was fluffy but firm and then spreading it over the top and the sides, topping the masterpiece with small bits of candied fruit and a sprig of artificial mistletoe. It looked a pretty thing, I thought. Then I took it home, where it sat in the pantry awaiting the Christmas Day knife.

My English friend Anna came over one Sunday, and she, Mrs. W., and I went for a walk in very cold weather. In the evening, our neighbor Mrs. Reese and I listened to a Beethoven concert at the Royal Festival Hall. Mrs. Reese and I had become friends, though she was at least twenty years my senior. Usually once a week, I went next door to have "elevenses" with her. Around 11:00 a.m., house-wives all over England took an elevenses break, put up their feet, and had a cup of coffee or tea. We'd sit in comfortable chairs, balancing our cup of coffee and maybe a small biscuit (cookie) on our laps, and talk about school, my boyfriend John, household chores, England, and Germany. Sometimes I made emergency visits to Mrs. Reese when I felt homesickness come on, especially at this time of the year.

I wrote thirty Christmas cards to family and friends in Germany though I con-sidered it a waste of money. I knew that people I didn't write to regularly, like Onkel Max, expected a card from me at Christmas. Mutti and Papa never sent Christmas cards except to people who lived elsewhere than Hamburg. This year, all my Christmas cards went to friends and family in and around Hamburg. It was the expected thing.

Two weeks before Christmas an Advent package dutifully arrived from home, containing black bread and liverwurst made by my Papa. Chewing on substan-tial, dense bread was heavenly in comparison to soft, white English bread. Other items sent were hazelnuts and candy as well as an angel candle holder with a can-dle. I was thrilled to have this token of love from my parents. Mutti also sent me a pound sterling which I put to good use buying more Christmas presents. Mrs. W. paid me two pounds a week, plus room and board, and I was able to cover many things with that amount, like theater tickets, tube tokens, hairdressers, books, and so on.

Mr. W. was coming home on December 15 and there was no anticipation in the air (he had spent time in France). He was not an involved father, rarely smiled, and spent most of his time at home in his study. He required a quiet house, so his homecoming put a damper on his sons. No more duels with dustbin lids and rakes that made such a racket that I sometimes had to intervene. The boys didn't sing Christmas carols as I did, for they just weren't in the habit of singing. But now and then Nigel and I would listen to classical music, like Han-del's Messiah.

In Germany, we would have celebrated at least three Advent Sundays by now, bathed in the warm scent of pine and oranges, so symbolic of a cozy Christmas season. It wasn't until years later that I could appreciate the British way of cele-brating Christmas.

Christmas preparations in my English family were in full swing. The drapes in the family room had to be taken down and washed at the launderette in prepara-tion for the holiday. We always seemed to do things at the last minute. Three days before Christmas, Mrs. W. and I cleaned the entire house in preparation for a dinner party that night. Then after lunch, we went to St. Paul's Cathedral for carol singing. Only one choir sang, and we weren't even allowed to chime in. This was disappointing to me, because I liked singing so much. I took Hugh and Nigel to the Whispering Gallery at St. Paul's while Mrs. W. investigated more of the cathedral. We had to climb 259 steps to the interior of the dome, quite a feat. Because of a quirk of construction, a whisper at any point against the gallery wall was audible to any listener whose ear was trained on a point diametrically opposite. We didn't stay very long, because Hugh and Nigel started whispering gross things and I made them leave.

The boys went on to the long-established bookseller Foyles on Charing Cross Road, while Mrs. W. and I hopped on the tube. Hopping on was overstating it, as we had to wait for three trains before we could even squeeze in. Nobody was impolite, and there was no shoving. (English people were amazingly polite!) Once home, we had to get everything set up for dinner that night, when a colleague of Mrs. W., her husband, and their son would be our guests. I helped serve, just like any member of the family would. We had a great time, wine being served with dinner and sherry afterwards, and when it was all over, there were mountains of dishes, but Mr. W., Hugh, and Nigel helped at this point. Then I dragged myself upstairs to my room.

Granny had been picked up by her other son-in-law a few days ago, so now the boys and I didn't have anyone fighting with us. We also didn't have anyone doing the dishes any more. So Hugh had to wash and Nigel to dry, and every night they would fight over who was going to do which. Their older brother John usually sneaked up to his room after a meal.

The most magical day of the year in Germany, December 24, *Heiliger Abend*, Christmas Eve, came and went without any of the German rituals I was used to. As children, Doris and I had spent the day in anxious anticipation of a visit by the *Weihnachtsmann* (Santa Claus), while Klaus helped my parents decorate the Christmas tree in the living room. When we were older, we would spend the day visiting my grandparents, having a cozy time with them in their farmhouse. Back home by evening, we would finally exchange gifts by candlelight, sing Christmas carols, and enjoy a simple meal. The candles on the tree shone brightly and cast warm shadows on our celebration back then.

Here in Mill Hill, a sprig of mistletoe was fastened to the doorway leading into the dining room, and whenever Hugh saw me coming into the room he would rush to kiss me. Soon we were making a game of it! The house had a Christmas tree in the living room, which the boys, Mum, and I had decorated, but it had electric lights on it instead of candles. This struck me as garish and I didn't like it, but having candles on the tree was considered a fire hazard. I called Mrs. W. "Mum" now, but only when I wrote about her in my diary. I felt very close to her but thought it would have been inappropriate to address her with that intimate name. As inclusive as she was, she probably wouldn't have minded, but my reserved nature kept me from asking her.

December 24th, Christmas Eve day, finally arrived, but for all its ordinariness who would have known? In the afternoon, Mr. and Mrs. W., Hugh, and Nigel, and I went shopping in downtown London. Most stores were already closed, but some were still open for bargain hunters such as us. We all had lunch at Lyon's Corner House and then went home to a house that lacked the Christmas spirit as I defined it. Mum was busy in the kitchen preparing the goose for tomorrow's dinner, the boys went to bed at their regular time, and Mrs. W. and John played chess in the living room. At 11:00 p.m. I went next door to the Reese's to watch choirs from England, Germany, Belgium, and France sing Christmas carols on television. And so transpired Christmas Eve 1960.

On the morning of December 25th, Christmas Day—in daylight, for heaven's sake—we opened presents that had been placed on the table in the living room. We were dressed completely casual in our pajamas. None of the festive atmosphere I was used to. On top of that, my overseas package (which was on its way, I knew that much) had not yet arrived, and I was doubly crushed until the door bell rang and the mailman (on Christmas Day!) delivered a giant package from Mutti and Papa, Doris, Anne and Klaus, and the Schütts (Hamburg neighbors). What I remember most about the package were the apples from our garden. Their fragrance made this first time away from home at Christmas a little more bearable. I could tell exactly which tree they were from, having often climbed it to pick apples. Or just to gaze out at the world.

Mum gave me a cookbook with fifty-four recipes, each of which could be prepared and cooked in fifteen minutes. The book was bound like a spiral notebook with a colorful hardcover. Almost fifty years later, I still have it, although I no longer cook from it chiefly because the ingredients are too fattening. The top of each page shows a black-and-white picture of the finished meal. All the ingredients and tools needed are shown on the side of the page, while the bottom shows step-by-step pictures and a description of each step, or the "tricky bits," to the accompaniment of a clock showing how many minutes of the precious fifteen had elapsed. The inside cover said, "They (the recipes) are ideal for deserted husbands (permanently or temporarily bereft), because they (the cooks) can just prop up the book and follow the pictures." Also, the recipes are "ideal for the hard-up and the weight-conscious because for each recipe a total cost and calorie value" is given. The calories were rather on the high end (such as 850 calories for thick back rashers (pork chops!), but back then, calorie-counting hadn't yet caught on. Or, rather, people were not yet fat.

The recipe list included English favorites such as tomato rarebit, kidneys and rice, and the more exotic kidneys au vin, fried whitebait, shrimp scramble, barbecued tongue, sausages and noodles, and, best of all, kedgeree (a concoction of boiled cod, chopped eggs and rice). I made several dishes from this cookbook for the family. Most of the recipes called for a heavy helping of fat, cream, and flour, which accounts for why I gained thirty-five pounds in one year!

The highlight of Christmas Day was the goose dinner. And then came the pièce de resistance—the Christmas cake I had made over the last several months that now sat on a pedestal plate on the table, ready to be cut. Since I had made the cake, I was allowed to cut it. Everyone was keenly attentive, anticipating a sweet delight. With a big cutting knife in my hand, I took a stab, and then another, and another, but the knife wouldn't cut through the blasted icing. I tried another knife, but still no penetration was achieved. It was as though the icing had become a petrified shield hiding all the goodness within it—the sugar, marzipan, rum, candied fruits, nuts, sherry, and fruit. So we had no choice but to use a saw, which handily split the icing open and let me proceed with cutting the slices. By this time we were all laughing so hard that I forgot to feel humiliated. The cake for its part was moist and scrumptious, and pieces of it were later served to everyone who came to wish us Merry Christmas. I even sent a slice of it home to Germany! But I have never been able to figure out why the icing was so tough.

Sometime during the day, Queen Elizabeth II broadcast a radio message to the nation. I think everybody in the family listened just so that they could imitate her royal accent and make fun of her, and this mockery had me in stitches. If I remember correctly, to them she was the "old bag" whom they supported with their tax money. I, of course, was fascinated by all the royal goings-on, and the Queen's accent was something a German girl could aspire to!

The whole family was on vacation for the Christmas holidays, but luckily the boys were not around the entire time because a schedule of plans had been made for them to visit relatives and friends. Before the boys went off on their respective trips, all of us except John attended the Lyric Theater in Hammersmith to see *Hooray for Daisy*. Though I don't remember the musical, I was able to understand most all of the lyrics, which meant that my listening skills were improving. The next day, Mum and I drove Hugh to the train station in Paddington, afterwards shopping the winter sales. Mum was always looking for bargains and this was the place to buy clothes on the cheap, into which the boys could change when they arrived home in their school uniforms.

Paddington was an impoverished area, so we saw many beggars sitting on the sidewalks. Eventually, we made our way to the British Museum, where Dad W. was doing research, the subject of which I wasn't privy to. Then on the way home, the car had a flat, at which I took the tube and bus home to fix tea for Mum and Dad W. when they arrived home an hour later.

On the last day of the year 1960, Mum took Nigel to the train that would transport him to her sister in Sussex. I thought he was a lucky chap to be able to stay with his aunt and uncle and cousins. I had never stayed overnight with any of my aunts, probably for the reason that they didn't have children my age as well as that their apartments were too small to accommodate overnight guests.

Mum and Dad W. went on to the house of the aunt who had died earlier that year, to pick up some of her possessions. They returned with a television set that was parked in the drawing room, to which everyone would adjourn for sitting and watching in the cold. Hugh especially was fascinated by this machine, even if it had only a very small screen, but I myself didn't really care for it and never watched much. Except when the whole family watched or I was bored and not in the mood to read.

On New Year's Eve there was a party going on next door, making me wonder if my family and friends were celebrating back home in Hamburg. If they were (and I'm sure they were) there would dancing and singing and midnight jumping off chairs to repeated yells of *Prost Neujahr!* I would love to be dancing again. And, to drink grog again and eat *Berliners* (jelly-filled doughnuts). But in the W. house, New Year's Eve passed as any quiet, ordinary English evening would. I packed my suitcase because tomorrow I would be off to Peterborough to visit Pauline and her family for a few days.

Singing for the guests the night before my brother's wedding,
August 12, 1960

My brother's wedding—August 13, 1960
From left to right—Doris, my mother, Anne, Klaus, Christel

Some of the places I visited in England

11

Au pairing in England

◆

1961

Mum and Dad W. dropped me off in Barnet, and from there I took the bus to Peterborough. Girlfriend Pauline's parents, Harry and Daisy Steward, had told me they would pick me up at the bus stop in Alwalton, a small town just outside of Peterborough. Well and good, but neither of the two bus drivers had the slightest idea of where this Alwalton was, so I fretted the entire trip that they would drop me off nowhere near Alwalton, just to get rid of my pesky self. To their credit, they must have studied their maps or called the bus garage on some kind of phone (the cell phone era was still years away), and in the end they found Alwalton. When the bus came to a halt, Harry and Daisy were already waiting for me.

Pauline, my friend, had long hair now that was even a shade blonder than before, but in other respects she hadn't changed at all. She was still the fun-loving girl I had known from our previous visits in Hamburg and Peterborough. Her sister Jo had grown a little plumper since I had first met her a year and a half ago. Mr. and Mrs. Steward hadn't changed at all and were as welcoming as ever. I slept in my old room, in the same bed, and felt totally comfortable. Pauline didn't waste any time going back to our old haunts and we started drinking ale at the "Grand." After a while, two of her male friends came and drove us to the "Gallon Club" where one of them ordered a double whisky for me. I pretended that I had had whisky before and chugged the double shot without letting on that this was my first whisky (not counting when I was a child and curious about stuff that people left in their glasses after a party, when I would sniff and drink and then have a coughing fit because the spirit burnt my throat). So when Pauline's friend ordered another double whisky for me, I politely declined, knowing my limits for holding alcohol. The good thing about Pauline's friends was that they all had cars, so we never had to wait for a bus. We were deposited at home by 11:30 p.m., where we talked for a long time. That is, Pauline talked about her boyfriends until my spirit-filled head was crammed with names and things all atumble.

I was allowed to sleep in and didn't wake up until 10:00 a.m. What luxury! Mrs. Steward wouldn't let me help her in the house, so Jo and I took the bus to downtown Peterborough and I had another look at the Cathedral. There we read about Mary Queen of Scots who had been buried here in 1587 after her execution at nearby Fotheringhay Castle. (Her body was later removed to Westminster Abbey.) We imagined her head rolling gruesomely down the stairs of the scaffolding, but failed to appreciate the majesty of Peterborough Cathedral built in its unique combination of Norman and new Gothic styles. In the afternoon, I hung around the house with Mrs. Steward and Jo (Mr. Steward and Pauline were at work), but I also managed to write a long letter to John. I loved him so much and thought constantly of him. In the evening, we picked up Annette, who earlier had been in Hamburg with Pauline, and headed back to the "Grand." This time we had to walk home and took this opportunity to stop at a fish and chips store. I couldn't get enough of that British staple in all its deep-fried deliciousness.

Since there wasn't much sightseeing to be done in Peterborough and I didn't have money to shop, I spent the next two days catching up on correspondence to friends and family in Germany. Mrs. Steward and I visited Daphne, a relative, who had a three-month old baby girl whom I loved looking at but was too afraid to hold her because in my entire life I had never held a baby. Having always been the youngest child in my whole extended family, I had never known any babies. In the afternoon I continued with my correspondence, and in the evening Pauline and I watched television which we interrupted only to rush out for chips. The mundane things of life.

The next day was my last with the Stewards. We had tea with Pauline's aunt Nip and then visited another aunt who was ill. On my last night we went to, of course, the "Grand!" On the way back, we stopped and bought chips, and I haven't since then eaten chips as delicious as these Peterborough-bought ones. Pauline came home from work at lunchtime on Thursday, January 5th, when we shared tearful goodbyes. The Stewards and Jo drove me to the bus station in Stamford, northeast of Peterborough, where the bus originated. Because the bus was a drafty old thing, I was miserably cold for the whole 2-1/2 hour trip, my head being sensitive to drafts even then. So I anticipated arriving "home," which is what living with the W. family had happily become. I felt really lucky to be part of this family, and most all to have such a warm and loving Deputy-Mum, as I sometimes called her. She was the second in command after my Mutti!

"Home" on January 6th meant washing the dishes, doing the laundry, making the beds, and just generally getting the house back in shape from the holidays. For one, the Christmas tree had to be de-decorated and discarded. The boys were still on vacation from school and were tearing up the house. They obviously needed something to do, so the next day, Saturday, Dad drove Hugh, Nigel, and me downtown (Mum was at a conference). Hugh went off on his own, but Nigel and I wandered down Oxford Street, had lunch at the restaurant "Fortes," spent at least an hour at Hamley's on Regent Street (a huge toy store), and ended up at Foyle's bookstore where we ran into Hugh, and together spent another hour perusing but not buying books. The three of us walked to the car park where we met Dad who drove us home. I liked spending time with the boys, rather like I was their big sister, but although I tried my best to rein in their overly energetic ways they didn't always listen to me.

On washday Monday, the kitchen floor got wet and Mum fell. She didn't break anything, but both she and I were shaken. Hugh and his friend Roger helped her up the stairs as I made a pot of tea for her. Dad was at the British Library, and when he was ready to come home he couldn't find his car keys. So John W. had to take another key to meet him in London. Dad W. was the perfect example of an absent-minded professor—always forgetting something, walking around with a preoccupied look on his face.

There was always something going on in the house. One night, Nigel wanted to cook one of the dishes from my cookbook. He chose the tomato rarebit which involved toast, cheese, tomatoes, and bacon. I handed him the tools, and he did quite a good job of it. As long as the boys were busy, they had less time to tear around the house or so it was reasoned. John W. never got up before noon and lurched around all afternoon while I was reading. At lunch the next day, he got upset with me because I hadn't made up the applesauce for his pork chops, at which I waxed indignant, telling him that I hadn't come to England to learn to cook but to learn English. And that was more important to me than making applesauce for him! "So make your own, why don't you," I said, and instead of getting mad back at me he proceeded to vent his contrariness on his brother, ordering Nigel to do the dishes. Mean older brother, that's what I thought of him sometimes. It was high time that they all got back to school. Their Christmas break was far too long for my taste.

I came down with a bad cold at which Mum gave me breakfast in bed, where I stayed until 11:00 a.m. reading *Major Barbara,* a title on the reading list for the new semester. The boys were back in school, except for John who was taking an exam for something, and the air was filled with heavenly quiet. Finally I had the house to myself again, with time to read. Before Mum left for work, she made me hot milk and ordered me to stay in bed with a hot water bottle. My Onkel Rolf, a musician friend of Papa's, sent me five Marks for a bottle of rum to cure my symptoms. Different ways to treat an ailment! The following morning, Mum again brought me breakfast, but soon I was up to clean part of the house. On Sunday, I slept until almost noon. Now Dad W. had the cold, putting him in a bad mood for a few days. He failed to make a fire in the fireplace, and soon after lunch he left without a word. The rest of the family sat in the kitchen until the fire caught in the drawing room, and then watched the telly. Dad W. returned for tea and took himself off somewhere in the house, probably his study. The rest of us sat reading and writing by the fire. There was nothing to be done when Dad W. was in a bad mood, but I often wondered how the boys could stand having a parent whose moods were so unpredictable.

On Sunday, February 5th, we rented a car (the W.'s "Austin claptrap," as we called it, didn't hold all of us) and drove to Surrey to celebrate Granny's 90th birthday. Granny lived with Mum's sister Kathleen and her family in a beautiful old farmhouse. While the adults visited, I spent time with Kathleen's three children and Mum's brother's son, rolling around on the lawn and playing hide and seek with them all. After lunch (Granny did the dishes), Mary, the childminder, Debbie aged seven, and I went for a walk in the countryside. We sat on the swings on some playground and Mary and I felt like children ourselves. At tea time, ninety candles were lighted on Granny's cake. She blew out the candles with a little help from the family and we all sang happy birthday. Ninety candles made quite a little blaze.

At home the next Sunday, from noon until dinner as the leg of lamb roasted in the oven, Mum and I cleaned out the shed in the backyard. It was used mostly for storing garden equipment though other, unused household stuff had made its way in there too, and it was packed so full that getting the lawn mower out proved a challenge. The boys took off, and Dad W. worked away in his study. The weather was unseasonably fine, perfect for lying out even though it was still February. Without any help from the four guys in the house, Mum and I managed to straighten up the mess. Now we could find the garden tools when we needed them.

On Sundays, the family usually had lamb, mashed potatoes, peas, and gravy. Maybe rolls, maybe brussel sprouts, maybe carrots. I had never eaten lamb in Germany and I ate my first leg of lamb (not the one with the flies!) with apprehension. Eating lamb not once but twice a week, I developed a fondness for it over time. For Monday's dinner, I sliced the leftover lamb, and made up the mayonnaise for the garnish. Making the mayonnaise usually took a while, because the oil had to be added drop by drop to the egg yolk. Now and then I got impatient and added the oil too quickly, causing the egg yolk to curdle, and I'd have to dump the mess down the sink and start all over again. The leftover potatoes and vegetables were pan-fried to produce a concoction called "bubble and squeak." When there weren't enough leftovers, Mum or I had to improvise and broil some tomatoes or add hard-cooked eggs. The leftover lamb was always eaten cold. In time I got used to this meal and the aftertaste of cold lamb on my tongue stopped making me automatically wish for some fried herring, which was my favorite fish.

◆　　　◆　　　◆

I recalled my Saturdays at home in Germany when I was about ten, and my parents would fry herring for the whole family for lunch (the main meal of the day). A fishy odor clung to the kitchen and eventually reached every room in the house. The smell of fish, melting butter, and oil made us even hungrier and we couldn't wait for the first bite. My mouth waters as I'm writing this just thinking of the crisp skin of the fish and the soft flesh. In postwar Germany, *Heringe satt* (enough herrings for all) was a blessing.

In my memory, Papa had walked to the fish store that morning, where he purchased twenty whole herrings that had probably been caught that morning somewhere in the North Atlantic Ocean and, *enfin,* whisked to the city by truck. Now they were ready for us.

My brother spread out a thick layer of newspaper on the kitchen table, and my sister armed us with paring knives. Each of us secured a herring with our bare hands and cut off its head and gills with one circular motion. Now five heads with milky eyes stared at us as we proceeded to scrape off the scales. This was a time-consuming task, because we had to scrape against the natural direction of the scales to pry them loose from the skin. The newspaper was now smeared with scales and blood and got even messier when we sliced open the belly of the fish, grabbed the innards and added them to the mess already on the table. Then we massaged the spine a bit, bent it back, and peeled it off. It was supposed to come out in one piece, but I was only ten years old and I was too gentle, so often I had to use the paring knife to loosen the parts of the spine that were still stuck to the fillet. Even when the fish were cooked, I could always tell which fillets I had cleaned because they looked like somebody had cut hills and dales into the flesh.

With the intestines and the spine removed, we then flattened the fish, which now looked like the wings of a skinny butterfly. Before we cleaned the table of the newspaper, scales, innards, and heads, Klaus had to do one last thing: stick his thumb and index finger into the head of a herring and make its lips move. It was a predictable part of the ritual, and he didn't get much of a reaction from us. But it was a sign for Peter the cat that he was about to have a feast. The innards and heads were placed in a bowl and put in the courtyard where Peter was quickly joined by two neighbor cats that jumped all over each other to get the first crunchy bite.

Now my siblings and I were done with our job and waiting for our first fillet. Papa and Mutti turned to the stove and filled the skillet, turning the fish to keep them from getting too dark. A dish of flour mixed with salt, and pepper was kept next to the stove to receive each fillet before it was placed in the frying pan. The butter and oil sizzled, splattering the stove, and the herring odor filled the kitchen. The cold potato salad that always accompanied fried herring sat on the table and got devoured instantly by our eyes. Doris and I set the table with a fork at each side of the plate because the custom was to eat fish with two forks rather than with knife and fork.

When the first fillet was set in front of us, we devoured it without really tasting it. But the next one we savored, eating it with the potato salad. (We didn't have tartar sauce, had never even heard of it.) We set to cutting through the crisp skin and the soft flesh of the herring, the process satisfying our eyes, mouths, and stomachs altogether. Mutti and Papa took turns eating because the fish couldn't be kept warm in the oven. It had to be eaten white it was hot and crisp. By now the house was enveloped in fishiness as were we, but we didn't mind. Stomachs full of herring and potato salad—we were happy.

In a matter of seconds this scene of our family preparing and eating herring together had flashed through my head as I readied the cold lamb dinner for my English family. The power of memory!

◆   ◆   ◆

Besides cooking and taking care of the house in Mill Hill, I often worked in the narrow backyard (the width of the semi-detached house) that was mostly grass, although there may have been some flower beds along the wooden fences on either side. The living room opened into this backyard via a pair of French doors. Raking and cleaning the beds reminded me of working with Papa in our backyard in Hamburg. My interest in gardening was definitely helped along by Papa showing me how to trim bushes and trees, how to pick plums and cherries, and how to maintain a *Misthaufen* (manure heap). So here in England I was regarded as the expert in the gardening department. Even the neighbor Mrs. Reese came to me for advice.

Mrs. Reese was always trying to get me to meet people my age. One night, her little son's godfather, a young man of twenty-one, and three of his friends picked me up, and we drove to a church in Edgeware where a youth group met on Saturday nights. There we played table tennis, had tea, and discussed the Jehovah's Witnesses because that religion was on the agenda for the evening. Because I had been exposed to the Jehovah's Witnesses and debated with some of its members back in Hamburg, I was able to participate fully in the discussion. And I received endless compliments about my good English, which swelled my head not a little.

Meanwhile, the new semester had begun. Tuesdays was reserved for grammar, vocabulary, and the like; Thursdays we studied literature; and Friday afternoon Life and Institutions, a course which covered political, governmental, legal, economic, and educational systems. There were eight people in my literature class, some of them from the previous semester. One of them, Dodo, was also from Hamburg, and she and I initiated a friendship given our mutual hometown. In preparation for studying Shaw's *Major Barbara*, our teacher Mr. Smith lectured about the great man, and I remember being impressed by his revolutionary thinking. A freethinker, a defender of women's rights, an advocate of income equality, he seemed to stir something deep within me, something I couldn't name then and there. I wonder if even back then I was on the road to becoming a freethinker myself in matters religious.

In the "Life and Institutions" class, we had to read seventeen books by the end of the semester, books about English political systems, elections, history, geography, and culture. To familiarize us with what we had to know by the end of the semester, our teacher Mr. Postlethwaite gave us a sample of the kinds of questions asked on the Cambridge Proficiency Exam from three years previous. Because students could choose between being tested on Literature or Life and Institutions, I already knew that I would opt for Literature because the Life and Institutions sample questions contained numbers, statistics, and dates which I could never, as hard as I tried, remember. But in retrospect, choosing Literature turned out to be a mistake.

Pronouncing Mr. Postlethwaite's name was a problem for several students, especially the "th." The "th" was usually a problematic sound for Germans, in whose mouths it ended up sounding like an "s." But for some reason, I had never had any trouble pronouncing English words containing a "th." The French girl in my class had quite a thick accent that was hard to understand but still rather charming. Instead of "ball" she would say, "bowl," resulting in a change in meaning. She pronounced his name "Posselsvet" which he obviously liked because he carried on a flirtation with her through the semester. I made a note in my diary that she had her attractions, i.e., she had big breasts. But then there was that vacuous look on her face, which proved (no further research needed) that men were more interested in a woman's appearance than in her mind!

In one class, Mr. Smith took us through a simulation of an oral exam. He had each of us read a page out loud and then he commented on our accents. He said that my pronunciation was excellent but that I didn't yet have the English tone and that he could still hear the foreigner in me. I wasn't sure I could ever learn the tone, but as for my pronunciation I hadn't yet come across any English person who had to ask me to repeat something because of my pronunciation and enunciation. I knew that my pronunciation was excellent; tone would have to wait. My spoken English was fluent and my vocabulary growing.

In Germany, I had been taught the Queen's English, and it wasn't until I lived in the United States that I was confronted with differences in word meaning between American and British English. For example, I would say variously that I "queued up" instead of "stood in line", that a "car park" was a "parking lot", and that a "dustbin" was called a "garbage can" in America. The word that produced hilarity in my American co-workers was "tinkle." When I asked someone to "please give me a tinkle," (a phone call) they just about peed in their pants with laughter because that's what it meant in America! But I had no such problems now in England with the use of British English words, having learned them before in my Hamburg English classes. Participating in conversation sessions at the British Council had further prepared me for English idioms ("not cricket" for "not fair;" "daft" for "stupid.") Now I always used the word "loo" for toilet, "telly" for television.

The months since my arrival in England had gone by swiftly and I had been barraged with so many new stimuli, but somehow I had still managed to keep up a steady flow of correspondence with family and friends. Letters arrived frequently from Mutti and Papa and less frequently from Klaus, Anne, and Doris. Friends from my first employer, Alexander Petersen, wrote and kept me up-to-date with who was doing what. My admirer, the old translator, was still there and still not washing his hands after using the restroom. I even had news from school friends and neighbors. All these letters, postcards, and even occasional visits from friends kept me connected to Germany. Sometimes, just one letter would help me get over my infrequent bouts of homesickness.

And, of course, letters from my beloved John lifted my spirits and turned the days when they arrived into giddy ones. I was still reliving every minute detail of our four dates and two phone calls. Each letter would be scanned immediately for an invitation for a date, preferably one in the near future, when we would finally see each other again. After that, each letter was read many times again until the next one arrived. I was still hoping that we would meet again in January or February. Our last date had been December 4, and I was longing for him. I had even enlisted God to help bring John to my side, but so far all my pleas and prayers had been to no avail. In fact, toward the end of January I received a letter that said he wouldn't be able to come to London until March 25. Not only were all my hopes dashed but fifty long days of longing and praying lay before me. I was so miserable that I decided to clean the gas oven and I was in the act of thrusting my head in it to reach the back panel when Mum called and suggested that I go for a walk. How did she know that I needed to get outside more than the bloody oven needed to be cleaned? It was a gloriously sunny but cold day and I walked for an hour and a half, thinking of John and inventing scenarios that made me blush and feel hot all over. I thought of being married to this man of my dreams, this gentle, loving, funny, intelligent man. I wondered what my parents would say if I married an Englishman?

The next three weeks were a roller coaster of hopes raised and hopes dashed. First he wrote that he might be in London on February 25, which would be eight days from the day I received the letter (he was student teaching in Buckingham-shire). Oh dear God, let it be true, I prayed. Five days later, he informed me that he was coming and my prayers were answered! I could have hugged the world, I was so happy. The next day, though, I received another letter dashing my hopes again. The plan had been for him and another teacher to take a busload of students to London and the other teacher would take them back. John would thus be free to see me in the evening. But now the other teacher was sick and so John would have to serve in his place. My disappointment was crushing, as there were now more than thirty days left before I would see him in March, which ironically had been the proposed date from the beginning. Then a miracle happened: something changed in the plans and he was coming after all. Only two more days—two days during which I prayed for this love to continue and grow stronger and the same two days during which I thanked God for making my prayers come true because who else but God could be guiding all this? I wonder if it ever occurred to me that the other teacher might have recovered or never even been sick and was taking the students back, leaving John free to see me. In any case, I gave God all the credit.

On the morning of Saturday, February 25th, I had my hair done, and Helen did an exceptional job for this enormously important occasion. For the rest of the day, I kept myself occupied by cleaning house rather than working on essays that were due shortly or reading assignments the following week. My mind was focused only on being with John. I arrived at Trafalgar Square at 5:30 p.m. and dashed into St. Martin-in-the-Fields church to pray for God's blessing for this evening. Standing at the foot of Nelson's Column, I watched cars spill into the round-about from The Strand, The Mall, Whitehall, and Charing Cross Road. Pedestrians were milling about or dashing across the square to other destinations. Pigeons liked this square, judging by the numbers of them fluttering around, covering lampposts and Nelson's column with white excrement. I had been here many times before because the National Gallery was located here with its entrance directly overlooking the square. Now I waited and waited, worried that something might have happened to him and feeling vulnerable walking around Nelson's Column time and time again. I passed and re-passed homeless people minding their own business, and though I was never accosted in any way I felt uncomfortable nevertheless.

At 6:45 p.m. John came bounding across the traffic and we fell into each other's arms. We left the square quickly and walked down dark side streets, stopping often to press against each other. We each hungered to feel the skin of the other. To merge, yes, right then and there, even if leaning up against a grimy building. Oh, to feel the warmth radiating from his body! My willpower was stretched to the limit even as my hands trembled, and my heart quivered to give him my all. Still, my head was afraid to lose itself in something that might not portend a glorious future. I couldn't lose my virginity without a guarantee of some kind of permanence!

We talked about the future over dinner at an Indian restaurant, and—it didn't look promising. In mid-April he was going back to Cambridge until June to finish his studies. He would then go home to Newark-on-Trent far from London. Then in September he would begin his first teaching job somewhere in Yorkshire, while in October I would go back to Germany. So for now, we set aside our future plans and paid attention to our sexual urges as we caressed and kissed our way through Soho until 11:00 p.m. when I had to dash to catch the last train. Now I was back to praying that I would see him again on March 25 and back to listening for each click of the mail slot. On the next day, Sunday, I spent most of the day in my room thinking about him, undisturbed and free to relive every minute detail of yesterday. I was the source of his desire and he of mine—how powerful love was!

I waited ten days for the next letter, and this one bore disappointing news. John had had a day off from student-teaching and had gone from Buckingham to Oxford. In my obsessive thinking I wondered why he hadn't rented a car and driven to London if there wasn't a Sunday train from Buckingham to London. Still, I had to be rational and consider the expense. After all, he was a student of limited means. But rationality aside, did he really love me? And if he did, wouldn't he have found a way to come to London? On one occasion, Dad W. beat me to the mailbox and called up to my room, "Three letters for you," but none was from John; another time, I was bringing inside the milk bottles that the milkman had left by the side door and, seeing the mailman leave the yard, I dashed to the front door only again to find nothing from John. Now I was keeping track of the days elapsed without a letter from him, praying for him to keep our date on March 25 and for his letters to come more frequently.

The next letter arrived within nine days, and he couldn't come on March 25! And not a word about why he was so late in writing. Plus why was his style so impersonal, as though he had nothing more to say to me, as though he were withdrawing from the relationship. I wouldn't reply right away and let him wait a little, but then recalled a particular Christian principle—the one that said to do unto others, et cetera.

While I was waiting on John's letters, and counting on getting one about once a week or so, I was also busy with school. We had finished reading and discussing *Major Barbara*. I had become fond of Bernard Shaw's writings, especially his humor, and continued reading other plays outside class. One day, *Major Barbara* was on the radio, and Hugh and I listened to it. In my class I had found it to be interesting and even amusing, but as a radio play it was rather boring and lacking real highlights. We had discussed this fact in class and I had thought we were doing Shaw injustice, but now I found it to be true. At least this particular play didn't translate from paper to voice.

I wrote essays on such topics as, "What provisions exist in Great Britain for the education of mentally and physically infirm children?", "An ideal excursion," "Compare the Continental and the British Sunday," and from Jane Austen, "Describe Emma's attempt to make a match for Harriet." In our Life and Institutions class, we were talking about English economic development when our teacher stopped the lesson before dismissal time, saying that he wanted to watch something on the telly. I found that to be very curious behavior for a teacher, but there were only three students attending that night and maybe he thought it wasn't worth staying either for him or for us.

My other teacher, Mr. Smith, gave me part of a proficiency exam from 1960, translating passages into and from German. It was hard work, and when I was done I showed it to Dad W., who proceeded to make quite a few changes. I realized that capturing the true meaning of a word or a phrase required a thorough understanding of language's idiomatic dimension. I had been toying with the idea of becoming a translator when my year in England was up, or at least translating letters for a future employer. Mr. Smith also had us write on the topic "walls" for ten minutes so we could get some experience of having a limited amount of time available during exams. I felt anxious doing an exercise like that because writing in a set amount of time had never been my strong point. Speed prevented thought. But as the words just wouldn't come, I realized that this was exactly the type of exercise I needed. So I began to time myself when I wrote homework assignments.

Besides school and an absent but ever-present John, I continued my new friendship with Dodo. We went to see *Romeo and Juliet* at the Old Vic Theatre, which had been founded over a hundred years ago and which had to be restored after it was damaged by the Nazis in World War II. That confounded war was omnipresent! Anyway, this was the first Shakespearean play I had ever seen and I was worried that I wouldn't be able to understand it. I had previously read a summary of the play, though, which helped me understand early modern English as spoken on stage. On the downside our seats in the gallery were uncomfortable and the place was draughty.

When I got home at midnight, I discovered that I didn't have my house key and all the windows and doors were locked. So I rang the bell once, twice, five times or more, but still nobody stirred. I was getting cold and not a little panicky. Then I thought of the kitchen door, hoping that the flap atop it wasn't closed all the way. I climbed on a bucket, and with some exertion I reached the doorknob and was able to unlock the door. Then I found out that Mum had forgotten I had gone to the theater immediately after school (or maybe instead of school) and fretted that I should have been home hours ago. So she worried about me just as my own Mutti would have! I didn't want Mum to worry about me, but nonetheless I was happy that she did.

Occasionally, Dodo and I spent time in the school cafeteria before we returned to our respective homes. On one particular day, Mr. Postlethwaite stopped by, sat with us, and began speaking German. After a few minutes a French teacher came in, and they began speaking French together. Then Mr. P. asked us if we wanted to come to his house for a cup of coffee. Dodo and I looked at each other and I knew that she felt the same discomfort I did. But we nodded yes. Why not? I was curious about Mr. P's German wife. So the four of us adjourned to his house after class, where he made coffee the German way (pouring hot water over ground coffee in a Melitta filter). But wait, his wife was at the movies! Fortunately, after about a half hour it was time for me to catch my train, and just as Dodo and I were leaving his wife arrived home with a girlfriend and the four of us exchanged quick hellos and goodbyes because by now we were in a hurry to clear out of there and escape our discomfort. Dodo lived in St. Albans, but instead of immediately going home she walked me to the train station and we agreed we would never do this again, as we felt as if we had done something behind Mr. P's wife's back even if it was no more than drinking a cup of her coffee. Mr. P. was in the habit of flirting with girls who were vastly more attractive than his wife, and Dodo and I speculated as to her lack of pulchritude being the reason for his flirtatious ways. When all was said and done, we decided we didn't like him as a person, mainly for his flirting or, as a teacher, for being boring and coming unprepared to class.

◆   ◆   ◆

It was early March. With all the activity at school, with voluminous reading and writing of essays not to speak of being challenged at every turn about my knowledge of English, world affairs, literature, Germany and World War II, I felt inferior to my classmates and cried off and on. Instead of appreciating what I did know, I obsessed over all the things I didn't know and all the things I had yet to learn, and I felt overwhelmed because I wanted knowledge all at once. Then again, I wanted to be a child again, to be cared for by Mutti and Papa. I didn't want to be a grown-up, out on her own. To hell with independence! Having this first inkling of what it would be like to be responsible for all my choices, I was intimidated by the sheer difficulty of it. What were my interests to be, what would I read, what kind of a career would I pursue? I think part of this questioning arose from knowing John, who was already working toward a career and studying at one of the best universities in the world.

Contributing to my feeling of being overwhelmed was the fact that I was constantly comparing England with Germany, evaluating the two countries' advantages and disadvantages and as a result felt torn, indecisive. I didn't know then that I was experiencing a phase of culture shock. I mean, what did it really matter that English people's view of Germany encompassed mountains, lakes, beer, and sausage? What if they didn't share my keen attachment to my beloved Northern German landscape—gentle hills, heather in sandy soil, villages surrounded by fields of grain as far as the eye could see, the rolling North Sea and its endless beaches?

I had never been particularly patriotic as I was growing up—showing patriotism was even frowned upon. After all, patriotism and prejudice had gone awry and devastated Germany. Funny thing, though, living in a foreign country had raised my level of patriotism though I kept the feeling inside because I felt uncomfortable with the whole notion that one country was better than another. In time, this patriotism subsided, coinciding with my acceptance of English ways.

And then again, I may simply have been homesick without recognizing it as such. But not wanting to admit it to myself, I instead became vulnerable to any criticism no matter how banal about Germany. One TV program the whole family watched on Sundays was "Sunday Break." On one particular Sunday the film was a passion play, performed by teenagers who used rock music to exemplify evil and anti-Christianity. During the play up popped an image of Hitler and marching Nazis. When we talked about it at tea time, I couldn't hold back my tears and cried bitterly. Why was it that when it came to naming an example of evil, Germany and the Nazis were always dredged up? Wasn't there a distinction between German and Nazi? My English family understood why I was upset and tried to make me feel better by saying that the British too had committed some hideous war crimes, for example, in the Boer War of 1899–1902. I had heard about this war, and now when I read up on it I learned that the British had rounded up Boer women and children as "collaborators" and put them into concentration camps. Then they burned the Boers' farms and starved the commandos into submission. But they didn't kill anywhere near six million people, I ruefully noted, as had Germany.

Apart from the emotional reaction to seeing Nazis depicted on television, I felt that I needed to educate myself about WW II because I had never been taught about it during all my years in school. But why had I waited until now to read and think more deeply about the war? That fact in itself seemed quite odd. And things were to get worse.

In 1961 there was more to come to thrust Germany and Germans into the spotlight again. In anticipation of Adolf Eichmann's trial, which was set to begin in April, the British press wrote extensively about his interrogation, which had begun in 1960 hard upon his capture. Eichmann was accused of crimes against humanity for transporting hundreds of thousands of victims to extermination camps. Papa wrote me a letter about Eichmann, which was supposed to make me feel better, saying that I shouldn't despair over all the reports about World War II. The British were no angels either, and what about all those countries that refused to take in Jews when they were driven out of Germany? But somehow even his reassurances failed to make me feel better about my country.

◆   ◆   ◆

With this heightened sense of misery over Germany's role in World War II, it was small wonder that my anxiety should transfer to the agony I felt over not seeing John. I worked myself into a state just waiting for his letters. In the meantime, with exams coming up in June, I had to work hard to keep up with my school reading. At the time I was reading such diverse literary works as *Macbeth,* Rumer Godden's *An Episode of Sparrows* (which was going to be on the exam), finishing *Emma,* and writing a 40-minute essay that would ask me to "Discuss, with illustrations, Jane Austen's powers in handling of either incident or dialogue in *Emma.*" Dad W. had given me the Austen assignment the day before and said I hadn't quite written to the topic, a major shortcoming of my writing generally, but he said my English was good and not to worry.

A couple of letters came from John in late March and early April, one of them informing me that he would be back in Cambridge on April 19. I was happy and immediately began to make plans, but the next letter informed me that immediately after his final exam in June he would be starting his first teaching job in Yorkshire because another teacher's resignation required filling without delay. In other words, my chances of seeing him were slim.

One evening Mum went to the "Ideal Home Exhibition" and Nigel, Hugh and I indulged in a telly-watching marathon from 6:00–11:00 p.m. The boys behaved themselves and went to bed without a fuss, although Hugh tried his old trick of pulling me down on top of him when I stood by his bed. Months earlier, he had tried this nightly when I, in my naivete, tucked the boys in at bedtime. Nigel was more of an enthusiastic bystander, but Hugh would take this opportunity to pull me down into bed with him. Hugh was thirteen, and when my brother Klaus was the same age I was only six and had no idea what thirteen-year-old felt about girls. Rather, when I was thirteen, I only wanted to beat up thirteen-year-old boys because I thought them so stupid. Now here was Hugh, feeling amorous and causing me to protest at tucking-in time. Knowing thirteen-year-old boys better than I did, Mum finally put an end to the nightly ritual. In my mind, I had only been saying goodnight to my brothers and was obviously still learning about the opposite sex. Sex was on John W's mind too, but it came out in other ways, for instance by talking about sex in terms he knew would shock me. In my opinion, he had a filthy mouth, and when he started in on his sex talk I would just stick my fingers in my ears or walk away.

Now and then, Mum, Mrs. Reese, and I went to the "pictures," as they called them in England. We saw *Saturday Night and Sunday Morning* with Albert Finney playing the role of a young working-class man living in Nottingham. Surrounded as I was by speakers of variant upper-class English, I had some difficulties with the rough dialect in the movie. I wasn't used to hearing people swallow their vowels and consonants and calling women "ducks."

Another evening, Mum and I went to Highgate School to see Nigel in W.W. Jacob's play, *The Monkey's Paw*. A mystery, as I recall. Nigel played the mother, Mrs. White, which was in fact the play's only female role. He wore an old dress of mine, my bra, and my shoes, and apart from looking hilarious he *was* hilarious.

The boys were now on vacation, and we were all—except Dad W.—going on a trip. Dad W. would meet us later at our destination in Godalming in Surrey. We took off around noon on April 6, after stowing away suitcases, bags, and fishing gear. Two and a half hours of riding scrunched up with the boys in the back seat and I couldn't wait to get there. Burningfold Hall Hotel was very pretty, a sort of English manor-house-turned-hotel. The gardens were well tended, and because the sun was shining everything looked twice as nice. I had a room of my own, of course, and after putting everything away and having tea, Mum and I strolled to the village, both of us happy to be free of making beds, doing dishes, and dusting. Sleep, eat, read, walk, be lazy—that was the ticket.

I was trying to read Iris Murdoch's *The Bell* in the lounge downstairs (the rooms were cold and the lounge had a blazing fire) but kept getting interrupted by other guests who wanted to talk. The telly was on in the adjoining hall and couldn't be turned down. Then there was a retired naval officer who liked to hear himself talk and would pick someone in the room and force them to listen, not to speak of a confused old woman with whom he did a noisy crossword puzzle every night. The officer tried daily to teach her something about puzzling, but by the next evening she would have forgotten everything and so he would start all over again. There was too a young couple with a sweet eighteen-month-old boy, a darling little child. And a refined old lady who took a shine to us as a family and who thought the boys well brought up. Plus an old gentleman who for some reason liked to talk to me about his family, a topic that didn't interest me in the least. However, with politeness being important, I would listen for a while and then try to bury myself behind the newspaper. The man was surprised when I told him that I was German as, in fact, everyone thought me a member of the family.

The next day Mum, John, and I went to Godalming to meet Dad's train. In the afternoon, I took photos of Nigel and Hugh playing croquet on the lawn behind the hotel, talked to the young couple, and played with the baby. In the evening, teenagers could attend a dance at the hotel, and since my room was directly above the ballroom I gave up trying to get to sleep and read instead, finally finishing *The Bell.*

Mum spent the whole next day with her friend in Horsham, and John and I went with Dad to neighboring Guildford because he had business there. At first, John and I were going to walk around Guildford, but we quickly found the town boring so we walked back to Godalming. Sometimes we had good conversations, but the details are lost now.

It rained all day the next day, boring me although I had plenty of reading to do. At dinner Hugh and Nigel tried really hard not to be gross, but in any case I was in a hurry to finish dinner because I wanted to catch *Panorama* on the telly. The show originated from Berlin, where the interviewer was asking young Germans about Eichmann and the Nazis. Oh God, I couldn't escape the topic. The young interviewees didn't know very much about the upcoming trial. When it was the turn of Willy Brandt (then mayor of Berlin) to speak, he said that thanks to the Eichmann trial young Germans had an opportunity to look at the past and make it more concrete in their minds. I wanted to say, Wake up, fellow Germans, and educate yourselves (myself included) about the atrocities done in your name. Some of the guests in the lounge shared their opinions about Eichmann and Nazi Germany, and we had an interesting conversation. Later in the evening, some of us watched a film about the Nazis in Norway, *Midnight Sun,* its main figure being a "good" German for variety's sake. Afterwards, we watched the opening of the Eichmann trial. It was fascinating to see how calmly he conducted himself in his bulletproof glass booth. The date was April 11, 1961, sixteen years after the end of World War II.

The weather was lousy, Dad went home to Mill Hill, and Mum and I went for a long walk. The old gentlemen who liked to talk to me now bought me candy and the next day knocked on my door and asked if I wanted a cup of tea. Instead of taking his attentiveness for a compliment, I grumbled about the fact that old men often seemed to show an interest in me. At Alexander Petersen & Co. the old translator, who had probably been in his sixties when I was in my teens, made it a point of stopping by my desk several times a day. He too bought me candy. I don't think I encouraged or flirted with old men, but then again maybe I did. I might have viewed them as harmless, whereas with young men all manner of uncontrollable urges could be unleashed by flirting with them.

Dad W. forwarded mail to us, among it several letters from German girl-friends and a package from home that brought a new blouse, stockings, an eye lash curler, Easter eggs, and magazines. I was inspecting everything when Nigel came barging in without knocking to look for Hugh, and John dropped by look-ing for his brothers. My room must have been a well-known meeting place! New guests arrived, among them a mother with her three daughters with whom the boys and I had become acquainted. John wanted me to know that he liked the oldest one and wanted to take her to the pictures. Oh the prospects, the feelings of spring all around! He had better hurry, though, because tomorrow we were returning to London. So there I was sitting in my room, longing for my darling John and wishing he were with me. In the meantime, the surrounding country-side was made for lovers—the woods kept secrets, hid indiscretions and sighs and kisses. Was it my destiny to wish rather than to experience? I felt like an innocent being longing to be naughty.

On the morning of our departure, April 13, Mum and I went out to pick primroses. They were beautiful, but I imagined they probably liked it better in their woodland home, a thought that led to my lifelong habit of leaving nature undisturbed.

Another letter from John arrived the next day and although this one wasn't yet postmarked "Cambridge," he said he would be there in a few days to start his last semester on April 19. I thought I might be heading to Cambridge soon.

One day when I was all alone I went shopping in Mill Hill and in the book-store came across a book called *The Truth About the Nazis*. Leafing through it, I came across appalling concentration camp photographs. How I hated Eichmann and that unspeakable war.

I bought a book called *Great Britain* by a Frenchman, an odd thing for me to do given that I would have to have known French customs to appreciate where the writer was coming from and I didn't know that much about France. I should have bought a book by a German, at which I might have been able to reject or affirm opinions I had formed about the British. The author stated that "public schools (which were really private schools) are gentlemen factories." I found that amusing at the time because on the surface it rang so true, but I would have had to dig in to learn exactly why this was true (were Nigel and Hugh really being made into gentlemen—you could have fooled me!) So I just took the Frenchman at his word and put the matter out of my mind.

When I browsed through the German Books Exhibition at the Royal Festival Hall, I decided that once back in Germany I would throw myself into reading my country's books. I had a lot of catching up to do in my reading of the classics as well as modern literature. Oh, my English family had awakened in me a love of reading I had not had before!

On April 24, I had a letter from John that said he hoped I could come to Cambridge but that he couldn't set a date yet. Eleven long days later he wrote he had wanted to invite me for Sunday, May 7, but that he had to lunch with his tutor (advisor). At least he wanted to see me even though his schedule was out of his hands. My disappointment was great even as I kept praying for a reunion with the man I loved. It didn't occur to me to make demands, or at least polite requests, for a date. I let the man do the asking, whenever possible.

At college, student trips were offered for Oxford or Cambridge for July 1, and because John wasn't going to be in Cambridge Dodo and I decided to visit Oxford for the cost of only ten shillings. Besides day-dreaming about John, I was writing about an essay a day, and Mr. Smith thought the quality of my writing to be improving.

It was the beginning of spring and although the weather was still somewhat chilly, the entire family with the exception of John went for walks. I took them because I wanted to lose weight. The British diet with its meat pies and sweet pies and bread fried in bacon grease had conspired to take its toll on my body. In the months since coming to England, I had gained at least twenty pounds. But it wasn't easy to diet, because Mum thought I should clean my plate. If I had fruit alone for lunch and she came home early, she would fix me whatever was available in the pantry and scold me for not eating more. When I came home from school and she was there, I simply had to eat. I could only get away with abstaining when she wasn't around.

Now that it was May, there wouldn't be any fires in any of the fireplaces until further notice—autumn—most likely. So it was chilly in those rooms, and when I was cold I couldn't concentrate on reading or studying, so I often ended up watching the telly in the cold drawing room along with everybody else. I didn't feel I could do like John W. did and hole up in my room all day; it wasn't polite to do that. But I envied him for being able to be alone when he felt like it. At home in Hamburg, I didn't have a room of my own to retreat to.

Pauline called to say that she would be in London in a few days (on Sunday) with her aunt and uncle. I thought she was calling just so she wouldn't have to write because answering letters had never been her strong point. So the opportunity to spend time with her was welcome news.

On May 14, I had a nightmare and I couldn't get back to sleep because the heat was unbearable. First chilly, then hot—like my relationship with John, I thought. It was a Sunday and I got up at 7:30 a.m. (the first time I had been up this early since last October!) and worked in the back yard. After a while, Dad W. came down and asked if I was okay. They actually thought I was sick; they had gotten so used to their au pair sleeping in on Sundays! Dad W. was leaving for Germany that day at 3:00 p.m., so we had to have lunch at noon. At 11:00 a.m. Pauline arrived by car with Nip, Tom, sister Jo, and the sweet, handsome young nephew John. We were really busy trying to get lunch on the table but Mum made coffee anyway, which I thought was nice. It was the kind of thing Mutti would have done. I was so lucky to have not one but two wonderful mothers.

After lunch, the boys had to do the dishes and John drove Mum, Dad, Pauline, and me into London, where Dad took a train to the airport, Mum went on to see her sister in the hospital, and Pauline and I walked from Victoria Station to Trafalgar Square where we met Sabine. We all sat in Regents Park until 4:30 p.m., when we met Pauline's relatives and had dinner at Lyons. While I was playing with little John, I kept thinking about my big John and when I would see him again. They dropped me off at home on their way back to Peterborough.

Two days later, Mutti wrote that my sister-in-law Anne was expecting a baby. Hurrah! She was in the hospital because she was bleeding a little, but otherwise everything was fine. Doris and I would be aunts for the first time, Mutti and Papa would be grandparents, and last but not least Klaus would be a father. Imagine my big brother becoming a father! I was so happy, proud to become an aunt.

◆   ◆   ◆

Two days after that, on Thursday, May 18, 1961, I finally had a letter from John, after not hearing from him since May 5th. It was a letter I didn't want. I couldn't believe what I was reading and yet somehow already knew it would come to this one day. He said,

> "What I am going to say now is not easy to say and I am afraid that you may misunderstand me. First let me emphasize that I am very fond of you, and that my feelings have not changed in this respect. But honestly, there doesn't seem much chance for us, does there? Immediately after my exams—now about 3-1/2 weeks away—I have to go up to Pontefract for six weeks. That leaves four weeks before you go home and some of that time I shall be in Scotland. I wonder therefore if it would not be much _easier_ for both of us if we didn't see each other again. I know that if I saw you again, it would make the inevitable parting much more difficult to bear. Don't you think this would apply to you as well? The last thing in the world I want to do is to cause you any unhappiness. I have given this a great deal of thought, and while I would love to see you again, and that is the absolute truth, I am convinced this way would be better. Please don't be upset: I am sure you will meet somebody much worthier of you than I am. I am only deeply sorry that things had to be the way they are. Please write and tell me that you agree with me: think the thing out calmly and rationally and I think that you will see that I am right. Anyway, let me know what you think about this suggestion. Much love, John."

I cried and cried. I wailed, I moaned, I thrashed about on my bed. I read his letter a hundred times but still couldn't think clearly. He didn't love me any more—this was the one sentence I kept repeating before I would burst into tears again. He wanted me to write him, but what would I write? Would I tell him how sad I was? Would I agree with him? Would I ever be able to think about his letter rationally and calmly?

Mum was in Ipswich overnight, so her friend Miss Burton was coming over to stay with the boys and me. My eyes were puffy and red from all the crying and the boys must have wondered what was going on. So for the night I had to control myself and pretend nothing wrenching had happened. The next morning I was up at 7:00 a.m. and made sausage and eggs for the boys. When they and Miss Burton left, I resumed my tears.

Only three short months ago, on our fifth date, John had seemed to want me with all his heart and soul. All his loving letters since then had reinforced that belief. So what was I to think? To be fair, it didn't sound as if he had planned this to happen.

When Mum came home in the afternoon, I made tea and told her what happened. She took me in her arms and I cried again while she consoled me as best a mother could (it didn't occur to me until years later that she had never been through this falling-in-and-out-of-love scenario with a daughter nor, at least up to that time, with the boys). She suggested that maybe John was afraid to love me too deeply, or maybe he just didn't want to commit himself. Looking at it from those angles diminished the pain a little. Maybe she was right and I should stop saying to myself that he didn't love me anymore. Still, I felt lovesick and listless. The waiting, the running for the mail, the anxious feeling I had all the time—gone! We had had such wonderful hours together, yes—hours, not days. I lay awake at night, composing the final letter. Yet now the silence between us increased with each hour and day to make it harder for me to tell him how I really felt.

I too had goals to accomplish before settling down. But how was I to do that in Germany and still stay in close contact with John when we couldn't even manage to do that living in the same country? It occurred to me that he may have been frustrated with my refusal to have sex, that possibly there was someone else who would accommodate him. Still, I really didn't think that was the case, and the more I thought of what Mum had said the more I thought she was right. I wanted to tell him how sad I was, how hurt, and how much I still loved him.

On May 25, a week after the first letter, I received a note from him: "Darling Christel, did you get my letter last week? If so, please let me have your views on what it contains. Hope all goes well with you. Love, John."

I wished I had never received the first letter and could stop reading it. Although I told myself that I would not read his letter again, almost every night I took it out of the leather case where I kept all his letters. Finally, on the afternoon of May 25th, I mailed my reply. The letter contained most of the thoughts I had been dwelling on since receiving that first letter. I don't think I would have pleaded with him to meet one more time let alone suggested that we could work it out. From somewhere inside me I summoned my pride to guide my answer.

Dad W. returned from Germany where he had had lunch with my Mutti and news for me that everyone in the family was well. A few days later I received a letter from Mutti that Anne had had a miscarriage, so I wouldn't be an aunt after all. I wondered if Anne was disappointed or relieved, because I knew that she and Klaus hadn't planned, mostly for financial reasons, on having a baby yet. Their apartment was very expensive.

Now that I had sent my letter to John, I was waiting for mail again. I really had to stop this, as well as the crying myself to sleep at night. My friend Dodo thought I should burn his letters and maybe she was right, but I wanted to keep them a while longer. The pages spoke to me of love and caring, and I didn't want to give the flame up yet.

The entire month of June was full of activities, such as attending lectures, picnicking with Dodo in Regent's Park on a spread of pork pies, apples, rolls, cheese, and biscuits (cookies), and writing essays on Jane Austen's *Emma* because it would be on the exam this year for the first time. The one event that dominated that month was the Cambridge Proficiency in English exam at St. Albans College, a very advanced exam—"perfect if you have achieved a high level of language skills and are able to function effectively in almost any English-speaking context" according to the University of Cambridge ESOL Examinations. Maybe I should have taken a less advanced course first and worked my way up to this level because I was beside myself doubting my abilities. When I enrolled, I must have told them that I had taken seven years of English in school, that I had used it on the job, that I had taken courses in business English at the Berlitz School of Languages in Hamburg, thus that I was placed appropriately. Now I doubted if I was ready to take the exam.

On the morning of June 7th, shaking with fear, I burned the prunes I was cooking, cut my finger, and nearly fell down the stairs. On the train to St. Albans I ran into another German au pair and we tried to encourage each other. At last, settled in our classroom, an official gave us a fairly easy dictation, after which the next order of business was the reading. The examiner gave me a sheet with a few paragraphs I was allowed to read through once while sitting on a chair in the hallway. He was astonished when I knocked on the door in less than two minutes. I read the paragraphs to him and then he gave me another, shorter piece on which I had to do a cold read. The third part of the exam tested my ability to interact in conversational English. The examiner and I chatted for a few minutes on a variety of topics, and then the oral exam was over. The written exam wouldn't be for another week. Time for me to study and fret and study and fret yet more.

On June 13th, the day before reckoning, Mr. Smith gave us some helpful instructions for the exam the following day. He stressed above all that we should read each question carefully and not to stay on one answer too long. I went to bed early and prayed to God, whom I believed decided how all human affairs turned out in the end. That was my first mistake.

The literature exam took place in a hall not unlike an auditorium, and shortly before 9:30 a.m. we were given a list of questions about the books we had read: *An Episode of Sparrows, Emma,* and *Major Barbara.* I found the questions disappointing in scope and therefore difficult to respond to with examples that could develop the points I wanted to make. Then at 2:00 p.m., the third part, Use of English, began. As far as I recall, it included, among other things, filling in words that fit in a given sentence. The stem of the word was given, after which I had to fill in the correct form in the context of that sentence. Then there was an exercise in which I had to choose a word that would make sense in each of three sentences. This time, the word was not given and I had to search my brain for a suitable insert. The most difficult part was summarizing a 350-word text in my own words, furthermore explaining the attitude underlying in the text. I will never forget the feeling of anxiety that gripped me when I had to read the text twice before I could begin summarizing and I worried that time would run out before I finished. I was so rattled that the words seemed to be jumping around the page as I read.

My first mistake was thinking that God had a hand in this exam, my second that I failed to see the final page of questions and therefore failed to finish this part of the exam. Too late, when time was up, I discovered the last page. And then when I got home after this most grueling day, I told the boys about some of the exercises and they didn't hesitate to let me know how many mistakes I had made. All I could do now was hope.

The following day, we had two hours in which to write an essay about a topic we could choose from a given list. The essay would be judged by its introduction, topical development, and appropriate conclusion. Viewpoints and opinions had to be justified. I chose to write about "holidays" in 300–350 words, comparing and contrasting the German and English versions. In sum, I felt that I had done pretty well. Now I could breathe again while awaiting the results, which wouldn't arrive until August.

For the entire duration of the exams, I thought I managed to suppress my longings for John, but once the academic pressure let up, the longing to be touched by his tender hands or to hold his beloved face in my hands swept over me again. If I could only see him one more time! About the same time I was finishing my exams, he was beginning his first teaching job. I wished him well in my never-ending thoughts about him. In fact, it was getting harder rather than easier to forget the times we had together, and I continued crying in my pillow at night.

Though the exam was over, classes continued until mid-July, and during that time we learned some elementary Old English, which I found difficult to decipher, but nonetheless enjoyable. Mostly, I felt like being lazy, catching up on my friendships, and sightseeing.

Dodo and I saw much of each other for the next two months. We celebrated June 17th, the Day of German Unity, with a picnic at the river Ver in St. Albans. From where we were, St. Albans Cathedral looked so much like King's College Chapel in Cambridge and my thoughts naturally drifted there. I told myself that I had to learn to live in the moment and not look back so much. But that's exactly what I was doing in so many other ways, looking back.

◆   ◆   ◆

The Eichmann trial was still going on, and reports of it appeared in the newspapers every day. For the first time in my memory, I was hearing about the atrocities committed by my countrymen. Why had my parents, relatives, neighbors, and friends of my parents been so silent about the holocaust? Why did they tell us only about how they had suffered? How scared they had been when the bombs fell, when they were starving and freezing and walking home from Czechoslovakia in the company of thousands of miserable men, women, and children? Wasn't that enough for anyone to handle? But now, what about the Jews? Here I was twenty years old and the questions were only now occurring to me. As a child I was too devastated by my parents' suffering to ask any questions that would sadden them all over again. Or if I did pose sticky questions, it was only to learn more about their plight and not someone else's. When they told their stories, they often cried. Maybe they cried for the ones that were herded onto trains, I don't know.

I had read *The Diary of Anne Frank* as a young teenager, but I never talked to my parents about it. They hadn't read the book and they never asked me questions about it. I guessed the silence meant I had to figure it all out myself. Or did I avoid discussing the fate of this young woman because I wanted to make-believe that what I was reading couldn't possibly have happened? Didn't I want to know the truth?

And even now, with the Eichmann trial proceeding, and my anger at being confronted in a foreign country by this horrific event from Germany's past, and my feeling of vulnerability on account of my country's shame, I managed to find a group of people, whom I called "greasy Southerners," to look down on. St. Alban's College hosted an end-of-semester dance in the same hall where we had taken our exam. I only danced four times, but I reasoned that it was better to dance four times with English boys rather than ten times with greasy Southerners, Italian men. It seemed that I had problems with Italian men, though my prejudice was based mostly on the way they greased their hair. Maybe I envied them for having fun in life, unlike Germans who seemed so driven to work excessively. My prejudices were not well-defined and based mainly on observations I made about appearances. For instance, when I opined that German men did not seem to have fun, I based that on my nearly non-existent experiences with German men. In other words, I generalized.

◆   ◆   ◆

Meanwhile at school, we began reading *King Lear,* a most difficult Shakespearean play. But without the pressure of an exam to push me, I'm afraid I took it easy. There were fun events coming up, like the school-sponsored trip to Oxford. In the morning of July 1, I took the train to St. Albans and from there my schoolmates and I and our teacher Mr. Smith traveled by bus for the two hours it took to get to Oxford. The first thing we did on arrival was to paddle down the river Cherwell. I'm almost certain that we didn't punt, because punting required skills that none of us had. I compared Oxford with Cambridge, and Oxford came in second place, not only because I found Cambridge more charming for its obvious romantic associations. It was a very hot day, and after Mr. Smith had shown us four colleges two other girls and I took off by ourselves, had a peek at Exeter College and the Sheldonian Theatre, and slowly made our way back to the river where we stretched out in the grass on this languid English day. Years later, when I revisited Oxford and Cambridge, Oxford looked even less charming, whereas Cambridge had kept that je ne sais quoi, fueled no doubt by my memory of happy days there.

One of the things I had neglected to do upon arriving in England was to register with the police, mandatory for all foreigners staying in England. I went to the police station in Edgeware but was informed that I needed to go to the main station downtown in Picadilly Place. It was even possible that I might have to pay a fine! The clerk was young and male, and joking around with him got me off from having to pay a fine or even to go to jail! While I was in the city, I decided to visit the House of Commons, getting in queue at 2:00 p.m. An hour and a half later I entered the hall, and at 4:00 p.m. I was finally in the chambers. The debate was on Angola, but apart from the speechmaking I listened to with one ear, I found watching the politicians was much more enjoyable. Winston Churchill, age eighty-seven, just happened to be there that day. I recognized him, of course, and

Hugh Gaitskill the Labor Party leader but nobody else. Churchill hadn't been prime minister since 1955, and I could only assume that he visited the House of Commons now and then because he found it difficult to stay away. I assumed that the members of parliament were brilliant and important people, representing their constituents in this august body, but I must say that I found their behavior rather odd. Some of the members slept, some held private conversations, and many of them had their feet on the tables. I was only able to stay an hour, because I had to get to St. Albans to a lecture on "The Law" in my last Life and Institutions class. Looking back, I should have stayed for the debate in the House of Commons, since I had the lawmakers debating right in front of my eyes. And I felt so privileged at having seen Winston Churchill, because he was a statesman I could admire even though he had given Germany hell in World War II.

Dodo called on a Saturday morning and asked if she could come over because she was bored out of her mind. I felt the same. I had been crying again and thought it was out of homesickness. Dodo felt the same. So it was more fun to be homesick together, and I was glad to have her company. I showed her the shops in Mill Hill Village and made tea at home. For tea, I usually prepared a variety of things, often leftovers, but also hard-boiled egg sandwiches on toast or beans on toast, sometimes bacon and fried bread, and sometimes again bubble and squeak from leftover vegetables (cabbage squeaks when it's fried). The more calories an item had, the better it seemed to taste!

Dodo was envious of the fact that I lived with a family with older children. She took care of a four-year old girl whose mother was pregnant and had to rest in bed most of the time. Dodo really liked my boys, especially Hughie. Hughie had a knack for keeping everybody entertained, mostly by being very clever with puns. At our expense, he imitated our German accents. When I took her to the train station that night, she said that she hadn't laughed as much as she had today, and we noted that our dour moods had lifted.

It was time for Granny to visit again, and now she didn't move around the way she had before, meaning that she was even slower! Dad W. said he didn't like old women and he mumbled nasty things about his mother-in-law while she was in the same room, knowing that she was hard-of-hearing. I told her that I was going home soon, and she gave me a pound sterling as a going-away present although I wasn't leaving England for another ten weeks. My departure date had not been set yet.

The day after Granny's visit was my last day of school and I felt sad to say good-bye to Mr. Smith, because I had had so much fun with him and considered him a good and caring teacher. On the other hand, it was easy to say farewell to Mr. Postlethwaite, who had kept asking Dodo and me to come over to his house again. (After that first time, we never did accept another invitation). Now that school was out, I was home alone with Granny until the boys' summer vacation began.

In mid-July, I met my friend Sabine at Schmidt's in downtown London for a last lunch before she left for Germany. Schmidt's carried authentic German food and had a deli attached to the restaurant. Before lunch, I picked up the makings for a real German dinner, with black bread, cheese, cold cuts, smoked fish, and even some head cheese. It wasn't so much that I wanted to treat the family to a German meal as that I was craving German food and just had to have it once in awhile. At Victoria Station Sabine and I exchanged teary farewells, since we wouldn't be seeing each other until September. She wasn't really ready to go back to Germany yet and would have preferred to stay for a few more months, but her parents had pressured her into coming home, she being an only child.

A couple of days later, I met Dodo at the train station in Harpenden north of St. Albans, and from there we walked to Ayot St. Lawrence in Hertfordshire, a distance of about five miles. Our destination was George Bernard Shaw's house. We walked along country roads, singing German folk songs and talking about everything and nothing. After an hour, we took a break and sat by the side of the road, filling up with delicious English cheddar, chunks of bread, apples, bananas, and tomatoes. We had just begun walking again, when a gathering thunderstorm threatened to douse us. Running to an abandoned Quonset hut for shelter, we thought we could wait out the downpour until we saw rats whisking by, and so we sprinted from cover and ended up soaked by the time we got to Shaw's house. As we were the only visitors just then, the housekeeper spent some time showing us around. The rooms were rather small, as I remember, and the furnishings not unattractive but not outstanding either. In the entrance hall, his cloak and hat were displayed on a coat stand, making me think that though he had died in 1950, he was waiting for us in the next room. The Nobel Prize which he had been awarded in 1925, all his works, masses of books, and pens he had used filled the study.

The house was not that big, and Dodo and I wandered through it in a short time. Since it was still raining cats and dogs and the housekeeper was a kindly person, she offered to make us a cup of tea and allowed us to sit on the covered terrace overlooking a gently sloping, expansive lawn dotted with huge trees. So there we sat, where the brilliant Shaw had sat only a little more than ten years before and where he had written most of his plays. I had fallen in love with his ironic tone, his "Shavian" wit that produced phrases such as, "England and America are two countries divided by a common language," and, "Christianity might be a good thing if anyone ever tried it." Having visited Shaw's house made me want to write, a feeling I had never before had except, of course, for diary writing. But the feeling didn't last, because my rational being took over and I had to admit to myself that I had never done well writing anything. Dodo and I ate the rest of our picnic food and waited for the rain to stop. Cold, wet, and far from home, we left when it was still drizzling and walked to a little cottage restaurant where we warmed up with a hot cup of tea. A hot bath was still a five-mile walk and a train ride away.

Anna, the English girl whose parents were friends of Mum's, came over the next day. She had visited us at least once a month since I arrived in England, and we were friends of sorts, though our friendship was more a forced kind and this Sunday afternoon seemed to go on forever. It was rainy, the telly wasn't working, and we didn't really have much to talk about. On top of that, John sneaked out and left me to make conversation. It's an art to talk about nothing, but that's what we did until it was time for tea. After all the time we had sat together over the past year, we never managed to click. My one and only English girlfriend was and still is Pauline, who was dear to me from the moment we met.

I guess Granny wasn't going to stay as long as she had the last time, because nine days after she arrived Mum took her home to Surrey and then stayed overnight with a friend of hers in Horsham. That meant that I had to take care of everything—cooking, washing, cleaning, and shopping. I was very quiet at lunch and Mum thought I was homesick, but instead I was in a foul mood caused by the fact that I had to do all that work. Clearly I was most upset about the cooking, because the preparation of meals from start to finish took up so much of the day. I shopped for food virtually daily, just the way my Mutti did in Germany, hauled the food home in bags, put the contents away, and then later in the day started preparing the food, cooked it, and set the table unless I got one of the boys to do it. Dad W. wasn't a big help clearing the table after dinner, and tonight again he left it to the boys to help me, while he slouched off to his study. That's when the bickering, the fighting over who was going to do what began. That made me boiling mad, because I assumed that the boys thought kitchen work was fun for me but not them. They were dead wrong—just because I was done with school didn't mean I wanted to be in the kitchen all day.

It all started the night before, when it occurred to me for the first time that I didn't want to be an au pair any longer. For once, I wanted only to enjoy a delicious, leisurely German dinner, preferably one cooked by my Mutti. I was mad at Mum for, in my opinion, favoring Nigel. At suppertime, there were only five chairs at the table and poor Nigel would have had to get his own chair from the living room (we ate in the kitchen) and Mum would tell John, "You could have got the chair because you were closer to the door." At that, I'd want to tell her what I thought but kept my mouth shut and silently sided with John. Nigel could be such a baby at times and was treated as such.

My internal ravings continued the day after Mum left, because it was a school day and everyone had to be fed and out on time. I knew how to do it, I just didn't want to do it any longer. John came home at noon and I made lunch for us, then cooked again in the evening. Blasted hell! I had had it up to the proverbial eyeballs, especially since they all wanted to be served and doubly so when their Mum was away. If they took comfort from my being there, I was uncomfortable with that sentiment. I didn't want to be their substitute Mum and looked forward to the coming week when Mum was going to be home and would hopefully do some of the cooking. When she came home that night, she must have sensed that I was fed up because she suggested that I take a vacation—like to the Lakes region of England the first week in September—but I didn't think I could do it for lack of funds.

I stopped ranting temporarily because the following week was a good mixture of fun and work. On a Sunday Mum, Dad, Hughie, Nigel and I drove to Cuffley, stopping for a picnic lunch on the way before driving around the area. When I was younger, I had gone on outings with my parents to lakes near Hamburg where we would picnic. We didn't call it "picnic" but simply "Mittagessen," (middle of the day eating), and all the bags of food and plates and forks and knives had to be carried there on trains and on foot. I liked the fact that for picnics in England, all the supplies were stowed in the trunk of the car and the hood served as the table. After our picnic, we drove on to Hatfield House, built for the First Earl of Salisbury between 1607 and 1611. Not only was the palace magnificent but the gardens were even more impressive. In the early 1600's, the botanist John Tradescant had brought back from his travels trees and plants never before seen in England, such as the roses and mulberries at Hatfield House. The gardens at all the castles I have visited have impressed me more than the houses, especially after reading about John Tradescant and his singular pursuit of nurturing all that is necessary for a beautiful garden.

On the following Wednesday, Mum had to visit a nursery school in Baldock. She said that since it was on the way to Cambridge we should go to Cambridge afterwards. I think she suggested this to please me. We proceeded to have lunch in the Union Society of Cambridge University, where John had shown me the results of the boat races. Memories of our happy times washed over me and I went into daydreaming mode in which from over the horizon John was running towards me, shouting "At last!" I left Mum by the river, sunning herself on this beautiful, sunshiny day fanned by the gentlest of breezes and wandered over to Pembroke College to gaze one more time at the buildings that held such brief but precious memories for me. The second time I had visited him here, we had finished our coffee, and as he was helping me into my coat he kissed me on the neck. I still remembered that loving, tender gesture, and the love I felt for him this day in Cambridge couldn't have seemed more tangible. It was time, though, to tuck it into a corner of my heart. And there it would stay, my second true love after Eberhard. After this day in Cambridge, I never mentioned his name again in my diary.

Time to be outraged again—at men, and specifically Dad W. Mum had to go to St. Albans one more time before semester break, and I did the usual domestic jobs. She got home rather late, and by 7:00 p.m. Dad was getting impatient with wanting his supper. Men, why were they so insensitive, among other things? I decided that I wouldn't want him for a husband for anything in the world. He was stingy, cowardly, and egotistical. He didn't show any interest in the upkeep of the house and couldn't even put a nail in the wall. So what if he had a good mind, where were his helping hands? Mum had to work to make ends meet, but she was also responsible for the house and the boys. Dad should have remained a bachelor, because he wasn't even a loving father. I would get incensed when he would say to the boys after a meal, "Well, let's do the dishes together because Mummy is tired" but then walk away and leave the boys to be Mummy's helpers. By George, he drove me up the wall! I kept comparing him to my Papa, who could repair just about anything that needed fixing, and I came to appreciate men who had that fix-it skill.

The next day must have been the day the boys' summer vacation began, because it was the last time Mum and I went to Highgate School for Speech Day. Hughie received a prize for something involving Latin and French, while Nigel showed off his fencing skills. The school was huge—perhaps 500 pupils—and had impressive buildings and playing fields. We had gone to the school after having lunch at home, and because we were in a hurry we had left the lunch dishes in the sink. So when we got home they were still there—Dad hadn't lifted a finger, although he had been home all afternoon. Oh Lord!

On Sunday afternoon, I met Dodo in St. Albans, where we sat by the cathedral and talked. We had discussed many times what we wanted to do about jobs after we returned to Hamburg, and today was no different. That long-buried wish to become a stewardess had returned with renewed interest, in part because Dodo wanted to be a stewardess too. Since airlines required fluency in two foreign languages, Dodo and I had talked about going to Spain as au pairs in the spring of the following year, to become fluent in Spanish. But now I wasn't so sure about this plan.

Since the eighth grade, I had spent hours at the *Amerika Haus* in Hamburg, reading about America and daydreaming about someday traveling and working in that land of opportunity. If my parents had only given their permission, I would have bypassed England altogether and become an au pair in America, but since I wasn't yet twenty-one years old and thus not on my own legally I had to postpone this wish of mine. Not for a single day did I regret having come to England rather than holding out for America, but I wasn't sure that I wanted to resurrect my dream of being a stewardess because I was still as afraid of flying as I had ever been. And I didn't like Spanish all that well. But it was fun thinking about going to Spain with a girlfriend rather than going to a foreign country all by myself. As it happened, our plans fell apart soon after because by September Dodo had fallen in love with an Englishman named Brian, and if things worked out she would be staying in England or Brian would be moving to Germany. So bye, bye, Spain! And hello America!

But first, a family trip to Wales was quickly coming up. So for the next four days, I was completely wrapped up in the preparations, mostly doing laundry and cleaning. I fell into bed at night and cried from sheer exhaustion. At breakfast, Dad W. asked, "You're so quiet, what's the matter with you?" "I'm a bit tired," I said. "Why?" he had the nerve to reply. Didn't he have eyes in his head? Had he seen me lounging around? No! Everyone was on vacation and waiting around to be fed. When the meals were done, there was still ironing and packing to do.

On the afternoon of August 4th, I sat down to sew a zipper in Hughie's pants (he wasn't coming with us but was staying with his aunt in Surrey), and so I was able to put up my feet for a short time. At 6:20 p.m., Nigel's French pen pal was supposed to arrive at Victoria station and Dad didn't want to go with us to pick him up. A big fight ensued, with shouting and banging doors. Although there had been noisy fights before, I had never seen Mum so enraged and felt sorry for her. Nigel, Mum, and I ended up going to the train station without Dad. My first impression was that Andre was cute like Nigel, sweet and devilish at the same time. Andre didn't speak much English yet, but thank God everyone in the family spoke at least some French. Maybe I could pick up a little too. Little did I know that sixteen years later, I would graduate with a bachelor's degree in French!

By 10:30 the next morning, Saturday, August 5, we finally had the car loaded up and were ready to leave. Dad drove, Nigel and Andre sat in the back seat, and Mum and I in the front with Dad (John was staying with a friend). We hadn't even made it through Hertfordshire yet when the car began to smell like rubber, and we were forced to stop and flag down an AA (Automobile Association) man, who worked on the car for thirty minutes. Then on we went through the pouring rain. Shortly before Banbury, about halfway between Mill Hill and Birmingham, the windshield wipers stopped working, but fortunately we found a place to park right away because Dad couldn't see anything for the sheet of rain running down the windshield. The convertible top had recently been replaced, but that didn't stop the rain from coming into the car. Dad cursed, and I was completely drenched on one side from sitting next to the window.

Dad managed to get the wipers working, we wiped everything down, and on we went through Stratford-upon-Avon, engaging in some out-loud wishful thinking about how nice it would be to stop and see Shakespeare's birthplace. However, we wanted to arrive in Tregarth/Wales before it was dark, and so there would be no time for Shakespeare. Halfway to Tregarth, IT happened: the wreck of a car just stopped and would not budge however hard we tried to revive it. Still, we were fortunate that a young man stopped and took Dad to a garage and from there a tow truck came and towed us to another garage somewhere near Wolverhampton. It took another hour before all the paper work was done and a cab was called to take us to North Wales. Great, the cab was much more comfortable and safer too but would be a long and expensive ride, about twelve pounds sterling. We finally arrived in Tregarth about 9:30 p.m., and after eating a small supper and doing the dishes (no dishwasher), we all went to bed exhausted from a day of misfortune and tension.

Mum and Dad W. had either rented the house in Tregarth, or else houses were being swapped. In any case, I was happy because only three beds had to be made! In addition, Mum took over most of the cooking for the duration of our stay. (She actually liked cooking!) We slept late, especially when it promised to be another rainy day. Even when the weather left much to be desired and the mountain tops were shrouded in clouds, it was refreshing to have breakfast while gazing at the peaks in distant Snowdonia National Park. I wasn't fond of mountains on the whole, preferring oceans and fields of grain and, most of all, a level horizon. Since I had never been to the south of Germany and so hadn't yet seen any mountains, I often wondered whether the mountains I had seen as a young child, when my family lived in the Sudetenland, had somehow imprinted themselves on my memory. But that memory never failed to evoke World War II.

Tregarth was a small village nestled at the edge of Snowdonia. It only had three tiny stores, and in order to buy food for the next few days the boys and I had to walk a mile and a half to Bethesda, a slightly bigger village. Nigel and Andre carried the groceries for me. The next day, Monday, was a bank holiday, a national holiday when not only the banks but stores would all be closed. Tourist places stayed open, though, and so we took a bus to the little fishing town of Bangor three and a half miles to the north. From the museum there, we had a terrific view of the Isle of Anglesey. The smell of the Irish Sea made me a little homesick for the North Sea but happy nonetheless to be gazing at a big body of water again. Busses to Tregarth left every hour and passed several villages with names like Llandygai and Llanllechid, the last one winning the prize for containing the most ls. Now I wasn't just listening to English, but to French and Welsh as well. A Celtic language, Early Welsh from the sixth century made way for Old Welsh, Middle Welsh, and Early Modern and Late Modern Welsh. I couldn't understand any of it, but I did try to pronounce it while I was there, only to forget it all once I was back in London.

The two weeks we spent in Wales were often wet and windy. On our third night, it began raining before midnight and didn't stop until the afternoon of the next day. We couldn't see the mountains, and the thick clouds turned everything gray, even the houses made of gray stone. Now they looked dark gray and almost threatening because of their darkness. Needless to say we stayed home all day and read or played games.

As long as there was even the possibility of a little sun, we were out and about climbing mountains. One of them was about 3000 feet high and took us all day to conquer. Sloshing through mud and heather and negotiating boulders, we finally arrived, if not at the top, then close to it. In my memory, we gazed down on a big and a small lake, both very clear and green and unbelievably beautiful. The stillness of it all was unnerving, almost depressing. For a while we sat on the boulders admiring the luminous water, but not for long because we weren't dressed warmly enough for the wind and freezing temperatures. Nor were we dressed for mountain climbing because our socks and shoes had not dried out from the previous wet days and now made squishy noises as our feet slid around in them. Mum and I wore skirts that day, and failed to take even a windbreaker.

On top of it all, the rain began, and we were glad to get back down as the fog was rapidly blanketing the mountain. On the way up, a Welshman climbing to a higher mountain gave me a small bunch of white heather meant, like German Edelweiss, to bring good luck. Suddenly I wished to see John one more time.

Another hike of about five miles on country roads took us to the village of Seion, where we spent the afternoon with friends of Mum's from St. Albans who had a cottage beautifully situated for a view of the mountains. Mrs. Newman took us home in her car, a luxury. Since we had arrived in Tregarth, the four of us—Mum, Nigel, Andre, and I—did all the hiking as a group unless a destination could be reached by bus. Dad W. stayed home waiting for the car to be fixed, which finally happened halfway through the vacation when he took a bus to Wolverhampton and drove the newly repaired car back to Tregarth. Now we were able to make good use of it, driving to the beach where we stayed almost all day because it was actually sunny. We enjoyed a picnic on the beach and then soldiered on to the twelfth century Caernarvon Castle. I had seen many castles in Germany, and visiting a fortress was boring even if it was in Wales! Crumbling stone walls reminded me of bombed out buildings in Hamburg, World War II being ever-present in my mind.

We had that one good day, and then the all-day rain began again. The next day was cold and windy again but we took off anyway and drove first to Llandudno, then Conwy, and on through the valley of Conwy to Llanrwst (by this time my tongue was rebelling), where we stopped and the boys and I competed at throwing skinny stones in the water to see whose would skip the most times. A game from my childhood. In Betws-y-Coed we beheld the mighty Swallow Falls. It cost sixpence to see this natural spectacle, this Swallowed Money Falls as I renamed it.

It rained again as we started our trip to Criccieth in Tremadog Bay. But it turned out to be the best day we had had so far, with bright sunlight and virtually no wind. The stony beach at Criccieth was hard to sit on, but we were in the water most of the time anyway, not swimming but throwing ourselves into the waves, Mum included but not Dad. In the early afternoon, he was urging us to get ready to leave, although we would get home much too early for tea, and although we hadn't had nearly enough time on the beach due to the bad weather. In the evening, Dad wouldn't let Mum turn on the telly because he wanted to read in the living room sitting in the only comfortable chair. I took Mum's side and filled with indignation. But she didn't say a thing, and I for my part couldn't understand why she didn't give him an argument. (She probably wanted to keep the peace and not argue in front of the French boy.) Mum only had a big vacation once a year, and even then she couldn't do what she wanted. What was even more astonishing was the fact that a few days after we got back to London, Dad was off to France, leaving Mum again to take care of the boys. Obviously, I didn't know enough of the underlying dynamics of their marriage to make these flash judgments, but I made them anyway.

To have two sunny days in a row was probably more than could be asked for, and the next day was accordingly miserable, the grayness of the mountains depressing. But soon enough we had another beautiful day which we spent in Treaddur Bay on a sandy beach with rocks to climb and little protected coves to lie in and soak up the sun. This was really the last day of vacation, because the next day Mum and I had to clean the house without the help of Dad and the boys who were excused because they would only be in the way. Since the house was small, we were done by noon and spent the afternoon in Beaumaris and Bangor shopping for souvenirs. When we left Tregarth the next day, it rained (what else?), and I had no difficulty saying goodbye to the mountains. The drive home was without incident—not even a flat tire!

While we were in Wales, two significant events had occurred, one in Israel and the other in Germany. After fourteen weeks of testimony, Eichmann's trial ended on August 14, 1961, and the case was given to the judges to deliberate. That meant that the Eichmann's name and crimes were no longer daily fodder for the newspapers. It also meant that I would no longer be confronted every day with my feelings about having grown up in a country that had murdered millions of people. How could I figure it all out now, not being among my own people? I needed to give myself more time, a lot more time to come to grips with how I felt about surviving the war when Jews and other despised peoples had been murdered. How responsible was I? I was nowhere near figuring it out at this time in my life, a month away from my 20th birthday.

The other event transpired in Berlin on Sunday, August 13, 1961. During the night, East German troops moved into East Berlin and began constructing an "anti-fascist protection barrier" intended, per the East German government to dissuade aggression from the West. Its real purpose, however, was to keep East Germans from escaping into the West, for in 1960–61 alone approximately 400,000 people had done exactly that. The Wall now physically divided the city and completely surrounded West Berlin, splitting families and cutting East Berliners off from their jobs. Initially, a barbed-wire fence was erected, but later in some sections of the city evacuated apartment houses were incorporated into the structure. A photo went famously around the world of an old woman climbing out of her first floor apartment window and being helped down by a man stand-ing in the ground floor window well below. The ground floor windows and apartment house door had been bricked over, so exiting from her first floor win-dow was her only means of escape into West Berlin. Eventually the Wall stretched over ninety-six miles, separating not only East and West Berlin, but cre-ating two Germanys. It was made of twelve-foot high sections of concrete, topped with barbed wire and guards watching vigilantly from their towers, and featured a death strip paved with raked gravel so that escapee footprints were easy to spot in addition to being mined and booby-trapped with tripwires.

I was enduring a boring, bad-weather day in Wales while the Wall rose in Ber-lin, but because I didn't have any relatives in East Germany, the Wall didn't have a great impact on me immediately. Still, the stories of escapes and the photo-graphs of people jumping from buildings broke my heart though it didn't dawn on me until years later how much courage it took for people to escape, not until a German physician-friend of mine who was in an English-as-a-second-language class I was teaching told me of her harrowing break for freedom curled up in the false bottom of a VW bus. I was angry at the Communists for the first time.

◆   ◆   ◆

The day after our return from Wales we took off again, this time to visit Granny in Surrey. John drove us, maybe because he had grown tired of cooking for himself while we were in Wales and maybe because he didn't want to stay alone in the house with his Dad given that the two of them didn't get along that well. I myself didn't get along with the little French twerp Andre, who was a pain to have around. He was always talking at me in French when he knew quite well that I didn't understand a word and had to get Nigel to translate for me. I proba-bly got back at him by speaking English more rapidly than I would have nor-mally.

Granny lived with Mum's sister in a big old house in Surrey. Kathleen was a teacher and her husband a baker. In this class-conscious country (even more so than in Germany), the odd union of an academically trained woman and a skilled tradesman doubtlessly seemed puzzling to me. In a country where dialect puts people in a social class and keeps them there or, even worse, keeps them from using their abilities, a marriage between two equally trained people seemed to be the ideal. But this particular union had worked for years, so obviously there were exceptions to the rule.

Andre, the French boy, was disgusting and especially so when he picked his nose right in front of us. I wanted either to give him lessons in how to behave himself in polite society or to pummel him until he was put out of his misery. As long as the two of them, Andre and Nigel, kept busy, I could at least tolerate them, so one day I took them into London and sent them off visiting museums while I looked for clothes, particularly a suit. Oxford Street had some rather high-priced stores on one end, but when I turned into Regent Street and entered Liberty's, I at last understood the meaning of the term high-priced. The suits I liked cost seventeen guineas, which was actually seventeen pounds seventeen shillings. In other words, almost eighteen pounds, though the stores figured that seventeen sounded better than eighteen. It was a beautiful store, true, but I didn't want to (or rather, couldn't) pay for the carpets as well as the clothes. Ten pounds was about all I could afford and that only with some help from my parents. In retrospect I'm not sure why I needed a suit, but I may have been thinking ahead to dressing up for job interviews once I returned to Hamburg.

One night at Kathleen's farmhouse I did a naughty thing—I read *Lady Chatterley's Lover* from cover to cover from under the covers! I had come across the book at the house in Mill Hill and had asked Mum if I should read it (D.H. Lawrence was, after all, a famous name in English literature), but she advised me to wait until I was a little older. That comment had intrigued me and now I had the perfect opportunity to act on a desire I had been advised (though not outright forbidden) not to have. So I pulled it from Kathleen's library shelf, snuck it in my room, and hid it under the covers. I couldn't wait until it was time to go to bed and read this intimate description of love and sex. Quickly I discovered the writing was so deliciously frank that I broke out in a sweat, blushing at the erotic fantasies it unleashed in me. The feeling lasted all night and day until I was done with the book. All of a sudden even John W. started looking good, and when he came back to Surrey bringing the mail and planning to stay the week, we spent a lot of time talking. That's all we did, though, while lying around on the lawn innocently talking, although my heart throbbed quite unexpectedly. But John left abruptly after two days and nobody knew why; he hadn't even told his mother that he was leaving. I was afraid to read anything into his sudden departure, but when Nigel and Andre were making their usual smart remarks at supper about this and that and talking about me, Christabelle, Nigel blurted out, "He (meaning John) is in love with Christabelle." I blushed instantly and then most likely told them to shut up. Did these testosterone-driven squirts know more than I did? No way was I going to fall in love again and especially not with John, my English "brother!" How embarrassing, and all because of a book of exciting prose!

In the mail that John had brought to me were the results of my exam. When I saw the first line, "This document is issued to *unsuccessful* candidates or to those who enter for part of the examination; it is *not* a certificate," I was annoyed and disappointed with myself. Now that I had the "Non-Certificate" in my hands, I could scarcely believe the results. I did best in the oral test, receiving a "B" for "good." In *Use of English,* and in *English Literature,* I passed with a "C." Even though I had missed the last page of the *Use of English* exam, I still passed to my great relief. The failing English Language grade, though, upset me terribly at first. I must not have developed the topic, "Holidays," failing to present my views and opinions appropriately. But writing essays had never been my strength, and writing within a time limit had always panicked me. I could have retaken this part of the exam but decided not to because I would be going home within a month and felt confident enough in my overall knowledge of English. If I were working for a company, I wondered how often I would be asked to write essays. I didn't quite realize then that writing anything, even business letters, required organization, that views or assertions needed proof, and that an appropriate conclusion was absolutely essential.

Well, then. I accepted the results and moved on. I would take more classes in English as soon as I got back to Hamburg, and this one non-certificate would not break my spirit. My English family was disappointed along with me but not in me, and nobody made any negative remarks.

Mum and I now passed time doing things together, things like blackberrying, spending a day in Brighton, and driving back to Surrey with the top down. What fun we had together. I think I had spent more time with Mum in this last year than I had with my own Mutti in the year before I left for England. Mum and I had more fun together, there being in us more levity than I had enjoyed with Mutti who, besides loving me, also had what seemed like the twenty-four-hour job of molding me into a respectable human being. Mutti didn't take her job lightly, which led to serious clashes between us. "Get off my back," I'd yell at her before she yelled back at me. Mutti was more volatile than Papa, and I was as volatile as or even more so than Mutti, so any remark or a raised eyebrow (not to speak of a "mean-eye" look) could set us off. With my English Mum I needed to be cautious so would often as not bite my tongue. She was my Mum but not my Mutti. I suspect the difference lay in the love.

The night before we were to return to Mill Hill, a water pipe broke and there was pandemonium in the house. I slept through it all and only learned about it when I discovered the plumber at work fixing things when I awoke. But there was the aftermath to clean up. So after packing every inch of the car with our stuff, I stayed on until 2:30 p.m., cleaned the house, and then went home on the train and tube. I was looking forward to sleeping in my own beloved room again.

John W. was at the airport picking up his Dad, and so blushing was postponed until he got home. Stupid me, even if I had told myself to get over my little crush. Next day he left for parts unknown to me for a few days. He had graduated from high school and maybe was off to some university he was thinking of attending. Before he left that morning, a girl called him twice (how dare she!) However, I didn't feel jealous and I took that as a good sign that I wasn't losing my mind. It is true, though, that I had come to think of him as a male as well as a brother. Now I didn't see so much his disheveled bedroom, the grimy sink he never cleaned, the unmade bed, the clutter of clothes and books—all those things that had annoyed me at the beginning. Instead, I saw a young man my age with typical pale English skin, stooped shoulders (his posture was terrible, maybe he had grown too quickly at one time). I saw the easy smile that stretched from ear to ear, and I remembered the great conversations.

More and more I was having happy thoughts about my return to Germany but at the same time feeling sad about leaving England. When the three young boys went into London, I walked to the travel agency in Mill Hill and inquired about the cost of a London-Cologne-Hamburg ticket. Papa was working with the band in Cologne and I wanted to see him first before I went home to Hamburg. Not wanting to think about leaving England but at the same time wanting to get on with my life—that was me now. It wasn't England so much that I was sad to leave as my English family, I realized.

Papa wrote and advised me to get a ticket to Hamburg that stopped first in Cologne. So I bought my reserved-seat ticket on September 11, 1961, for eight pounds eighteen shillings. It wiped out most of the money I had saved up, but with the rest of it I bought a pipe for Papa. It would be a present for him when I arrived, because on the day I left England he was turning fifty-six. I would leave London on Sunday, October 1, at 3:00 p.m. and arrive in Cologne at 3:00 a.m. Now began my worrying that Papa wouldn't hear his alarm clock and that I would be stranded at the train station. Big girl, me.

On September 6 Andre returned to France, and France was welcome to have him back! He had been getting on everyone's nerves, not just mine. The things I wouldn't miss were just teenage-boy things, like not cleaning up after himself. I had been raised to believe that sloppiness was not to be displayed by a non-member of the family. Visitors needed to be vigilant of their behavior at all times.

There were only twenty-four days left and most of them I spent doing ordinary things, but between the ordinary things my friend Dodo and I managed to see each other fairly frequently. One day we took a boat down the Thames (the river is quite pretty past Kew) to Hampton Court Palace, munching on bread and cheese in the most magical gardens surrounding an old, musty, and boring sixteenth century palace!

I began feeling tired all the time and took a nap every day to the point where I started getting teased about it. I think I was feeling depressed about leaving and napping was a way of escaping that feeling for a short time.

For my twentieth birthday on Sunday, September 17, I invited Dodo and her boyfriend Brian over. They were seriously thinking about getting married, whereas I was single and fancy-free, just the way I liked it for now. Marriage was not part of plans for my immediate future and I was not in the least bit envious about Dodo and Brian's bliss. Becoming even more independent than I had been when I left Germany, I was more concerned with how resuming living with my parents would work out. In fact, I felt anxious about it. This time around would Mutti treat me like a grown-up or like her little girl? I swore that I wouldn't let her get away with treating me like a little girl. Other times I thought about seeing her again soon, at which love for her filled my heart.

The last few days I spent in England seem rather a fog, and I can't today recall how the send-off went. I remember that Mum had asked me weeks earlier to stay on and that I had been adamant about returning to Germany. I'd like to think that they all came to Victoria Station to see me off and that there were hugs all around—even a few tears. I didn't have the feeling that I would never see them again, because the fare to England was reasonable and I would soon be making money. Yes, I could always come back for a visit, for I had truly grown to love this family and I would always thereafter refer to Mrs. W. as "my English Mum."

When my train pulled into the Cologne station at exactly 3:00 a.m., there was Papa! We hugged and kissed, happy to see each other again. He was staying in a *Pension,* a boarding house, with the rest of the band, so I got to meet the band members and I even revived an old collecting habit of mine, asking Papa to get me autographs from the singers appearing with the band. Sometimes they were well-known German artists and sometimes not, but I just liked looking at their photographs and their dedications to me.

Papa and I spent part of one day visiting Cologne Cathedral, the building of which had begun in 1248 and continued until about 1560. I don't know if the Catholic Church ran out of enthusiasm, but nothing much again happened until

1842, when the construction was resumed and it finally saw completion in 1880. It was bombed in World War II but quickly reconstructed, by 1956. Papa and I saw the completed cathedral in the fall of 1961, when Cologne still had far too many ruined apartment houses. Papa and I talked then about the millions of Marks that had been used to rebuild a cathedral when people had been waiting for almost any housing. Papa never did put much faith in churches, Catholic or otherwise, that spent so much money on themselves.

The cathedral was huge and impressive and, as I recall, had stalls positioned all over the place enticing visitors to purchase one cheap souvenir or another. Papa remarked, "They only need a hot dog stand in here and the fair would be complete." Truly, it felt more like a busy tourist stop than a place of worship.

At one point, while I was telling Papa about my experiences in England, he asked, "Christelchen (using the diminutive of my name), what's the matter with your German? It sounds like *Kauderwelsch.*" Gibberish, he meant. Apparently, I was still thinking in English because that is what I had done almost exclusively for the last twelve months. Now I was mixing things up a bit, especially word order. So one day when I went to get a haircut, I decided just for the fun of it to pretend not to know German. I was reasonably sure that the beautician wouldn't know any English. Once I was seated, I gestured with my fingers and said, "Short," and my bangs, "So," and the back "So," and when she said something in German, I shrugged my shoulders and held up my palms in a helpless I-don't-understand gesture. And then I listened to the mundane conversations around me until one of the ladies said (in German), "I don't know why the English can't learn German!" I jerked my head around so fast that I almost got scissors stuck in my neck! Still, in reacting so strongly I had almost given myself away though I managed to recover and stayed in character until I left the salon, grinning over my successful charade as I meandered down the sidewalk. Maybe there was a little of my playful grandfather in me.

I stayed with Papa for two or three days before it was time to take another train to Hamburg, where the whole family met me at the station. The happiest person was Mutti who was sure she had me back forever. It seemed strange to see my house again, as though I had been gone much longer than a year. Still, it was unchanged. And now I had to share a room again, after having had the luxury of my own space. Nor was Doris any too thrilled to be sharing our *Kinderzimmer* again. After all, it had been hers alone during my absence. She hadn't changed much of anything in the room, though, except for taping a few more posters to the walls, one of them of James Dean. My Mutti looked the same at first glance, and I failed to see the tiredness around her eyes until I had been home for a good month. Then I noted that her lips were often tinged bluish and, more than once, her hand sliding a little while pill under her tongue. Her heart was acting up in some way, but she didn't want to go to a doctor. She still worked for our family friend the pharmacist and would continue for another four months or so, when Papa finally stopped playing in the band. A good friend who had once worked with him at the *Vereinigte Deutsche Metallwerke* and who was now in management offered him a job in the drafting department which Papa accepted. For the first time in a very long time, my parents could depend on the same amount of income every month.

◆   ◆   ◆

I had to get busy finding a job and did so by reading the want ads in the "*Hamburger Abendblatt*" and answering ads for bilingual secretaries by sending my resume to the companies, mostly import/export trading companies. My resume was short—after all, I had only worked for one company so far and at that only for eighteen months. Still, I had an excellent recommendation from Alexander Petersen & Co. to help in my search for just the right company. Because my English was excellent, I could afford to be choosy and, as far as I can recollect, the Deutsche BP AG, headquartered in Hamburg, was the only company that interviewed me: they offered me a job on the spot! All I knew about BP was that the company owned gas stations, and our old neighbors Tante and Onkel Schütt owned one of them.

My job was to take dictation in German and English for the Purchasing Department, file various documents, and make sure that memos from other departments got seen by my bosses and then forwarded to the appropriate personnel. This was an entry-level position, and the only part of the job I felt excited about was that I was going to be working with two Englishmen, with whom I could practice my English skills and possibly help them with their German. My monthly salary was 450 Marks, up from the 250 Marks I had received at Alexander Petersen & Co. Even after paying for room and board at home, I felt positively rich. I needed to invest some of my earnings in a completely new wardrobe, having dressed mostly casually for the past year, but I did this slowly by adding a piece or two every month.

Even before I began working for BP on November 1, 1961, I enrolled in the Berlitz School of Languages to work on a certificate in foreign correspondence and interpreting, the written and oral parts of translating. My goal was to become either an executive secretary for an important company man or a translator. But I wasn't exactly sure if I would work for a company or a consulate or just how I would use my language skills. So in June of 1962 I earned a certificate as a foreign language correspondent after eight months of classes meeting six hours a week. My grades were good, and I now possessed a certificate which would impress a potential employer. It was important at that time in Germany to have as many certificates as possible in one's portfolio. Germans seemed to value diplomas and the like.

Most important to me was that I liked my job, got along with the people I worked for, had money to spend, continued my education, and held on to my dream of going to America. I felt that I had matured in England and that I had a plan for the future, though this plan was flexible.

From living in England I knew that I was able to function around strangers; that I was able to survive emotionally any separation from family and friends, and that I was open to accepting other peoples' customs and behaviors. The maturation I had undergone in the last year would surely help me in any future adventures.

Now I wanted to have fun with my friends. After an absence of a year, I called former co-workers and met them for coffee, lunches, and sipping coca colas and rum and dancing at night clubs. I renewed my friendship with Dickus, and we met often for lunch because we both worked downtown. She had just met a young man and was seriously in love. And it wasn't too long before Doris hooked me up with a friend of a friend, and I and this young man dated. He was an engineer with a good future ahead of him; I was twenty, and somewhere deep, deep within me was the longing to find a mate. The feeling didn't surface that often, however. My friends were all still single, but I noticed that more of them were in relationships when in the past we had had more group dates. I came away from visits to my brother Klaus and sister-in-law Anne believing that they had the perfect marriage and the perfect apartment, something I could aspire to should a longing for domesticity surface.

My English Mum and I in the backyard in Mill Hill, 1961

Mrs. W. with Nigel and Andre in Wales in 1961

At a party in Hamburg with my German friends, 1961

Doris and Christel having fun at the Baltic Sea, 1962

My nephew Sven's baptism, 1962
Anne, Christel with Sven, Klaus

My best friend "Dickus" (Ingrid) and I

Christel in the backyard of our home in Hamburg, 1962
Ready for the world

12

Off to America

✦

1962

1962—Since 1961, 562,000 apartments have been built and the most acute shortage of living space since the end of the war is over. Since 1946, about 812,000 Germans emigrated, mostly to the U.S., Canada, and Australia. The ballpoint pen slowly gathers popularity, but is not allowed in schools where only ink pens are permitted. The twist is in. Twenty-eight East Berliners escape from East to West Berlin via a twenty-seven-meter long tunnel. Adolf Eichmann is hanged on June 1.

It wasn't until January 9, 1962, that my next life-changing event occurred. After returning from England, my life had settled into a routine of working, taking English classes, dating, and participating in English conversation groups at the British Council where Mr. Clark welcomed me back with open arms. Now, instead of listening most of the time and talking only occasionally, I was one of his best talkers, and he often relied on me to keep the conversation going when participants ran out of things to say or lacked the necessary vocabulary to say what they wanted.

A few days before January 9 I received a phone call from one of my Mormon friends asking me if I would be interested in attending a dance. She had heard that the American consulate in Hamburg was organizing a dance for the crew of the visiting American aircraft carrier USS Essex and needed lots of girls to attend. I wasn't all that interested at first and truthfully speaking was put off by the idea, feeling that I would be used to give a bunch of American sailors a good time. But Margo kept at me, explaining about how much fun it would be. And where would they get the girls if not through the consulate's network of companies? So reluctantly I agreed and met Margo at the designated time on Tuesday, January 9, in front of the American Club where the dance was being held. From the

American Club it was possible to see the imposing hulk of the aircraft carrier docked at the pier across the street. The sidewalk around the American Club was already packed with sailors in their navy blue uniforms. I had understood that we would be dancing with officers dressed in smart jackets, but these guys seemed to be enlisted men in their winter blues, of which I remember the peacoats and pants with their multitude of buttons instead of the single zipper that only became fashionable a few years later. A peacoat I owned later was always my most favorite coat.

The USS Essex was in Hamburg on a ten-day "goodwill" NATO cruise and was accompanied by its fleet of submarines, destroyers, and frigates. Not content merely with showing off its naval force, the Americans (about which I had gotten so much information through the *Amerika Haus* over the years) had planned visits with German families for American sailors. So that the victors and the vanquished could get to know each other! I did not know about all this planning at the time, probably because I was neither reading the newspaper regularly and we didn't have a TV set at home.

In any case, Margo and I and perhaps a hundred other German girls showed up to dance, which meant that we would be sitting at tables, drinking coca cola (no alcohol, as I recall), and waiting until we were politely asked for the pleasure of a dance and all that. Which is exactly what didn't happen, at least to me, when a tall American planted himself in front of me, smiled broadly, held out his hand, and asked, "Wanna dance?" Do what? Didn't these Yanks have any manners? What happened to the boy's "May I have this dance?" and then, after a suitable delay, the girl's acceptance with an extended hand? But I didn't have time even to say no if I wanted to, for he grabbed me by the hand and just like that I was up and dancing. We danced a jive so didn't have time to talk, and after that first dance he was back again and again for a whole evening of fun. Then how we talked, although I had some trouble understanding his American dialect. It sure wasn't the Queen's English. The sailor's name was Jerry, and at dance's end I think he took me to the subway station, only two minutes away, along with Margo and her new American friend. Before we parted I gave Jerry my phone number because he wanted to arrange for my parents and me to tour the ship. During the ten-day U.S. presence, thousands of Hamburgers were to visit the aircraft carrier known in the military as "The Oldest and the Boldest" and "The Fightingest Ship in the Navy." And I was to be one of them!

My parents were as excited as I was to see what an aircraft carrier looked like, although my excitement may well have had more to do with seeing Jerry again. He soon called, and on Monday, January 16, Papa, Mutti, and I met him by the ship and he took us on board. I'm not sure how much attention I paid to the ship, the size (872 feet in length) of which probably left me and all Germans dumbstruck. I of course was the one in our party to translate from English to German and German to English, and my Papa asked a lot of questions because he was fascinated by this huge ship. Mutti was less curious, but I could tell she was really taken by the young American. She let me know later that he had glanced at me every time Papa wasn't asking a question. I glanced at him, too—he had the bluest eyes and the widest smile.

Jerry told us that as the U.S. fleet was sailing up the river Elbe it scraped bottom and temporarily got stuck. The aircraft carrier Essex was the largest ship that had ever come up the river. Sailors lined the flight deck and waved to the people on shore, who waved back. Banners on nearby homes and office buildings further welcomed the crew. From the mouth of the river near Cuxhaven, the ship glided past small towns and villages on either side of the river where it wasn't that wide, and the sailors on the flight deck could actually see the people who were waving to them. Jerry said that the crew was sometimes allowed to wave back, though not all the time. It must have been cold on deck, but he claimed he didn't mind, finding the changing countryside views interesting. It must have been quite a sight to reach this busy harbor where all the other ships were waiting to welcome the fleet with booms of ships horns. On one Sunday alone 50,000 Germans visited the ship, and the crew was amazed at the sheer numbers of people interested in witnessing this powerful display of American might.

Of course, Jerry didn't know that Hamburgers had ships in their blood. The harbor was our lifeline to the world, bringing ships loaded with food when we needed it most after the war. Now ships that loaded and unloaded raw materials and supplies were making Hamburg's seafaring tradition burst with energy. And what this particular aircraft carrier brought would change my life, for one.

At the end of the tour, my parents invited Jerry to visit us at our home, which he did and just a few days later. He had never been in a German home before and such a small one at that, with only 614 square feet of living space, including a primitive bathroom. The details of this occasion are lost in my memory, but I do remember leaving home with Jerry and taking the subway back to the ship. Along the way we stopped at the American Club for a beer and then walked the rest of the way to the ship, stopping now and then for a kiss. There was a definite spark between us. He had my address and I had his, and we promised each other we would write.

Which we did! I was astonished when Jerry's the first letter arrived, because sailors are notorious for making promises and then leaving town for the next port, never again to be heard from. In this first letter I learned that he almost hadn't attended the dance where we met but went after all because another sailor in his department was willing to go with him, and I replied to him in my letter that I had almost said "no" when he asked me for a dance because he hadn't asked properly. But in a split second I had changed my mind and my life.

Between January and October 1962, I received at least one letter a week and often two or three. "Did I get a letter?" was the first thing I would say when I got home every night, prompting my parents to start lining up the letters that had come that day on top of the china cabinet in the living room. The red and blue-striped border of the American air mail envelope thus became a familiar and treasured sight. Sometimes my parents would play games with me and say "no" when I would ask "Did I get a letter?" Then they would whip out two from behind their backs and say "Not one. But two!" (The arrival of several letters at once was a quirk of the military postal service). He wrote almost every day, and I did the same.

I told Jerry of my plans to visit the United States, and he expressed pleasure at the prospect of seeing me again. Very slowly, over the next few months, I began to think increasingly about leaving Germany for a while, coming to think of my homeland as a place too small for me to remain in. Small in space and thinking, narrow-minded, tethered to the war and all the reminders of it, especially in the ruins that everywhere lay around us. I couldn't spread my wings here, or at least that's how I came to think of what motivated me to take my next steps. I didn't let on to anything at home, but my Mutti and Papa sensed that I was falling in love with Jerry and had a hunch where that would lead.

In February, I was moved to the Sales Promotion Department, and now I worked for the husband of one of the granddaughters (or perhaps great-grand-daughters) of the last German emperor, Kaiser Wilhelm II. At first I was impressed, if a little frightened at working for such an important man (he was not royalty himself), but fairly quickly my prejudices and expectations about royalty were confirmed: he proved to be lazy, tardy, and absent a lot of the time. Maybe he was charged with showing up at outside sales events and thus couldn't be expected to sit in an office. I much preferred to work with Mr. Roberts, my British boss, who was a humorous person and always ready for a good laugh, as was I.

Not that I was dissatisfied with my job. Everything was going quite well, so well in fact that now and then I was asked to substitute for the executive secretary to one of the board members. All board members had their offices in one wing of the top floor of the BP building. After all, they were the top executives and everyone treated them like your-highnesses. Whereas my regular office (which I shared with another secretary) had merely a linoleum floor, all board members and their secretaries' had offices with plush, wall-to-wall carpeting. In addition, the windows were graced with drapes, and the outer office (where the secretary worked), had a sink and drinking glasses in a cabinet. The furniture was of rich, dark wood, lending the offices an air of elegance and importance.

Whenever I was called to work for Dr. H., I went with anticipation but also a good dose of trepidation because I wondered if I fit in with these exalted people. Would I be able to give off the same aura of professionalism and even a certain arrogance? (I called it arrogance, but it could just have been self-confidence that they exuded). Could I fill the shoes of the regular secretary and give my temporary boss the same quality of work he was accustomed to? When the phone buzzed, I grabbed my steno pad and pencil, knocked on the door separating our offices, and Dr. H. would commence dictating. I didn't want to appear ignorant and ask too many questions, so at times I wrote down what I had heard only to discover later that I hadn't heard correctly, at which I had to re-type the letter. Some dictations took a long time and included all the correspondence for that day.

When I got back to my desk, I quickly typed a rough draft of what I had scribbled on the pad, worrying that if I waited too long to look at the notes I wouldn't be able to read my near-illegible marks! I never hesitated to clarify matters with Mr. Roberts, or that quasi-royalty boss of mine, but I was reluctant to bother Dr. H. as he had so much else on his mind. Sometimes when I couldn't read a shorthand symbol, I'd use a word that fit in the context of the sentence. In particular, I would improve on letters dictated in English, all thanks to my previous language training. But when I was totally perplexed at what I had written down and had to knock on his door and ask for clarification, I usually broke out in a cold sweat. A quiet, reserved, middle-aged man, he was usually very kind and helped me out, but still I felt that I wasn't serving him very well with what I considered to be my inadequate secretarial skills. It never occurred to me to blame him for mumbling or changing his mind three times about what he wanted the letter to say.

Many times he was in meetings, leaving me with nothing to do but daydream about Jerry and write letters to him. I was all alone in my ante-chamber with no one to talk to. When my stints ended I was always happy to get back to my own office. Little did I know then that Dr. H. was impressed with my skills, becoming the only employee ever to fill in for his secretary.

◆   ◆   ◆

A catastrophic event occurred during the night of February 16–17, 1962. Hamburg and its North Sea coast were hit by a tidal wave that reached a height of over eighteen feet above mean sea level. Winds of more than 125 miles an hour had driven the North Sea into the Lower Elbe! The sea overflowed the dikes and covered a large area south of Hamburg, and thousands of people in densely populated parts of the city like Wilhelmsburg were cut off by the flood water for days. 17,000 had to be evacuated and 315 people died along with countless pigs, chickens, goats, cats, and dogs this icy-cold, stormy night, swept to their deaths by the salty brown water. About 15,000 lost only their homes and belongings.

Seventeen years after the war, this part of Hamburg housed many Germans who had fled from Eastern Europe plus those who had lost everything to the war and were still living in jerry-built huts. Those who since the war had moved to newly-built apartment houses were luckier, especially if they lived on the upper floors.

Among other losses to the flood were all the apple, pear, and cherry trees in an area called the "Altes Land." Now these trees were covered with seaweed that had to be removed quickly if they were to survive. A call went out to churches for volunteers, and several of my friends and I answered the call on a cold February day when we caught a bus from the parish church St. Gabriel and headed for the area where we were to work. On the way there, I saw destruction the likes of which I hadn't seen since the war: houses where walls had caved in and abandoned rooms were exposed, furniture still in place. The orchards were a mess—a tangle of trees covered in muck and seaweed.

At first, my friends and I pulled from the trees all the flotsam and jetsam we could reach, but I recall that we also climbed into the trees to free as many branches from the seaweed that would otherwise have choked the nascent buds. Our work was but a small part of the help thousands of volunteers provided. It made me feel good to have answered the call, but nonetheless I got into big trouble when I got home because I had worn Doris' favorite green sweater without asking her. She had been at work, and this heavy sweater was the warmest piece of clothing I could find for the cleanup. Now, however, it was black and stank of moldy sea bottom, and I had to soak it for days and then wash it several times to get the smell out. Doris threatened to kill me if her sweater didn't get back to its original condition!

It was at about this time that my childhood friend Dickus learned she was pregnant. She and her boyfriend married quickly, and immediately after their civil wedding the ship's engineer bridegroom left for a year at sea. Dickus would be alone during the pregnancy and birth of her baby in October 1962, then to await her husband's return to his new family. At least that is how I remember the sequence of events. She was definitely growing up faster than I was, what with the coming physical demands of caring for a baby at her age (twenty) as well as with having total responsibility for another human being, but she seemed to take this unexpected turn of events in her stride. In the early sixties, it was still unacceptable to be pregnant out of wedlock—thus the sudden wedding. To "have" to marry would have made me nervous, but she and her new husband seemed to be genuinely in love. Now he was gone, though, and she was reduced to waiting for his letters. Just what I was doing! But whereas Jerry wrote frequently, Dickus sometimes had to wait for a whole month before she would hear from her husband. She would try to justify this dearth of correspondence by saying that he was kept too busy on the ship and that mail was posted only when the ship anchored in a port. But she was sad about not hearing from her husband more often, especially since she was carrying their child. I was the one mad at him for not writing more often.

Before I learned of Dickus's pregnancy, Klaus and Anne announced that they were expecting a baby in August of 1962. This time the pregnancy seemed to proceed normally, and I was looking forward to becoming an aunt.

I was still dating the same man I had been seeing when I met Jerry, but now I dated him half-heartedly. So, with Jerry increasingly on my mind, it wasn't long before the relationship ground to a halt. The letters between Jerry and me were now full of plans for the future—our future—and by April of 1962 I was ready to undertake the next step.

◆   ◆   ◆

First, I called the American Consulate General in Hamburg to find out what papers I would need to work in the United States, at which time I learned about the requirement of having a sponsor. I could work as an au pair for an American family, I could have a friend vouch for me and my good character, or I could find employment with an American company. The first choice was out of the question—after the year in England I had no desire to be an au pair again. The second choice would not work either because I didn't know anyone in the States except for Jerry, who was in the military and couldn't sponsor me. Or he couldn't sponsor me because he hadn't known me long enough! The third choice was the only one that would work for me, but how was I to find employment with an American company?

The first thing that came to mind was the *Amerika Haus*, for there I would be able to study the want ads in American newspapers. This I did for a time even though the newspapers were not always up-to-date. Nor could I find any ads for bilingual secretaries as it hadn't occurred to me that bilingual secretaries would be rarities in America, the only language required of my American competitors being English unless they worked for a company doing business with foreign customers.

What to do? Then it crossed my mind that I had access to people who might be able to help me in my quest. First, I ran my plan by my English boss, Mr. Roberts, and he thought it an excellent idea. I didn't say anything to my parents because they were not business-type people, and I didn't want to be subjected to any negative feedback. I spent days and days rehearsing what I would do, feeling that the only way to move my plan along would be to forge ahead and hope that the response would be positive. I had to let go of my fears and insecurities. Oh, I was scared. But I did it!

I called the office of Dr. H., my sometime boss, and made an appointment with his secretary for whom I had often substituted. I let her in on what I wanted to do, and she thought it couldn't hurt. Then on the appointed day and hour, with my heart pounding out of my chest, I walked from my humble office down the plush carpet path of the executive wing to Dr. H's office. The secretary, who could see how nervous I was, hugged me, then knocked on his door, opened it, and announced my arrival.

He was curious as to why I was there, it being an extraordinary occurrence for a secretary from another department to come and see him. But he motioned me to sit down, and I sat where I had so often taken dictation. Then I commenced telling him about my plan to further my work experience in America. Given that the German BP had contacts in the U.S., I made so bold as to ask him if he would be willing to use his influence and talk to his contacts in New York about employing an ambitious young German woman.

When I left his office it was by no means certain that American employment could be found for me, but Dr. H. did assure me that he would try. I was vastly relieved because I had fantasized that he would fire me on the spot or at least think ill of me because I wanted to leave BP. And was I really sufficiently qualified for him to be sticking his neck out in my behalf? After all, I had less than two years of experience working in a bilingual capacity. It wasn't as if I would be able to assist a company with my vast pool of knowledge.

It was time to wring my hands. I had no Plan B so I would just have to wait and see what developed. In the meantime, I went out with my friends to escape from my anxiety, though when I tried to imagine how I would miss them, probably never seeing them again, my stomach tied up in knots.

I finally told my parents that I had spoken with Dr. H. about getting a job in New York City and my mother alternated between not saying a word about it and trying to talk me out of it. She believed that America was a dangerous place, gun-toting and uncivilized in a cowboy-and-Indian way. I was uncertain where she was getting her information from and when I tried to tell her what I knew about America she clammed up, not wanting to hear about it.

One Saturday, when I was helping her sand the living room floor, which she was still doing with a steel wool pad under the sole of her shoe (how backward, I said to myself, this is not how they would clean a floor in America), she burst out in tears and pled with me not to go so far away from Hamburg. But I wasn't listening to the ache in her heart because at the time I didn't know what to listen for. So I didn't hug her and tell her not to worry, I'd be back in a couple of years, because I couldn't imagine what a mother would feel about her child moving so far away. Instead, I was annoyed that Mutti was only making it harder for me to leave. Such was my mindset at twenty years of age. My heart aches for her now as I write this, and I cry hot tears.

Come the end of June I was on top of the world, having received a letter from the M.W. Kellogg Company offering me employment at their headquarters office in New York City. In my secretarial position I would earn $80 per week, based on a 37–1/2 hour week. The letter contained other information intended to satisfy the Immigration Department, such as, "This employment is of a definite duration and should be considered that of a permanent nature. You will be assigned to one of our engineering departments located at our headquarters office, 711 Third Avenue, New York." That would inform the Consulate that this firm was offering me a permanent, not temporary, job and that they had a definite idea of where to use my services. Dr. H. had contacted a person he knew at this particular company, because M.W. Kellogg was in the petroleum-refining, petrochemical-processing, technological, engineering, and construction businesses and was therefore closely linked to BP.

I had picked up an application for an immigrant visa at the U.S. General Consulate in advance of receiving the letter from Kellogg, just in case they would decide to employ me. Now I was able to sit down and fill it out as well as to begin the process of obtaining the required copies of various documents—among others, my birth certificate and a report from the police department stating that I had never been charged with any misdemeanors or other crimes. I underwent the medical examination required by the U.S. Foreign Service, including blood work, a chest x-ray, and a revaccination for smallpox. I didn't have tuberculosis or leprosy or any of the other dangerous contagious diseases they were checking for: gonorrhea, ringworm of the scalp, or mental conditions such as insanity or drug addiction. I was a healthy human specimen and received a clean bill of health on July 26, 1962.

The application was four pages long and by no means a complicated document to fill out. It asked for the usual personal information including height, weight, eye and hair color, and present occupation. The questions were stated in German and English, and I answered them in German. My occupation was translated by the Consulate as "correspondent for foreign languages." I listed my complexion as "white," which they later translated into "fair." (Two questions about race and ethnic classification appeared on the application but were crossed out.) The question about the length of time I intended to remain in the United States I answered with "Approximately two years." In my mind, I was not emigrating, but just visiting the U.S. But in the back of my mind, there was Jerry. My purpose in going to the United States was, I stated, to further my career. My sponsor was the M.W. Kellogg Co. My evidence of support was stated in their offer of employment.

I wasn't sure at the time how much $80 per week would buy me. Of course, I would have to wait and see how much I would have to pay for rent and food. Initially for a few days, the company would pay for a room at a YWCA somewhere on Lexington Avenue in Manhattan. I could stay there indefinitely or until I found a better place to stay. Later I would pay $50 a month to room with a coworker.

The next two pages of the application were filled with questions about moral conduct, use of drugs, membership in subversive organizations such as the communist party, military service, polygamy, and prostitution. Twelve questions had sub-questions so that in total I answered a mere thirty-eight questions. I signed the application on July 26, 1962.

Now I had to wait again for the Consulate to notify me that my application had been accepted and a visa issued. But because all the paperwork was in order and I had the all-important offer of employment, this was no nail-biting time. My plan was to depart for America toward the end of September. So I had all of

August and September to wrap up my life in Germany, and to get a freighter lined up.

I daydreamed about seeing my sailor Jerry again, and our letters back and forth only fueled that desire: they were full of love, courtship, and sexual undertones. He was at that time stationed in Providence, Rhode Island, but would be able to visit me in Manhattan when he was off-duty. We could actually have dates, talk, and smooch.

While I was still in Hamburg, I wanted to see as much as I could of my friends, especially those who had kept in contact with me through my year in England. I guess that I was hoping they would keep up a correspondence during my sojourn in America. Was I anticipating homesickness? I don't today recall feeling sad at the thought of leaving family and friends behind, thinking more in terms of missing my friends because we had had such a good time together. With a group of friends from Alexander Petersen, my first employer, I went to the Hamburger Dom and gorged on my favorites, the things that I wouldn't be able to buy in America—pickled herring on a roll, the soft, spongy, sugary squares called Hamburger Speck, and *Lebkuchen* hearts. I reasoned that if I ate those things just before I departed Hamburg, I would remember their taste and the memory would comfort me. I lamented that I wouldn't be going to the Dom one year hence.

For the first time in years, my parents took a train to a vacation destination in Austria. In one photo, Mutti sits on the balcony of their hotel room and smiles happily into the camera. She looks suntanned and relaxed. In another photo, she is wearing a favorite flowered dress against a backdrop of mountains and shimmering lake. But behind the smiles she was agitated enough to make Papa agree to come back early: her first grandchild was due at the end of August, and her youngest child was leaving her forever (as she envisioned my American adventure). She didn't want to be in Austria, she wanted to be at home.

On August 30, 1962, Klaus and Anne welcomed their baby boy, Sven. His face mirrored the fine features of his handsome father. At his christening on September 23 I became his godmother, receiving a brief document that stated the duties of a godparent. Among others, it stipulated that the godparent should be a person who prays. I still prayed at the time and considered myself a church-going Christian (which Sven's parents were not), so it would be up to me to keep Sven on a god-fearing path, even though I wasn't really sure how I would accomplish that while living across a wide ocean. Still, it made me feel important to be Sven's guiding light, and somehow I would not let the distance deter us from being god-child and godmother. Somehow it would work out. At the christening, I held my little nephew proudly when the pastor sprinkled holy water on his forehead. I found it most extraordinary that Klaus was now a father, as though somehow he should still be that soccer-playing, fun-loving boy I once knew, the one who would go to the lake with his buddies and take me along. Or the one who would wrestle with Doris and me.

After the christening, Mutti and Papa gave a party at our house for the immediate members of both families, and in photos of the event Mutti beams broadly while holding her grandson. Anne, the new mother, hovers attentively nearby.

A week before the christening, I had a big 21st birthday party, at which I said farewell to friends and family because on Wednesday, September 27, I would set sail for America, embarking on my quest to see the world.

On that crisp and clear day, Papa and Mutti ordered a cab to take them and me and my two steamer trunks to the docks. The Italian freighter, *M/V Polinnia* with its gleaming white, green, and red smokestacks rose out of the river Elbe to dwarf all of us. How often had I daydreamed about this moment? Every-one—family, relatives, and friends exclaimed at the size of the ship, so colossal and intimidating. In my memory, we are all standing around in little groups; even Onkel Max is there, but not my Oma and Opa because I had already said goodbye to them at their house. We are waiting for the captain to give us a signal that it was time to break off our exchange of fond sentiments (every word of which I have forgotten) and board promptly. But I know for sure that I was sad and excited simultaneously. It was a huge step I was taking, and I was aware of it and yet strangely oblivious to it. I was headed to a city much bigger than the one I had grown up in, to a huge country completely unknown to me except through books and movies and one male person who I knew little about and, at that, mostly from letters. It seemed a little crazy even to me, who had been working so diligently toward this very moment. Yet there I was, setting off for America with only the $150 that I had borrowed from my parents because the one-way freighter ticket had taken all my savings. I had decided on going by ship rather than by plane, because even a one-way air ticket would have been beyond my means. In the end I paid 600 Marks (at that time 150 dollars) for a one-way ticket to Norfolk, Virginia.

The captain gave us the signal and the other twelve passengers and I queued up to board. I did and didn't want this moment to arrive: Mutti and Papa hug-ging me and stroking my hair, holding my hands, and all the while crying. This interminable moment lasted until I absolutely had to walk up the gangway or miss my boat. From the deck I leaned over the rail and waved and waved, even when the ship began moving forward, until everyone began walking away from the dock to become blurs in my memory. Then I walked slowly to my cabin.

Afterword

I arrived in Norfolk, Virginia, on October 6, 1962.

Just eleven days later, my mother died of heart failure, her wish to die at home, in her bed, with my father by her side, fulfilled. For many years thereafter, I believed she had died of a broken heart. Broken over me.

Jerry Ervin and I were married on January 18, 1964, in his hometown, Kawkawlin, Michigan. I became a naturalized U.S. citizen on April 24, 1967.

Eventually Jerry and I had two daughters, Julie and Amberley. For a while we lived a happy life in Flint, Michigan, until our marriage broke down.

In 1971 I enrolled at the University of Michigan-Flint and received a B.A. in German and French. At thirty-five, I finally had the degree I hadn't gotten in Germany.

I met my second husband, Dick Gehlert, at the Flint, Michigan, Unitarian-Universalist church. I had by now realized that for me religion was not God-worship but the belonging to a community of people who emphasized the here and now.

Dick's love of the German language had a great deal to do with choosing my native tongue as my major, and it was with his encouragement that I became a teacher of German.

Dick and I were married on February 14, 1976, in Grosse Pointe, Michigan. My daughters and his son Keith and daughter Amy now made up our new family.

Because German teaching jobs were hard to get, I worked for three years for Volkswagen of America as a bilingual secretary, experiencing first-hand the problems that occur when people from two countries work together.

In 1971, I joined the women's movement, and two other women and I started a NOW chapter in Rochester, Michigan, where my family then lived, as well as an Oakland University-Rochester Campus chapter. I marched in Michigan and Washington, D.C.

By 1979 I had embarked on a master's degree in Linguistics, out of which emerged my small consulting business that prepared translations in English, French, and German and gave cultural support to businesses dealing with foreign clients. At the same time, I got the chance to teach German and Latin.

I visit my "English Mum" whenever I am in England.

Dick and I are now grandparents to Oliver, Makenna, and Elena.

Now in Fort Wayne, Indiana, I became involved in the German Heritage Society and Sister Cities International. Here I helped establish a now thriving relationship between Fort Wayne and Gera, Germany, which through student exchanges promotes peace and understanding on both sides. I have been a pacifist my entire adult life.

Writing about growing up in post-war Germany has freed my mind from the constant din of idly recollecting the war. Calling up the memories was painful, but I feel better for having done it. Now I can redouble my volunteer activities, reading, gardening, tennis, golf, ballroom dancing, and world travel.

978-0-595-46145-5
0-595-46145-X

Printed in the United States
118967LV00003B/61-99/A